Ethnography and Qualitative Design in Educational Research

SECOND EDITION

Ethnography and Qualitative Design in Educational Research

SECOND EDITION

Margaret D. LeCompte
School of Education
University of Colorado
Boulder, Colorado

Judith Preissle
Department of Social Science Education
College of Education
University of Georgia
Athens, Georgia

with

Renata Tesch
Qualitative Research Management

ACADEMIC PRESS, INC.
Harcourt Brace Jovanovich, Publishers
San Diego   New York   Boston   London
Sydney   Tokyo   Toronto

This book is printed on acid-free paper. ∞

Academic Press, Inc.
1250 Sixth Avenue, San Diego, California 92101-4311

United Kingdom Edition published by
Academic Press Limited
24–28 Oval Road, London NW1 7DX

Library of Congress Cataloging-in-Publication Data

LeCompte, Margaret Diane.
    Ethnography and qualitative design in educational research /
Margaret D. LeCompte, Judith Preissle, with Renata Tesch. – 2nd ed.
        p.   cm.
    Preissle's name appears first on the earlier ed.
    Includes index.
    ISBN 0-12-440575-4
    1. Education–Research.   2. Ethnology–Methodology.   3. Education–
Evaluation–Methodology.   I. Preissle, Judith.   II. Tesch, Renata.
III. Title.
LB1028.L36   1993
370'.78–dc20   92-28787
                                                                   CIP

PRINTED IN THE UNITED STATES OF AMERICA
92 93 94 95 96 97   MV   9 8 7 6 5 4 3 2 1

Contents

Preface

Second editions owe a considerable debt to everyone who talked back, agreed or disagreed with, or otherwise responded to the first edition. We are grateful to the colleagues across the human sciences who entered into dialogue with us—in print, in person, or through other media. While we ourselves are responsible for all the extensions, elaborations, and changes of mind in this revision, our work is, nonetheless, a reflection of this interchange.

This book still is a treatise on how to do qualitative and ethnographic research. Like our first edition, it addresses ways to collect data, methods for assuring the quality of data, the roles researchers enact in the course of their efforts, and techniques for organizing results, conclusions, and interpretations. Like the first edition, the second also emphasizes the role which theory plays in every step of the research process.

Like our first edition, this one evolved from resources we developed for use in field research methods courses we taught to graduate students in education. Above all, we undertook a representation of the whole research process. We discussed social science investigation from initial stages of problem formulation through the last phases of analysis, where statistical manipulation may be appropriate. We also addressed interpretation and assessment of results. We have endeavored to demonstrate the interrelatedness of investigative traditions; to some degree, psychologists, anthropologists, and sociologists all engage in naturalistic studies. Each discipline has its own terminology for such studies; all use similar methods, yet cordon off their respective disciplinary bailiwicks in a way that sometimes distorts the integrated reality of human existence. Our work represents a practical effort toward a melding of disciplines in that we address concerns that are central to research in anthropology, psychology, and sociology, but are rarely shared among them.

This second edition differs, however, in some significant ways from our first endeavor. First of all, our own thinking has evolved. Second, immediately after the publication of the first edition, the use of qualitative and ethnographic research in education and the social sciences exploded; it now enjoys considerable legitimacy. No longer can we describe our reference list as exhaustive with confidence. No longer is it appropriate to expend any effort defending the legitimacy of ethnographic approaches to research. No longer is the analysis of qualitative data a low-tech, manual effort. And ethnographic and qualitative designs themselves are by no means uniform; they have undergone considerable evolution, both epistemologically and methodologically. To that end, we have enlarged our list of references considerably. Our theory chapter has been moved and completely revised. We now include critical, postmodern, collaborative, and feminist perspectives on the purposes and implementation of research as well as on the stance researchers adopt in interaction with both participants and their research data. We also have added a section on construction of the literature review. We have "unpacked" many of our examples, using tables and figures to explicate some of the more opaque sections of the original text. We also expanded our use of concrete examples to include a range of studies, from community ethnographies to classroom studies. We asked Renata Tesch to contribute a chapter on the use of computers in the analysis of qualitative and ethnographic data. Our last chapter, on evaluation of ethnographic and qualitative research, differs considerably from our first edition and reflects our own current thinking as well as that of other theorists.

Chapter One places ethnography and its related qualitative research variants within the context of scholarly investigative styles and social science traditions. The historical development of ethnography is traced from cultural anthropology and field sociology to its present use in a number of disciplines. Purposes for and variations in educational ethnography are discussed. Influences on educational ethnography are identified from educational anthropology, educational psychology, educational sociology, and evaluation research.

Chapter Two is a discussion of problem selection and research design. It provides a framework for the remaining chapters. It addresses how research design facilitates the seven decisions any social science researcher makes: (1) formulating a problem, (2) selecting a research design, (3) choosing who and what to study, (4) deciding how to approach participants, (5) selecting means to collect data, (6) choosing how to analyze data, and (7) interpreting data and applying the analysis.

Initial phases of qualitative and field research are introduced in Chapter Three. These require an investigator to match who and what to study with why and how they are being studied. This chapter addresses the issues involved in choosing relevant populations and in selecting and sampling qualitative data. It describes how populations are conceptualized and distinguishes between probability sampling and criterion-based selection. The variations of these two techniques are discussed and illustrated.

Chapter Four describes the special ways that the roles assumed by a researcher in an ethnographic study differ from those assumed by investigators from other traditions. Particular attention is devoted to the way personal relationships affect data and how the ethics involving treatment of human subjects apply to ethnographers. The interaction of roles internal and external to the research site is examined in the context of their impact on the execution of a study, the construction of meanings within a research site, and the results obtained; and specific skills of boundary spanning, or communication and negotiation, necessary for successful completion of an ethnographic research project are defined. The final portion of the chapter addresses the ways ethnographers and qualitative researchers initiate field residence and begin data collection: locating study sites and collectivities, obtaining access and entry, and mapping groups and social scenes.

Chapter Five is devoted to the ways in which theory informs the definition, collection, and interpretation of data. We examine the levels of theory, both formal and informal, personal and scientific; we also discuss how different theoretical frames lead to different kinds of research questions and designs.

Chapter Six discusses methods used to collect data by qualitative and ethnographic researchers. The chapter is divided for convenience into two sections: interactive methods, which include interviews and surveys and participant observation; and noninteractive methods, which include nonparticipant observation and collection of artifacts. Different kinds of data are illustrated, and extended examples of various kinds of data are presented. Throughout this chapter, the integration of data collection methods with roles assumed by researchers is emphasized, and the coordination between data collection and data analysis is anticipated. Most significantly, we highlight interplay of data collected simultaneously through different, but complementary, avenues.

Chapter Seven focuses on analyzing and interpreting ethnographic and qualitative data. It integrates themes and decisions described in the preceding four chapters. Three categories of analytic processes are described and discussed. These are generic modes of manipulating information, or theorizing—perceiving, comparing, contrasting, aggregating, ordering, establishing linkages and relationships, and speculating—and two formal and systematic conventions for analysis. The first is sequential selection; these strategies are means for guiding data collection with emergent analytic constructs. They include negative case selection, discrepant case selection, theoretical sampling, and theory implications selection. The second involves general analytic procedures used throughout the research process; these are analytic induction, constant comparison, typological analysis, enumeration, and standardized observational protocols.

The second section of the chapter demonstrates how these varying processes are used to build an ethnographic analysis. These same operations guide the researcher's final task: interpreting and integrating ethnographic data. We present examples of how four approaches to this activity are used by investigators: theoretical consolidation; theoretical application; formulation of metaphors, similes, and analogies; and synthesis of results with other literature. Triangulations of analytic tools with combinations of data collection methods, selection techniques, and conceptual frameworks are stressed throughout this chapter.

Chapter Eight, on the use of computers and related software for the analysis of qualitative data, has been contributed by Renata Tesch. In this chapter, we discuss what computers can and cannot do in the research process and review the principal qualitative data analysis software packages available for IBM, IBM-compatible, and Macintosh personal computers.

The book concludes with ways to assess ethnographic and other qualitative research in Chapter Nine. It synthesizes the material discussed in earlier chapters for use by both investigators evaluating their own activities as they proceed and scholars judging the merit of studies reported in the literature. The research tasks discussed throughout the text each are examined for a variety of criteria for quality.

We would like to acknowledge some of the people who have contributed so considerably to the production of this book. First, Joe Ingram, the former Academic Press editor who supervised the first edition of the book and initial work on this edition, continues to be a stalwart friend and supporter of our work and ourselves. Nikki Fine, our current editor at Academic Press, is owed a debt of gratitude for continuing to encourage us and to support the project. Our students, faculty, administrators, and staff at the Universities of Georgia and Colorado–Boulder inspired, encouraged, and stimulated our efforts. Our colleagues, Kathleen Bennett DeMarrais, Doug Campbell, Donna Deyhle, MaryCarol Hopkins, Ann Nihlen, and Mary Ann Pitman have been generous to a fault with their time and creative thinking. They reviewed our work, held our hands, and spurred us onward. Special thanks from Georgia go to JoBeth Allen, Diane Brook, Linda Grant, Mary Jo McGee-Brown, Xue Lan Rong, Tim

Seiber, and Banghu Wang. From Colorado, thanks are owed to Margaret Eisenhart and Ken Howe, who helped to clarify—but who are not responsible for—substantive dilemmas, and to Mary Ellen Wiertelak and Sue Reissig, who went far beyond duty and loyalty in producing graphics and a giant reference list. Our families, friends, and companions deserve acknowledgment for their support as well as their timely diversions—especially Sergiu Luca, Mark Toomey, and Pete Preissle.

Margaret D. LeCompte and Judith Preissle

List of Tables and Figures

Characteristics and Origins of Qualitative and Ethnographic Research in Education

Introduction

> You're an anthropologist? I've always wanted to go on an archeological dig . . . Oh, you say you're an *ethnographer*. You guys *do* dig up old bones, don't you? . . . What? You study *schoolchildren*? What kind of tribe is *that*!

Welcome to the world of the educational anthropologist, whose methodological stock in trade is *ethnography*,[1] or writing about people. Probably no one who works in schools or studies them would be mistaken for a hard rock archeologist. However, there probably are as many approaches to anthropology, ethnography, and qualitative research in education as there are practitioners of the craft. The authors of this book have been "doing ethnography" in schools and writing about *how* to do it for almost 20 years, and we present this text as an introduction to our field. In so doing, we hope to entice you, the readers, into participating with us in what we believe to be one of the most fulfilling and exciting ways to study human beings in their natural settings. We begin by telling you a bit about ethnography itself.

Ethnography is both a product—the book which tells a story about a group of people—and a process—the method of inquiry which leads to the production of the book. The former consists of the body of literature—results, conclusions, interpretations, and theories—amassed from field studies of schooling and other educational processes. Broadly conceptualized, it includes studies of enculturation and acculturation from anthropology, studies of socialization and institutionalized education

---

[1] From *ethnos*, or race, people, or cultural group, and *graphia*, which is writing or representing in a specific way a specified field.

from sociology, and studies of sociocultural learning and cognition and child and adult development from psychology. Educators often use the terms *ethnography* and *ethnology* synonymously; however, for our purposes, ethnography is *not* ethnology. We make the same distinction between ethnography, as the study of a phenomenon conceived of as an individual entity, and ethnology, as the comparative analysis of multiple entities, that mainstream anthropologists make. Much work which uses individual ethnographic studies for interpretive purposes or for the generation of theories is, in fact, ethnology.

Ethnography also is an investigative process which social scientists employ in different ways to study human behavior, depending upon their discipline. In the pages which follow, we describe the early development of general ethnography as a research model, identify the purposes for and variations in educational ethnography, trace the origin and development of the model within its parent discipline of educational anthropology, and delineate the intersection of influences from psychology, sociology, and educational evaluation. We hope that this discussion emphasizes the fluidity of the ethnographic process and underscores the hazards of overstereotyping and rigidifying it as a specific research model.

Origins of Ethnography in Anthropology

Social scientists associate ethnography with cultural anthropology and particularly with the structural–functional theoretical perspective (Kaplan & Manners, 1972). This association derives from the insistence of anthropologists on defining ethnography in terms of the culture concept (Goetz & Hansen, 1974; Wolcott, 1975; LeCompte & Preissle, 1992b).

In this volume the term *ethnographic research* is used as a shorthand rubric for investigations described variously as ethnography, qualitative research, case study research, field research, or anthropological research (Smith, 1979). Although we use ethnography as the research model structuring this text and indicate how many aspects of investigative processes are shared across research designs, we distinguish ethnography from research that involves the investigator in other ways, is executed differently, and is designed for other purposes.

Ethnographies are analytic descriptions or reconstructions of intact cultural scenes and groups (Spradley & McCurdy, 1972). Ethnographies re-create for the reader the shared beliefs, practices, artifacts, folk knowledge, and behaviors of some group of people. An ethnographic product is evaluated by the extent to which it recapitulates the cultural scene studied so that readers envision the same scene that was witnessed by the researcher (Beals, Spindler, & Spindler, 1973; Wolcott, 1975). The ethnographic researcher begins by trying to examine even very commonplace groups or processes in a fresh and different way, as if they were exceptional and unique. Erickson (1973) calls the process "making it strange"; it allows even investigators who study very familiar scenes to discern the detail and the generality necessary for credible description. The practice of "making it strange" by a researcher studying a familiar culture is equivalent to the practice of "making it familiar" engaged in by an anthropologist studying an exotic culture.

Traditionally, ethnographers have concentrated on single research settings. They have focused on recording in detail aspects of a single phenomenon, whether that phenomenon is a small group of humans or the operation of some social process. However, studies of a phenomenon, particularly an organizational innovation, over a number of sites have become more common (e.g., Cassell, 1978; Herriott, 1977; Herriott & Gross, 1979; Huberman & Miles, 1983; Louis, 1982; Rist, 1981; Wax, 1979). Whatever the scope of the study may be, the task is to reconstruct, in what Lofland (1971) calls loving detail, the characteristics of that phenomenon.

In addition to being a product, ethnography is also a process, a way of studying human life. Ethnographic design mandates investigative strategies conducive to cultural reconstruction. First, the strategies used elicit phenomenological data; they represent the world view of the participants being investigated, and participant constructs are used to structure the research. Second, ethnographic research strategies are empirical and naturalistic. Participant and nonparticipant observation are used to acquire firsthand, sensory accounts of phenomena as they occur in real-world settings, and investigators take care to avoid purposive manipulation of variables in the study. Third, ethnographic research is holistic. Ethnographers seek to construct descriptions of total phenomena within their various contexts and to generate from these descriptions the complex interrelationships of causes and consequences that affect human behavior toward and belief about the phenomena. Finally, ethnography is multimodal or eclectic; ethnographic researchers use a variety of research techniques to amass their data (Wilson, 1977; Goetz & LeCompte, 1984). Although these strategies are most common in sociology and anthropology, they are used to some extent by all social science disciplines when mandated by the research goals.

History of the Ethnographic Research Model

Ethnography as an investigative model is rooted in anthropology and particularly in the desire of late nineteenth and early twentieth century culture theorists to discover what the non-Western-European world was like. During this period, social scientists tried to discover for human behavior the same kinds of laws and underlying patterns that natural scientists had begun to identify in the physical universe. They used descriptive and taxonomic studies of natural history, because it seemed to provide an investigative model appropriate for the study of human behavior; in fact, many early ethnographers initially were trained to be natural historians—the precursors of biologists and botanists. Thus, early anthropology had a strongly comparative and taxonomic bent. Constructs developed by anthropologists in Western societies were tested and refined in the context of data and beliefs about non-Western societies, both to investigate their generalizability and to refine analysis and understanding of the structures and functions of both the Western and the non-Western world. However, the social science data produced by these methods were not nearly so complete or well codified as those of natural scientists, nor were methods for defining, eliciting, and classifying usable data as well developed. Often the empirical data upon which early analyses were based were collected haphazardly and unscientifically.

During the nineteenth century, cultural theorists used descriptions of cultures written by travelers, missionaries, adventurers, and natural scientists. These data included diaries, memoirs, letters, interviews, and material from questionnaires sent to colonial administrators on the behavior of the tribes and peoples under their particular jurisdictions (Hayes, 1958). They varied from descriptions as dispassionate and detailed as those of any well-trained contemporary anthropologist to sensational exposés of so-called primitive behavior. The gaps and inadequacies of this record and the difficulties in generalizing from it convinced anthropologists of the need for firsthand field study. Wax (1971) suggests that the action-oriented research of European social reformers during the eighteenth and nineteenth centuries also provided a catalyst for field study. The European tradition relied upon reports developed from systematic observation of social problems to publicize and ameliorate poverty, crime, and immorality; the surveys, participant observation, and questionnaires which the Europeans used now form the multimodal staples of contemporary ethnography.

Researchers also had other purposes for doing field studies in other cultures. For some investigators, field study had intrinsic interest—it appealed to desires for adventure, challenge, and mystery. It was a means to understand the structure of Western society by comparing it with other human groups. Researchers thought they could discover the source for universal patterns of human thought and activity by documentation of the variety of human cultures. They used comparative analyses and syntheses to test certain theories about human history, particularly orthogenesis. Modeled on biological evolution but omitting the notion of natural selection, this theory postulates that all human societies pass through unvarying stages as they become civilized. Researchers felt that studies of so-called primitive societies, as they recapitulated the stages, could shed light on the development of industrialized societies. Finally, after World War I, field study became particularly critical as a means to preserve some knowledge of aboriginal groups that were fast disappearing. "Salvage anthropology" in fact was the catalyst for the American school of ethnography, initiated by Franz Boas at Columbia University in the 1920s.

Early anthropologists disagreed on the goals and the specific investigative methods of their field. Some, like Franz Boas, felt that given the tenuous data base and dearth of substantive organizing constructs, anthropologists simply should continue to gather rich descriptive data for in-depth studies of small, discrete groups (Stocking, 1968). Others were more interested in establishing patterns and relationships among groups. Some felt that anthropology, as a discipline, could provide insights to improve human life. Others opposed both the use of anthropological data in applied settings and the involvement of anthropologists in politics or practical affairs.

Although they disagreed on basic philosophical approaches to their field, these researchers did agree that the major task of anthropology is to describe cultures. Because culture is defined as everything having to do with human behavior and belief, they had to describe everything—language, kinship patterns, arts, crafts and technology, rituals and beliefs, economic and political structures, child rearing, and life stages. This is why cultural anthropology is preoccupied with holism. The scope of investigation mandated residence in the community and strongly suggested that studies should be conducted in the native language of the participants. The ethnographer was to study a society from the perspective of a child, by first learning its language and basic behavior patterns (Burnett, 1974b) and gradually becoming inducted into its life ways. This immersion in another culture allowed researchers access to the phenomenological views of participants. However, realities of funding, time, and language facility meant that even the strongest proponents of fieldwork often learned little of the language and spent limited time in the field (Wax, 1971, p. 32). More commonly, they used interpreters, hired informants, and made numerous, relatively short visits to their chosen peoples.

Most neophyte ethnographers got their training on the job. They learned to be ethnographers by doing an ethnography. Actual research techniques were not codified explicitly; coursework often was designed to give students a theoretical grounding rather than practical experience. The tools with which an ethnographer entered the field were lists of phenomena to investigate (e.g., Royal Anthropological Institute, 1964) rather than a systematic research design and set of instruments. Not until the publication in the 1920s of Malinowski's work on the Trobriand Islanders (1922) did fieldwork begin to be described systematically and technically. Even so, the descriptions primarily stressed the researcher's relationships with participants and provided only minimal guidance for data analysis and interpretation; accounts emphasized successful fieldwork, omitting review of problems and avoiding discussion of projects that failed altogether (Wax, 1971, p. 279).

SOCIOLOGICAL FIELDWORK

In the 1920s and 1930s, while anthropologists were exploring fieldwork techniques, something very much like ethnography began to emanate from the sociologists at the University of Chicago. Confining their investigations to contemporary North American settings, sociologists such as Robert Park, Everett Hughes, and Louis Wirth of the Chicago school used field studies to document life in familiar, usually urban, communities (Stein, 1960). Like anthropologists, they borrowed the methods of natural historians, living in the field among the people they were studying, collecting specimens, looking for patterns and regularities, developing systems of classification for what they observed, and generating hypotheses about what they had found. They applied sociological rather than anthropological constructs to their work, speaking of society and socialization rather than of culture and enculturation; they used organizing concepts such as social role and structure and norm, and were more concerned with issues of power and class. By contrast, ethnographers used functional analytic categories such as kinship, language, trade, and the like.

By the 1950s, individual investigators such as William F. Whyte (1955) and Herbert Gans (1962) were being claimed by both anthropology and sociology. Although these boundary-spanning scholars failed to leave their own disciplinary community totally, they did study ethnic enclaves within maintream society using the long-term residence in the community and participant observation familiar to anthropologists. These practices foreshadowed partial fusion of the two fields. Societal forces have contributed to such developments. By the 1950s fewer and fewer aboriginal groups were isolated from industrial society. Anthropologists found they no longer had access to societies that were relatively untouched by Western culture; rather, like sociologists, they had to consider cultural contact and change, industrialization, and assimilation in their studies. Both disciplines had to adapt their research to an industrial, rather than a preindustrial, society. Thus, the populations of interest to and the problems addressed by anthropologists and sociologists began to converge.

Major differences in approach and method persisted, however. As a mainstream discipline, sociology continued to emphasize research technology—sampling, instrumentation, and statistical analyses. These concerns derived from the sociologists' usual focus on populations too large to study in their entireties. Anthropologists stressed the interpersonal aspects of research, such as gaining access to the field, selection of and working with informants, and ethical relationships with participants, a preoccupation that reflects the critical and peculiar nature of the researcher's role in anthropological studies. This is not to say that anthropologists ignore technique and sociologists are oblivious to their respondents. However, ethnography as practiced by anthropologists has retained characteristics of both art and science, while sociology has concentrated more upon technical or scientific aspects of the research enterprise. Anthropologists have retained their traditional approach because cultural reconstruction, like historical narrative, is rendered more clearly and credibly by sensitivity to the nuances of human meaning and activity and by fluent and aesthetic use of language. Anthropology is a literary science; a well-done ethnography is always a well-written ethnography. In addition, comparability and legitimacy of ethnographic studies require precisely described methodological systems and systematically recorded accounts of how fieldworkers proceed. In recent years, however, methodologists in anthropologists anthropology have begun to address the technical and methodological foundations of ethnographic design as well as its human and artistic foundations (e.g., Powdermaker, 1966; Williams, 1967; Spindler, 1970; Freilich, 1970; Wax, 1971; Pelto & Pelto, 1978; Spradley, 1979, 1980; Agar, 1980; Goetz & LeCompte, 1984).

Evolution of Educational Ethnography

George Spindler (1982b, p. 3) has underlined the eclecticism of ethnography in education by identifying by discipline three varieties of ethnography: anthroethnography, socioethnography, and psychoethnography. We add as well the category of critical ethnography (Anderson, 1989;

Carspecken & Apple, 1992; Gitlin & Smyth, 1989; Quantz, 1992). In the pages which follow, we discuss the purposes of educational ethnography and describe how these varied influences have combined to form a multifaceted investigative model.

PURPOSE OF EDUCATIONAL ETHNOGRAPHY

Educational ethnography has been used to describe educational settings and contexts, to generate theory, and to evaluate educational programs. It has provided rich, descriptive data about the contexts, activities, and beliefs of participants in educational settings. Such data represent educational processes and their results as they naturally occur and in context; they rarely are limited to isolated outcomes. However, studies purporting to be educational ethnographies vary widely in focus, scope, and methods of execution. Some are classics, clearly recognizable as traditional ethnography. They are characterized by the investigation of a small, relatively homogeneous and geographically bounded study site (Goetz & Hansen, 1974), by long-term and repeated residence of the researcher at the site (Wax & Wax, 1980), by use of participant observation as the preferred data collection strategy supplemented with a variety of ancillary techniques (Wilson, 1977), by creation of a data base consisting primarily of field notes (Spradley, 1980; Bogdan & Biklen, 1992; Sanjek, 1990), and by a preoccupation with the interpretive description and explanation of the culture, life ways, and social structure of the group under investigation (Wolcott, 1980, 1988; Spradley, 1979). Such work is typically inductive, generative, and constructive. As they construct the social world of the school, researchers use a judicious balance of objective and subjective data. Examples include Wolcott's study of the principalship (1973), King's study of a residential Indian school in the Yukon (1967), Peshkin's study of the effects of schooling on children in a traditional African culture (1972), and Ogbu's study of minority schooling in Stockton, California (1974). Ethnographic work includes studies of change and innovation in school systems, such as Rogers' study of desegregation in the New York City schools (1968) or Metz's work on power and control in desegregating schools (1978); studies of language use in schools and communities (Heath, 1983); and studies of socialization to adulthood (Eckerd, 1988; Foley, 1990; Holland & Eisenhart, 1990; Lesko, 1988; Roman, 1988).

Contrasted with works like those described above are studies that some researchers contend are not at all ethnographic (Rist, 1980; Wolcott, 1980). These deviate from the classical design in that they focus on small subsets of larger cultural systems; they include microethnographies of single classrooms and dyadic studies done by sociolinguists (see examples anthologized in Spindler, 1982b, and described in Erickson, 1984, 1986, 1992, and Gee, Michaels, & O'Connor, 1992). Such studies eschew the multimodality of traditional ethnography and base their designs on a single data collection technique without triangulating or corroborating from multiple data sources. They include research derived from life history or biographical interviews (e.g., Fuchs, 1969; Herr, 1991; Anderson & Herr, 1991), studies using tightly structured and limited schedules for observation (e.g., Kounin, 1970), or designs incorporating a short period of field observation to provide contextual data for a survey or experimental study (e.g., Ginsburg, Meyenn, & Miller, 1980; Weis, 1988). The investigations most seriously contested as nonethnographic are those Wolcott (1980) prefers to label descriptive; these studies adopt some or all of the methods common to classical ethnography but do not use the interpretive, conceptual, and theoretical frameworks of cultural anthropology. Studies like these are quasiethnographies, as are those which use traditional ethnographic concepts and methods but combine them with other methods and theoretical frameworks in an interdisciplinary approach.

Many investigators are vague about what ethnography is, even when they assert they are doing it. As Rist (1980) has observed, the enthusiasm for ethnography in educational research has resulted in the formulation of such anomalies as "blitzkrieg" ethnography, relying on 2 or 3 days of fieldwork, or studies which ignore the culture of the people under investigation. At times the use of any so-called qualitative methods—especially those involving sustained interaction with participants—appears to be the criterion for labeling a study an ethnography.

Educational ethnography is neither an independent discipline nor, as yet, a well-defined field of investigation. It is, however, an approach to studying problems and processes in education; substantively, it represents an emergent interdisciplinary fusion because it has been practiced by researchers from different traditions. No consensus among these traditions has been reached, however, about what should be the proper scope and method for ethnographic studies in education; the various methodological influences on the field come from areas as varied as educational anthropology, educational psychology, educational sociology, evaluation research, and literary criticism. (See LeCompte, Millroy, & Preissle, 1992, for a collection of essays describing each type and its traditions.) To facilitate an understanding of the origins of this debate, we devote the next part of this chapter to a discussion of the disciplinary influences on educational ethnography.

EDUCATIONAL ANTHROPOLOGY

The earliest form of educational ethnography developed within cultural anthropology and studies of small intact communities. Analyses of child-rearing practices and enculturation processes were a necessary component of these studies. The anthropologists' mandate to investigate culture in all its manifestations focused attention on how children and adolescents were inducted into the practices and beliefs of a group. The child's relationships within the family, patterns of informal learning and instruction, acquisition of roles and statuses, and a group's conceptualization of and prescriptions for appropriate development from infancy to adulthood revealed the mechanisms of cultural transmission. Much of what is known of educational practices in traditional societies can be gleaned from early monographs depicting enculturation within the complex tapestry of group life (e.g., Malinowski, 1929; Stayb, 1931; Powdermaker, 1933; Blackwood, 1935; Heckel, 1935; Firth, 1936; Opler, 1941; Nadel, 1942). Viewing the transmission of culture as the foundation of social continuity (Malinowski, 1927), other researchers focused attention on this area (e.g., Kidd, 1906; Whiting, 1963; Raum, 1940; Ammar, 1954; Richards, 1956). Among these, Margaret Mead (1928, 1930, 1935) took child rearing and adolescence as a major field of concentration. Influenced by Boas (1911, 1928) and Benedict (1934, 1938), Mead sought to document variation in life-cycle patterns, in cultural influences on individual personality, and in the interplay of human knowledge, attitudes, and values with cultural styles of behavior, interaction, and activity. Mead's work stimulated successive generations of scholars to examine the diversity and limitations of human plasticity and adaptability. Her work also led to an analysis of the interdependency of societal institutions and other social structures for its influences on enculturation.

Although cultural anthropologists focused their fieldwork on pre-literate and nonindustrialized groups, they also made applications to and comparisons with their own societies throughout this period. Vander-walker (1898), Hewett (1904), and Montessori (1913) had emphasized the cultural context of educational processes and had advocated a central role for anthropology in the development of educational theory and research as well as in the professional preparation of teachers. Elaborating on this tradition, Mead (1943, 1951) and her colleagues (Bryson, 1939; Benedict, 1943; Herskovits, 1943; Redfield, 1945; Wooton, 1946) used cross-cultural comparisons to interpret and assess educational structures and functions in U.S. society.

Simultaneously, social continuity and stability throughout the world were being challenged by multiple cultural contacts, acculturation of traditional hunter–gatherer and peasant societies, and the inexorable conflicts generated by rapid social change. Anthropologists concerned with cultural transmission—enculturative and acculturative—inevitably took their fieldwork into schools, traditional institutions as well as colonial and missionary facilities. Murray's (1929) examination of schooling in Africa was followed by Harley (1941), Watkins (1943), Little (1951), Laye (1959), and Read (1955). Institutionalized education was investigated in the Pacific region (Wyndam, 1933; Elkin, 1937; Embree, 1939; Thompson, 1941), in the Middle East (Granqvist, 1947), among native peoples in the Western hemisphere (Erikson, 1939; Redfield, 1943), and finally within mainstream North American society (Fox, 1948; Brameld, 1958, 1959). Anthropological investigation of schools and schooling in industrial societies received additional impetus during the 1950s through the work of Jules Henry (e.g., 1955, 1957, 1959, 1963). Although not an anthropologist, Henry examined rituals, culture, and social structure, treating elementary school classrooms and high schools as if they were tribes. From his observations in U.S. suburban schools, Henry inferred patterns derived from and supportive of the wider cultural context of his participants. Many of these patterns were drawn from Henry's own knowledge and experience as a member of the culture rather than through extensive fieldwork to establish the linkages he posited; but such inferences demonstrated unequivocally how schools and schooling were integrated with their cultural contexts—just as Vanderwalker, Hewett, and Montessori had asserted so many years before. Wylie's (1957) ethnography of a French school within its village milieu, Spiro's (1958) analysis of education in an Israeli kibbutz, and Hartshorne's (1943) study of U.S. college students likewise documented the interrelationship of schooling with a society's belief systems, modes of perceptual and conceptual meanings, and predominant political, economic, and social structures.

During the 1950s, the interdisciplinary area of educational anthropology began to crystallize. The accumulation of fieldwork research and of comparative interpretation, cited above, provided a body of literature using anthropological constructs and research design to investigate educational phenomena. Major efforts to analyze and synthesize this material and to examine its applications were undertaken during this decade (e.g., Brameld, 1957; Rosenstiel, 1954).

The two scholars whose activities were the greatest catalyst to the formalization of educational anthropology were Solon Kimball, then at Teachers College, Columbia University, and George Spindler at Stanford University. Kimball advocated including anthropology in public school education and using it in educational policy making and research (e.g., 1956a,b). In later decades, his efforts culminated in a comprehensive review of educational anthropology (1974), a theoretically informed critique of education in the U.S. with McClellan (1962), and the creation, with Burnett (1974b), of an anthology of investigations into the influence of culture on human learning and cognition. Spindler, too, promoted culture theory and anthropological perspectives in educational decision making (e.g., 1955a) and in curriculum content and teacher training (e.g., 1959). His anthologies of current scholarship and empirical research in educational anthropology (1955b, 1963b, 1974b, 1982b, 1987; Spindler & Spindler, 1987) reflect the diversification, elaboration, and intensification of work in the field. His work focuses on ethnography as an alternative way to study schooling in the United States and provides examples of the wide range of cultural perspectives on what happens in schools, as well as strategies for discovering and documenting these patterns.

During the 1960s and 1970s, educational ethnography flourished within anthropology (Brameld & Sullivan, 1961; Shunk & Goldstein, 1964; Wolcott, 1967a; Sindell, 1969; Gearing & Tindall, 1973). Some researchers continued the tradition of Mead, studying child rearing and enculturation in traditional societies (e.g., Read, 1959; Kaye, 1962; Landy, 1959; Jocano, 1969; Williams, 1969; Honigmann & Honigmann, 1965; Howard, 1970; Deng, 1972; Grindal, 1972; Leis, 1972; Peshkin, 1972; Moore, 1973; Kawharu, 1975; Erchak, 1977; Freed & Freed, 1981).

Like earlier work, such studies followed enculturation throughout the life cycle from birth to death, within the cultural framework of social organization and belief systems. More frequently, however, the vagaries of Westernization and urbanization required examination of acculturation as well as enculturation. Where appropriate, ethnographers followed their participants into schools and documented variation, confluence, and conflict among the formal education of schools, the informal education of kinship and community networks, and the nonformal education of village groups and governmental agencies (LaBelle, 1975).

Other anthropologists examined enculturation and socialization within industrialized and industrializing societies, further clarifying distinctions between schooling and education (e.g., Dore, 1965; Warren, 1967; Brameld, 1968; Spindler, 1973; Peshkin, 1978). Such studies focused on forces contributing to both cultural change and cultural continuity, emphasizing the impact of modernization and urbanization on the values and ideologies of communities throughout the world. The comparative, concurrent analyses of six cultures—villages in New England, Kenya, Okinawa, India, the Philippines, and Mexico—represent a complex elaboration of the central Meadian tradition (Whiting, 1963; Whiting & Whiting, 1975) in focus, in research design, and in the melding of anthropological and psychological constructs to illuminate patterns of human behavior and belief.

Grounded within the tradition of community studies, a major thrust during these decades was the ethnographic examination of education in subcultural and ethnic enclaves within industrialized societies. Many of these were conducted in the United States; they include George and Louise Spindler's (1971) work among the Menominee; Murray and Rosalie Wax's studies of the Sioux (e.g., Wax, Wax, & Dumont, 1964) and the Cherokee (e.g., Wax, 1971); Hostetler & Huntington's analysis of the Amish (1971); Collier's investigation among Alaskan Eskimo (1973); Parmee's study of the Apache (1968); Hendricks's tracking of migrants to New York City from a village in the Dominican Republic (1974); Gallimore, Boggs, & Jordan's assessment of schooling in a Hawaiian-American community (1974); and the studies of U.S. blacks by Ogbu (1974) in an urban neighborhood and by Ward in a rural settlement (1971). Investigations of education in minority communities elsewhere include a collection of studies of Canadian Indians (King, 1967; Wolcott, 1967b; Lewis, 1970), Modiano's analysis of acculturation among the Indians of the Mexican Chiapas (1973), and Shimahara's fieldwork among the Japanese Burakumin (1971).

Since the early 1970s, educational anthropology has diversified substantively and methodologically, and it contributes increasingly to the use of ethnography and other qualitative designs in the study of educational phenomena. The culture concept remains a unifying construct of this tradition. Anthropologists study language and other formal symbol systems through which culture is transmitted, maintained, and transformed (e.g., Cazden, John, & Hymes, 1972; Green & Wallat, 1981; Wilkinson, 1982). They study the stratification of culture in industrialized societies as it is expressed in schooling (e.g., Leacock, 1969; Hakken, 1980; Eckerd, 1988; Foley, 1990), education of religious groups (e.g., Lesko, 1986, 1988; Peshkin, 1986; Schoem, 1982), age cohorts (e.g., Goodman, 1970; Sieber & Gordan, 1981), and racial and ethnic identities (e.g., Ogbu, 1978; Rist, 1973; Rosenfeld, 1971; Delgado-Gaitan, 1988; Gibson, 1988; Deyhle, 1986). They document the consequences for education, schools, and students when governmental policy changes existing patterns of cultural stratification and diversity. Examples include studies of desegregation in the United States (e.g., Fuchs, 1966; Rist, 1978, 1979; Wax, 1979; Clement, Eisenhardt, & Harding, 1979; Rowley, 1983; Schofield, 1982).

Anthropologists study both explicit social structures and organizations and tacit conceptual systems—such as the hidden curriculum in schools—underlying the cultural and subcultural processes that maintain these units (e.g., Au, 1980; Au & Jordan, 1981; Philips, 1983; Deyhle, 1992). They examine patterns of language use, interpersonal interactions, transactions, relationships, and participation through which cultural processes are expressed and created in educational settings (e.g., Borman, 1982; Erickson & Shultz, 1979; Heath, 1983; Moll & Greenberg, 1990). Using the conceptual tools of cultural relativism and diversity, they have offered scathing critiques of schooling and educational policy (e.g., Eddy, 1967).

Most significant for the design of educational ethnography, anthropologists have begun to investigate mass schooling in urban societies by selecting units narrower than an entire community and its educational systems. These units are more arbitrary than was the custom in the community study tradition, but they are units whose scope lies more within the resources of most researchers. These studies can be divided into six groups, depending upon the analytic unit selected.

1. Career and life histories or role analyses of individuals (e.g., Wolcott, 1973).

2. Microethnographies of small work and leisure groups within classrooms or schools (e.g., Leemon, 1972; Au, 1980; Gearing & Epstein, 1982).

3. Studies of single classrooms abstracted as small societies (e.g., Schultz & Florio, 1979; Cox, 1980; Spindler & Spindler, 1982).

4. Studies of schools or school districts that treat the inhabitants of the units as discrete communities (e.g., Singleton, 1967; Johnson, 1980; Peshkin, 1986; Foley, 1990; Eckerd, 1988; Chang, 1991).

5. Studies of small communities or subgroups defined by their relationship to schools or schooling [Adler & Adler's (1991) study of collegiate basketball players].

6. Conceptually controlled comparisons of any of the preceding five units (e.g., Eddy, 1969; Fuchs, 1969; Lancy, 1980; Moore, 1967; Kapferer, 1981; Schwartz, 1981; Holland & Eisenhart, 1990).

These six designs are controversial. Because researchers using them deemphasize broad contextual and cultural factors external to the examined unit, some anthropologists label them as "not ethnography." This judgment is justified further by the interdisciplinary overlap so common in such designs; the investigators supplement anthropological perspectives with constructs drawn from sociology and sociologically informed studies of Third World countries, psychology, and educational evaluation.

INFLUENCES FROM EDUCATIONAL SOCIOLOGY

Some of the earliest sociologists, notably Durkheim (1947, 1961) and Weber (1947), were concerned with schools and schooling, particularly as they were said to facilitate nation building and moral development. Both Durkheim in France and Dewey (e.g., 1916) in the United States wrote extensively on schooling; Durkheim (1947) used cultural transmission to frame the issue of the role of formal schooling. He identified the process of differentiation that socializing and enculturating agencies undergo as societies industrialize, emphasizing the development of formal schooling as one product of that process (1947). This work was, however, preeminently prescriptive and analytic rather than empirically based in fieldwork. In a more theoretical vein, Weber (1947) developed a taxonomy of ideal–typical socioeconomic systems and the types of school systems which were associated with them. He suggested that knowledge of a society's elite structure would predict its patterns of formal socialization or education because the latter was designed, consciously or unconsciously, to provide recruits for and to reinforce the existing structure of social stratification.

Sociologists from the fieldwork tradition generally ignored education and schools through the first half of the twentieth century. Research in educational sociology and its conduit—the *Journal of Educational Sociology*, founded in 1926—emphasized survey research, experimental investigation, and quantified measurement (Bogdan & Biklen, 1982). Much other writing took a somewhat reformist bent; educational sociologists were concerned that schools receive substantive input from sociology so that, better understanding the nature of society, they could socialize children to create a better world. Waller's publication, *The Sociology of Teaching* (1932), stood alone as a data-based descriptive study of the school as a community until the 1960s. By midcentury, however, sociologists investigating the towns and cities of the United States began to include schools and schooling as significant components within the social fabric. Hollingshead's *Elmtown's Youth* (1949), a landmark work from a field sociologist, examined how formal high school training affected adolescents. This study explicitly addressed the way small-town culture was reflected in and reinforced by educational practices. In addition, portions of community studies such as *Yankee City* (Warner, Lloyd, Low, Lunt, & Srole, 1963), *Middletown* (Lynd & Lynd, 1929), *The Levittowners* (Gans, 1967), and *Small Town in Mass Society* (Vidich & Bensman, 1958), like the ethnographic monographs provided by anthropologists, dealt with rearing and socialization of children and included data on schooling. The educational component of much of the work identified above remained descriptive. Few attempts were made to tie it to structural or theoretical frameworks. Mainstream sociologists criticized the genre for its lack of theoretical underpinnings, its failure to generate statistical correlations among the variables and constructs explored, its lack of generalizability, and its alleged subjectivity. Few studies in educational sociology originated with educators, nor did they address directly practical concerns that educators had about teacher behavior and effective instruction.

Only within the past two decades have descriptive studies of schools and schooling become acceptable within mainstream sociology. The initiation of ethnographic studies may have been impeded by the reservations, both legitimate and spurious, that hard-line quantitative researchers had about the rigor of community studies; sociologists also believed that educational issues were matters for practitioners to explore, not scholars.

CROSS-CULTURAL INFLUENCES ON EDUCATIONAL SOCIOLOGY: THE IMPACT OF THIRD WORLD COMPARISONS

In the 1960s, some sociologists became concerned with the effects of schooling on the social class structure. Drawing from Durkheim's and Weber's notions of the relationships between sociopolitical structure and educational practices, and using the data from both European and Third World nations as examples, political scientists, economists, and sociologists began to examine the relationships among schooling, cultural change, and levels of economic and cultural development in nations (e.g., Havighurst, 1961; Harbison & Myers, 1964; Shils, 1965; Anderson & Bowman, 1965; Foster, 1965; Kahl, 1968; Inkeles, 1974; Inkeles & Smith, 1974; Brownstein, 1972; Clignet & Foster, 1966; Labelle & Verhine, 1975; Heyneman, 1976). The data included large-scale attitudinal surveys which linked educational and occupational aspirations and expectations of individuals to demographic and economic data from government archives in many countries. The researchers relied on controlled manipulation of masses of data in ways that required extremely sophisticated statistical and analytical techniques, none of which would have been possible without computer technology. Methodological empiricism, so called by Karabel & Halsey (1978, p. 16), also was used to examine the relationships between sociocultural variables like ethnicity, socioeconomic status, and parental education on one hand and occupational or educational attainment on the other (Coleman, Campbell, Hobson, McPartland, Mood, Weinfeld, & York, 1966; Blau & Duncan, 1967; Jencks,

Smith, Acland, Bane, Cohen, Gintis, Heyns, & Michelson, 1972; Bowles & Gintis, 1976). The preoccupation of sociologists with causal modeling and statistical manipulations led to an emphasis on quantification and derogation of small-scale descriptive research, particularly in field sociology and ethnography.

By the late 1960s and early 1970s, however, several factors converged in sociology to enhance interest in studies that were termed qualitative, field-oriented, observational, cross-cultural, or ethnographic. This is because the questions researchers were asking had changed. Sociologists and evaluators wanted to discover not only what was happening and how phenomena were connected, but whether processes and outcomes were occurring as predicted. For explanations, a synthesis was needed. If the quantitative studies could be criticized because they had not entered the schoolhouse, ethnographic and field studies could be faulted because they had not emerged from it. Earlier fieldwork efforts had been restricted to the small communities in which the schools studied were located. The new approaches emphasized the in-depth microanalysis of instructional effectiveness, as well as questions about links between schools and the broader social, economic, and political structure.

The first reason that a new approach was required was that neither the experience of students and teachers nor school-related factors affecting student outcomes could be addressed using the procedures of the methodological empiricists. Rather, in-depth small-scale studies were needed, and just as the University of Chicago had been a focal point for community-based field research in earlier decades, so also it served as a base for educational field study during this period. Becker, Geer, Hughes, & Strauss's *Boys in White* (1961) and Becker, Geer & Hughes's *Making the Grade* (1968) remain classic examples—albeit in higher education—of students' reactions to and interactions within formal educational institutions. Informed by clearly designed theoretical perspectives, designed to substantiate relationships discovered among categories constructed, and reported with methodological precision, these investigations offered explanations for what happens in schools. Combining qualitative strategies with more traditional approaches, other Chicago scholars investigated elementary school classrooms (Jackson, 1968) and the teaching profession (Lortie, 1975). Elsewhere, sociologists studied the operation of high school counseling as a means of social differentiation (Cicourel & Kitsuse, 1963), the effect of role sets on teachers' interactions with students (McPherson, 1972), and student peer interaction as a function of high school social structure (Cusick, 1973; Gordon, 1975). Sociologists had begun to address a gap in their knowledge base resulting from inadequate descriptive data and process analysis; it had confounded efforts to explain intriguing correlations between classroom processes and other social phenomena.

A second reason for change was that experience in and cultural knowledge of other countries had been gained by scholars who first became interested in studies of national development. To collect their data, they had lived abroad. They began to discover the gaps and misfits that occur when models generated in Western societies are grafted onto societies with different cultural infrastructures.

A third reason was that although the sophisticated and elegant studies of the methodological empiricists had established relationships among social variables and various aspects of schooling, they failed to account for why the relationships existed. Clearly, schooling acted on individuals and groups, and schooling was, in turn, acted on by many social factors. However, the studies stopped at the schoolhouse door. How and why the effects observed were manifested were still unknown, and large-scale studies could not provide the answer.

INFLUENCES FROM FRANCE AND ENGLAND: THE NEW SOCIOLOGY OF EDUCATION

In the 1970s such questions generated a revisionist critique of traditionally static structural–functional sociocultural models of the relationship between education and society. This movement was called the New Sociology of Education (Young, 1971).

Beginning in Europe and using observational methods that had been developed in major studies of early primary and elementary education (e.g., King, 1978), New Sociologists linked the systematic differences in educational attainment among subgroups, particularly disadvantaged subgroups within the society, to cultural patterns and social structures (e.g., Lacey, 1970; Stubbs & Delamont, 1976) of schools. By contrast, the old sociology of education focused on social stratification theory at the macroeconomic level. The New Sociology of education was informed by the sociology of knowledge, conflict theory, and symbolic interactionism and emphasized the school as a transmitter and processor of cultural information. It examined both overt and covert messages conveyed in the curriculum and management systems of schools (e.g., Dreeben, 1968; Jackson, 1968) and was enthusiastically embraced by investigators who called themselves variously ethnomethodologists, phenomenologists, and symbolic interactionists (Karabel & Halsey, 1978).

The New Sociology posited that researchers had to understand what happens inside the school before they could establish and make explicit

linkages between school effects and macrosocial and economic phenomena (Apple, 1978). Such studies combined ethnographic techniques with
historical and structural analyses to connect the meanings and constructs
developed in the process of schooling with existing equalities and inequalities in the larger society (e.g., London, 1978). They concentrated on the
actual and hidden content of schooling (e.g., Metz, 1978), processes of
teacher–student interaction within classrooms (Keddie, 1971; Hargreaves & Woods, 1984; Willis, 1977; Furlong, 1976), and common-sense
categories that educational participants use to order, guide, and give
meaning to their actions (Apple, 1978). Most made direct reference to
the inextricability of schooling and its effects from the larger societal
context, especially the linkage between educational success and occupational or social class status (e.g., Willis, 1977; Carew & Lightfoot, 1979;
Lacey, 1970). Although most of these analyses involved very small groups
of students or students and teachers (e.g., Mehan, 1976; Furlong, 1976;
Willis, 1977), some examined schools within their community contexts,
explicitly addressing class, power, and cultural structures of that community (e.g., Sharp & Green, 1975).

INFLUENCES FROM
EDUCATIONAL PSYCHOLOGY

Although they rarely call themselves ethnographers, the work of some
psychologists draws heavily on observational data and ethnographic techniques and has had a profound effect on educational ethnography. The
interchange between anthropology and psychology (Harrington, 1979)
frequently centers on issues relevant to educators, and such interchanges
have resulted in creative design alternatives for educational researchers.

The primary qualitative design tradition in psychology is the clinical
case study, used by Freud and his psychodynamic successors (for a review
of psychodynamic theory and the research designs that generated it, see
Hall & Lindzey, 1970). Although the clinical interview constitutes the
core of data collection in this tradition, it is supplemented by painstaking
observation, by interviews with others significant to the client subjects, by
projective devices and other psychometric instruments, by interpretive
examination of public and private documents, and by introspective analysis of the therapist/researcher's own responses and experiences.

Psychodynamic theory and its clinical research methods influenced a
generation of cultural anthropologists and contributed to the subfield of
culture and personality. Among them were investigators whose work was
fundamental to educational anthropology: Margaret Mead, John and
Irma Honigmann, and O. F. Raum (Haring, 1956). Although the clinical

case study and the comparative analysis of collective cases have been neglected as legitimate design alternatives in educational research (for a recent exception, see Borg & Gall, 1983, pp. 488–490; see also LeCompte & Preissle, 1992a), this tradition continues to produce creative perspectives on education, schooling, and child and adult development. For example, Coles' investigations (e.g., 1967, 1971a,b) of disadvantaged children in the United States are based upon clinical studies of children in culturally induced crises. Vaillant's (1977) examination of the lives of men considered to be mentally healthy is grounded in longitudinal case histories of individuals enrolled in a liberal arts college in the 1930s and 1940s who were studied through the mid-1970s. Erikson's (1968) theory of human development draws from his cross-cultural fieldwork (e.g., 1939), his clinical observations, and his psychoanalytic biographies of such figures as Martin Luther (1962).

In the 1920s and 1930s the interest of other psychologists in the cognitive and emotional development of children resulted in the child study movement. Unlike the anthropologists of that era, who studied children in their social and cultural contexts, the child study investigators concentrated on generating exceedingly dense descriptions of individual children's behaviors in a variety of settings, including schools (e.g., Monroe, 1932). However, they generally neglected cultural and other background data. Taken together, their data provide an empirical basis for delineating stages of development in children; methodologically, they provide examples of how streams of behavior (Barker & Wright, 1951; Wright, 1960; Barker, 1963) can be recorded and categorized.

At the same time, Piaget's observational work with his own children provided an impetus for studies of the ways children learn. Piaget's approach to the questions he posed was inductive, generative, and constructive. His research designs illustrate how these modes of investigation have contributed to the advance of social science theory (Piaget & Inhelder, 1969).

Another influence on educational ethnography has been cross-cultural psychology (Cole & Scribner, 1974). Its emphasis has been the discovery of differences in cognition and perception in Western and non-Western societies; it relies heavily for explanation of its results on ethnographic data collected to supplement experimental manipulations. Examples of the use of ethnography in cross-cultural psychology include Gay & Cole's (1967) study of cultural differences between American and Kpelle children in the acquisition of mathematics concepts; Kleinfeld's (1979) examination of the effects of a bicultural education program on the achievement, social relationships, and values of Eskimo adolescents; and Tharp & Gallimore's (1988) synthesis of Vygotsky's Soviet activity theory with pedagogical and curriculum theory and knowledge derived from ethnographic work with native Hawaiian children.

Closer to traditional ethnography is the work of ecological psychologists (Lewin, 1951; Barker & Gump, 1964; Barker, Gump, Friesen, & Willems, 1970; Bronfenbrenner, 1970) and sociologically informed psychologists like Louis Smith (Smith & Geoffrey, 1968; Smith & Keith, 1971) and Joan Roberts (1970). They have focused on behavior, social structures, and beliefs and interaction patterns in schools and classrooms. Bronfenbrenner's explicitly cross-cultural analysis illustrates work indistinguishable from that of anthropologists focusing on the same units. Such work underscores Harrington's (1979) assertion that research techniques need to be separated from the disciplines to which they traditionally have been assigned; effective research design is founded in methods appropriate to the questions posed. Thus an investigation may be no less ethnographic for having been executed by someone who is not an anthropologist.

EVALUATION STUDIES

Governmental funding always has been an important catalyst for educational research, affecting not only the questions asked, but also legitimizing specific research methods (Karabel & Halsey, 1978). During the 1960s, systems-analytic approaches (Rivlin, 1971), commonly used in economics and industry, dominated federally funded educational research in the United States. They emphasized measurement of easily scaled or quantified variables that generate highly reliable data. This approach was the driving force behind most educational research, in large part because of the impact of heavily funded and mandatory evaluation components attached to government-funded social projects. By the late 1960s, however, dissatisfaction with the systems-analysis model had become substantial.

In many cases, the systems-analysis approach was inappropriate to the phenomena under investigation and produced data of uneven and questionable validity (e.g., Guttentag, 1971; Helfgot, 1974; House, 1979; LeCompte, 1970). The results failed to satisfy those involved in programs and their evaluations, to explain success or failure of innovations, or even to define success adequately. Constructs and models lacking meaning for participants were used in evaluation designs; goals assessed often were insignificant to program planners; and final reports addressed few questions important to participants. Process data on problems and successes of program implementation rarely were reported.

By 1969, techniques for elicitation of implementation, process, or formative evaluation data began to show up in some research projects. These procedures required data collection techniques familiar to ethnographers even though the practical nature and often relatively short time span of the projects were not entirely congruent with classical ethnographic fieldwork. Ethnographic evaluation, so called, became extremely popular in the late 1970s and has been the genesis of much evaluative and basic research in education since then (e.g., Hess, 1991; Fetterman, 1984; Fetterman, 1988b; Fetterman & Pitman, 1986; Koppelman, 1979; Patton, 1980, Chapters 1–5; Patton, 1990b; Pitman & Maxwell, 1992; Willis, 1978).

It is interesting to note that the little observational research that was initiated by educators in schools and classrooms prior to the early 1970s did not originate in the social science disciplines. For the most part, it came from a tradition of teacher evaluation, in which standardized protocols were used to determine the quality of instruction, affect, or classroom management practiced by teachers (Medley & Mitzel, 1963). Although educators were interested in whether instructional programs improved pupil achievement and whether teachers and administrators were effective, they tended to rely for their information not on naturalistic observation, but on standardized instruments and upon prescriptive statements and quasiexperimental research designs. Very little emphasis was placed upon what has come to be called process data (Stufflebeam, 1978), which explains why programs developed as they did or examines classroom phenomena in detail. The integration of ethnographic data collection strategies into research on schools during the 1970s made it possible for researchers to examine these phenomena more fully.

Ethnographic techniques now are used in curriculum and program evaluation in two ways: comprehensive adoption of the entire ethnographic process or strategic selection of a few data collection techniques (for a statement of problems and issues in ethnographic evaluation, see Knapp, 1979). The objectives of the research determine which of these alternatives a researcher will choose. If the researcher wants to document shared beliefs, practices, artifacts, environments, folk knowledge, behaviors, subtle patterns of interaction, and a comprehensive inventory of program effects, then the appropriate choice is to do an ethnography of the entire intervention program. Smith & Keith's (1971) analysis of the establishment of an innovative elementary school; Wax's documentation (1979) of the process of desegregation in five public schools, and Deyhle's study (1986, 1989, 1991, 1992) of dropouts and dropout prevention programs among native American students are ethnographies comparable to traditional investigations conducted by anthropologists and sociologists. They offer implicit or explicit explanations to account for the patterns observed. Such ethnographies of organization or curricular innovations differ from community and tribal studies only in their focus.

A second alternative is to use only one or a few ethnographic data collection techniques in what is otherwise a traditional quasiexperimental or survey design. Even these limited applications provide data that strengthen the validity of standardized instrumentation. For example, Hall & Loucks (1977) used limited nonparticipant observation to assess the validity of a teacher questionnaire designed to determine the extent to which instructors actually use educational innovations in their classrooms. Limited use of ethnographic techniques also can highlight specific program effects of interest to developers or program participants. Applications such as these have the advantage of reducing required time and resources while producing useful results soon available to policy makers.

INFLUENCES FROM CRITICAL STUDIES, POSTMODERNISM, AND POSTSTRUCTURALISM

Since the mid-1980s, ethnography and qualitative research designs have moved from marginal, or merely complementary (Jaeger, 1988), methods in the social sciences and education to a position of assured legitimacy. However, debate over how and why such methods should be used or in what form their results should be presented persists. Central to this debate is a critique of the universal application of positivistic canons to research in education—a debate which began in the natural sciences in the 1930s, swept through the social sciences in the 1950s, and profoundly influenced American educational research in the 1980s and 1990s. Erickson's (1986) article in *Handbook of Research on Teaching* verified mainstream acceptance of "interpretive" approaches, which Erickson equates with "ethnographic, qualitative, participant observational, case study, symbolic interactionist, phenomenological, constructivist or interpretive." This research includes any use of participant observation whose primary focus is "interest in human meaning in social life and its elicitation and exposition by the researcher" (p. 119).

Erickson's focus on methods and the stance of the researcher toward subject- or participant-constructed meanings did not move far enough beyond positivism to satisfy researchers steeped in critical theory, whose questions followed soon after. A heated debate has raged ever since over differences between positivists, interpretivists, and critical theorists with regard to research questions, epistemology, researcher stance, research goals, and subject—or participant—roles. In Table 1.1 we clarify the differences between these approaches to inquiry.

Since the mid-1980s, critical theorists, including feminists, neo-

TABLE 1.1
A Comparison of Ways of Knowing and Inquiring

	Positivistic approaches	Interpretive approaches	Critical approaches
Role of Researcher	Detached, objective	Involved, subjective	Educative, analytic, transformative; Active teacher/learner
Role of Researched	Passive informant	Active collaborator	Educative, collaborative; Active learner/teacher
Procedures	Definition of terms (researcher) Description (researcher) Classification/codification (by researcher) Enumeration Correlation Verification Prediction	Definition of terms (subject) Description (subject) Classification/codification (by researcher subject to member checks) Enumeration Correlation/association Interpretation (by researcher in conjunction with subject) Communication (between researcher and subject)	Definition of terms (researcher and subject) Description (researcher and subject) Classification/codification (by researcher subject to member/checks) Enumeration Correlation/association Interpretation (researcher in conjunction with subject) Communication (by researcher) Action/transformation (researcher and subject)

Goals	1) *Generalization* of results to subsequent similar events and phenomena 2) Development of universal laws which govern human behavior in all settings	1) *Comparison* of results to similar and dissimilar processes and phenomena 2) Development of workable and shared understandings regarding regularities in human behavior in specific settings	1) *Analysis* of results to unmask inequities in processes and phenomena 2) Development of emancipatory stance toward determinants of human behavior
Concern	Self as defined by society/form/social structure (i.e., what's going on outside individuals)	Society/form/social structure as defined by self (i.e., what's going on within and between individuals)	Self as defined by the structure of domination (i.e., what's going on within and between individuals as a consequence of their given material and historical conditions)
Process	Achieving control of behavior by modeling its study after procedures used by scientists studying the physical universe	Achieving understanding of behavior by analysis of social interaction, meaning, and communication	Achieving change in structure and behavior by exposing hidden patterns of meaning, communication, and control
Origins of knowledge	By definition, by deduction from laws or theoretical statements, from experience	From shared understandings, negotiation, historical and social context	From differential access to knowledge regarding historical context and political, economic, and social conditions
Focus	Observable behavior Measurement and quantification Controlling variance and bias	Elicited meanings for observational behavior Intersubjective understanding Explaining variance and bias	Structural asymmetries, critical consciousness, hidden meanings and assumptions, patterns of oppression Exposing variance and bias

Marxists, postmodernists, and poststructuralists, have integrated the methods of cultural anthropology and fieldwork sociology with an activist critical theory in an approach they term "critical ethnography." Critical theory, the tradition underpinning critical ethnography, traces its roots to Marxism and neo-Marxism and seeks to illuminate how the distribution of power, privileges, resources, status, authority, leadership, and decision making affects society, culture, technology, and science itself. Most particularly, critical theory is directed to examining how inequitable distributions lead to inequalities among groups and individuals (Bottomore, 1984). It seeks to identify contradictions between actual and perceived conditions of material life, using them as leverage for initiating change in existing power asymmetries. Taking this critical perspective, scholars have reexamined both the practice of human research (e.g., Bredo & Feinberg, 1982) and the practice of schooling in Western societies (e.g., Giroux, 1981) to assess their role in perpetuating political and economic inequality.

Critical ethnography has been especially important in research on education and schooling, examining how groups use symbols, social practices, myths, and rituals of schooling to create and maintain inequitable distributions of power, prestige, and resources (e.g., Apple & Weis, 1983; Anderson, 1989; Brodkey, 1987; Gitlin, Siegel, & Boru, 1989; McNeil, 1988a,b,c; Popkewitz, 1990; Popkewitz & Tabachnick, 1981; Quantz, 1992; Quantz & O'Connor, 1988; Roman, 1992; Sharp, 1981; Weis, 1988; Woods, 1992).

Feminist theory also derives from the critical tradition. While it is concerned with political dimensions of both public and private lives, it focuses on how these play out differently by gender (Christian-Smith, 1988; Holland & Eisenhart, 1990; Lesko, 1986, 1988; Roman, 1988, 1992). Smith (1987), for example, insists that what she calls the standpoints, including gender, of all the players in human research— investigators as well as participants—be represented in what is studied and written. She emphasizes that the experiences of individuals, whether powerful or powerless, must be represented in any adequate theories of society and culture. Feminist scholarship in the human sciences is responsible for revealing, rediscovering, and rescuing documentation of women's lives and related gender patterns across societies (e.g., Belenky, Clinchy, Goldberger, & Tarule, 1986; Hammond & Jablow, 1976; Harding & Hintikka, 1983; Keller, 1983; Keller & Grontkowski, 1983; Leacock & Safa, 1986; Reiter, 1975; Rosaldo & Lamphere, 1974). Qualitative research in education has been especially receptive to feminist theory (e.g., Aisenberg & Harrington, 1988; Grant & Sleeter, 1986; Harper,

1979; Hoffman, 1981; Holland & Eisenhart, 1990; Lesko, 1988; Valli, 1986).

All these persuasions have in common a rejection of traditional science, especially the emphasis in positivism on control, the omission of context, and the objectification of subjects being studied. They often place their practitioners within what has been termed a "postmodern and poststructural" approach to inquiry, two terms often, and erroneously, equated. Both postmodernism and poststructuralism have their origins in the critical tradition. Postmodernism, however, addresses issues of power and specifically rejects all existing authority. It suggests that the voices currently expounding the accepted canon, even in aesthetics, achieve their legitimacy because they hold social, economic, political, or cultural power, not because of any inherent correctness of the rules or truths they espouse. In other words, those who have the power to pay the piper call the tune. Postmodernism, then, questions the *content* of rules and the legitimacy of those who *make* the rules in every aspect of modern life.

By contrast, poststructuralism is a more narrowly construed term. It refers to the rejection of rules in the social sciences. Specifically, poststructuralism questions the structural–functional concepts and analytic categories underlying all traditional social science inquiry. Critical, feminist, and poststructural epistemologists have begun to question the premises underlying objective social science research. Some even question the possibility of striving for an objective science. In rejecting accepted canons for social science, poststructural researchers also reject accepted concepts and terminology. They find that the language of poststructural science is full of concepts with multiple meanings, some of which may contradict each other. Standards and definitions are mutable. Relationships between researcher and researched are negotiable. And reality itself has no stable existence; rather, it becomes a function of those who experience it. As might be imagined, these different perspectives on research have generated healthy and heated debate among investigators. Both postmodernists and poststructuralists call for giving voice to viewpoints and persons who hitherto have been marginal or silenced. They ask questions which have never before been formulated and try to address them with unconventional methods. They interpret their results through new lenses and present them in novel ways which are intended to portray more adequately the multiplicity of viewpoints now recognized to constitute the reality of any social setting. In these efforts, the techniques of ethnography and qualitative research have been crucial, because, as Erickson (1986) states, they *involve* the researcher with participants, and emphasize the *meanings* which human beings use to structure and construct their existence.

Summary

Ethnography and its qualitative design variants provide educational and other social researchers with alternatives for describing, interpreting, and explaining the social world and the operation of educational phenomena within this world. Substantive constructs generated within the various social and applied sciences that influence educational ethnography provide diverse perspectives toward education and contribute to the authentic portrayal of a complex, multifaceted human society.

Educational ethnographers examine the processes of teaching and learning, the intended and unintended consequences of observed interaction patterns, and the relationships among such educational actors as parents, teachers, and learners and the sociocultural contexts within which nurturing, teaching, and learning occur. They investigate the variety of forms education takes across cultures and among subgroups within society, the manifest and latent functions of educational structures and processes, and the conflicts generated when socializing agents are confronted by rapid social change. They document the lives of individual teachers, students, and administrators for unique and common patterns of experience, outlook, and response.

The outcomes of educational ethnography contribute to improvement in educational and school practice in several ways. They strengthen the overall research upon which many innovations and policies are based. Ethnographic and other qualitative accounts convey to teachers, administrators, and parents the diversity to be expected from children, students, and school communities and encourage these educators to respond more flexibly and appropriately to their charges. The ethnographer's focus on the vagaries of everyday life and on the perspectives of those involved confirms the reality experienced by educators and demonstrates concretely the connections among research activity, educational theory, and pragmatic concerns (Brown, 1982a). This is facilitated by the rich, descriptive data of ethnographic reports, traditionally written so as to be accessible to the public. Finally, the complexity of educational phenomena and their entrenchment within broader sociocultural milieus are revealed consistently in ethnographic accounts. These allow policy makers and educational consumers to formulate more accurate and judicious expectations about what schools, families, and other agencies can do to direct and enhance education and socialization.

Having provided, in good ethnographic fashion, a historical context for the research design, the remaining chapters of this book present principles, guidelines, and alternatives for (1) formulating research questions and choosing theoretical perspectives appropriate for ethnographic investigation, (2) selecting sites, people, and other research units that comprise an ethnographer's data sources, (3) negotiating the intricate relationships upon which valid and reliable information depends, (4) anticipating and modifying the data collection tactics used to elicit such information, (5) developing, borrowing, or adapting analytic strategies relevant to the data acquired and to pertinent redirections of research questions, and (6) assessing and evaluating the ethnographic process and its resultant products.

CHAPTER TWO

Considerations on Selecting a
Research Design

In this chapter, we address the question of research design. Research design, most broadly conceived, involves deciding what the research purpose and questions will be, what information most appropriately will answer specific research questions, and which strategies are most effective for obtaining it. A distinguishing characteristic of qualitative and ethnographic research design is that it facilitates a fluid and developmental process of investigation.

We begin this discussion by distinguishing among terms applied to qualitative and ethnographic research design. We hope that such distinctions will facilitate clear choices between models for investigation.

Clarifying the Language of Research Design

The term *research design* is somewhat confusing. Social science methodologists have failed to make clear and definitive distinctions among research designs or to clearly discriminate among theoretical frames, research designs, and data collection methods. Some descriptors applied to designs often are presented as opposing poles of a dichotomy—phenomenological research versus positivistic research, naturalistic research versus experimental research, or qualitative research versus quantitative research—even though it could be argued that the first two of these pairs are natural opposites and the last pair is not.

Distinctions between qualitative research designs are further confused by the synonymous use of terms such as phenomenological, naturalistic, nonmanipulative, observational, qualitative, and ethnographic research. These designations refer not to design, but to quite different aspects of the inquiry process. While ethnographic research *is* nonmanipulative, naturalistic, and often phenomenological, not all nonmanipulative, naturalistic, or phenomenological research is ethnographic. Describing studies as either "qualitative" or "quantitative" is misleading, because much ethnography uses quantitative data and many quantitative studies use what are termed qualitative data collection techniques. Finally, novice researchers often describe their research as "descriptive." We believe, however, that there is no such thing as a descriptive *design* because, by itself, the term tells us nothing about how the researcher plans to do the work. All research is, to some extent, descriptive. If it isn't, the reader will not know what was studied.

Qualitative research and ethnography often are erroneously described as "not empirical" by people who are trying to say that they are neither experimental nor "quantitative." However, the term *empirical* has nothing to do with numbers or manipulation of variables. Rather, it refers to whether or not phenomena are capable of being found in the real world and assessed by means of the senses. Since both qualitative and ethnographic research are preeminently concerned with observation and recording of real-world phenomena, they clearly *are* empirical. In fact, all social science research, especially ethnography, is empirical. Philosophy, by contrast, is not.

Ethnographic and qualitative research often is equated with hermeneutic or interpretive research, though not all hermeneutic or interpretive studies are ethnographies. These terms refer to very different aspects of the inquiry process. A concern with hermeneutics involves a concern with meaning. The term comes from a Greek word meaning "to translate"; a *hermeneut* was an interpreter. Contemporarily, hermeneutics is concerned with ways to explain, translate, and interpret perceived reality. In contemporary research, a concern with hermeneutics is a concern for interpreting and recounting accurately the meanings which research participants give to the reality around them. Ethnographers are concerned with interpreting cultures accurately, but because they can only see portions of a cultural reality, they also struggle with the issue of portrayal. Many ethnographers believe that the "reality" of a cultural scene is the product of multiple perceptions, including that of the researcher and that produced by the interaction between researchers and the people they study. The problem becomes one of determining how much of whose reality is portrayed, how it can be portrayed, and with what degree of adequacy (see Clifford & Marcus, 1986; Geertz, 1988; Marcus & Fischer, 1986).

Interpretive research shares with hermeneutics a concern with meaning. These studies are framed by descriptions of, explanations for, or meanings given to phenomena by *both* the researcher and the study participants rather than by the definitions and interpretations of the researcher alone. These studies emphasize analysis of language and discourse; they use semantic description rather than probabilistic statistics for proof (Erickson, 1986).

ISSUES OF SIZE, SITE, AND METHOD

Names given to research designs often refer to wildly different—and noncomparable—logistical aspects of the investigation. For example, selection defines the term *case study;* a case is the number of units—one—studied, whether the unit is a formal organization, a psychotic child, a community, or an encounter group (Merriam, 1988; Stake, 1988). Because they are reconstructions of a single culture, ethnographies *are* case studies, by definition. Most ethnographies also, by definition, are field studies. Field studies are defined by the *site* of the research, usually the natural habitat or customary environment of the participants. Case studies are used in a variety of disciplines, from industrial and clinical psychology to education. Case studies can be quantitative as well as qualitative; like field studies and ethnographies, they may take place either in naturalistic settings or in artificial laboratory-like settings. Both case studies and field studies may involve researcher-initiated manipulation or participants, or natural experiments—accidental occurrences interrupting the normal flow of events—that can be studied as if they were experiments.

Observational research can be used in all kinds of studies. It indicates that the researcher is observing participants and collecting data on what they are doing, whether or not researcher and study participants interact in any way.

The term *survey* refers to a method of data collection, whether it takes place in the field, in a lab, among the participants of a case study, or among the thousands included in a Gallup poll. In general, good surveys are preceded by field work. Ethnographers use surveys, in the form of both interviews and questionnaires; they also use participant observation. Surveys can stand alone as a design or can be used in conjunction with other data collection techniques.

ISSUES ASSOCIATED WITH
DISCIPLINARY TRADITIONS

Social scientists generally use variations on one of seven research models: ethnography, case study analysis, survey analysis, experimentation, standardized observational research, simulation, and historical or document analysis.

Each of these models captures different aspects of the human experience. For example, case study analysis is appropriate for intensive, in-depth examination of one or a few aspects of a given phenomenon. By contrast, survey analysis usually addresses fewer individual aspects of phenomena, but does so across far more instances. An experimental study might be able to tell a researcher if a specific program achieved its stated goals, but it would not give much information on *how* the program was implemented or to what to attribute its success. Thus, the naturalistic, phenomenological, and holistic emphasis common to ethnography can be contrased with the customarily controlled, positivistic, and particularistic emphasis in experimentation. While both are oriented to analyzing the content and meaning of human behavior, experimentation and ethnography differ from historical and document analysis in that the latter rely principally upon written artifacts which recorded past human behavior, whereas the former use current behavior—verbal and nonverbal—as their dominant source of data.

Each of these research designs also is typically associated with particular social science disciplines: psychology with experimentation, sociology with survey designs, anthropology with ethnography, economics with simulation strategies such as mathematical model building, and political science with comparative case studies. Table 2.1 shows the various social science disciplines and the research models which are associated with them, usually because the "ancestors" of the disciplines used these models in the infancy of the field. It is important to note, as we have emphasized throughout this chapter, that contemporary researchers in every discipline borrow models from each other with impunity in the interest of better research.

Variation in choice of research models also is associated with subfields within a discipline, as, for example, in the association of controlled field studies (manipulation of specific behaviors in an otherwise natural setting) with social psychology. The models themselves have developed within conceptual frameworks specifying the nature of legitimate data, assumptions about causal relations, and theories of human behavior (Smith, 1979). Thus, behaviorists in psychology emphasize experimentation as the model of choice. Likewise, psychodynamic theorists depend upon the clinical case study, whereas ecological psychology relies heavily upon standardized observations made in unmanipulated natural settings. While Piaget and other developmental psychologists used manipulated observations to address their research questions, most psychometricians have conducted surveys with various standardized tests and protocols.

TABLE 2.1
Research Designs Customarily Associated with Social Science Disciplines[a]

	Economics	Psychology	Political science	Sociology	Anthropology	History
Mathematical models	X					
Simulations	X					
Controlled experiments		X				
Controlled field studies		X−				
Standardized tests and observational protocols		X				
Surveys	X	X+	X	X		
Linguistic elicitation					X	
Case studies		X*	X	X	X	X
Ethnography					X	
Analysis of documents and records			X	X#		X

[a]X−, naturalistic psychology (ethology); X+, social psychology; X*, clinical psychology; X#, demography.

Some variation is associated with the historical development of a field. Anthropology originated in biology or natural history; its methods mirrored the studies of plants and animals carried out by biologists. Descriptive, comparative, taxonomic, and inductive in their intent, they relied to a large extent on observation and recording of events and behavior as they naturally occurred in field sites. Ethnography and physical anthropology still rely on these methods.

As with psychology, entire schools of sociological thought frequently have been generated from research studies using, for the most part, a single general research model. Sociological research began as case studies of organizations, theoretical treatises on macrosocial phenomena, or secondary analysis of demographic and census material. It moved subsequently in two directions. One direction relied upon the survey model as an extension of demographic analysis. The other, which evolved in the 1920s at the same time as ethnography in cultural anthropology, came from the so-called Chicago School of Sociology. It used the same participatory observational techniques employed in anthropology, but was informed by the symbolic interactionism of G. H. Mead and Robert Blumer and others. The Chicago School researchers carried out case studies of specific groups, usually in urban settings in North America and Western Europe. This model also was used among industrial psychologists in their analyses of worker groups; both types of study eventually came to be associated with the data collection strategy of participant observation. Some subdisciplines like social psychology began by using small-scale field observations and opinionnaires for research on groups; they moved increasingly toward experimental and quasiexperimental design models.

Despite the preference, legitimate and otherwise, for certain general research models by individual schools within social science disciplines, some of the most creative research uses models eclectically, combining aspects of various models to produce more valid research designs. In many circumstances, the most desirable design involves the amalgamation of two or more of the seven ideal–typical models in a kind of triangulation. Designs applied by social scientists often employ elements derived from more than one model, although a single one may predominate. Over the past few decades, the practice of combining models has become more common, facilitated by technological advances such as computers which permit consideration of multiple variables within a single experiment, the blurring of strict disciplinary boundaries which once obviated alternative approaches to inquiry, and methodological and theoretical advances which encourage eclecticism in research design (Eisner & Peshkin, 1990; Jaeger, 1988; LeCompte *et al.*, 1992; Sherman & Webb, 1988).

Campbell & Stanley's quasiexperimental designs (1963) (for an updated version, see Cook & Campbell, 1979), applied extensively by educational researchers, combine the rigor of laboratory experimentation with the naturalistic lack of manipulation in the field environment. Similarly, Piaget's manipulated case study observations, noted above, combined elements of experimentation and case studies. Much of Milgram's research in social psychology (e.g., Milgram, Mann, & Harter, 1965) incorporates both naturalistic observation and manipulation of key experimental variables. Ethnographers, for example, may combine ethnographic data collection with strategies from survey or experimental models. Such models and their various combinations and simulations are alternative means for addressing an initial research question. The variants discussed in Chapter One as quasiethnographies result from this eclectic approach to research design (for diverse forms of the qualitative case study, see Bogdan & Biklen, 1992). Even farther afield are policy, critical, and applied researchers who explicitly enter the field intending to change it. They eschew injunctions about researcher detachment altogether and build into their designs negotiation of research problems, access, conditions of study, relationships with subjects, and even how the final results will be used (Anderson, 1989; Giroux, 1988; Giroux & Simon, 1989; Gitlin & Smyth, 1989; Partridge, 1987; Schensul, Schensul, Gonzales, & Caro, 1981; Schensul & Schensul, 1992).

SUMMARY

Research designs may be defined by any of the following factors (Le-Compte, 1990):

— The type of research site (field studies versus lab studies)
— The number of units selected (case studies)
— The role that the researcher plays vis-a-vis study participants (participant observation)
— The number of items studied and their amenability to statistical analysis (quantitative studies)
— The method of data collection (survey research, participant or nonparticipant observation)
— The degree of control exercised by the researcher over participants (experiments, naturalistic research)

Questions to ponder in selecting research designs are listed as follows:

— With what theoretical orientations (see Chapter Five) and disciplinary affiliations is the desired research design typically associated?
— Which of the seven typical design models in the social sciences most effectively address the goals of the research project?
— Does the research require extensive examination of a few cases or extensive analysis of many cases?
— Does the research require a holistic focus or does it focus on particular aspects of the phenomenon?
— Must the phenomenon being studied be examined in its natural context, or can it be more clearly illuminated through researcher manipulation in a laboratory setting?
— Are the theoretical orientations implicit in the design compatible with, contradictory to, or irrelevant to the research questions?

Formulating Research Purposes and Questions

One of the most difficult tasks a researcher faces is coming up with an operational research question, framed within a valid research purpose. Distinguishing between the purpose and the research question is the first problem.

THE DISTINCTION BETWEEN RESEARCH PURPOSE AND QUESTION

The initial formulation of a research question or problem defines the topic of interest and establishes parameters for the research design. Many researchers confuse research purposes and research questions. This may be because in ethnographic research, the formulation of questions and problems is complicated by the variety of ways initial objectives may be extended, modified, or redefined in the course of the study. Distinguishing between the purpose or goal of a study and the question investigated is essential to communicating both a study's conceptual significance and its empirical content. Although research purposes and research questions are related and often overlapping concerns, they are not synonymous.

Statements of research *purpose* or *goals* delineate what is to be the overall, ultimate product of the research. These statements describe what is yet unknown which a study will reveal and how it will fill gaps in an existing knowledge base, expand the knowledge base, initiate investigation in a neglected line of inquiry, or facilitate integration of an emerging conceptual field. They also suggest how the research results might be used. Statements of focus and purpose should reflect the conceptual and theoretical frameworks that guide and inform the research process. Ethnographers frequently develop or redefine purposes as they proceed through the research activity in the analytic mode we have termed "recursivity" (see Chapter Seven); consequently they must address both a priori and a posteriori goals with consideration for how and why modifications occurred.

The research *questions* investigated, by contrast, define how the purpose or goals will be carried out. They delineate the specific hypotheses or problems addressed in a study. In contrast to the conceptual abstractness of statements of purpose, research questions are phrased as concretely as possible in empirical or operational terms. They describe relationships sought or tested, facts discovered, proved, or disproved, and constructs or concepts generated. They also spell out exactly where, with whom, and how a study will be carried out. Careful specification of what the initial questions investigated were constitutes a succinct summary of what the researcher intended to do or actually accomplished in the study.

Research questions are more amenable to modification, reformulation, and redirection during the course of an ethnographic study than research purposes. To avoid giving the impression that the conclusions reached at the end were actually intended at the beginning of the research project, some ethnographers refuse to provide succinct summaries of the initial questions they addressed. Others are reluctant to express their work in the form of questions because the work has been "merely" descriptive, rather than guided by any form of formal or informal hypothesis or hunch. Such research often aims toward preservation; simply providing an accurate account of phenomena often has been considered a sufficient and legitimate research goal in cultural anthropology. However, a good research report describes both the questions which the study actually answered and the initial questions which were found to be inappropriate, unmanageable, or irrelevant.

Below, we enumerate a number of the questions which ethnographers and qualitative researchers must ask in order to identify and clarify their research purposes, goals, and questions.

— What topics, problems, or issues does the study address?
— What are its objectives?
— What is the scope of this investigation?
— What is to be included and excluded?
— Is the study oriented to abstract objectives or more concrete ones?
— How precisely or vaguely must the goal be articulated?
— Is the topic an applied issue or one involving basic research?
— To what extent are the research goals and questions amenable to extension, modification, or redefinition?
— What are the researcher's intentions for the study's results?
— How may the study's findings be used?
— What gaps in the existing knowledge base will the study address or expand?
— What new lines of inquiry might be opened?
— How may the study's conclusions contribute to the integration of existing concepts and propositions?

Theoretical Influences on the Research Purpose

Other factors having to do with the way data will be analyzed and interpreted and how research results will be used also affect the choice of design. These are guided by sets of assumptions characterizing various approaches to inquiry and are best illustrated by comparing ethnography with its most commonly asserted opposite, experimental design. In the pages which follow, we describe these distinctions and sets of assumptions.

PREDICTION VERSUS DESCRIPTION

In general, the initial design decision a social science researcher must make is whether the research is to be *predictive* or *descriptive*. The purpose of predictive research is to measure precisely the impact a specific activity or treatment has on people and to predict the chances of being able to duplicate that impact in future activities or treatments. The purpose of descriptive research is to document exactly what happened, whether the researcher is describing an experimental treatment or something occurring in the natural habitat of study participants.

Ethnography always is descriptive; it also always involves the study of an interplay among empirical variables as they occur naturally, rather than as they may be manipulated or arranged in advance by an investigator. Its process rarely emphasizes experimental treatments or manipulations except insofar as they are part of an overall context. Credibility and effect are established by systematically identifying and examining all possible causal and consequential factors attendant to an event (Scriven, 1974). The process involved differs from post hoc analysis that provides contextual information in experimental traditions. The naturalistic setting both facilitates on-the-spot and holistic analysis of causes and processes and precludes precise control of so-called extraneous factors.

By contrast, in predictive research, which requires focusing on the examination of effects caused by a specific treatment, the researcher needs considerably greater control over the phenomenon under study. The researcher establishes credibility of the research design and power of the treatment effect by holding constant or eliminating as many of the extraneous and contextual factors as possible. Sometimes ethnographers accidentally become involved in a manipulation, as when a *faux pas* is committed. In these cases, the ethnographer subsequently observes the ensuing interplay of natural normative sanctions. Occasionally, ethnographers may deliberately create an informal experiment by manipulating settings to elicit participant sanctions for the violation of social norms or to provoke other reactions from participants in a study (e.g., King, 1967; Rosenblatt, 1981; Rosenfeld, 1971). These data constitute a supplement to the ethnography. However, such manipulation is risky because it may embarrass participants, violate their trust, and ultimately jeopardize the study.

While predictive and descriptive studies may, in fact, use many of the same data collection techniques—and, in fact, many researchers, especially applied scientists and evaluators, mix predictive and descriptive elements in their projects—predictive and descriptive approaches differ in both the operations executed by researchers and the assumptions underlying how they proceed. To place themselves on a continuum between descriptive and predictive research, researchers need to ask themselves the following questions:

— How much control will I have over the subjects and the context of the research, and how it is to be executed?

— Is the phenomenon I am studying sufficiently well-understood that all the variables which might affect its course are known and can be controlled or explained?

— Given the goals of the study, does planning a predictive study make any sense?

— What kind of information do I need, and from which sources can I get it?

— Do I really need a controlled study to obtain the data?

Once the researcher has addressed these questions, an examination of the sets of assumptions governing various research designs is necessary before the researcher can make clear choices among ethnography and other designs. Similar to other investigators, ethnographers share common assumptions about ways to identify, organize, and process data and the ideas that explain them. These characteristic ways of thinking influence the choice of design.

General Assumptions Governing the Choice of Social Science Research Design

Social scientists define knowledge and truth according to assumptions they have about what constitutes a legitimate way to define, discover, construct, and explain reality. One way of conceptualizing these assumptions is by framing them in the four dimensions outlined in Fig. 2.1.

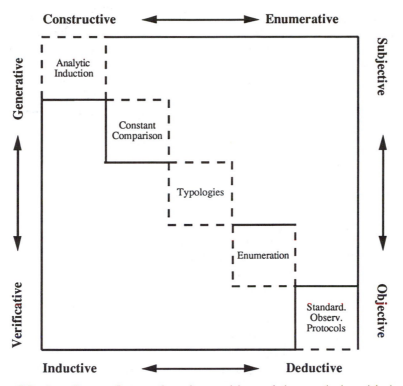

Figure 2.1 A continuum of assumptions characterizing analytic strategies in social science research. Broken lines indicate that the strategy varies on a dimension; solid lines indicate invariance.

These include an inductive–deductive dimension, a subjective–objective dimension, a generative–verificative dimension, and a constructive–enumerative dimension. Cultural reconstructions requiring congruent research strategies—phenomenological, empirical and naturalistic, holistic, and multimodal—are more likely than other research products to reflect assumptive modes of induction, generation, construction, and subjectivity. Ethnographic research, then, typically is located closer to the generative, inductive, constructive, and subjective ends of the continua. Ethnographers attempt to describe systematically the characteristics of variables and phenomena, to generate and refine conceptual categories, to discover and validate associations among phenomena, or to compare constructs and postulates generated from phenomena in one setting with comparable phenomena in another setting. Hypotheses developed by induction, or causal propositions fitting the data and constructs generated, then may be developed and confirmed. Although an ultimate goal may be the discovery or development of causal relationships, ethnographers commonly avoid assuming the validity of a priori constructs or relationships.

By contrast, experimental research is oriented to the deductive verification or testing of causal propositions developed outside of the specific research site. Having hypothesized causal relationships between variables, experimenters test the strength or power of causes on effects. Designs such as experimentation are located more commonly toward the opposite ends of all four continua.

INDUCTION TO DEDUCTION

The inductive–deductive dimension refers to the place of theory in a research study (Camilleri, 1962; Homans, 1964). Purely deductive research begins with a theoretical system, develops operational definitions of the propositions and concepts of the theory, and matches them empirically to some body of data (Popper, 1968). In a sense, deductive researchers hope to find data to match a theory; inductive researchers hope to find a theory that explains their data. Purely inductive research begins with collection of data—empirical observations or measurements of some kind—and builds theoretical categories and propositions from relationships discovered among the data (Becker, 1958; Kaplan, 1964). That is, inductive research starts with examination of a phenomenon and then, from successive examinations of similar and dissimilar phenomena, develops a theory to explain what was studied.

Examples of inductive research are Smith's intensive analysis of William Geoffrey's classroom in an inner-city school (1968); Shirley Brice Heath's (1983) 10-year study of black and white children in two Piedmont communities in Virginia, and Ogbu's (1974) study of Stockton, California. Smith observed for months, trying to isolate components of Geoffrey's strategies for managing students. He and Geoffrey then developed a set of concepts describing the classroom processes, which subsequently were used to create a tentative theory of instructional organization. Heath studied how children acquired language in the two communities. She also observed how black children and white children used language differently, and differences in language use in home and school in both communities. She subsequently isolated those differences which most dramatically illustrate differences in school talk and home talk.

At the adult level, Ogbu (1974) examined the strategies for articulating with jobs and opportunities which people used in the community he studied. In particular, he observed the role they believed education played in achieving success for themselves and their children. He theorized that minority students did not achieve educational or occupational success because of a "job ceiling" above which certain minority groups could not rise. The job ceiling consisted of a specific level of occupational attainment and had been determined by long-established patterns of racial discrimination.

GENERATION TO VERIFICATION

The generative–verificative dimension refers to the position of evidence within a research study as well as to the extent to which results from the study may be generalized to other groups (Denzin, 1978). Verificative research verifies or tests propositions developed elsewhere; it attempts to provide evidence that a given hypothesis usefully applies to several data sets. It also commonly attempts to generalize beyond the scope of a single study. The goal of verificative research is to establish not only the extent to which a proposition obtains, but also the universe of populations to which it is applicable (Zetterberg, 1966). Generative research, on the other hand, is concerned with discovering constructs and propositions using one or more data bases as the source of evidence (Glaser & Strauss, 1967; Smith, 1974).

In the examples cited previously, researchers first determined what overall categories could be developed in which to subsume the individual behaviors observed in the classroom, schools, and community. Their data bases consisted of observational field notes, interviews, teaching records, documents, artifacts, reconstructed summaries of each day's events, and other information. Chunks of this data base were sorted and classified until the researchers were able to identify relevant constructs and categories.

Generative research often is inductive just as verificative research frequently is deductive. Generative research may be initiated with no particular theoretical framework; it also may be informed by theory. Likewise, although verificative research customarily begins with some theoretical proposition, it may be initiated with no theoretical framework whatsoever—a criticism directed to certain social science and educational studies (Kaplan, 1964; Rappoport, 1970; Shaver & Larkins, 1973).

CONSTRUCTION TO ENUMERATION

How a study's units of analysis are formulated and delineated constitutes the constructive–enumerative dimension of an investigation (Zelditch, 1962). A constructive strategy is aimed at discovering what analytic constructs or categories can be elicited from the stream of behavior; it is a process of abstraction in which units of analysis are developed in the course of observation and description. Enumeration is a process by which the researcher subjects previously derived or defined units of analysis to systematic counting or enumeration; it usually is preceded by the constructive process described previously. Smith and Geoffrey did not engage in enumeration; however, the typologies they created can be used by other investigators in an enumerative fashion. For example, their category of "ringmaster behavior," in which the teacher establishes and maintains control over a multitude of simultaneous classroom activities, may be applied to other teachers and its incidence can be counted (1968, pp. 104–105).

SUBJECTIVE TO OBJECTIVE

Finally, research designs may be characterized along a subjective–objective continuum (Wilson, 1977). Ethnography builds the subjective experiences of both participants and investigator into the research frame, thus providing a depth of understanding often lacking in other approaches to research. This practice is a self-conscious attempt to balance observer bias and reactivity of participants (see Chapter Nine). One approach to ethnography advocates that researchers seek no advance knowledge about their research sites, but enter them ignorant or naive about the phenomena under investigation. Another suggests that ethnographers attempt to suspend preconceived notions and even existing knowledge of the field under study. The former, we think, is unwise, and the latter almost impossible to achieve. A third approach integrates the knowledge of both the researcher and the participants. We believe that the most realistic approach is some combination of the second and third alternatives. Although fieldworkers may be familiar with related empirical research and use general theoretical frameworks to initiate studies, they generally assume that detailed description can be constructed more accurately by not taking for granted facets of the social scene (Erickson, 1973). Thus ethnographers attempt to enter unfamiliar settings without generalizing from their own experiences to the new setting and to enter familiar settings as if they were totally unknown. This suspension of preconceptions permits ethnographers to focus on participant constructs, whether subjective or objective, and sensitizes researchers to their own subjective responses; it contributes to the phenomenological orientation of most ethnographic design. Ethnographers also are aware that the perceptions of the people they study inevitably color their own, including those they present in the research report.

In their reports, ethnographers present both their initial assumptions and their subjective reactions to events, often presenting audiences with both preconceptions and "postconceptions." Ethnographers address the issue of researcher subjectivity by trying to incorporate it; hence, they study participants. Experimental researchers are equally as concerned with the effect of preconceptions and expectations on the outcomes of their investigations. However, unlike ethnographers, they approach their subjectivity by trying to expunge it. They control for biases with design and statistics, not analytically or behaviorally. Precise construction of an a priori design, ubiquity of the null hypothesis, and elimination of sources of treatment contamination are strategies crucial to demonstrating lack of researcher bias and reliability and validity of experimental results.

Ethnographers who describe cultural and behavioral patterns as they are viewed by the group under investigation reconstruct the categories that participants use to conceptualize their own experiences and world view (Erickson, 1973, 1986). Using the participants' own constructs to frame a study is an emic, phenomenological, or subjective approach. It contrasts with objective approaches that use conceptual categories and explanatory relationships created or identified by the researcher or other external observers to structure the analysis of particular populations. (See Scriven, 1972, for distinctions between quantitative and qualitative meanings for subjectivity and objectivity.)

The distinction between subjective and objective data is translated by some anthropologists into the categories emic (from "phonemic," having to do with meaning and referring to subjective or participant meanings) and etic (from "phonetic," having to do with objective or researcher meanings) (Pike, 1967; Harris, 1976; Pelto & Pelto, 1978). However, these distinctions do not mean that the categories used by an etic researcher are meaningless to the participants. For example, the categories that Smith used to describe what Geoffrey did in the classroom were those that made sense to and were recognized by Geoffrey himself. These were given name and form during the course of extensive conversations between Geoffrey, the participant observer, and Smith, the nonparticipant observer. A less collaborative, more objective approach might have involved taking a set of classroom management behaviors developed by Smith or someone else, observing Geoffrey's classroom, and then determining the extent to which that set matched Geoffrey's behavior.

Even the degree of collaboration practiced by Smith and Geoffrey has been challenged by some critical theorists and phenomenologists who argue that the use of researcher constructs puts words in the mouths of participants and presents a view more congruent with the researcher's status position and perspectives than it is of the people being studied.

Some researchers argue that adhering to the researcher perspective has promoted an androcentric, Eurocentric science, one which has made invisible or nonexistent the experience of women and minorities (see Harding & Hintikka, 1983; Ellsworth, 1989). Some researchers consider it arrogant to presume to speak for or tell the story of others (Asad, 1986; Deloria, 1969; Said, 1978); other researchers view the problem of defining reality as one of negotiating a shared view (Lincoln, 1990). Still others struggle with the problem of presenting multiple viewpoints within a single monograph (Clifford & Marcus, 1986; Roman, 1992; Roman & Apple, 1990). All of these perspectives contribute to the current epistemological and literary debate over the topics, form, purpose, and execution of qualitative inquiry.

SOME FURTHER CONTRASTS WITH EXPERIMENTAL DESIGN

Ethnographic and qualitative designs can further be contrasted on the basis of their approach to the legitimacy of data, the ways in which credibility of results is established, and the ways different types of data are used. All these must be considered in the choice of research design.

The Distinction between Qualitative and Quantitative Data

We agree with Reichardt & Cook's (1979) statement that the practice, appearing so frequently in methodological literature, of polarizing social science research into qualitative ("soft," "subjective," and "inferior," even "feminine") and quantitative ("hard," "objective," and "superior," even "masculine") paradigms is a parody unduly dichotomizing research designs (Harding & Hintikka, 1983; Lincoln, 1990; Smith, 1990). On one level, the existence of such a dichotomy implies that serious, rigorous, and competent researchers will use only quantitative designs and that only such designs produce legitimate research. At another level, adherents to the dichotomy allege that the qualitative paradigm, encompassing such designs as ethnography, case study analysis, and historical or document analysis, appeal only to those who assume that reality is ever changing, that knowledge consists of understanding, and that the goal of research is examination of processes. Those who assume that reality is fixed, that knowledge consists of explanations and prediction, and that the goal of research should be verification of outcomes will be attracted, in contrast, to the quantitative paradigm and its associated designs—experimentation, survey analysis, standardized observational research, and simulation models.

Although philosophical allegiances undoubtedly affect researchers' choices of designs, Reichardt & Cook (1979) emphasize correctly that these beliefs about the nature of reality and knowledge are, in fact, shared by researchers whose disciplines span the so-called paradigms. Nothing in the experimental model, other than professional stereotyping, precludes psychologists from examining a dynamic reality to discover processes that enhance human understanding. Likewise, anthropologists—who are most comfortable with ethnographic methods—heatedly disagree about the nature of reality, the function of knowledge, the intentions of researchers, and the goals of science (Clifford & Marcus, 1986; Manners & Kaplan, 1968; Marcus & Fischer, 1986; Said, 1978).

Establishing Comparability and Translatability

While experimental researchers focus on the generalizability of their results, ethnographers are concerned with comparability and translatability. Comparability and translatability contribute to effective generalization regardless of research design; however, they are of paramount importance to the legitimacy of ethnographic research. Establishing comparability requires that, to the extent possible, the ethnographer use standard and nonidiosyncratic terminology and analytic frames. Furthermore, the characteristics of the group studied or constructs generated must be delineated so clearly that they can serve as a basis for comparison with other like and unlike groups (Wolcott, 1973; Rosenblatt, 1981; Borman, LeCompte, & Goetz, 1986). Translatability assumes that research methods, analytic categories, and characteristics of phenomena and groups are identified so explicitly that comparisons can be conducted confidently and used meaningfully across groups and disciplines. Assuring comparability and translatability provides the foundation on which comparisons are made. Both function for ethnographers as an analog to the goals of more closely controlled research: generalizability of research findings and production of causal statements.

For comparative purposes, ethnographers may choose phenomena to study because they are similar or because they differ systematically along particular dimensions. In either case, the intention is the generation, clarification, refinement, and validation of constructs. This method can be used to compare phenomena identified in a single research site (Glaser & Strauss, 1967), or it can be used by researchers engaged in ethnographic study of special phenomena in a number of research sites (e.g., Cassell, 1978; Herriott, 1977; Herriott & Gross, 1979; Ogbu, 1988; Pitman, Eisikovitz, & Dobbert, 1989; Tikunoff, Berliner, & Rist, 1975; Stake & Easley, 1978; Wax, 1979; Whiting, 1963).

Triangulating and Converging

Unlike many other research designs, ethnography is eclectic in its use of data collection and analysis procedures (see Chapters Six and Seven). Ethnographers use many kinds of data collection techniques, so that data collected in one way can be used to cross-check the accuracy of data gathered in another way. Just as a surveyor locates points on a map by triangulating on several sites, so an ethnographer pinpoints the accuracy of conclusions drawn by triangulating with several sources of data. Triangulation prevents the investigator from accepting too readily the validity of initial impressions; it enhances the scope, density, and clarity of constructs developed during the course of the investigation (Glaser & Strauss, 1967). It also assists in correcting biases that occur when the ethnographer is the only observer of the phenomenon under investigation.

Multiplicity of data sources and means to collect and analyze information are hardly the exclusive domain of ethnography. Triangulation is equally common in historical research, some survey designs, and many secondary analyses or meta-analyses of experimental results; it also is used for establishing convergent validity for psychometric instruments. Nevertheless, triangulation is less frequent in single-study experimental research. This is because the precision required for isolating treatment effects mandates designs that eliminate other sources of information and converge on the specific effects at hand. Sampling assumptions often are based on demonstrated equivalence among data sources; treatment and control groups either are drawn from the same population or are analyzed statistically along salient dimensions of expected difference. Multiplicity of data collection methods requires complex procedures such as Campbell and Fiske's multitrait–multimethod matrix (1959) or multivariate analyses that some experimenters find too cumbersome or too elaborate to use.

Experimental studies that amplify or extend some well-defined line of investigation often require uniformity with prior studies, and the strictures of experimental control mandate a more rigid design than is common in exploratory inquiry. Modifications in an ethnographic design are common, even after data collection has begun. This is because triangulation of data sources often turns up new and fruitful directions for study after the investigation has been initiated. However, similarly modifying an experimental design after treatments have begun violates the assumptions upon which such studies are based. Consequently, the analog to ethnographic triangulation in the experimental tradition is the serial experiment—a chain of experimental studies on a given topic in which strategies are deleted or added, substituted or refined.

Below we list some questions ethnographers must consider as they select a research design.

— What designs have social scientists customarily used to address this research area?

— Would alternative models contribute new perspectives to the topic, illuminate unexamined assumptions or gaps in this line of inquiry, or merely provide redundant data?

— Which particular research model most effectively addresses the philosophical assumptions about reality, knowledge, value, and the place of theory implicit in the research questions?

— Are the assumptions about human behavior inherent in or typically associated with the design the researcher wants to use congruent with those implicit in the research goals and questions?

— Which research models best match where the research goals and questions fit on the continua of research from generative to verificative, inductive to deductive, constructive to enmumerative, subjective to objective?

— Does the research emphasize descriptive, correlational, or causal relationships?

— To what extent must the design establish time order, covariation, and eliminate rival hypotheses so as to generate, refine, or verify causal relationships?

— Is reactivity a problem with this design and these research questions?

SUMMARY

We characterize each of the characteristic sets of assumptions as a continuum. They delineate the common distinction between quantitative and qualitative research (Rist, 1977). By quantitative research, people mean that a study is deductive, verificative, enumerative, and objective; qualitative research is understood to denote inductive, generative, constructive, and subjective processes. Our position is and our experience tells us that the quantitative–qualitative distinction is inexact and artificial (Reichardt & Cook, 1979). For this reason, we have substituted the preceding continua. Formulating distinctions as continua denotes their quality or relativeness and rejects interpretations describing them as mutually exclusive dichotomies. The majority of social science studies lie somewhere between the extremes of each assumptive mode. A particular study may combine both constructive and enumerative units of analysis, and certain complex studies may begin by generating propositions that are subsequently verified. Furthermore, any one of the four sets of assumptions may be found in combination with the other three. Recognition of the assumptions underlying theoretical perspectives and research topics permits investigators to choose research strategies that are compatible with overall design considerations.

Differences in overall design between experimental and ethnographic research do not preclude legitimate sharing of research strategies (Denzin, 1978). Ethnographic techniques may be supplemental, augmenting reliability or validity of an experimental design. Such strategies enhance the replicability of a treatment by providing a processual and contextual frame for the experimental manipulation. They strengthen the validity of results by confirming the salience of constructs to real-world situations. Likewise, experimental techniques may increase the credibility of an ethnographic design. Such techniques enhance generalizability when multisite investigation is used. They strengthen the reliability of results when standardized measures are used to portray variables in a natural context.

Dichotomizing the ethnographic and experimental traditions is useful for heuristic purposes; it provides a clear way to compare and contrast two approaches to inquiry. Unquestioned assumptions and conventions are highlighted; novices are aided in comprehending and applying the models. Nevertheless, studies reported in both the experimental and the ethnographic literature are too variable to match the stereotypes exactly, and the most creative designs among these may be those that conform least to the archetypes.

For some few researchers, using alternative designs may be so alien a notion that they prefer to change their research questions rather than to adopt an unfamiliar research model and its associated epistemological baggage. For the most part, however, educational ethnographers, especially those whose work is informed by the active interdisciplinary context discussed in Chapter One, individualize their research designs. They may, for example, substitute more controlled or quantitative forms of investigation when ethnography is inappropriate, or adapt their research designs to better address their objectives by incorporating relevant dimensions of case study analysis, historical or document analysis, survey analysis, experimentation, or simulation design.

TABLE 2.2
A Data Collection Planning Matrix

What do I need to know?	Why do I need to know this?	What kind of data will answer the questions?	From which sources or people must the data be elicited?	Where can I find the data?	Whom do I contact for access?	Timelines for acquisition
Question A	Rationale A_1 Rationale A_2	Data A_1 Data A_2 Data A_3	Data, source, or person A_1 Data, source, or person A_2	Organization A_1 Organization A_2	Name, phone #, address A_1 Name, phone #, address A_2	Month/day/year to Month/day/year
Question B	Rationale B_1 Rationale B_2	Data B_1 Data B_2 Data B_3	Data, source, or person B_1 Data, source, or person B_2	Organization B_1 Organization B_2	Name, phone #, address B_1 Name, phone #, address B_2	Month/day/year to Month/day/year
Question C	Rationale C_1 Rationale C_2	Data C_1 Data C_2 Data C_3	Data, source, or person C_1 Data, source, or person C_2	Organization C_1 Organization C_2	Name, phone #, address C_1 Name, phone #, address C_2	Month/day/year to Month/day/year
Question D	Rationale D_1 Rationale D_2	Data D_1 Data D_2 Data D_3	Data, source, or person D_1 Data, source, or person D_2	Organization D_1 Organization D_2	Name, phone #, address D_1 Name, phone #, address D_2	Month/day/year to Month/day/year

TABLE 2.3

Adaptation of the Data Planning Matrix for a Study of American Indian At-Risk High School Students[a]

What do I need to know?	Why do I need to know this?	What kind of data will answer the questions?	Where can I find the data?	Whom do I contact for access?	Timelines for acquisition
What are the truancy rates for American Indian students?	To assess the impact of attendance on American Indian students' persistence in school	Computerized student attendance records	Attendance office; assistant principal's offices for all schools	Mr. Joe Smith, high school assistant principal; Dr. Amanda Jones, middle school principal	August: Establish student database October: Update June: Final tally
What is the academic achievement of the students in the study?	To assess the impact of academic performance on American Indian students' persistence in school	Norm and criterion referenced test scores; grades on teacher made tests; grades on report cards; student portfolios	Counseling office	High school and middle school counselors; classroom teachers	Compilation #1: end of fall semester Compilation #2: end of school year
What is the English language proficiency of the students?	To assess the relationship between language proficiency, academic performance, and persistence in school	Language assessment test scores; classroom teacher attitude survey; ESL class grades	Counselor's office; ESL teachers' offices	Counselor's test records; classroom teachers	Collect test scores, Sept. 15 Teacher survey, Oct. 10–15 ESL class grades, end of fall semester and end of school year
What do American Indian students dislike about school?	To discover what factors lead to antischool attitudes among	Formal and informal student interviews; student survey	Homeroom classes; meetings with individual students	Principal of high school and middle school; parents of students;	Obtain student & parent consent forms, Aug.–Sept.

Research question	Purpose	Data sources	Setting	Respondents	Timeline
	American Indian students			homeroom teachers	Student interviews, Oct–May 30 Student survey, first week in May
What do students plan to do after high school?	To assess the degree to which coherent post-high school career planning affects high school completion	Student survey Follow-up survey of students attending college and getting jobs	Counseling office; Tribal Social Services office; Dept. of Probation; Alumni Association	Homeroom teachers; school personnel; parents; former students; community social service workers	Student survey, First week in May Follow-up survey, summer and fall
What do teachers think about their students' capabilities?	To assess teacher expectations of student success	Teacher survey Teacher interviews	—	Building principals; individual classroom teachers	Teacher interviews, November (subgroup) Teacher survey, April (all teachers)
What do teachers know about the home culture of their students?	To assess teacher's cultural awareness	Teacher interviews Teacher survey Logs of participation in staff development activities	Individual teachers' classrooms and records	Building principals; individual classroom teachers; assistant superintendent for staff development	Teacher interviews, November (subgroup) Teacher survey, April (all teachers)
What do teachers do to integrate knowledge of the student's home culture community into their teaching?	To assess the degree of discontinuity between school culture and home culture	Teacher's lesson plans; classroom observations; logs of participation in staff development activities	Individual teachers' classrooms and records	Building principals; individual classroom teacher; assistant superintendent for staff development	Lesson plans, December–June Observations, Sept. 1–May 30 Staff development, June logs

[a] Research problem: To what extent do various at-risk conditions contribute to dropping out for American Indian students?

Down to the Nitty-Gritty: Determining "Who?" "What?" "Where?" "When?" "Why?" and "How?"

We now move to some practical suggestions for constructing a design. Once considered the principal questions guiding sound journalistic practice, the above interrogatives also are sound principles for qualitative researchers considering the kind of data collection they will use. *What* kind of data will you need from *whom; where* can the data be found and *when* is it accessible or conveniently obtained; *how* should it be recorded, collected, or stored, and most important, *why* is it needed anyway? What does it add to a study and do I have the resources to collect it?

Qualitative researchers balance between two problems: too much data and too little data. If the data are too thin, the researcher has insufficient evidence to substantiate results. If the data base is too big, the researcher will be overwhelmed and never finish the project. Very often, novice researchers propose to collect all kinds of data, often simply because they are interesting, fun to do, or easily available. They also may be encouraged to do so by mentors interested in a particular technique. Doing so invites disaster; the extended time needed to analyze mountains of data deranges project timelines. Researchers also can spend undue amounts of time collecting data which do not really address the problem under investigation or add to the power of the results. A word from experienced researchers is in order:

> The researcher should be considering resources as she struggles with the conceptual framework and design issues of a study. For example, a researcher cannot decide to conduct a multisite, multiperson project with no prospect of financial resources in sight, nor can she prudently plan to conduct a long-time, intensive participant observation study when she knows she must continue to work full-time and cannot possibly devote the necessary time to the study. [Marshall & Rossman (1989), p. 122]

Answering the cautionary questions which follow can help to avoid these problems.

— What do I want to learn? What is my research purpose? What are my goals?

— What questions am I asking and what presuppositions am I making? What are my conceptual, theoretical, and philosophical frameworks?

— Who and what am I examining? What are my populations and how might I select and sample from them?

— What is my relationship to whom and what I am studying? What ethical principles should guide my conduct?

— How can I obtain the information I want?

— How can I learn what I want to know from the data I collect?

— How will I interpret what I may learn?

— Do I possess the skills and knowledge necessary to implement the contemplated design?

Reflecting on these questions will lead researchers to develop an overall approach to their inquiry. However, researchers should take care that checklists such as the preceding do not stifle creativity or the search for alternative approaches to the project, or force the investigation into overly routine patterns. One way to avoid this is to approach data collection as if it were the construction of a legal argument, every alternative of which had to be considered and every step and stage of which had to be justified to a jury. Use of a planning matrix, such as Table 2.2, will help a researcher design a project which is both elegant and economical, collecting all the data necessary to answer the questions without going off into time-consuming—and informant-annoying—tangents.

Notice that the construction of such a table serves a number of purposes. First, it helps the researcher define what is possible. Some data which would be nice to have may not exist or be available to the researcher. Second, as the researcher continually asks "why" each type of data might be needed, what the research problem really is becomes clearer. Further, the matrix promotes parsimony; once a clear rationale for each piece of data has been established, some data originally thought critical to the project may well prove to be unnecessary. The matrix does not have to be adhered to precisely in order to be useful; Table 2.3 shows how one of us adapted the matrix for a proposal to study dropouts.

Summary

Research design involves putting things together, bringing to conscious-ness—and to the notebook—as many aspects as possible of the research's planning and preparation for inquiry. We now assume that our reader has made a creative and judicious choice of design and is ready to move to a discussion of specific techniques used by qualitative and ethnographic researchers to select participants for the research project.

Selecting and Sampling in Qualitative Research

The first chapter of this book traced the varied origins of ethnographic and qualitative design in educational research and provides examples of the issues and questions customarily addressed by researchers using these approaches. Chapter Two described the process by which researchers choose an appropriate research design. Both chapters indicate criteria used to determine whether ethnography or some variant of ethnographic design is appropriate to a given focus and orientation. Now we are ready to assume that researchers have chosen ethnography or a related qualitative model as the most appropriate design to investigate their initial research questions and to apply the conceptual or theoretical frameworks that inform their preliminary speculations.[1]

At this point, researchers are ready to decide who they are going to study. A common misconception is that ethnographers do not use samples because they study entire intact groups. However, all qualitative research, including ethnography, uses both selection processes and sampling. The former involve defining what kinds of people and how many of them can be studied, as well as when, where, and under which circumstances they will be studied; the latter involves selecting a smaller subset from the original population to assure representativeness, to generalize from a group of key informants to the large population, or to reduce the size of the group under study. The flexibility and adaptability of selection and sampling decisions, as well as their continued implementation throughout the research process, are hallmarks of the ethnographic research model.

[1] The linear, step-by-step process implied in this paragraph, and indeed, in the structure of our text itself, is presented as a heuristic device. Our experience has been that, in practice, ethnographic and equalitative research seldom evolves in such an orderly fashion!

Choice of whom to study is an interactive process which takes place first in the initial phases of a qualitative or field study, hence its introduction and elaboration in this chapter. Many anthropologists initiate research by identifying a group—a tribe, a village, an urban scene—that poses some personal, empirical, or conceptual interest. They then obtain access to the group and develop subsequent selection and sampling solutions on site within the context of generating research foci and questions and gathering additional data (See Chapter Six) and identifying relevant analytic, conceptual, and interpretive frameworks (See Chapter Seven).

Thus, all ethnographers confront problems and issues of selection and sampling. In this chapter we define the terms selection and sampling, discuss how they are distinguished from each other, and examine both their relationships to data and data sources and the issues they pose for ethnographic design. We end with an identification of the varieties of selection and sampling strategies used in social science research.

Choosing Data Sets

In all research, investigators are faced with deciding which items from some array or collection to study. Selection and sampling are two ways of making these decisions. Selection refers to a more general process of focusing and choosing what to study; sampling is a more specialized and restricted form. This distinction is relevant because the term *sample* too often is used inappropriately to describe any collectivity under study; furthermore, such uses place undue and misleading emphasis on issues of statistics and probability. Selection requires only that the researcher delineate precisely the relevant population or phenomenon for investigation, using criteria based on theoretical or conceptual considerations, personal curiosity, empirical characteristics, or some other considerations. Selected phenomena customarily include people, events, traits and responses of people, artifacts and other objects, time segments, and settings. Once the population has been defined and identified, a researcher may or may not decide to sample from that population. These decisions and the constraints governing them are a function of the history and development of ethnography as a research model.

As discussed in Chapter One, ethnography and its counterpart in sociology, community field study, were developed to investigate small, homogeneous groups of people whose natural sociocultural boundaries were limited to face-to-face interaction (Goetz & Hansen, 1974). These small groups of participants—clans, tribes, villages—were assumed to share a cultural or subcultural tradition distinguishing them from their neighbors. Such groups constituted distinct populations. In these situations selection issues revolved around the initial choice of a research group or site, and sampling problems were restricted to an adequate representation of the individuals and subsets who composed the group. Anthropological ethnographers and field sociologists limited their responsibility to the accurate and valid reconstruction of the group under investigation. Underlying this objective was the assumption that human groups are infinitely variable and that the researcher's responsibility is to document the group's idiosyncratic, distinctive, and singular characteristics and processes. Generalization of findings from specific groups studied to other populations was relegated to ethnologists and other scholars interested in comparative analysis.

Classical ethnographers resolved the sampling problem by restricting their investigations to populations viewable in their entirety. They interviewed all the people in a group—a village, union, or classroom—and observed all the events that transpired in the factory, school, or tribe. To allow for variation over time, they studied units over several years. In their reports, researchers customarily designated whom they observed and interviewed, how many participants were involved, and how and why these individuals were chosen. Such information allowed an assessment of possible biases resulting from selection effects: distortions in data or interpretation resulting from inadequate generalization from some individuals or subsets to other individuals, other subsets, or the entire group (see Chapter Nine). Random and stratified sampling were used only where important segments or elements of the social scene could not be examined entirely.

The world in which researchers operate has changed, however. With the numbers of relatively isolated, homogeneous human groups growing ever smaller and with the increased interest in examining segments of industrialized and developing populations, ethnographers and field researchers have had to seek study populations elsewhere. This means they confront problems of sampling individuals and groups from larger populations to which they intend to generalize results (Schatzman & Strauss, 1973; Pelto & Pelto, 1978). In addition, researchers from other disciplines have sought to integrate qualitative or ethnographic research techniques into their designs to corroborate and provide context for findings obtained by more experimental or positivistic means. All of these influences have resulted in the borrowing and refinement by ethnographers of more sophisticated selection and sampling procedures developed by researchers such as survey analysts.

Although some current educational ethnographers continue to investigate small, distinct populations (Chang, 1991; Foley, 1990), researchers more commonly choose groups that are subsets of larger populations: university undergraduates (e.g., Becker *et al.*, 1968; Holland & Eisenhart, 1990), urban secondary students (e.g., Cusick, 1973; Weis, 1990) or young adults entering the labor force (Borman, 1991; Valli, 1986), black elementary schoolchildren in the rural South (e.g., Rowley, 1983; Heath, 1983; Goetz & Breneman, 1988), collegiate basketball players (Adler & Adler, 1991). Such groups rarely are homogeneous or culturally discrete. When ethnographers study such groups, they clearly delineate the larger population that the selection is assumed to represent or to which it legitimately can be compared. The reasons and methods for identifying the subset are specified, and the size of both subset and population is calculated or estimated. In essence, the investigator reports the number of participants, the way they were selected, the size of the subset selected, and the characteristics of the original population. Procedures for choosing participants and other units vary from rigorous randomized or stratified strategies to semistructured techniques such as critical case selection (Patton, 1980, 1990b) to informal strategies of volunteer or convenience selection. Whichever procedures are used, the investigator's initial task is to identify the populations or phenomena relevant to the group under examination and to the research focus being proposed or developed. This is done by establishing and defining its boundaries.

CONCEPTUALIZING CHOICES

Conceptualizing the boundaries of whatever it is a researcher wants to study is the ethnographer's first task. Researchers identify populations for investigation using whatever criteria are relevant to establishing the boundaries of the phenomena. Both logistical and conceptual constraints affect the choice of groups. The criteria for selection include lists such as the following: Spanish–English bilingual teachers in ethnically diverse elementary schools close enough to the university to visit biweekly (Reyes & Laliberty, 1992), or a specific Navajo extended family in a community whose school district asked the researcher to carry out a study of dropouts (Deyhle, 1991, 1992). These descriptors constitute boundaries because they distinguish between people to be studied and those to be excluded from consideration. Some of the descriptors are conceptual; bilingual teachers or extended families are concepts embedded in the research questions. Other descriptors are logistical; availability and accessibility to the researcher, for example, are conditions necessary to the feasibility of any study.

Populations and Their Subsets

Once its boundaries have been specified by the researcher, the entire population or a smaller subset of it may be selected for study. The distinction between a population and a sample is important: A sample is a subset of a larger population. The term *sampling* denotes extracting systematically from a larger group some smaller portion of that group so as to represent adequately the larger group. Samples are designed according to principles of probability such that the sample can, with some measurable margin for error, be asserted to represent the whole group from which it was extracted. Sampling is undertaken when studying an entire population is too unwieldy, too expensive, too time consuming, or simply unnecessary.

Smaller subsets from a population may be chosen nonprobabilistically. These are not, strictly speaking, samples. We refer to them as selections, or populations. For example, Reyes' bilingual teacher both fit her selection criteria and consented to be observed; Deyhle's family was the only one which permitted an Anglo lady professor to live with them at their summer sheep camp.

Selection, then, may be neither representative nor extractive. Researchers who study a whole population or some special subgroup of a population may deem it inappropriate to sample probabilistically. Thus, although selection procedures may be designed to reflect principles of probability, they do not require use of such guidelines; more important is that the criteria used for selection be clearly defined.

Units of Selection

Although the process may take place throughout the research process, the way data are defined and divided into units determines what populations will be considered relevant to researchers and how they will choose their selection and sampling procedures. The term *population* commonly is used to refer to potential human respondents or participants in a study, but nonhuman phenomena and inanimate objects also are potential populations. Groups of people conduct their activities within finite and specifiable settings and contexts, time periods, and circumstances. Each of these factors comprises a bounded population from which ethnographers select and sample. Locating potential data sources within study sites and collectivities depends upon how populations have been conceptualized. This requires that researchers translate into concrete, empirical descriptors phenomena that are abstractly characterized in research goals and conceptual frameworks. For example, studies proposing to study adolescent alienation must define what behaviors characterize alienated people, determine what kinds of adolescents exhibit such behavior, and then locate individuals who possess those characteristics, who are accessible, and who are willing to be studied. These terms help to constitute initial *selection units* that designate who or what—in this case, adolescents who exhibit certain kinds of behavior characteristic of alienation, and who are willing participants in the research—is the primary source of data. Selection units are usually humans, individually or in groups, viewed as interactive wholes or as exhibiters of particular behaviors, traits, or beliefs. In some instances, however, units are conceptualized as artifacts, events, or contexts. Locating potential sources of data requires the researcher to address the problem of where, when, and how such units may be found. Regardless of how they are defined and wherever they may be found, selection units are characterized by their boundedness, such that they can be distinguished from one another. Any item, person, trait, or belief chosen to constitute a unit must be clearly distinguishable from all other units.

Boundedness of Populations

Identification of units of analysis is affected by the boundedness of populations. Studying any group requires locating it and differentiating it from other groups. This can be difficult when no list of its members exists or can be created. Some populations are naturally bounded. They exist independently of researcher interest and are formed, or at least recognized, and confirmed by their constituent participants. Naturally bounded groups include the classrooms studied by Carew & Lightfoot (1979), the village studied by Spindler (1973), the council-affiliated Southern Baptist ministers studied by Walker (1983), and the basketball team studied by the Adlers (1991). Other populations are artificially bounded. These are groups identified by researchers, scholars, or policy makers as collectivities of individuals sharing common attributes. Although such individuals may recognize their commonality in occasional encounters, they do not together form socially designated groups. Artificially bounded groups include the illiterate men studied by Gill (1982). Although these individuals shared the attribute of being unable to read, they neither gathered together in groups nor formed associations. Some groups have attributes of both natural and artificial boundedness. For a multiple-case comparison of highly talented adolescent males, Safter (1992) sought individuals whose creativity on intelligence measured in the top 0.1% of the population. Locating highly intelligent individuals posed few problems; these students are often organized by schools into special gifted education classes. Highly creative students, on the other hand, rarely are served by such special programs. Those who lack high scores on intelligence tests are scattered throughout the student population.

Naturally bounded groups. Naturally bounded groups who share a common geographical location—villages, schools, factories—offer the advantage of being finite and discrete. Such units can be arrayed as entire, complete populations from which selection and sampling can be conducted with confidence and certainty. Eventual generalization or comparison to the larger population is thus facilitated. Naturally bounded groups that share no common geographical locations or that change geographical locations pose greater difficulties. Citizen protest groups, professional associations of educators, student activist groups, or even dispersed ethnic groups may form voluntary associations or informal interactive groups with no single physical location at which to meet, yet they may recognize one another as forming common groups. Formally organized groups maintain membership lists through which their constituents may be contacted. Protest and activist groups are generally more informal, and members may be located only through direct participation and interaction. Whether organized formally or informally, such groups pose special problems for researchers. Individuals may be distributed across other, wide populations; for example, members of many professional educator groups are distributed across the United States. For most researchers, this restricts contact to written forms of data collection and necessitates some form of sampling procedures. Protest and activist groups are also widely distributed, but their locations are frequently geographically concentrated. Because these groups depend on direct, face-to-face interaction, selection procedures are often more feasible than sampling methods.

A final problem shared by all bounded groups is the flexibility with which participation is defined. People move into and out of groups frequently, and many individuals who share their interests and objectives never associate with them directly and formally. Researchers studying high school mathematics teachers, for example, may locate many such individuals through the national mathematics education organization, but only a portion of mathematics instructors associate with this group. Those who do may be only approximately representative of the larger population. Locating naturally bounded groups who share no central geographic site requires familiarity with the group as well as flexibility in selection and sampling. In his study of the Seattle tramps, for example, Spradley (1970) located informants at three different sites where they often were found: a court, an alcoholism treatment center, and a local skid-row area.

Artificially bounded groups. Artificially bounded groups pose the most serious difficulties for location. Teachers suffering from professional exhaustion or burnout (Dworkin, 1987), school dropouts (LeCompte & Goebel, 1987), and schoolchildren whose families are geographically mobile are examples of such groups. Another example is the negative prediction defiers studied by Boardman, Harrington, & Horowitz (1987). These are individuals born and raised in socially and economically disadvantaged families who, as adults, achieved the status of doctors, lawyers, bankers, and other professionals. Rigorous sampling strategies can be used with these groups only when they are clearly identified within some other bounded population. For example, researchers may test or survey all of the teachers or students in a school district to identify special categories of either group. Other artificial populations may be selected or sampled through the special services they solicit; for example, people with problem marriages or pregnant teenagers may be located through family counseling centers. Researchers may seek participants through media advertisement and through their own networks of personal and professional contacts. Because of these special approaches to location, however, both generalization and comparison of findings are affected.

Locating sources of data, then, depends on the boundedness of populations, their sizes, and their substantive attributes. The larger the size of a population, the greater the necessity either for widely distributed probabilistic sampling procedures or for multiple-site selection methods. Substantive characteristics of populations also affect locatability. These are designated by the conceptual or theoretical frameworks that inform a study. They also are discovered through empirical examination of groups. Such attributes include demographic features, recognizability, stability, and permeability (the ease with which members enter and exit a group). Less permeable, unstable, or poorly defined groups often require more preliminary fieldwork and selection rather than sampling methods.

Issues of boundedness are not limited to human populations. Artifacts, events, and contexts are also bounded. Some of these phenomena are grouped by the people who produce them. Others are grouped only by the researchers and scholars who study them.

EXPERIENCING CHOICES

Educational researchers commonly study naturally bounded, geographically located groups; classrooms, schools, and school districts are frequent units of analysis. Their identification rarely poses problems for researchers. Difficulties with these units revolve around selection and sampling alternatives and entry problems. Investigators reduce the biases such problems cause by identifying and describing the settings and circumstances constructed and maintained by participants and by explaining how their selection and sampling influence data collection, analysis, and interpretation.

Populations also may consist of time and time periods. Because the lives of groups and individuals are too long to study in their entireties, researchers select or sample from the time stream or from designated time periods. Each time segment constitutes a unit of analysis. To assess the rate and direction of change across time, ethnographers use time-sampling procedures. They identify factors intervening in the social scene over time and retrospectively trace the origins of phenomena isolated in the final phases of a study. In situations where data are required from the preentry period of a field study, ethnographers use informant reconstruction and information located in a variety of documents. They may revisit sites at subsequent intervals to verify the time-dependent nature of various phenomena. Investigators typically describe and justify the time frameworks of their studies by specifying how long and how regularly they were engaged in fieldwork and by accounting for any unusual or unique events occurring within that time period. Investigators also identify those time periods or segments that people themselves define as important or tied to their customary ways of living (e.g., the Christmas holidays, school vacations, the fall football season, or the first salmon run). Describing how these were chosen allows for the assessment of selection effects associated with the time periods in which data were collected.

The researcher's task, then, is to determine the groups for which the initial research question is appropriate, the contexts that are potentially associated with the research question, the time periods to which the research question may be relevant, and the artifacts particular groups of interest to the researcher have produced. In each case, the researcher sets parameters. For most ethnographers, this developmental process is susceptible to refinement, modification, and redirection throughout the research process.

Reconceptualizing and Redefining Populations

Problems with access to, and expectations of, populations and subsets may result in alteration of research questions. For example, soon after her entry to the field, Gibson (1976, 1982) redefined her initial focus from ethnic group relations to sex-role socialization. Among the schoolchildren whom she studied in St. Croix, gender was more salient to school achievement than ethnicity. The population she had chosen was inappropriate for the study of differential achievement among ethnic groups, so she reformulated her research goals.

Sometimes both site and focus change. Wax (1971) cites the experiences of several anthropologists whose comprehensive and thorough preparations for the study of identified groups were disrupted by obstacles to access and entry in the field; each adapted by redefining the focus to an alternative group. LeCompte was unable to conduct a proposed study of political values among schoolchildren in Latin America because her chief contact in the country she chose was placed under house arrest in the course of an unexpected revolution. The project was reformulated as a study of work-related values and relocated in the safer environment of New Mexico (LeCompte, 1975).

Once assured of access and entry to the identified group and of the salience of the research focus intended or developed, investigators proceed with selection and sampling decisions. Although such decisions are similar to those made by other social scientists, using an ethnographic or qualitative design entails special considerations.

Guidelines for Selecting and Sampling

Researchers who use ethnographic and qualitative approaches use sampling and selection somewhat differently from investigators interested in generalizing their results to large populations. The latter begin their investigations with sequential strategies to create for their study a product, the sample, that resembles the larger population as closely as possible. In such cases, sampling is a necessary precursor to the research. Once the sample has been drawn, assuming that its population has been identified clearly, concern with selection and sampling procedures ceases and the real study begins.

Choosing recursively. Ethnographers, however, view selection as recursive; it is dynamic, phasic, and sequential (Zelditch, 1962) rather than static. Their concern with selection and sampling does not end with the creation of the initial group of study participants, events, or traits. Ethnographers do use selection and sampling to define the initial population so it can be handled conceptually and logistically. They also use selection and sampling methods to expand the scope of the study, refine the questions or constructs under investigation, or generate new lines of inquiry. Although some phenomena can be identified and characterized as being salient prior to entering the field, many others emerge only as the fieldwork proceeds. Consequently, selection in ethnographic research is a developmental, ad hoc procedure rather than an a priori parameter of research design.

Choosing and generalizing. How generalizations are created and used varies. Statistically random sampling procedures are used to improve the degree to which formal inferences can be drawn and generalizations made from smaller to larger groups. Ethnographers may use statistically random sampling within the community under study so as to generalize to its entirety, but they use other processes of inference and generalization differently. Rather than making statistically based inferences only at the conclusion of a study, they use induction and sequentially logical inferences based on accumulation of many corroborative sources of data over time. In addition, inferences made by ethnographers tend toward explanation of phenomena and relationships observed within the study group; generalization outside the group is limited by the extent to which comparable studies with comparable groups can be found and analyzed for similarity.

This distinction between statistical and logical inference is, however, honored more in the breach than in practice (Reichardt & Cook, 1979). Most social science researchers generalize findings to larger groups, regardless of whether their selection and sampling procedures justify doing so (Polkinghorne, 1991). Many researchers select a group because it is conveniently located and resembles a larger population of interest—for example, low-income urban ninth graders in the middle school closest to the university, or female freshmen psychology majors. Having sampled or assigned randomly from that group, researchers then publish the results as if the group studied were typical of all low-income urban ninth graders or all women in the United States. They use the same informal logical inferences all scholars use when they generalize, but they often do so without acknowledging the constraints of comparison and without making explicit the informal logical inferences they used.

Choosing and gaining participant assent. How people become participants in a research study is partly a function of selection and sampling. Conditions of recruitment and giving assent vary (see Fig. 3.1). Participants selected for a study may or may not see themselves as the researcher does, and their enthusiasm for the project may not be as high as that of the investigator. Typically, researchers develop a set of criteria that constitutes a portrait of the group they want to study. They then search for groups possessing those characteristics, request access to the group, and seek permission to do the study. In these instances, participants have no voice in deciding whether they meet the desired criteria, because the

1.	Please come study (with) me.
2.	Yes, you may study (with) me a. because I already know you. b. because I want to/am interested in what you are doing. c. because I want the compensation you are offering. d. because I feel compelled to let you.
3.	What? You mean someone's been studying me? Without my consent?
4.	Some combination of 1-3.

Figure 3.1 Levels of assent.

researcher has, a priori, categorized them as members of the study group. Refusal to participate may be difficult, as in the case of college students whose professors wish them to be subjects of an experiment. Some people may decline to participate, but they have no voice in deciding whether they qualify for selection. They also may be sought and investigated as nonrespondents; they are, therefore, included in the final report despite their refusal to participate.

Second, a researcher may develop criteria and then advertise for willing participants to select themselves. In this case, potential participants make two choices. First, they decide whether they possess the desired characteristics. Are they indeed sedentary women, or might they decide to start jogging next week? Are they really happily married couples, or did last week's fight disqualify them? Next, they decide whether to contact the researcher to volunteer. In this instance reluctant participants are unlikely, but whole subsets of the desired group may be lost because people failed to see the researcher's advertisements or because those who did see them did not define themselves as the researcher would have.

A third option involves cases where participants search for a researcher. Individuals administering innovative programs or experimental projects may find the lure of documentation and possible publicity irresistible and seek a researcher to evaluate or investigate their activities. Other individuals who believe they have had interesting or exceptional life experiences may seek a researcher to construct their life histories. Alternatively, research and evaluation may be a condition of funding for a program. This self-selection guarantees willing participants, at least initially, but it requires different forms of inference and reporting. Sampling to create a research group is irrelevant in these cases; however, sequential sampling and selection within these groups for investigative or analytic purposes may be quite appropriate.

Researchers must consider the following questions as they do their selection and sampling.

— With what populations and in what contexts may the research design be most effectively implemented?

— What facts or data are to be sought?

— What phenomena or categories of phenomena are to be examined, and how can these be conceptualized and bounded?

— What relationships among these categories can be expected, sought, or foreshadowed?

— Can the research be done at a single point in time—a synchronic study—or must events and behavior be selected, sampled, and analyzed over time—a diachronic study?

SUMMARY

Ethnographers and other qualitative researchers develop parameters used to define populations and to select and sample from these populations throughout the research. Sampling and selection are crucial to establishing the authenticity of descriptive analysis because, as described in Chapters Seven and Eight, they are the means by which the researcher systematically seeks and discards alternative descriptions or explanations of the phenomena observed. They are critical to the logical inferences that support comparability and applicability. The credibility of these inferences is affected by the extent to which participants volunteer cooperation or are compelled to acquiesce in a research study. The degree to which people are willing participants sets boundaries and constraints within which ethnographers make particular sampling and selection decisions. In the next section, we define and give examples of common selection and sampling strategies and assess them for their strengths, weaknesses, and implications for overall design credibility.

Using Sampling and Selection

We have grouped all methods for choosing participants and other research units under two general rubrics: probabilistic sampling and criterion-based selection. We define these terms and then delineate the variations of each kind of strategy. We present the distinction between sampling and selection here for heuristic purposes; in practice, most researchers use both approaches.

CRITERION-BASED SELECTION

Criterion-based selection requires that the researcher establish in advance a set of criteria or a list of attributes that the units for study must possess. The investigator then searches for exemplars that match the specified array of characteristics. Some researchers (e.g., Manheim, 1977; Patton, 1980) label this purposive sampling to distinguish it from probabilistic sampling. That label is misleading because it implies that probabilistic sampling is nonpurposive. On the contrary, random and other probabilistic sampling strategies are highly purposive; sampling is based on specific parameters. Thus the term *purposive* applies across selection and sampling procedures and should be contrasted only with completely haphazard means of selecting data or data sources.

Ethnographers use criterion-based selection in choosing the group or the site to be studied. From the research problem and questions and from relevant empirical and theoretical influences, fieldworkers develop a set of attributes or dimensions characterizing a group or setting. They choose the first such person, group, or setting that both matches those criteria and permits the study. Some ethnographers, however, locate several alternatives and choose from among them the one most suitable (e.g., Wolcott, 1973; Carew & Lightfoot, 1979; Tobin, Wu, & Davidson, 1989).

Criterion-based selection is the starting point for all research. It precedes probabilistic sampling. In positivistic traditions, once the research question has been formulated and the population to be studied identified, choice of data sources proceeds probabilistically. Studies using sampling procedures to generalize to a larger group from a smaller subset must rely on previous work in the field for enumeration of population characteristics. If such characteristics are unknown, the researcher must either build such activities into the research design or choose another group to study. We present the distinction between sampling and selection here for heuristic purposes; in actual practice, most researchers use both.

Ethnographers use a sequence of selection strategies throughout the research because their studies customarily are exploratory and open ended. Criterion-based selection is used to identify the population; as the research study unfolds, it also is used to establish new sets of phenomena to examine. Thus a variety of selection processes is used fruitfully throughout the stages of problem identification, data collection, and analysis. As is indicated later (see Chapters Seven and Eight), they may be used as well in the final stages of a project, while refining and corroborating the results of a study. A number of researchers have discussed the selection and sampling procedures used by ethnographers. These have been termed convenience sampling, comprehensive sampling, and a collection of purposive sampling techniques such as critical-case sampling and sensitive-case sampling (Patton, 1980). Negative-case sampling (Znaniecki, 1934; Robinson, 1951) and theoretical sampling (Glaser & Strauss, 1967) are usually included, although these techniques are analytically oriented and are less useful during preliminary phases of research (see Chapters Eight and Nine). In our discussion we use the distinctions other scholars make among types of selection when the differences are clear and help to discriminate among selection procedures. We have collapsed others, like critical-case sampling and politically sensitive case sampling (Patton, 1980), and subsumed them under one rubric because they appear to be identical. Finally, selection on bases such as ease of access, convenience to the researcher, availability of population lists, and other fortuitous or accidental factors frequently has been termed convenience sampling (Manheim, 1977). Patton (1980) even groups convenience sampling as a strategy with purposive sampling. However, all researchers choose populations or samples that are, for whatever reasons, as convenient as possible—either because they are nearby or, if far away, because they afford an opportunity for exotic foreign travel or the chance to have a personal tribe to study, unspoiled by earlier investigators.

Criterion-based selection has a number of variations. Simple criterion-based selection requires only that the researcher create a list of the attributes essential to the selected unit and proceed to find or locate a unit matching the list. Variations in simple criterion-based selection may be divided into two groups. The first is composed of strategies used to locate an initial group or setting for study or to select units from populations determined to be relevant during early phases of research. This includes comprehensive selection, quota selection, network selection, and selection on the basis of extreme cases, typical cases, unique cases, reputational cases, ideal–typical or bellwether cases, or comparable cases.

The second group of selection strategies involves progressive and sequential processes and includes negative-case selection, discrepant-case selection, theoretical sampling, and selection and comparison of cases testing theoretical implications. Because these strategies are used in later phases of research during analysis, hypothesis generation and refinement, and interpretive elaboration, they are discussed and illustrated in Chapters Eight and Nine. Figure 3.2 displays both types of criterion-based selection, how they are related, and when they are used in the

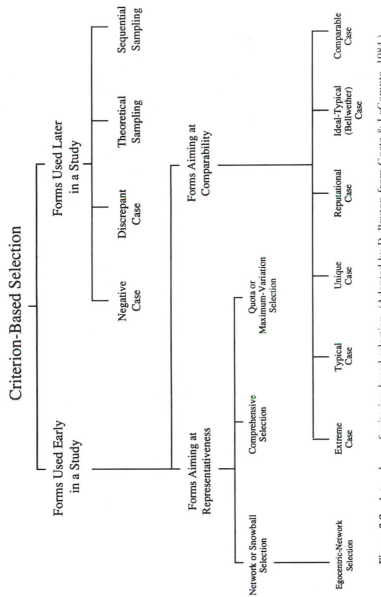

Figure 3.2 A typology of criterion-based selection. (Adapted by D. Bruton from Goetz & LeCompte, 1984.)

research process. In the following pages, we discuss the types of selection in each of the two categories: (1) selection of the initial study population, and (2) subsequent elaborative strategies.

Comprehensive Selection

Comprehensive selection strategies are the ethnographer's dream. Using them, researchers examine every case, instance, or element in a population. Representativeness is guaranteed by virtue of universal coverage. Ethnographers who study small, bounded populations over long periods of time are able to sample comprehensively across the populations of participants, events, settings, and other relevant phenomena. Each pertinent population is manageable in size, and the effort to select subsets requires more resources than does examination of every instance. Historians and sociologists may be confronted with similar situations when studying some narrowly defined public role, such as the United States' Secretary of Education, formerly the Director of the Office of Education. A researcher examining the relationship between this office and trends in national educational policy would sample comprehensively across office holders because the total population is so small.

A second reason for selecting comprehensively occurs when a population is composed of elements so heterogeneous that selection and sampling processes would result in the loss of important variation. For her investigation of individuals who enrolled in an adult fitness program, Jones (1983) studied everyone who registered in the program during a 6-month period. The population was sufficiently diverse that comprehensive selection was mandated. This happens most frequently when a population is still poorly understood. For example, autism is a mental condition incompletely conceptualized. Cases are rare and vary from one individual to the next (Quay & Werry, 1979). A school district evaluating its facilities and programs for mainstreaming autistic children would need to select all the children for study to assess its offerings adequately.

Resources to select comprehensively are rarely available, and populations sufficiently small to examine totally are rarer still. When probabilistic sampling is inappropriate and comprehensive selection is precluded, researchers use simple criterion-based selection or one of its variants.

Quota Selection

Like comprehensive selection, quota selection, sometimes called maximum-variation sampling (Patton, 1980), is intended to be representative. However, quota selection is restricted to a representative subset of some larger population. It was commonly used by early survey researchers and opinion pollsters who knew the general parameters of the population whose attitudes they wished to tap but who had no access to population lists from which to draw random samples (Rossi *et al.*, 1983). In this procedure, researchers first identify the major, relevant subgroups of some given universe. A school ethnographer may divide a high-school student population into groups by grade level, sex, and race. The researcher then proceeds to obtain some arbitrary number of participants in each category, such as black male seniors, black female seniors, and white male juniors. Where these groups comprise differential percentages in the population, the quota may be weighted to reflect these ratios. Quota selection provides a subset that approximates a population. It does not supply the precise representation provided by random and systematic sampling, but the selected units do correspond to relevant dimensions characterizing the population.

The classic and most ambitious model for maximum variation or quota sampling in educational anthropology is Whiting's (1963) investigation of child-rearing practices in six different cultures. Six small communities, scattered throughout the world, were chosen for the cultural variations they represent. Asia, the most populated area of the globe, provided sites in India, Okinawa, and the Philippines. Remaining sites were located in Kenya, Mexico, and the United States. Although each of the six teams of field researchers produced an independent ethnography, preentry planning and collection of standardized data for other phases of the study resulted in six investigations of comparable phenomena, analytically incorporated into a multimethod, comparative investigation (Whiting & Whiting, 1975; Whiting & Edwards, 1988). More recent multisite studies (e.g., Cassell, 1978; Herriott, 1977; Herriott & Gross, 1979; Rist, 1981; Stake & Easley, 1978; Tikunoff *et al.*, 1975; Wax, 1979) are variations of the Whitings' design. Still other contemporary researchers have begun to devise procedures for systematically establishing consistency of collection, analysis, and interpretation of data across ethnographic research sites (Dobbert, 1982; Pitman *et al.*, 1989; Ogbu, 1988). Criteria for site selection, time spent on site, central integration of data collection and analysis processes, number of field researchers per site, and nature of final products differ across these studies. Each exemplifies some form of criterion-based selection, but they vary in the extent to which their results may be generalized confidently to the broader populations from which they were chosen.

Network or Snowball Selection

Network selection is a strategy in which each successive participant or group is named by a preceding group or individual. The researcher thus collects a selection of respondent groups or individuals on the basis of participant referrals. Network configurations vary. Some may be conceptualized as links in a chain. This occurs most frequently when a respondent or group possessing the attributes required by a researcher suggests as potential respondents an individual or group possessing the same attributes. For example, Harrington & Gumpert's (1981) investigation of negative prediction defiers—people who have achieved advanced occupational success despite the low socioeconomic status of their families of origin—was based on selection through networks. Each respondent was requested to name others who fit the profile of a negative prediction defier.

This strategy is useful in situations where the individuals investigated are scattered throughout populations and form no naturally bounded, common groups. Network selection often is the only way that researchers can identify such people. Other network configurations may resemble chains linked along nodules or groups of informants. Researchers studying such groups as reconstituted families, remarried individuals with children from previous marriages, or members of stigmatized groups such as homosexuals, drug users, dropouts, or members of clandestine organizations may obtain some of their respondents from groups known to and named by those already investigated. In other situations, groups may be bounded naturally, and informants may serve as access contacts from one group to another. For example, researchers studying high school clique groups (e.g., Cusick, 1973; Varenne, 1982) often obtain access to successive cliques by introductions from individuals who are members of two cliques or who have close relationships with members of other cliques.

The most sophisticated network configuration may be conceptualized as a latticework of interlocking webs. Labeled egocentric network analysis (Pelto & Pelto, 1978), this procedure is a data analysis technique as well as a selection strategy. It is described as *egocentric* selection because the network chosen has as its focal or initial point a single ego, or individual. Researchers use the procedure both to obtain access to participants and to investigate the relationships that hold together the fabric of human interaction. In these cases, researchers request individuals from a group, for example, a family or household, to name those outside the central group with whom they have significant relationships. Each relationship thus leads into other comparable families or households, and the process is repeated until the selection is complete. Burnett (1973) used network selection in her study of Puerto Rican youths in Chicago; an initial selection of 30 individuals—chosen by stratified, random sampling—was interviewed, and networks consisting of their family, peer, and school relationships were constructed and investigated.

Researchers elaborate on the criterion-based selection procedures they use for a variety of purposes. In each variation selection is based on comparison across cases or across dimensions of cases. Whereas probabilistic sampling and both comprehensive and quota selection address representativeness, the following variations facilitate acquisition of data used comparatively.

Extreme-Case Selection

Extreme-case selection involves first the identification, whether explicitly or implicitly, of the norm for some characteristic of interest to the researcher—academic achievement, for example. Then the extremes of that characteristic are defined, and all potential cases are arrayed on the resulting continuum. The extremes, or poles, of these continua become the focus of the study so that comparisons against the norm may be made and salient dimensions of more moderate cases may be explained. An example might be a comparison of attitudes and behaviors of students who score extremely high and extremely low on standardized tests. At another level, a comparative case analysis of a very large school and a very small school (Barker & Gump, 1964) allowed researchers to identify factors common to both and shared with schools of all sizes, as well as distinguishing factors that are affected differentially in schools of varying sizes. To identify their extremes, however, Barker and Gump first had to determine the mean size for public high schools.

Typical-Case Selection

A similar process is undertaken in selecting for the typical case. In this procedure, the researcher develops a profile of attributes possessed by an average case and then seeks an instance of this case. Wolcott (1973) sought a typical elementary school principal for a role analysis of that institutional status. Using a demographic profile of principals developed from a national survey, Wolcott created a description of the typical elementary school principal. He then eliminated from consideration women, people who were too young or too old, single males, and other individuals atypical of those holding elementary school principalships. His task was then reduced to finding a real-world match who would permit himself to be studied.

Unique-Case Selection

Unique-case selection involves the choice of cases that are unusual or rare on some dimension. Whatever other attributes such a case may share with a larger population, this dimension sets it apart. It is used when researchers want to examine some dimension or attribute that functions as an experimental treatment but that would be precluded from actual experimental manipulation by ethical proscription, its accidental occurrence, or empirical or historical impossibility. Unique cases can be historical events providing researchers with opportunities to examine divergent social processes and group response to them. The migration of Southeast Asians to the United States during the 1970s supplied Finnan (1982) with a population of children whose life experiences served as a contrast or pseudotreatment by which to compare those of children born in the United States. In this situation, the researcher capitalized on the consequences of an historical development affecting large numbers of individuals. This permitted her to contrast spontaneous play patterns of children born in the United States with the more rule-governed activity of Vietnamese refugee children.

Other researchers choose unique cases that constitute historical microevents. Fuchs (1966), for example, studied two interracial incidents—a school boycott and a community protest effort—that occurred at inner-city schools during the height of the 1960s civil rights movement. Schools or districts may be chosen for their unusual success in particular programs or for adoption of an exceptional innovative program, for example, Wolcott's (1977) study of technology in education or Hess's (1991) analysis of radical school decentralization in Chicago. Although such analyses are limited by the impossibility of close replication, they highlight the underlying group processes and functions that contribute to social behavior and belief (for example, Precourt, 1982).

More commonly, ethnographers and other field researchers select cases for unique or rare attributes inherent in a population. Student groups may be selected for some unusual ethnic composition, for example, Guilmet's studies of Native Alaskans (1978, 1979); for their relationship to an unusual community, for example, Peshkin's study of a fundamentalist Christian school, (1986), Foley's study of the students in a politically active Hispanic town (1990), Guthrie's study of Chinese-American students in San Francisco (1988), and Gibson's study of the adaptation of Pujabi Sikh students to a California high school (1988); or for patterns of behavior, such as Roman's study of young women participants in punk slam dancing (1989) or the Adlers' (1991) study of a collegiate basketball team. Teachers may be chosen for singular background characteristics, as, for example, Au's (1980) study of teachers of Native Hawaiian children and Erickson & Mohatt's (1982) comparison of Anglo-Canadian and Odawa teachers in a Native American school.

Reputational-Case Selection

Reputational-case selection often is a variation of extreme-case or unique-case selection. In this procedure, the researcher chooses instances of a study population on the recommendation of experts. In seeking public figures in a southeastern city who best exemplified charisma, Hall (1983) requested nominations from journalists and from members of a local leadership council. Principals may be asked to recommend their most competent teachers. Dillon & Searle (1981) amplified this procedure in their analysis of student language use in a first-grade classroom. They chose the teacher they studied on the basis of the teacher's reputation for excellence among her supervisors, her colleagues, and the school's parents. State education officials may be requested to recommend the most or least successful of a state's dropout programs. In some instances, researchers discover that the reputation attached to a case by experts may be undeserved. Spindler (1974c), for example, demonstrates how a "well-adjusted" child chosen for examination by a group of teachers was a victim of cultural preconceptions; investigation revealed the child to be suffering from both emotional maladaption and social marginality.

Ideal–Typical Case Selection

Ideal–typical case selection is a procedure in which the researcher develops a profile or model for the best, most efficient, most effective, or most desirable example of some population and then finds a real-world case that most closely matches the profile. Tikunoff *et al.* (1975) used a variation of ideal–typical selection in their choice of 20 elementary schoolteachers demonstrated to be more effective in reading and mathematics instruction than 20 less effective peers. In this instance, ideal–typical selection was grounded in the broader framework of extreme-case selection, a common process whether it occurs explicitly or implicitly. A variation of ideal–typical case selection is the bellwether version, typified by the statement: "If it won't work here, it won't work anywhere." Such instances are most likely to be revealed by serendipity rather than being actively sought by researchers. They may involve populations who actively seek out a researcher to document their activities. Hanna (1982), for example, initiated her study of a desegregated elementary school because of interactional difficulties among the children that she had observed as a parent. An underlying theme emerges clearly throughout her analysis, however. Despite the conflict that initially led her to the study, she unexpectedly discovered that the school embodied many of those conditions considered ideally supportive of desegregation. Hanna's demonstration of social dissonance within such a setting is all the more striking. In contrast, Warren (1982) selected a southern California elementary school because of its 8 years of stable operation and incremental program development. This allowed him to document an instance of educational success and achievement in a bicultural, bilingual program.

Comparable-Case Selection

Comparable-case selection constitutes the ethnographer's version of replication. Although researchers engaging in multisite studies often use this approach, it also may be used by a single researcher across a career of studying a variety of groups or sites sharing central, relevant attributes. For example, Goetz's second ethnographic site (1981a,b) was chosen for attributes it shared with her first site (1976a,b): a rural consolidated elementary school serving a rural transitional population dependent on surrounding urban areas for economic livelihood. Less commonly, a researcher may replicate the work of a predecessor by choosing a comparable group or site. Whether operating in teams or singly, ethnographers may study several units simultaneously, chosen on the basis of comparative factors and operating as concurrent replications. LeCompte's examination (1978) of the normative behavior of four elementary schoolteachers was predicated on her selection of individuals who shared multiple characteristics, personal and professional. Despite some few attributes that varied—by researcher choice and by incidental occurrence—the results were consistent across teachers; in their normative messages to children, all four teachers emphasized the value the school district placed on conformity to authority, time, work, achievement, and order.

PROBABILISTIC SAMPLING

Probabilistic sampling, as introduced previously, involves extracting from an already well-defined population a subset for study approximating the characteristics of the group from which it was derived. It requires a mathematical procedure for assuring that the smaller group is representative of the larger.

Random and Systematic Sampling

Two kinds of probabilistic sampling procedures are used by human science researchers: systematic and random sampling. Simple random sampling, which uses mathematical procedures to assure that no unit has any greater chance for inclusion in a subset than any other, is the best understood form of sampling. It is used less commonly than other strategies because the conditions necessary for its use are difficult to achieve. It requires that the population to be sampled be selected first, that every unit in that population be identified, and that each unit be accessible to the researcher for study. This is to assure that each unit has an equal probability of being selected (Fowler, 1984; Kalton, 1983; Pelto & Pelto, 1978; Rossi, 1983).

Systematic sampling is a more commonly used probabilistic strategy. Systematic sampling requires the researcher to select an element from the study population at some appropriate interval, determined by the ratio between the needed sample size and the size, calculated or estimated, of the total population. For example, every fifth name from the telephone directory or every ninth student from a high school class may be selected (see Jaeger, 1988). The ordering principles used may vary; they may be numerical, chronological, spatial, or alphabetical. Although the entire population is sampled at the given interval to guarantee representativeness, this procedure does not require that all units in a population be identified in advance of selection, that they be immediately accessible, or that the exact size of the population be known. For example, if the population to be studied is a set of social interactions—flirting in high school hallways, for example—the total number of such interactions in a given day might be unknown, but a researcher could systematically select for analysis every third such interaction from a videotape recording. A major difficulty with this strategy is establishing that the sampling interval is unaffected by some confounding fluctuation or variation in the population (Gordon, 1975). A school ethnographer, for example, who observed every fifth day throughout the school year, might conclude the study with an excellent analysis of end-of-the-week school days, but the data would have questionable relevance to other periods during the school week.

Although all human science researchers use both systematic and random sampling for a variety of purposes, ethnographers use these procedures specifically to assure internal validity in their studies. When observations are planned across time periods, settings, events, or individuals, ethnographers sample these units randomly to ensure that their findings are representative of these entire populations. More commonly, however, variations on simple random and systematic sampling are used. These are either cross-sectional or longitudinal strategies. Cross-sectional strategies include stratified sampling and cluster sampling. Longitudinal strategies include trend analysis, cohort studies, and panel studies. Figure 3.3 displays the types of probabilistic strategies. All five of these variations eleborate and diversify probabilistic sampling procedures; they also form the basis for variants of criterion-based selection.

Cross-Sectional Sampling

Cross-sectional strategies are appropriate when researchers are interested in a population at only one point in time. Among them, stratified samples are mandated for those populations composed of discrete and differentiated subgroups. Stratified sampling requires that the total population be divided into relevant subsets or strata and that individuals be

Probabilistic Sampling

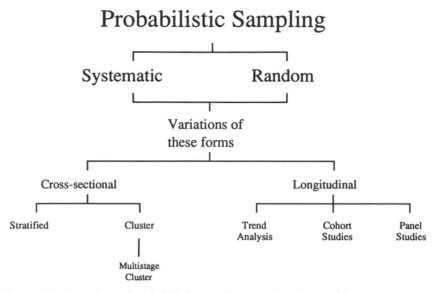

Figure 3.3 A typology of probabilistic sampling strategies. (Adapted by D. Bruton from Goetz & LeCompte, 1984.)

selected from each subset. It is used with either random or systematic sampling techniques. Units may be selected from each stratum or subset equally. They also may be weighted in some way to match representation of subgroups within the population or to achieve minimal representation of small subsets that otherwise might be missed. The school ethnographer described previously, for example, would have achieved a more representative sample of school days by first stratifying the school year into weeks and then sampling by weeks or days of the week.

Cluster sampling also may be applied randomly or systematically. It is used when the population to be studied can be aggregated, naturally or analytically, into groups that are similar. After all the aggregated groups are designated, a sample of them is drawn; then all or some sample of individuals from within the selected clusters are studied. Cluster sampling is useful when selecting from large populations or where sampling individuals from a population is disruptive. For example, school researchers frequently take classrooms, rather than individual students, as the unit for study because interrupting individual students at their lessons is objectionable and because schoolchildren are found in naturally occurring groups of similar size and composition. A variant of this procedure, multistage cluster sampling, occurs when clusters are successively defined and sampled prior to identifying the specific group to be studied.

Cluster sampling requires that researchers account for any biases introduced by the initial division of population into aggregated units. It frequently is used by researchers such as demographers and survey analysts who need samples representing large populations. Initially designated clusters may be naturally occurring and mutually exclusive units that are equally heterogeneous for the targeted population, such as city blocks, neighborhoods, towns, factories, or schools. When obtaining a sample of student respondents, school ethnographers use cluster sampling on a small scale. For example, dividing a school into clusters of classrooms, randomly choosing a sample of classrooms, and sampling students only from those classrooms can provide ethnographers with data representative of overall student opinion, of common student social customs, or of patterns of student academic work habits.

Longitudinal Sampling

Longitudinal studies are mandated when a researcher wishes to assess change in a population over time. Hence, the goal is to sample as much as possible from the same population at different points in time. The first of these strategies, trend studies, involves successive sampling—random or systematic—of a population defined by particular characteristics or by a common geographic location. A disadvantage of this strategy is that the elements composing the population are different at the succeeding time intervals. Although sampling a school faculty at 2-year intervals over a 10-year period supplies data approximating the same kinds of individuals, school faculties change over time. Successive samples include not only those who remained for the 10-year period, but also individuals who were present at some stage and left, as well as their replacements. Nevertheless, this may be an efficient way to assess changes in faculty over time.

A more sophisticated approach to the investigation of faculty change is the cohort study. Here, populations are defined either by age or by some uniform length of experience. An ethnographer may survey, randomly or systematically, a group of first-year teachers in a school. Five years later, the school's fifth-year teachers may be sampled; and 10 years later the tenth-year teachers may be examined. A cohort design allows a more precise distinction between changes resulting from life-cycle influences and those reflecting general historical trends, thus strengthening internal validity. Like trend studies, this strategy suffers from the disadvantage that the successive populations are composed of somewhat different elements because of attrition and accretion.

When this poses a serious threat to the legitimacy of results, researchers choose a third alternative, the panel study. This procedure requires that a population be sampled at some point in time and that the sampled elements be followed over succeeding periods. For example, a researcher may select individual graduates randomly from a teacher-preparation program and interview them at designated time intervals to assess life-cycle changes. This strategy also has disadvantages. Mortality remains a problem. The representativeness of the sample becomes more question-able the longer the interval between original sampling and successive data collection.

Although the variations of cross-sectional and longitudinal strategies were developed for random and systematic sampling, they may be adapted for criterion-based selection. Many ethnographers use trend, cohort, and panel designs by returning to their original study sites from time to time to assess change or by systematic selection of data represent-ing populations at times prior to a field residence.

The classic instance in educational ethnography of site revisiting is Hollingshead's return (1975) to his Elmtown site and the accompanying analysis of changes that occurred over a 30-year period (cf., Mead, 1956; Wylie, 1974). Wolcott, in his examination of education in a Kwakiutl Indian village in Canada (1967b), supplemented his year-long participant observation with extended visits during the following two summers and by retrospective interviews with village informants and educators who had taught in the village school prior to his tenure (cf., King, 1967; Hostetler & Huntington, 1971; Modiano, 1973). Ogbu's study (1974) of an inner-city neighborhood traces the 10-year history and development of the education rehabilitation movement in the community's schools through both interviews and the collection and analysis of pertinent documents. Finally, the most extensive site revisit in the school ethnogra-phy literature is Smith's return (Smith, Dwyer, Prunty, & Kleine, 1986, 1987, 1988) to Kensington Elementary School, originally studied in the late 1960s during its innovative early years (Smith & Keith, 1971).

CHOOSING BETWEEN SAMPLING
AND SELECTION

Like other researchers, ethnographers use statistical sampling proce-dures—simple random or stratified—when they wish to study a small group possessing the same distribution of characteristics as the larger population to which they intend to generalize. Statistical sampling may be inappropriate, however, under circumstances frequently encountered in ethnographic research. In cases such as the following, other forms of selection are mandated: (1) when characteristics of the larger population have not yet been identified, (2) when groups possess no naturally occurring boundaries, (3) when generalizability is not a salient objective, (4) when populations are composed of discrete sets and characteristics are distributed unevenly among them, (5) when only one or a few subsets of characteristics of a population are relevant to the research problem, (6) when some members of a subset are not attached to the population from which the sampling is intended, or (7) when researchers have no access to the whole population from which they wish to sample.

Certain research goals may make statistical sampling irrelevant. These include studies where initial description of a hitherto little known or singular phenomenon is desired; where social constructs—to be tested later in more stringently controlled designs—are to be generated; where the goal of the research is explication of meanings or microsocial processes; or where the subject of an investigation is an entire population. For researchers studying special institutions, regions, or populations, selection criteria differ from those required to generate a representative or stratified random sample. The goal under these circumstances is the development of findings that may be compared and contrasted with many other groups. Statistical sampling also may be inappropriate when excluding any member of a population is too risky, as is the case in some epidemiological studies, or when logistics or ethical considerations preclude sampling at all. For example, including every member of a population in a study may be cheaper and easier than sampling, which may cost more time and effort than the improvement in data is worth. Finally, selecting some members of a group and not others for study may be obtrusive or offensive (see "Sampling: How to Fix the Odds—Part I," 1980). Where statistical sampling to ensure representativeness is obviated by research circumstances, ethnographers aim for comparability and translatability of findings rather than for outright transferance to groups not investigated (see Chapter Two). Assuring comparability and translatability rests upon the systematic application of nonstatistical selection procedures and provides a foundation for making inferences about similarities and differences among groups.

Summary

Most educational research is a complex combination of the variants of criterion-based selection and probabilistic sampling. Choice of selection and sampling strategies depends on the goals and questions formulated by a researcher, the nature of the empirical unit to be studied, the overall theoretical and conceptual frameworks informing the study, and the credibility intended or sought by the researcher in generalizing or comparing obtained results. Terman (1925), for example, used extreme-case selection in choosing highly gifted children to follow over time in what became a criterion-based, panel selection (Terman & Oden, 1947, 1959). Likewise, many survey analysts and experimenters use criterion-based selection to delineate a group or population, from which they then sample randomly.

Because most ethnographers study characteristics and behaviors of human groups rather than the effects of specific treatments, ethnographic participants are chosen for relevance to specific interests. When these interests are served by locating data sources representative of a larger population, researchers use probabilistic strategies to choose study groups. More commonly, however, such groups are chosen by some variant of criterion-based selection. Criterion-based selection is particularly effective in examining little-known or extremely heterogeneous, highly permeable and diffuse, or extremely small or rare populations. In these cases, the precision required in delineating criteria for selection provides the researcher with the dense detail essential for eventual comparative analysis.

Once they have entered their research sites, ethnographers use methodical and sequential internal selection and sampling to assure that data adequately represent the varied characteristics and behavior within the group being investigated. Such sampling and selection may take the form of cross-informant interviewing for confirmation and validation of interviews, structured questionnaires, or findings derived from participant observation across the spectrum of subgroups and factions.

This mapping process, which is detailed in Chapter Four, facilitates how researchers characterize the groups they study. They engage in (1) thorough documentation of relevant attributes and features within the study site or group, including the role played by the researcher; and (2) specification of how the data collected during the mapping process affect the overall results of a study. Most important, they also become alert in the initial mapping stages to which roles they may assume, the forms of data collection that are most feasible and relevant, and emerging techniques for analyzing and interpreting the data obtained. All these involve criterion-based selection.

Although some ethnographers plan and conduct their research according to the linear fashion in which we present research decisions in this volume, the majority of qualitative investigators find the process to be reflexive and interactive. However conscientiously the researcher might define and characterize populations in preliminary phases, data collected in the field "talk back," providing empirical information that mandates modification of initial expectations and strategies. Likewise, selection and sampling procedures anticipated prior to field entry must be refined as conditions warrant. It is during the initial stages of fieldwork—especially those of locating a study site, gaining access and entry, establishing residence, and mapping fields, populations, sites, and collectivities—that many of these early decisions are reviewed and redirected. These kinds of sampling issues are discussed in Chapter Four.

CHAPTER FOUR

The Role and Experience of the Researcher

Among the social sciences, anthropology was one of the first disciplines to acknowledge how much who an individual researcher is affects research design, findings, and interpretations. Although scholars in the humanities have grappled with the relationship between artist and art for centuries, in the sciences a very different ideal has been sought. This ideal is the interchangeability of those practicing science. The premise is that if procedures are applied precisely and documented exactly, then anyone with similar training can replicate a study, and therefore science can be conducted with no concern for individual variation in researchers. In addition to replication this premise supports the goal of objectivity. One criterion used to assess the objectivity of a study is that it renders the same results regardless of who conducts it. Although positivist criteria have served the natural science with success, they have always been suspect in the social and human sciences. Vico (1968), writing in 1725, may have been the earliest scholar to insist that these criteria, at that time newly emerging from the Scientific Revolution, were unsuitable for inquiring about humans.

Those who study humans are themselves human and bring to their investigations all the complexity of meaning and symbolism that complicates too precise an application of natural science procedures to examining human life. This difficulty has been recognized for millennia; Greeks like Herodotus (Stambler, 1982) questioned the histories of people written by observers from differing perspectives. As the social and human sciences developed at the end of the nineteenth and beginning of the twentieth centuries, the relationship of the studier to the studied was discussed and debated by figures such as Weber (1949, 1968) and Dilthey (1988).

Some traditions in the human sciences, such as experimental psychology and survey sociology, did attempt to emulate closely natural science practice and sought to develop researcher-proof methods and techniques. However, early in the development of anthropology and field sociology scholars began to reflect on what many considered to be the unavoidable and inevitable effects on research of the individual who conducted it (e.g., Malinowski, 1935, 1967). By the middle decades of the twentieth century qualitative methodologists and scholars (e.g., Schatzman & Strauss, 1973; Schwartz & Schwartz, 1955; Williams, 1967) customarily discussed a number of topics under the rubric of researcher role and experience. These topics include the fieldwork tradition in general and the problems for investigators of conducting face-to-face research in the natural environments of those being studied. They also include researcher conduct in the field and the conditions affecting roles and experiences of ethnographers and other fieldworkers. In this chapter we discuss each of these topics; we then conclude with a section on establishing first contact with participants and entry to the field. This section provides a bridge to the following chapters on qualitative methods of collecting data.

Researcher Conduct

Accompanying the stereotype of the scientist as a disinterested observer of natural and human events is the myth of investigator-as-amoral-altruist. Investigators are accorded the authority to make decisions on the basis of training and purpose. Advancing science and knowledge are seen as a goal justifying the use of humans and other animals, one somehow outside the pantheon of other values, morals, and ethics framing human behavior. Scientists are assumed to have been prepared by their training to make decisions about when the benefits to science, and presumably to humankind, justify deception, invasion of privacy, manipulation, and other practices considered questionable in a variety of moral and ethical codes. Milgram's demonstration (1974) of how the identity of scientist can influence people to behave in ways they ordinarily would regard as reprehensible illustrates the pervasiveness of the myth of scientist-as-amoral-altruist.

Perhaps when scientific communities were small and reputations easily communicated, informal social controls prevented widespread abuse of scientific authority. However, the atrocities committed by Nazi physicians and subsequent revelations of abuses elsewhere perpetuated in the name of science brought the laissez faire period of scientific practice to a close in the United States. During the past 20 years those natural and human sciences that study or use humans and animals in their work have begun to develop standards for the treatment of and conduct toward both.

As a result guidelines for personal conduct during research have been adopted by groups such as the American Anthropological Association (1971), the American Sociological Association (1989), the American Educational Research Association (1991), and the American Psychological Association (1981). Parallel to these efforts are institutional constraints on the conduct of research. Any institution in the United States accepting federal funds for research on humans, animals, and recombinant DNA is required to maintain compliance offices to monitor and advise such activities. Many private funding agencies also require evidence of monitoring before monies are delivered to institutions. The development and dissemination of such guidelines and constraints have taken years, however, and the limitations they pose provide problems for most investigators at some point in their studies. Not the least of these is the adjustment required of researchers accustomed to autonomy in the conduct of their affairs.

As we have emphasized previously, it took some decades for human scientists to develop a well-organized tradition of fieldwork (see Chapter One). In the discipline that pioneered this area, some of the most influential early anthropologists did little, if any, fieldwork. They relied on the data they analyzed on surveys and questionnaires about native peoples sent to colonial administrators and missionaries as well as on stories collected from travelers to or visitors from exotic lands (Hayes, 1958). With some notable exceptions—Frederick LePlay's 1855 study of the European working class (cited in Nisbet, 1966) and work done among the urban poor on both sides of the Atlantic (see Bogdan & Biklen, 1992; Deegen, 1988; Wax, 1971)—even less face-to-face research was done by early sociologists.

In these situations social scientists interacted with the groups they studied much as historians related to documents and records. Of course many investigators who did do fieldwork were concerned with the relationships they had with their participants, but no codifications of guidelines for field workers were available at that time, either for what ethnographers should look for or for the ethics that they should use in their relationships with participants. Under these circumstances, some native peoples not only were embarrassed by well-meaning but naive investigators; they were browbeaten and robbed by anthropologists who were unable to understand why tribal people would not part with artifacts or tell them stories about sensitive aspects of their life and culture.

The Fieldwork Tradition and Face-to-Face Conduct

Although personal predilection may have kept some early anthropologists out of the field, with the advent of Malinowski's (1922) carefully documented work on the Trobriand Islanders and the increasingly large body of work done during the 1920s and 1930s by students of Franz Boas, it became difficult to avoid face-to-face contact with participants. By the 1930s, few researchers could call themselves anthropologists without first having accomplished the rite of passage that initial experience in the field constitutes (Kluckhohn, 1944; Spindler, 1970; Wolcott, 1975). During the same period, 1910 to 1930, Robert Parke and Ernest Burgess were supervising the many field studies from the University of Chicago that laid the groundwork for qualitative sociology, and their students were facing similar challenges (Adler & Adler, 1987).

Fieldwork and its face-to-face characteristic raises problems and questions less significant in research conducted at a distance.

— How can I communicate meaningfully with my participants?

— How are they and I affected by the emotions we evoke in one another and how should I handle these feelings?

— How are my participants and I similar and different—in personal characteristics, resources, and power—and how do the similarities and differences affect my relationship with them and my investigation among them?

— What is my responsibility to my participants, both as a researcher and as a member of their community, however temporary my residence there may be? What is the relationship between these responsibilities and those to other interested parties?

How investigators address and resolve these issues varies according to who the investigator is, who is being studied, and what the purpose of the research is. This is one of the sources of the idiosyncratic and the idiomatic in qualitative research. Each researcher handles these problems differently from other researchers. Furthermore each investigator handles the issues differently from one study to the next and across the course of a research career, for most with the hope of doing it better with each successive attempt. The personal tailoring of the interaction between ethnographer and informant is simultaneously a strength and a weakness of this approach to human science. It is a strength because it promotes the collection of data that more richly represent the experiences of the participants; it is a weakness because it makes comparison and replication more difficult.

Like all human science research, qualitative inquiries involve complex moral and ethical dimensions, most of which are public issues concerning any informed citizen (cf. Mills, 1959). Researchers, for example, who use standardized tests to study school achievement are well aware of the risks and dangers of characterizing groups of students by their performance on such instruments. These investigators rarely confront the misuse of their results on an individual level. They do not have to face these issues in their private, domestic worlds. Unlike qualitative researchers, investigators using conventional procedures from detached positions do not have to consider the effect of their private values on their research efforts.

Fieldworkers, in contrast, live out their ethical and moral choices in personal, day-to-day interaction with their participants. The public issues and values permeating all social science research (Weber, 1949) are complicated by the myriad personal issues that face-to-face contact entails. The special conditions of fieldwork and other intensive means of collecting qualitative and ethnographic data both complicate and enrich an investigator's conduct of research.

Conditions of Fieldwork

The circumstances and contexts within which human scientists conduct their inquiries vary. Research occurs in libraries, in laboratories, through the mail, in investigator's offices, and in the environments of those being studied. Fieldwork is the name given to the latter circumstances—research conducted in natural settings, the places where people are found going about their customary affairs. Each of the places where research occurs has its strengths and weaknesses, its advantages and disadvantages. In this section we describe how six conditions affect research conducted in the field: personal issues, participatory issues, advocacy issues, role relationships, boundary spanning, and ethical issues and political ideology.

PERSONAL ISSUES

Ethnographers and other qualitative researchers are, first of all, individuals with human personalities and preferences, family histories, varying states of physical and mental health, and a myriad of personal experiences, talents and skills, and strengths and weaknesses (Wengle, 1988). These individual characteristics affect research activities in ways immediately recognizable, ways that become apparent only over time, and ways that may never be known. (Peshkin (1982), for example, speculates on the extent to which his interest in studying small communities may reflect his positive experiences growing up in a tightly knit urban neighborhood. Patton (1990) discusses how he believe his mental and physical conditions affected some of his research projects.

Disciplinary Identity

As we will indicate in Chapter Five, an important part of personal identity is the researcher's professional background and position as a scholar within an academic discipline. These attributes include being an advocate of a particular method of study, an investigator wishing to justify the value of studying a particular group of people and asking a specific research question, and an entrepreneur in search of funding.

It is usually in the early stages of a project that researchers most closely attend to their roles as members of an academic discipline and as colleagues to other scholars interested in the research problem or the group under study. If the researcher is a graduate student, the research process is used by advisors and mentors as an opportunity to impart and reinforce the culture of the given academic discipline; professors may tell the student how to conduct the project, how to behave in the field, and even how to think. This process usually leaves an indelible imprint on the logical processes and future research of its participants.

Although the disciplinary constraints on an individual's later research may be less obvious and heavy handed, they still are significant. Prior research in the field influences the questions still to be asked; it may encourage some of the investigator's ideas while discouraging others. Colleagues, and journal editors, may have to be convinced that a particular set of research procedures is valid and appropriate, that a given research question is significant, or that investigating some group of people is valuable. Researchers and the work they produce are expected to represent generally the approaches typical for that discipline. If they do not, the work may be defined by other members of the discipline as outside the field, even though it may be recognized as good research. For example, if cultural anthropologists do quantitative or experimental research, other anthropologists may define the work as not anthropology, saying that the errant anthropologist is not behaving, or thinking, like a member of the tribe.

The Researcher-as-Instrument

The personal characteristic, however, most affecting conduct of qualitative research is the investigator's identity as the "essential research instrument" (Wolcott, 1975, p. 115). Ethnographers are data collectors, or "sensitive . . . observer[s], storyteller[s], and writer[s]" (p. 116); like human videotape recorders, they record as faithfully as possible the phenomena they see. The identity of data collector mediates all other identities held and roles played by the investigator.

Doing fieldwork raises many problems inherent in living in alien cultures or unfamiliar venues of a native culture. The roles the researcher assumes within the culture and the researcher's identity and experience are critical to the scientific merit of a study. They are part of the research design because researchers are dependent on and involved with participants over a sustained period of time and in ways far more intimate and complex than simply filling out questionnaires (Schwartz & Schwartz, 1955). Ethnographers share houses, raise their children, become ill, and have emotional crises among the peoples they study. To the extent that they become a part of the community and have the same experiences as natives do, the quality of their data is improved. Many have written of cultural insights that occurred to them as they grappled with personal and domestic problems encountered. Wylie (1957), for example, deciphered a French teacher's treatment of and perception of intellectual differences among children while watching his own child become the teacher's pet; Metz (1981) had to reassess her relationships with participants because the school she was studying was consolidated with one attended by her son.

Researcher Subjectivity

Qualitative research is distinguished partly by its admission of the subjective perception and biases of both participants and researcher into the research frame. The subjectivities of participants are usually a major part of what investigators seek to capture in their records. The subjectivities of the researcher serve multiple purposes. As Erickson (1973) emphasizes, affective reactions to what we are observing can be significant clues to things that need to be examined and analyzed further. For example, Shostak (1981) describes her initial objections to supplying her !Kung informants with tobacco; in addition to health concerns, she worried about the impact of fostering her informants' dependence on this and other goods supplied by the ethnographers. Her attention to her feelings about these issues, however, also appear to have sensitized her to the centrality in !Kung communities of reciprocal gift giving and the sharing of resources so often sparse on the Kalahari desert.

Researchers' subjectivities are also essential to establishing and building the intimate relationships with participants that permit trust and confidence. Finally subjective reactions and responses are often sources for methodological decisions. For example, researchers who find confrontation difficult are unlikely to elicit information from informants by using the "adversary and discombobulating tactics" that Douglas (1976) first describes and then admits he rarely uses. In addition to the problems these tactics create, Douglas says his aversion to them is "no doubt partly a personal thing" (p. 178).

As we will indicate in Chapter Five, the metatheoretical predispositions of ethnographers as well as their personal and professional interests form the basis for initial questions and choice of participants. Ethnographers use their own cultures implicitly to make comparisons with the one under investigation, clarifying both by comparing what is observed with what they have experienced in the past (Campbell, 1979). Thus, although it is not an explicit intent of fieldwork, researchers often become better aware of the structure of their own cultures and lives by virtue of their work in another culture or community.

PARTICIPATORY ISSUES

A second condition of fieldwork is intimated in the preceding section—fieldworkers customarily participate in the lives, experiences, and communities of those they study. They interact as fellow humans with the people under investigation.

Kinds of Participation

The degree of participation varies from one study to another and within studies as well. Gold (1958) categorizes participation according to the kind of interaction in which the researcher engages and how aware participants are that they are being studied: the complete participant, the participant-as-observer, the observer-as-participant, and the complete observer.

The complete participant is a researcher who assumes an insider role in the group being studied and whose research identity is not known to the group. This, of course, requires deception; the hidden, complete participant is working under cover. This raises ethical issues; furthermore, the undercover researcher's access to the whole group is limited by the role chosen, management of data collecting and recording is complicated by having to conduct it surreptitiously, and some of the balances to bias and oversubjectivity possible when research is conducted openly are precluded by covert research.

The participant-as-observer enters into the social life of those studied, sometimes assuming an insider role, but often playing the part of a snoop, shadow, or historian—roles not normally found in the group but familiar enough to participants to allow comfortable interactions. Under these circumstances, the participant-as-observer is known to be a researcher, can address ethical issues more directly, and can request access to the whole group, to negotiate data collecting and recording and to seek feedback on what is seen and how it is interpreted.

The observer-as-participant is also known as a researcher to the group, but has more limited interactions with participants. Gold suggests that interviewers who schedule a single session are observers-as-participants. They do enter into the lives of those they study, but social interaction is brief and focused around the question-and-response format of the interview.

The complete observer position, like that of the complete participant, is also covert. Participants go about their business, not realizing that they are being observed through a one-way mirror or by a hidden camera. The complete observer is removed or distanced from the social field inhabited by the participants. Although it provides the advantage of leaving the social field relatively undisturbed, this position shares many of the limitations of complete participation.

Our experience with these positions is not only that they characterize a researcher's overall stance toward the people studied, but also that they represent the range of participation throughout a field study (cf. Ball, 1990). The balance between observing and participating varies according to what is happening, and people's awareness of being studied comes and goes. Furthermore, when field residence extends over a long time, people forget that the fieldworker is studying them and begin to treat the researcher as a complete participant.

Adler & Adler (1987) offer a different version of Gold's distinctions among kinds of participation. Their categories for memberships researchers may have in groups being studied are peripheral, active, and complete. They associate a preference for these memberships with three traditions in qualitative sociology: the Chicago school, existential sociology, and ethnomethodology. Like Gold's categories of participation, each kind of involvement in participants' lives has benefits and limitations for research.

Participant Languages

An important dimension of any kind of membership and participation in others' lives is familiarity with the language or idiom of those studied. To achieve the degree of understanding required for unraveling the behavior and belief patterns under study, many trainers of fieldworkers insist that no researcher really can hope to study a people adequately through interpreters. Paul Radin (1933) points out that in-depth understanding of a culture requires near-native fluency in the language as well as extensive and intensive participant observation. Radin's position is an ideal case; most investigators have had to rely to some extent on native speakers for translation. A more behavioristic approach adopted by some investigators (Harris, 1980) diminishes the importance of native language fluency. These researchers feel that observable behavior is the most important aspect of a culture for investigators to consider, because what people say about what they do is less important than what they actually do.

We believe that the issue of language fluency is critical. Even ethnographers working within their own language and culture may find that meanings they attribute to sayings or actions may not be the same as those given to the same things by their participants. Researchers studying teenagers, for example, may note that without some careful groundwork in adolescent argot, it is impossible to get beyond polite indifference. Willis (1976), for example, was able to analyze incipient patterns of social stratification among British schoolboys by discussing with them the relationships between their slang names for subgroups among the boys and the behavior connected with the use of those terms. This led to a detailed study of differences in patterns of preparation for the work force.

Natural Settings

Above all, ethnographers must work in settings where behavior occurs naturally. They must go to their participants; they cannot rely on laboratory settings for purity of design or captive audiences for convenience. Over a sustained period of time, they must maintain constant interaction with participants. Often ethnographers have no real role or plausible reason for being in a setting other than the desire to study it. They are dependent on participants for friendships; they may be dependent for services and access to additional participants as well.

Initial days in the fieldwork setting can be exhilarating, as everything observed is something new to be learned about. They may be trying, as necessary arrangements for the study move with glacial slowness through barely understood procedural channels specific to the culture. Hostility usually comes from some quarters, and it may be difficult to avoid acquiring roles or friendships that, because of their unique status or stigmatizing qualities, may bias perceptions or preclude access to important sources of information at a later date (Argyris, 1952). Ethnographers may find that their first informants are self-selected individuals who are eccentrics or have low status within the group under study. They seek association with the ethnographer as a means of enhancing their prestige. Powdermaker (1966), for example, found that she had to fire a key informant in her first fieldwork because his need for her approval led him to exaggerate greatly the material he gave to her. Attribution of an unexpected role by the classroom teacher initially biased behavior of participants in LeCompte's 1975 study; she found that her elementary school participants had been informed that she was writing a book about them (see Chapter Seven for a more detailed description). Basing their behavior on popular TV programs, the students proceeded to perform in ways they believed would make good copy.

Tensions in Participation

Involvement with participants creates a number of problems for the field worker—tensions that most researchers address by seeking balances. Most obvious is simply maintaining the capacity for objectivity. Occasional absence from the field is useful when things begin falling apart; it facilitates perspective, especially when it is combined with an opportunity to review field notes and perceptions with other colleagues outside the research setting (Whyte, 1955).

Ethnographers' involvement with their participants is, however, also governed by an informal tradition that expects a special kind of commitment from the researcher. This involves sympathizing and identifying with the people studied to the extent that the materials produced represent the participants' life ways in ways that are not just true to life and authentic to outsiders, but that are legitimate to the participants themselves. People have experienced emotions ranging from dismay and anger to amusement on reading descriptions of themselves by anthropologists, even those who were generally sympathetic to the participants (Deloria, 1969; Yoors, 1967). A good example of an anthropologist who violated both the ethic of commitment and caring and canons of dispassionate reporting is Turnbull (1972). He lived among the Ik, but found their—to him—callous and unloving social relationships to be so offensive that he was only able to describe the tribe in ways that clearly displayed his revulsion. He could neither speak on their behalf nor remain objective in his presentation of their culture.

ADVOCACY ISSUES

The commitment to participants expected of fieldworkers often developes into advocacy. This may be an inevitable outcome of a research stance that involves participation, although many natural and human scientists are deeply committed to what they study. Qualitative researchers are often outsiders who come to reside partly within a culture. In the course of their work, they first acquire roles and status within the community. Then the excitement and bloom of first discovery fades into the everyday drudgery of note taking, interviewing, and observation of increasingly familiar phenomena. Maintaining a constantly high level of interest and openness becomes difficult in the face of boredom; more critically, it may be increasingly difficult to maintain the tension between friendship and dispassionate observation without taking sides (Miller, 1952). The outsider changes from stranger to friend and member of the family (Powdermaker, 1966; Wax, 1971) and, as such, is expected to share the same passions and crises as other members of the community.

Fieldwork brings tests of commitment and objectivity that call on the researcher to become an ally in family or community disputes or to speak on behalf of the community to outsiders. As understanding develops, investigators may become reluctant to document more unusual or seamy aspects of participant lives. It also may become more difficult to view with understanding practices that repulse the researcher. These need not be as obvious as food habits or hygiene. How participants treat categories of people in the community, such as women or the disabled, may offend the researcher's sense of equity and fairness. Ethnographers studying schools, for example, almost inevitably observe teachers or school administrators treating students in ways the observer believes are inhumane or unfair.

Advocacy issues, then, often revolve around the researcher's peculiar stance as both insider and outsider. As outsiders we seek to document and describe the lives of people as dispassionately and fairly as possible. As insiders we seek to understand the lives of others from their points of view. This is inherently a schizophrenic task. We risk losing the outsider's perspective by overidentifying with participants, and we risk losing the insider's perspective by underidentifying with them.

Changing Views of Advocacy

How fieldworkers in the social science disciplines handle advocacy issues has changed over time. In the 1920s and 1930s interest in psychodynamic theory affected anthropologists' relationships to participants. Early anthropologists had tried to match a study of so-called primitive minds with what was erroneously believed to be the evolution of civilized people. The culture and personality school of anthropology, heavily influenced by psychodynamic theory, encouraged a more sympathetic and systematic analysis of beliefs, symbols, and cognitive processes among non-Western people.

In some cases this occurred because anthropologists became, through their study of native peoples, conscious of the abuses to which some people had been subjected by colonial powers. In other instances, they foresaw commercial and industrial exploitation of resources in native territories and sought to ameliorate the impact such changes would have on native cultures and lifeways. War and politics also intervened. Some leading anthropologists felt impelled to speak out against the pseudoso-cial-science theories that inspired Nazism and other racially oriented national policies (Boas, 1938); they also became involved in facilitating communication for military personnel from European cultures who came into contact with tribal or feudal peoples during wartime. This type of culture conflict could have been predicted. However, during the second World War even contacts among Europeans and Americans, though the cultures were not so different from one another, were fraught with culturally generated misunderstandings (Benedict, 1946; Mead, 1942, 1959).

Comparable issues generated similar concerns among other human scientists committed to face-to-face interaction with those they studied. Much of the work produced by the Chicago school sociologists during the same period, for example, focused on individuals and groups whose powerlessness, poverty, and victimization placed them at risk physically, mentally, and emotionally. Researchers' documentation of the lives of tramps, gang members, and addicts placed these investigators in the position of speaking to the rest of society on behalf of those unable to do so for themselves (e.g., Anderson, 1923; Lindesmith, 1947; Shaw, 1930).

Speaking for Participants

Advocacy issues usually begin to develop toward the end of a study when the researcher has developed sufficient familiarity with the group studied to be considered a legitimate spokesperson. These relationships often continue long after the initial project has been completed; they sometimes provide an impetus for further studies, which expand on questions raised originally. Researchers may be sought as expert witnesses on behalf of people they have studied. Traditionally, the people studied have called on researchers to intercede with social or governmental agen-cies in issues opaque to the participants but well understood by research-ers because of their greater familiarity with contemporary institutional life. Although the increasing sophistication of peoples once thought to be traditional or primitive has made this practice less common, a variant has emerged in contemporary popular literature that purports, for exam-ple, to explain Japanese and Chinese business practices to American entrepreneurs, presumably for the benefit of the latter (Ouchi, 1982).

How researchers speak on behalf of participants varies. They may act as interpreters of language or behavior that the ethnographer under-stands but that outsiders of the same general culture of the ethnographer do not. Thus, ethnographers may be asked to broker between street gangs and the police, between Appalachian mountaineers and government bureaucrats, or between teacher groups and their administrators. The problem the ethnographer has in these cases is to speak for one group to another without becoming identified as part of either. Davidson's work (1981) is an example of failure to achieve that balance; following the publication of his book describing the experience of illegal Mexican migrants to Texas, he was arrested and indicted for allegedly smuggling in Mexican aliens, despite documentation from authorities indicating that he was a legitimate investigator.

In other cases, anthropologists may be asked to intervene on behalf of their participants, as Deyhle (1989, 1991, 1992) was when Navajos in the community she studied asked for her data on dropouts to support a lawsuit against the school district where she did fieldwork. Becoming advocates in this way surely alters the relationships held with participants; whether a success or a failure, the intervention cannot avoid affecting how the ethnographer is viewed by participants.

The advocacy position implicit in much qualitative research further complicates relationships that are both scientific and personal. It makes the political views and commitments of the researcher directly relevant to all such research. Investigators with conservative agendas ask different questions and interpret the answers they obtain in different ways from liberal or radical investigators. Although academia has been stereotyped for generations as the hotbed of radicalism (e.g., D'Souza, 1991; Kimball, 1990; Sykes, 1988), scholars do vary in their politics, and this variation accounts for considerable disagreement and controversy about the knowledge they generate.

Asymmetry in Field Relationships

Equally significant is that scholarship and research are themselves political activities. Relationships between the studier and the studied are rarely symmetrical. For most of this century people with more power, resources, and information have examined those with much less of all three. The relationships often border on patronage; researchers may not only speak for those they study, they may also control the interaction and discourse of their participants with other outsiders. In any event the relationship between a participant and a researcher has typically been uneven. Even when the researcher is a student, the position of candidate for a doctoral degree with its attendant expectations of entering the professorate confers on the investigator a status higher than that of many research participants. This asymmetry in the relationship between researcher and researched has been challenged in past decades. More anthropologists, for example, have been engaging in what they call "studying up" (Nader, 1972; Roman, 1992; Roman & Apple, 1990). Studying up is investigating those with more power, prestige, resources, and status than academics ordinarily achieve (Daniels, 1980; Harrell-Bond, 1976; Hoffman, 1980). Wealthy philanthropists, politicians, top corporate executives, celebrities, as well as physicians and attorneys are examples of the categories of participants more powerful than most researchers, student or faculty. The relationship between researcher and participant continues to be asymmetrical, but the balance of power is reversed. The advocacy issues in studying up are less likely to be the temptation to speak for participants than the enticements of being co-opted by the powerful, feeling obliged to apologize for them, or even avoiding the exposure of their clay feet.

A second practice creating a shift in the conventional asymmetry of researcher—researched relationships is what has been called collaborative research (Gitlin & Smyth, 1989; Johnston, 1990; Miller, 1990; Oja & Smulyan, 1989; Reason, 1989; Schensul & Schensul, 1992). Centered principally in research on schools and education, it is based on balancing the relationship between investigators and their participants by conceptualizing the study as a collaborative effort between an outside researcher, typically an academic, and an inside researcher, typically a member of the group being studied. Ideally (see LeCompte, 1993), problems defined by insiders are given precedence. Inside and outside researchers work together to define the purpose of the study and to design, conduct, and report the research. Exact symmetry in relationships may be impossible, and imbalances between the insider and the outsider may remain, in professional status or experience with doing research, for example. However, collaborative research seeks to even out power and control over the investigation itself such that both inside and outside researchers have equivalent commitments to and interests and stakes in the study; risks, responsibilities, and rewards are all shared. The advocacy issues in collaborative research are complicated because the insider—outsider positions are held by individuals who may themselves be simultaneously insiders and outsiders in the research project.

ROLE RELATIONSHIPS

All the relationships acquired by and ascribed to the fieldworker in the course of interaction with study participants constitute roles. These include roles that give the researcher a legitimate reason for remaining in the study site as an observer and others that permit appropriate social interaction with the participants under study.

Establishing Roles

Some fortunate fieldworkers have been able to legitimize themselves simply as observers who want to learn all they can about a culture. This is a useful role to hold if it can be achieved. It creates fewer perceptual screens in the minds of the participants, screens that give participants notions about what observers really want to or should know, given their statuses. In some cases, however, people cannot act toward others until their statuses, and the behaviors attendant to those statuses, have been made clear. Researchers are able to elicit little interaction with participants until they acquire a specific role from the array of relationships available to the group. In other cases, researchers have had to invent a role that is familiar to the participants and compatible with collection of the data the investigator seeks. These include newspaper reporter, government medical officer, evaluator, writer of a book, or sponsor—someone who presents a sympathetic view of the particular group to the outside world. Depending on the purposes of their research, the roles fieldworkers assume can vary. However, we believe that the variation involved is more one of relative emphasis placed on a collection of acquired roles than it is additions or deletions from the list.

Qualitative researchers must communicate their projects and needs effectively to members of the group being investigated. They must also communicate effectively to subgroups of the study group whose ascriptive characteristics such as gender, race, and age, with their associated cultural patterns, may differ from those of the researcher. It may be necessary to establish linkages with agencies or individuals, such as school administrators or officials of the Bureau of Indian Affairs, who are gatekeepers and supervisors of the people under investigation. In many cases, these functionaries may have well-established belief structures about the motivations and behaviors of the group being studied; a researcher whose study does not confirm those beliefs may be viewed with suspicion. Ethnographers doing evaluation studies encounter additional problems; although they are held to many of the same strictures on roles as other sociocultural researchers, they may be obligated to communicate what they discover to participants and often to external agencies in what is seen as a timely manner. Insofar as the findings do not coincide with beliefs the participants hold about the flow of events and behavior, they may offend informants in ways that affect the researcher's access to information. By contrast, the classical ethnographer left the field and wrote the results of the study later. This job did not require transmitting conclusions as soon as they were formulated, regardless of the degree to which they flattered the participants of the research.

Social and Personal Dependencies

Once an ethnographer has spent considerable time in a culture, the roles and friendships acquired create a network of mutual dependencies between researcher and participant. Although these are critical to the research project, they may be less socially and personally important to investigators than they are to informants, who rely on the ethnographer for commodities as disparate as salaries, protection, status, entertainment, emotional support, medicine, or contact with a more complex, modern, or adult culture. This creates a dilemma: To do the research, an investigator must have a role, but having roles inevitably leads to the kinds of relationships that need delicate handling when terminated. The presence of the ethnographer may give participants a kind of relationship never before experienced, one that is exhilarating or lucrative. Its loss may be far more devastating to participants than to researchers; researchers return to their own cultures, often with relief and sometimes with the triumph of a job well done. The participants, however, have certainly lost a diverting social contact; they also may have experienced something tantamount to a death in the family. Thus, qualitative researchers must consider how to disengage from fieldwork in ways that cause as little disruption to the culture as possible (Snow, 1980).

Disengagement can, of course, pose risks to people involved in any kind of research, but it is especially serious when unanticipated or delayed effects of a treatment may occur. Researchers are admonished to explain these in advance, to obtain consent where necessary, and to work with subjects until all reasonably foreseen repercussions are ameliorated. The federal guidelines on involving human beings in research, discussed at the beginning of the chapter, mandate such practices. The same strictures apply to ethnographers. They may be even stronger because qualitative researchers can predict in advance neither the effect they may have on participants nor the importance that their informants may attribute to relationships with them.

BOUNDARY SPANNING

In addition to accommodating to a variety of roles achieved or ascribed to them in the research setting, qualitative researchers must move from sets of roles appropriate in one setting to others different because they were developed in different contexts for different reasons. They also must communicate as legitimate and convincing representatives of that role or status to others who hold positions similar to each of their multiple identities. For example, an anthropologist, in the role of trusted confidant

of village elders, may be asked, as a technical expert familiar with government bureaucracies, to intercede in negotiations with a visiting medical
team for the solution of an intractable health problem. The request for
intercession could, of course, be made in the opposite direction—the
medical team may ask the anthropologist to intercede with the villagers.

Skill in communicating within and across cultural groups has been
termed *boundary spanning* (Schensul *et al.*, 1981). Because ethnographers
almost always study groups whose cultures are not identical with their
own, boundary-spanning skills are critical to the success of a research
project. Boundary spanning in some senses is similar to cultural brok-
ering, insofar as ethnographers often act as intermediaries or go-
betweens for several groups, each of whose actions or motivations must
be explained to the other.

Multiple Constituencies

Boundary spanning goes beyond the passive role of translating from
one culture to another performed by cultural brokers. Boundary spanning involves active participation in the variety of cultures that are involved with and impinge on a project. Its utility is not limited to research
projects, but a qualitative researcher needs those skills not only to survive
in the research site, but also to facilitate execution of the study at every
stage. This is because so many constituencies develop a vested interest in
the project at different times. These may include professional associations, funding agencies, the participants of the study, other academics,
and policy-making institutions.

Successful boundary spanning requires familiarity with, or at least
the ability to become familiar with, the behaviors, goals, and beliefs of all
constituencies that influence a project. It also necessitates being recognized as a legitimate representative from at least one constituent group
in a project and the ability to operate dispassionately at the margins of
several other such groups without loss of credibility. In a sense, the ability
to span boundaries means that the researcher is in many groups but often
is not a full-fledged member of any of them. The titles of a number of
research methods books written by ethnographers illustrate this tension
between belonging and detachment: Powdermaker's (1966) *Stranger and
Friend,* Freilich's (1970) *Marginal Natives,* and Agar's (1980) *The Professional Stranger.*

Negotiating across Cultures

Boundary spanning also involves a broader definition of the term
culture than is often used. Most discussions of research projects involve
two cultures: One is easily recognized—the one under study—and one

is at least implied—that of the researcher (Campbell, 1979). However, all human social enterprises—occupational, familial, social, or institutional—form groups that establish stable or enduring rules and regulations, interests, behavior patterns, and ways of viewing the world, which, insofar as they are adopted by group members, constitute identifying characteristics for that group. Such groups may be described as having a culture (Goodenough, 1976), even if the membership criteria vary. For example, membership may be somewhat transient, as in governmental bureaucracies, where a formal structure dictates roles whose incumbents are more or less interchangeable. Another case involves groups whose members are subsumed by no single formal association. An example is an academic discipline such as anthropology, where a common culture is imposed by coursework, training, and apprenticeship, but no single professional association includes all anthropologists.

Groups like these are critical to a research project in that their members may be involved individually, with the researcher as a colleague, or collectively, as a body like a funding agency with which the researcher must negotiate. In any case, both the skills researchers possess in negotiation and communication, as well as the researcher's depth of understanding of the nuances of the cultural group influencing a research project are critical to the execution of a study.

Another concern during the early stages of a project is funding agencies. Funding agencies also constitute cultures; they, in turn, are accountable to boards of directors or legislative agencies with their own belief structures. All are embedded within a lay community, various components of which may at times have interest in, but little understanding of, the people under investigation. A researcher may believe that an agency is a likely source of support, but only if his or her interests can be translated into the lexicon used by the agency and made to be salient. At times, a proposal is written so that the agency's interests may be addressed at the same time that the investigator's research project is piggybacked with it (LeCompte, 1970). For ethnographers who are doing contract research or who are employed as evaluators or documenters by an agency (Fetterman, 1984, 1988a; Fetterman & Pitman, 1986), early negotiations also may involve bringing traditionally hierarchical bureaucratic working styles and norms into some convergence with traditional qualitative working styles and norms (Everhart, 1975). Whereas agencies typically want problems and data collection procedures to be delineated and time lines established at the beginning of a project, qualitative researchers need the autonomy to define and explore questions as they arise. Even when initial understanding is reached about how an employed researcher will do the work, vicissitudes in project leadership and public policy may dictate ongoing negotiations over project execution throughout its duration (Fitzsimmons, 1975).

Once the project is completed, a variety of audiences needs access to the data. Depending on the purposes of the project or the motives of the investigator, presentation of results should be tailored to the needs, interests, and background of the constituency (Pitman & Maxwell, 1992; Schensul & Schensul, 1992; Schensul *et al.*, 1981). An academic constituency wants a lengthy technical monograph detailing how the data were collected and how the results affect future theoretical or empirical considerations; policy makers have very little interest in how the data were collected but a great deal of concern over the implications a study has for legislation or administration. Project directors and practitioners, still another constituency, are less interested in the philosophy of participants than they are in the effectiveness of a given project (Schensul *et al.*, 1981).

As qualitative researchers move away from traditional small-scale, grant-funded studies toward work that is more applied and often executed by multidisciplinary teams, and to the extent that they address concerns germane to large, modern, urban settings, the number of constituencies with whom they must communicate expands. No longer can ethnographers feel fairly certain that their participants will never read the monograph; nor do they have the splendid—and lengthy—isolation, which earlier anthropologists had to spend in long and arduous meditation over their data. A wide variety of agencies sees the techniques of study and the insights garnered by the ethnographer to be increasingly useful; such utility imposes new constraints and challenges on fieldwork and its practitioners. The skill with which fieldworkers are able to relate to, communicate with, and transcend their own and other cultures is critical both to the legitimacy and comprehensiveness of research results and to the ability of investigators to continue to do fieldwork in the same and different sites.

ETHICAL ISSUES AND POLITICAL IDEOLOGY

As we described in Chapter One, researchers' increasing recognition of and sensitivity to the political nature of their relationships to their work, to those they study, and to scholarship in general has resulted in the past 30 years in a literature of review and critique enriching consideration of the knowledge generated by human scientists, its sources, and its applications (e.g., Anderson, 1971; Gouldner, 1970; Hymes, 1972; Punch, 1986; Weaver, 1973). Critical theory and feminist theory, especially, have contributed to the bulk of recent thinking about the politics of research. Although it may be more accurate to label these traditions in the plural—critical theories and feminist theories—to represent the diversity of factions they encompass, both of the frameworks share common concerns, as we discuss in Chapters One and Five.

Additional factors contributing to consideration of the ethics and morality of qualitative research are advocacy issues, qualitative researchers' dependence on personal relationships for much of their data, the changing ethical climate for all research, studying up and collaboration, and the emphasis in critical theories and feminist theories on domination and subordination in human affairs. Central to such consideration are questions of risk and vulnerability, disclosure and informed consent, loyalty and responsibility, and possession of the data collected and results reported.

Risk and Vulnerability

Risk refers to the possibility of any ill consequences of a research study—the chances of injury, damage, harm, or losses to anyone associated with an investigation. The two groups most frequently considered here are the participants in the research and those who are studying them. Both are subject to varying amounts of risk according to what is being studied and how it is being studied. Investigators usually initiate the research; the risks they undertake are considered to be known to them, weighed carefully by them, and freely undertaken. These conditions are not always met, of course. Novice researchers are often naive about the risks they incur, and even experienced investigators can be misled by the occasional encounter with unscrupulous funding sources (e.g., Glazer, 1972; Rynkiewich & Spradley, 1976).

Participants rarely initiate research. Since it is their lives being examined, the risks they incur are considered to be the most serious. Consequently one convention observed by most qualitative researchers is the assurance to participants of confidentiality. Confidentiality is withholding participants' real names and other identifying characteristics from others—from published and unpublished reports as well as from casual conversations and formal and informal talks. Investigators customarily use pseudonyms for all proper names of people, groups, communities, and such. In some cases personal characteristics are not only withheld, but may be disguised to further protect participant identity. Disguises, however, have to be planned so as to avoid confounding patterns in the data; researchers have to be sure that the dimensions chosen for disguise are not relevant to research questions and findings. If a researcher is able to collect from people information that cannot be identified—through a mailed survey, for example—then participants may be protected by anonymity. Anonymity is withholding identity because it is truly unknown; it is a stronger protection than confidentiality but is usually precluded in qualitative designs where researchers have face-to-face contact with participants and consequently are able to identify who supplied what data.

In both instances, however, the identity of participants is often recognizable to the person represented in the report; that is, anonymity and confidentiality may protect identities from outsiders but not from participants themselves—they may recognize themselves and others should they read the research reports. Ordinarily this self-identification is an asset. Investigators believe they have got it right when their portraits are recognizable to participants. Whether this poses an additional risk and requires further protections depends on the situation. For example, researchers in schools typically attempt to protect students from retribution by teachers and to protect teachers from retribution by administrators. The question to be asked is whether data and information revealed in a report place participants in positions that make them vulnerable to risks. Finally, even data not reported—field notes, audio tapes, and such—are susceptible to legal risks. Unlike physicians and lawyers, researchers and the information they collect enjoy no special protection from legal review. Any data collected by an investigator is open to subpoena by the courts. Although such material is rarely demanded, researchers should be aware that their material is vulnerable.

Other groups associated with research projects also undertake risks, and their involvement should be recognized: funding agencies such as governments or private foundations, sponsoring agencies such as universities or research companies, and the larger population represented by the participants selected—all teachers, all teenagers, all parents, all administrators, for example. Funding agencies risk money and prestige; personnel backing the wrong idea may lose jobs. Likewise universities have many competing constituencies; support for some through research or provision of programs may risk the support of others.

The customary principle used in weighing risks is that whatever the potential damage is should be balanced by potential benefit. Furthermore these potential risks and benefits should be known to all involved, so that individuals may elect freely to participate or not. This free choice is affected by two further issues, vulnerability and disclosure.

Vulnerability is a characteristic of participants in research whose freedom to choose may be limited by age (the very young and the very old), by health (mental and physical disabilities), by social constraints (inmates of prisons, hospitals, and similar institutions), or by such other conditions as having been the victim of a violent crime or engaging regularly in activities deemed criminal, shady, or socially unacceptable—even merely embarrassing. The more vulnerable the participant, the more care is expected in seeking and obtaining consent. Guardians or other gatekeepers may be asked to agree to the consent on behalf of the participant. In these situations, the study of children, for example, researchers may also request indication of children's assent to participation for which parents have given consent.

Disclosure and Informed Consent

Agreement, whether assent or consent, is dependent on disclosure—revealing to participants and others involved what is being studied, how it is to be done, and what the risks and benefits are expected to be. This is an issue with a long history of debate among human researchers. One problem is that the more participants and subjects may know about the research, the less naturally they may behave. Additionally, even knowing that the research is occurring may create a risk otherwise avoided. For example, if a researcher reveals to teachers that some of the students being observed in classrooms are illegal immigrants, this knowledge might place teachers in legal jeopardy for aiding and abetting in a crime (cf. Davidson, 1981, cited previously).

The debate between the relative values of overt and covert research thus has ethical and moral dimensions as well as methodological ones. Conventional research design assumes that the less participants and subjects know about what is going on, the better. In medical and other experimental designs, disguising or hiding the research activity is labeled a blind study. Further disguising activity from those collecting or analyzing the study is called a double blind study. In qualititative designs such covert design has been used when researchers have muckraking intentions, when overt research would not be agreed to by participants, when overt research would so distort natural behavior that findings would be regarded as hopelessly contaminated, or, as noted above, when overt research creates more risks than covert research. Researchers disagree on the extent to which they condone covert research. Some believe that no covert designs are acceptable; others weigh potential benefits against the harm such designs may incur; still others believe that covert research may be mandated by political considerations—revealing corruption and abuse in mental hospitals, for example—or by theoretical and methodological considerations.

These issues are complicated by the extent of disclosure. Our position is that disclosure is relative. It is not merely a function of researchers telling participants what they are up to. In qualitative designs especially, purposes evolve; researchers do not always know themselves all that they will be up to. Participants are not always interested in full disclosure. For example, in Goetz's first attempt at ethnography (1976b), her complex, and probably convoluted, attempts to explain her purpose to a class of third graders was finally reduced by them to the satisfying and simple explanation that she was writing a book about them. Informed consent thus becomes a function of how much researchers disclose to those they study. How informed and knowledgeable a participant may be in consenting to participation in research is itself arguable. Schein (1987), for example, takes the position that consent is never meaningfully informed unless researchers are studying other researchers; only researchers understand what participation entails, and only researchers should be responsible for any risks undertaken in the process.

Loyalty and Responsibility

Responsibility and loyalty are issues made especially crucial by the personal, face-to-face nature of much qualitative research. The ethical and moral question is to whom a researcher owes primary loyalty. Whose interests predominate in any conflict? Those of the researcher? The scientific community? The public? The funding and sponsoring agencies? The participants? All have a stake in scholarship. In the code of conduct adopted in 1971, the American Anthropological Association specified the principle that an ethnographer's first loyalty should be to those studied. This can result, of course, in ill consequences for others. Whatever the ethical guidelines adopted by a researcher, one question that must be considered is priority of loyalties and responsibilities.

Ownership of Information

Related to these questions are issues of ownership of data and findings. Through most of this century the information collected by ethnographers and other fieldworkers has been considered the possession of the researcher. Although many investigators eventually donated their material to publicly available data repositories like the Human Relations Area Files and although the human sciences share with the natural sciences a premise that data should be available for public, or at least scholarly, scrutiny, field notes and other material have been considered to belong to whoever obtained them. This convention worked because investigators often operated alone and because the people they studied were frequently illiterate and semiliterate.

The idea that information may also belong to the people from whom it has been gathered accompanied the decolonization movements abroad and the minority rights movements in the U.S. Recognition that knowledge, whether manifest or tacit, about people is something that may belong, first and foremost, to the people themselves is a recent development among scholars. Furthermore, with the large-scale funding projects undertaken in the 1960s and 1970s and the spread of team research, other groups such as funding agencies began to make claims to ownership of data. Where possession of the data has not been clarified at the beginning, ethnographers have found themselves in the unsettling position of being expected to hand over field notes that they recorded as private documents. These conflicting claims to possession further complicate issues of risk, loyalty, and consent.

Summary

As discussed previously many professional organizations have sought to develop guidelines to assist researchers in making decisions ethically and morally. The compliance offices required by such funding agencies as the U.S. government also contribute procedural requirements intended to protect the public from being placed unnecessarily at risk or being unwittingly exploited. However, because most ethical issues that arise in research are complex and situational, decisions are rarely clear-cut and easy. Each decision involves a different set of circumstances and priorities than every other decision. Consequently, we believe that the responsibility for these decisions must rest with the individual researcher. Only the researcher in the field has the information and the perspective to permit wise decision making. Guidelines and reviews provide researchers with what the community of scholars and its publics designate as ethical and moral; we believe that individuals should acknowledge these and be aware of when their own principles conflict with shared principles. We also believe that differences should be publicly aired should conflicts arise in particular situations. Most important, we also believe that researchers whose ethical and moral conduct is questionable should be ready to defend and argue their positions and should know that they are liable for censorship as a consequence of their decisions. That is, we believe that individual researchers not only have the responsibility for making ethical decisions but also have the responsibility for accepting the consequences of those decisions.

The fieldwork tradition and face-to-face contact and the moral, ethical, and advocacy issues they raise mandate that ethnographers, because of their special relationships with and knowledge about participants, give more thought than other investigators to the roles they hold vis-a-vis participants. As we emphasized at the beginning of this chapter, the roles of the ethnographer and other qualitative researchers differ from those of investigators in other traditions. Although we believe that the considerations discussed here should be addressed by all researchers, they are particularly important to ethnographers and qualitative researchers.

Access and Entry

Once potential sources of data—sites, groups, or individuals—are located, researchers face the problem of gaining access and entry. They must decide who to contact, how to initiate contact, and how to maintain the contact. Guidelines for access and entry in sociological and anthropological research are plentiful (e.g., Agar, 1980; Fetterman, 1989; Kahn & Mann, 1952; Schatzman & Strauss, 1973; Shaffir & Stebbins, 1991; Wax, 1971). All are offered tentatively; all require flexibility and adaptability. Furthermore, just as locatability is affected by the boundedness of data sources, so are access and entry.

The issue of whom to contact to initiate collection of data requires researchers to identify gatekeepers—people who can facilitate access to the desired group of people. Contact with data sources may be initiated formally or informally. Formal contact involves approach through official, often professional, channels. Informal contact is initiated through personal networks of relationships. Both formal and informal contacts may be conducted face to face or in writing. Generally, informal, face-to-face contacts are more effective. People are more likely to respond positively to direct, interpersonal appeals, and informal networks are often trusted more than official channels. Such guidelines, nevertheless, are situation specific. Participants may be reluctant to cooperate without official sanction or may perceive an initial written contact to be less threatening than a face-to-face encounter.

Researchers can approach varying segments of a group through single or multiple contacts. Formal, hierarchically segmented organizations may be approached through single or multiple avenues at one or more status levels. Contact through top-level officials can ensure organizational sanction for the research and often is required by school districts and other groups that wish to limit researcher access to internal affairs. However, overidentification with high-ranking officials can be a problem if it alienates the lower-ranking participants whom the researcher wants to study. Single status and unsegmented groups are often approached more easily because they possess no central authority to deny access, but the issue of multiple- or single-avenue approaches remains. Most researchers find multiple-access approaches more effective; however, these do not obviate the problem of becoming overidentified with initial contacts or prevent researchers from being torn between allegiances to competing or hostile sets of informants.

Access to individuals whom the researcher has designated as the group to be studied also is facilitated by introductions from third parties known to both researcher and participant. Third-party introductions may be used regardless of the nature of the study group. Third parties may ease access, especially if they are valued by people the researcher wishes to study. However, if the third party is not well regarded, intended participants may refuse to grant access to researchers. Therefore, researchers should seek whatever information is available about the relationship between a third party and a potential participant prior to requesting an introduction. In those cases where no common acquaintance can be found, researchers must introduce themselves.

Both initiating and maintaining contact require researchers to present themselves as sincere individuals who have a commitment to the study group. Most ethnographers recommend that researchers genuinely assume a stance of naivete—one which approximates the relationship of novice to expert. Someone who knows everything does not need to be told anything, while there is no end to the information that a learner needs to acquire from more knowledgeable participants. The opportunity to be teachers not only helps to convince participants of their value as data sources, but also sensitizes the researcher to phenomena that might otherwise be overlooked or discounted.

Many researchers also offer participants some reciprocation for data obtained. Although this may constitute something as concrete as money or tasks accomplished for a group, intangibles also are effective. Attentiveness, empathy, and the documentation of individual or group life ways are often far more compelling rewards than goods or services exchanged. They also avoid long-term, material dependence of participants on the researcher. Finally, contact is facilitated when participants and respondents view the research purposes as valuable or at least harmless and the researcher's motives as benign.

The most significant elements in obtaining access and entry are researcher flexibility and sensitivity to nuances of participant response. These necessitate that investigators present their purposes as simply and as tentatively as possible. The fewer the initial requests, the more likely participants are to respond positively to later, more elaborate appeals. Finally, identifying, initiating, and maintaining contacts should be documented as thoroughly as possible. This experience itself provides data; its record facilitates comparison and replication, and it constitutes the beginning of the mapping procedures preliminary to more thorough data collection.

MAPPING GROUPS AND COLLECTIVITIES

We refer to the initial stages of an ethnographer's entry to the field or the interviewer's approach to respondents as an informal process of "shagging around" (LeCompte, 1969). Shagging around is sometimes designated as mapping (Schatzman & Strauss, 1973); however, it refers to getting a picture of the social, as well as the physical, environment. Shagging around involves "casing the joint": getting acquainted with participants, learning where they congregate, recording demographic characteristics of a study group, mapping the physical layout of a site, and creating a description of the context of the phenomenon under consideration. In other words, shagging around provides baseline data. In qualitative research relying only on interviews, mapping is addressed by questions that elicit general profiles and by the interviewer's fishing expeditions—broad, open-ended questions intended to reveal serendipitous data.

More formally, shagging around consists of taking a census of the people involved in a group or collectivity—determining such factors as their number, ages, training, socioeconomic status, sex, racial and ethnic identity, and relevant organizational status positions, both formal and informal. It involves eliciting participant constructs by means of careful listening and subsequent recording of what has been heard. In this way, the investigator examines how people categorize themselves and each other, the central issues of importance to participants, and any potential areas of group conflict and accord. By shagging around group sites, researchers can identify key informants and develop a map of time use and daily events so that parameters may be established for later, more detailed mapping strategies.

Shagging around facilitates the development of more formal means of data collection such as structured and unstructured interviewing. When the focus of research is a group, a context, or an event, it permits researchers to begin the significant sorting and categorizing of the people who constitute primary data sources. These categorizations form some of the internal units from which researchers further sample or select. Explicit documentation of these procedures is integral to data analysis (see Chapter Seven) and is essential to assessment of the study's design (see Chapter Nine).

Wax (1971) emphasizes that the disciplined investigator seeks and maintains contact with the diversity of participants, despite personal preferences and prejudices, as a strategy for correcting bias and distortion. Because different informants represent different groups of constituents, they provide researchers with access to some people but preclude access to others. Thus, by associating with one group on a field site, researchers may forfeit information about the life experiences of people in other groups. For example, in Cusick's ethnographic study (1973) of student culture in a midwestern high school, his initial association with a clique of senior athletes facilitated his entry to groups with whom the athletes associated but hindered his access to other cliques and to student isolates. Berreman's retrospective analysis (1962) of fieldwork in India provides a classic example of the extent to which information gathered is a function of the persons who give it. For these reasons, careful documentation of participant characteristics, their friendship and kinship patterns, and relationships they hold with the researcher are critical to establishing reliability and validity of a study.

Participants who gravitate toward ethnographers and other field researchers may be atypical of the group under investigation; similarly, those sought by ethnographers as informants and confidants also may be atypical (Dean, Eichhorn, & Dean, 1967). This may be necessary because people who speak languages comprehensible to researchers, who understand the analytic categories used by ethnographers, and who are introspective and insightful about their own lives are rare. These qualities, which make them valuable as informants and research assistants, may mark them as deviant from their own groups. Consequently, although marginal individuals and other extreme types among a study group may serve as liaisons for entry and initial investigation (Kahn & Mann, 1952; Vidich, 1955), ethnographers should follow Wax's guidelines for interactions with as diverse a group of participants as possible. For example, in her analysis of the impact of a state-mandated curriculum on the staff of a school district, Brown (1982a) verified perceptions of the innovation reported initially by a few teacher informants through subsequent questionnaires administered to all involved teachers.

Ethnographers commonly initiate field residence with mapping procedures that establish the range of possible informants and participants in a group and the variety of situations in which they are found. This assures that data are obtained from all participant types under naturally occurring circumstances. In his study of attitudes toward formal education held by native American parents and students, Riner (1979) first identified the categories of families sending their children to school and then sampled from that typology. Deyhle (1989) used a three-step selection process. First she located all the native American students who dropped out of school between 1980 and 1988; then she sampled to obtain a smaller population to whom to administer in-depth interviews; and finally, she selected a single dropout's family to live with as a participant observer. Similarly, conclusions reported by Clement & Harding

(1978) and Clement, Eisenhart, & Harding (1979) in their analyses of student relationships in a desegregated elementary school and by Becker and his colleagues (1961) in the study of student culture in a medical school are based on observations sampled from the initially established range of events, activities, and settings identified in the field sites.

MAKING IT STRANGE

The tendency for the exotic to be more obvious initially than commonplace events and behaviors is a constant problem facing the fieldworker. It affects the events and activities the ethnographer maps as well as the selection of informants. It is tempting to record only bizarre, unusual, or compelling phenomena and to forget to document the boring regularities and structure of everyday behavior. The commonplace is always the same; it recedes into the background and gets forgotten. Such structure is, however, the warp and woof of social life; it often represents the normative underpinnings of human existence.

The problem of the ordinariness of everyday life is particularly acute among educational researchers, who are, after all, studying an institution with which they have been intimately associated for decades, as students, teachers, or even parents, and whose every nuance seems all too familiar. Erickson (1973) suggests that the task of the ethnographer is to make the familiar strange—to try to look at events, behavior patterns, interactions, and artifacts as if they are occurring on a different planet. In that way, we may be able to look at them afresh and understand them and their consequences in a new light.

Summary

Mapping a field site or group and delineating the characteristics of a collectivity of individuals involves (1) thorough documentation of relevant attributes and features within the study site or group, and (2) specification of how the data collected during the mapping process affect the overall results of a study. Most important, initial mapping strategies alert researchers to the roles they may assume, a major topic in this chapter. Mapping also points to the forms of data collection most feasible and relevant and to emerging techniques for analyzing the data obtained. These topics are explored in the following chapter.

C H A P T E R   F I V E

The Role of Theory in the Research Process

Introduction

Whether consciously or not, early ethnographers realized that theory and method were inextricably linked. They understood that theoretical frameworks, intentions, or purposes with which researchers approached their investigations not only determined which questions were important, but also determined the methods which should be used to collect the data which would answer them. Certain standard practices which drew implicitly on functionalism as a theoretical framework evolved from the practical business of surviving in an alien society. Ethnographers spent a great deal of time determining patterns of kinship and the names people had for each other and their social roles, so that they could interact appropriately with their subjects. They also learned languages to improve communication and they classified much of the observable material around them—house types, ceremonies, agricultural and subsistence practices, dress, and patterns of warfare. However, until recently, books specifically devoted to ethnographic and qualitative research methods, as this one is, did not exist. With few systematic guidelines, researchers simply learned how to "do" ethnography by doing it. According to Margaret Mead, learning occurred by osmosis—in the act of watching or assisting others like her mentors Franz Boas and Ruth Benedict—or by intuiting which procedures had been used by carefully examining the kind of data presented in manuscripts (Mead, 1959). In those days, theory, not methods and techniques, was emphasized in graduate training. In some ways, theory was seen to be akin to what we now call design and methods—a way of looking at the world and deciding what things are important and, hence, what data to collect. In Ruth Benedict's course, research methods in the Anthropology Department at Columbia University in 1933 was really a course in theory. To Margaret Mead she wrote:

116

> I've worked considerably on the theory course, i.e., "methods," so-called. I organized it into a consideration of methodology in historical reconstructions, tropical studies (Westermarck Marriage, Beaglehole Property, Boas Art etc.), functional studies. [Benedict quoted in Mead, 1959, p. 332]

In other words, "methods" involved studying how specific individuals with known theoretical perspectives and personal idiosyncrasies approached questions and collected data on given topics. Adequacy, at least for Boasians, was based upon whether or not the researcher had garnered "sufficient" data (Mead, 1959).

Because we feel that a mere "tools and techniques" approach to ethnographic methods and design is inadequate, we shall use this chapter to return a bit to past practice, discussing methods and design as they are linked to theory. First, we will define what theories are and how they are created. Second, we will examine predominant theoretical perspectives in social science research and discuss how they shape the research done under their aegis. Finally, we will describe how theories affect the perceptions researchers have about the world and the research questions they ask.

"THEORY ANXIETY"

A sign observed in a dentist's office reads, "Ignore your teeth and they'll go away." Some things do disappear when they are ignored, but most are ignored at one's peril. Among those things that persist despite the best efforts to the contrary are theories. This is because humans think theoretically: Theory is embedded in human thought.

It is hard for most of us to recognize this, because most of us are afraid of theory. Theory is something done by brainy intellectuals in ivory towers, something too mysterious to be comprehended by ordinary people. Or, theory is characterized as rash speculation, to be avoided by rational people. In the United States in particular, theory—bad, fanciful, esoteric—often is contrasted with practice—good, useful, sensible. Such sentiment is illustrated by statements like, "Don't confuse me with theory; just show me how to do it," or "That's too theoretical; show me something practical."

It is true that many theories are complex and difficult to understand. It also is true that all scientific theories are speculative to some extent; that is, they are held tentatively, as generalizations. This is what distinguishes theory backed by science from certainty backed by religious faith. In addition, some theories are indeed poor ones which do not contribute much to the practice they are supposed to inform, while no practical application may yet have been found for other, perfectly good ones. These problems lead many people, including researchers in the human sciencies, to ignore or avoid theory. While most scholars do study theory as part of their academic preparation, many regard their coursework as an inoculation. Once they have been exposed to the course, they can ignore the danger of contact! In fact, many researchers eschew contact with theory altogether; they treat the process of developing a theoretical framework as little more than the collection of a few corroborative empirical studies into what could pass for a literature review and proceed directly to collect data. They leave a concern for theory to "great men," but they do so at the peril of poor work. To avoid such an eventuality, we begin with a definition of theory.

What Is Theory?

Theories are statements about how things are connected. Their purpose is to explain why things happen as they do. Theories vary in size, density, abstractness, completeness, and quality. They also come in various forms. Mathematicians, natural scientists, and some social scientists prefer to express their theories in mathematical formulas such as "$e = mc^2$." Some scientists present their theories as a series of related propositions, like classic logical syllogisms. These are constructed as a series of "if . . . then" statements, which present a major premise followed by several minor premises. Durkheim's (1951) theory of suicide is such a theory, stating that *if* the level of social disorganization reaches a certain level, *then* the social norms guiding behavior and belief will begin to break down. *If* social norms break down sufficiently, *then anomie,* or a state of normlessness, will increase. Anomie creates intense anxiety in individual members of the society, as they cease to understand what is right and wrong and how to act. *If* anomie proceeds unchecked, *then* suicide rates will tend to rise. Other theories are expressed in narrative prose in the form of a statement describing a phenomena followed by elaboration consisting of examples, anecdotes, or descriptions. An example comes from ideas on reading competency: Children who are better readers are those whose parents are literate and who read to them regularly as children.

Theories also vary in their underlying premises. Theories which explain general phenomena may be predictive ("every action causes an equal and opposite reaction"). They also may be retrodictive or descriptive. Retrodictive and descriptive theories are similar in that both are explanations of phenomena tied to particular situations, but they differ in their time referent. Retrodictive theories address things which happened in the more or less distant past, such as historical explanations of the causes of specific revolutions; descriptive theories are more oriented to things close in time, such as an explanation of how a given university faculty responded to the policies of a new dean.

Theories which explain individual cases do not generalize; they cannot be used to predict the cause of a different kind of case. For example, a theory which explains the causes of one particular revolution or the responses of one faculty to a new dean cannot be used to predict the causes of another revolution or the responses of a different faculty to a new dean or even of the same faculty to another new dean. However, they can be used in comparative fashion to alert researchers to themes or events which might be common to similar phenomena under different conditions.

Theories also may center on understanding and interpretation of the meaning of constructs rather than explanation of phenomena. These theories address interpretive rather than sensory phenomena. Psychodynamic theories, such as those of Freud and Jung, are good examples; constructs like the Id, Ego, and Libido are inferentially derived rather than directly observed. However, their impact upon behavior and belief can be elicited empirically, and from these data have been constructed theories of their origin and role in human life.

THE FORM OF THEORIES

Scientists often use special terms called concepts or constructs in their theories. These name classes of highly complex processes, arrangements, patterns, emotional states, or entities; they help scientists to group together or explain various items of behavior and institutional arrangements that may have interested them (Kaplan & Manners, 1972, p. 14). Even the simplest theories can be broken into two parts: the things to be connected and the connection itself. The things to be connected are the concepts, which at the simplest level are the classes of phenomena and their characteristics which humans use to organize their world. Essentially, they are names, or labels with definitions, which we attach to things which are salient to our own culture. They may be concrete—milk, go, dog, mother—or abstract—food, activity, animals, family. They also may have abstract referents—ethics, faith, government, alienation, love.

Concepts and constructs can be grouped into categories which share similar characteristics. To be of use to a researcher, whether grouped singly or taken together, concepts and constructs first must be identified and described. That is why the first question with which ethnographers begin their work is, "*Is* there anything going on out there?" The second question, then, is, "*What* is going on out there?" The distinction between the two questions is important, because by asking the "yes–no" question first, one avoids the danger of assuming the presence of a phenomenon which may not, in fact, exist in the given setting. Failure to make the distinction can cause embarrassing surprises. For example, before she began her fieldwork, LeCompte (1975) assumed that teachers did reinforce the intrinsic value of academic achievement and she created coding categories accordingly. She failed to ask herself *if* intrinsic valuing were going on and subsequently failed to find a single example of it in a whole year of observation. Similarly, Valli (1988) entered the Catholic high school she studied expecting to find that academic tracking led to low morale and high rates of failure among students not selected for the highest tracks. Because she failed to begin her study by observing if and how tracking affected morale, she was surprised to find, in fact, that high levels of esteem prevailed among students in all seven academic ability levels.

The second part of a theory is the connection, or relationship, which shows how concepts, categories, or constructs can be linked together once they have been identified. These linkages or relationships can express time order, causality, correlation, description, or explanation, or they can represent any action occurring between the concepts. For example, children observe that plants undergo sudden growth after a rainfall and learn to link water causally with the growth of vegetation. Einstein equated energy with the speed of light multiplied by itself, and the educational level which children achieve is correlated with that of their parents. The connections themselves are generalizations; theories are constituted of groups statements made up of such concepts linked by generalizations.

THE PURPOSE OF THEORIES

The purpose of theories is to help us sort out our world, make sense of it, guide how we behave in it, and predict what might happen next. Theories are created by developing a set of propositions, postulates, or generalizations which establish relationships between things in some systematic way. Theories are *human* constructions; they are derived from information which people collect by seeing, hearing, touching, sensing, smelling, and feeling. This information is put together into formal or informal theories by means of cognitive processes, or thinking. We call this type of thinking, or set of cognitive processes, "theorizing." (See Chapter Seven for a more detailed discussion of theorizing.)

At an informal level, theories or notions about how the world operates guide how and when we get up in the mornings, find our way around in the world, and do our daily work. At a formal level, theories structure the world of science. Scientific concepts and theoretical frames differ from lay concepts and theories in that those in science are developed in a systematic and rigorous manner, following canons of the scientific method and the constraints of logical reasoning. They also must be intelligible to and amenable to challenge by a relevant community of scholars within the given discipline. However, both formal and informal theories are grounded in our experience. As such, they structure our expectations about the world and our response to phenomena within it. The theories we hold also shape our research questions.

Tacit, Informal, or Personal Theory

The informal explanations we use to guide our daily life as well as the hunches we have about why things work as they do are *tacit*, or lay, theories. They derive from our own cultural background, academic training, life experiences, and individual personality traits. They have a profound effect on the research process. They also constitute significant sources of potential researcher bias.

PERSONAL CHARACTERISTICS AND LIFE EXPERIENCES

Ascriptive characteristics which we cannot shed, such as sex, age, ethnicity, country of origin, economic status, and social or occupational role shape the questions researchers ask and the kinds of information which informants feel appropriate to pass on to them. Research studies almost always contain themes which reflect a preoccupation with these facets of a researcher's personal identity. For example, Ruth Benedict discovered patterns in other cultures as she searched for patterns in her own culture to explain her personal beliefs, behavior, and personality development. Franz Boas salvaged records of dying North American cultures in the wake of the dissolution of his own culture during World War I. This "bias in the biography" (LeCompte, 1987) can be seen in the "identity work" (Anderson & Herr, 1991) of current attempts by members of ethnic minority and other stigmatized groups to explore the conditions and genesis of their marginality.

Any inquiry process, scientific or otherwise, is affected not only by ascriptive characteristics but also by a researcher's personal history and the general sociocultural frameworks and philosophical traditions in which he or she lives. Implicitly or explicitly, these affect the assumptions researchers make about the nature of reality, knowledge, and values (Bredo & Feinberg, 1982), as well as the research *questions* they formulate. Researchers may be attracted to a particular theory because it is compatible with conceptual frames and preferences they already have. Goetz's examinations (1981a,b) of sex-role enculturation in a rural elementary school and LeCompte's analysis (1978) of work norms in school settings are explicitly related to social values and controversies that intrigued the researchers. These included how girls and boys in school come to construct their identities as men and women in the workplace and family structure. Some questions are lodged within ideological commitments of ethnographers. Apple and Weis's (1983) collection of studies on schooling and curriculum reflects their concern with the origins of pervasive inequalities in education and society.

Feminist commitments and their own social class background led McRobbie (1978), Kelly & Nihlen (1982), and Roman (1988, 1992) to explore the developing work and gender identities of young working-class women and the ways in which their limited future choices came to be constructed, justified, and/or resisted. Other descriptions of the function of ideological commitments in investigators' choices of research problems include Hammond's collection (1964) of sociologists' reflections on research design and Wax's (1971) and Powdermaker's (1966) analyses of the reasons they undertook each of their periods of anthropological field work. Ideological commitments also are evidenced by work of feminist theorists on research methodology (Gilligan, 1982; Delamont, 1989; Belenky *et al.*, 1986; Harding & Hintikka, 1983; Lather, 1986). While the work derives explicitly from the tensions which women scholars have experienced as they "crash" hitherto male-dominated academic domains, it also has facilitated the development of new ways of framing research questions and collecting and interpreting data.

Other questions derive from curiosity about ordinary phenomena or personal experiences. Wolcott's experiences as a former elementary schoolteacher contributed to the formulation of research problems in three school-related studies: culture conflict in a Kwakiutl Indian elementary school in Canada (Wolcott, 1967b), role transactions of an elementary school principal in the United States (1973), and an analysis from multiple perspectives of an educational innovation in the United States (1977). McPherson (1972) drew from her ongoing employment as an elementary schoolteacher to focus on teachers' negative perceptions of their tasks, while Gumport (1992) used her experience as an untenured professor to study the effects of budgetary retrenchment on institutions of higher education. Employment is not the only experience which facilitates research; Wolf (1990) turned a love of motorcycles and a thoroughgoing rebellion against authority into extracurricular activities which led to his ethnography of a West Coast biker gang.

Similarly, problems and ideas identified by others in real-world contexts may generate speculation that leads to the creation of a research project. Smith & Keith (1971) initiated their examination of the development of an innovative elementary school program upon the invitation of participants who sought to record and analyze their efforts. Occasionally this may occur within the context of an ongoing study. Participant-defined problems may provide the initial thrust of a research project or may redirect goals as people being studied begin to "correct" the investigator's initial framings of the problem. Research studies and theoretical treatises produced by their colleagues stimulate many researchers to formulate research questions; thus research projects frequently are formulated as extensions, modifications, responses to, or reversals of the work of other investigators.

CULTURAL BACKGROUND OF THE RESEARCHER AND RESEARCH PROJECT

Cultural context also affects the formulation of research questions as well as the interpretation of results. Far more studies of social class structure, for example, have been done in England, where social class differences were visible and salient in everyday life, than in the United States, where equality is a cultural ideal and class differences tend to be ignored or treated as an embarrassment. By contrast, the racial heterogeneity of the United States has been a catalyst for studies of race relations, which have not been nearly so common in more ethnically homogeneous England.

Belief in science itself is an artifact of Western European culture. It includes a view of causality as rational and of time as linear. Westerners and those assimilated to scientific culture give little credence to magical, paranormal, mystical, or supernatural explanations of phenomena of Western Europe and North America. "The security of the scientifically oriented person rests in his faith in the logical nature of the universe and in his faith in human ability to attack it and overcome it . . ." (Dobbert, 1976, p. 214). This cultural belief system is all the more powerful because it is unconscious. As C. P. Snow (1963) put it:

> . . . without knowing it, we are more than we think children of our time, place and training. [p. 62] . . . scientific culture really is a culture, not only in an intellectual but also in an anthropological sense. That is, its members need not, and of course often do not, always completely understand each

other; biologists more often than not will have a pretty hazy idea of contemporary physics; but there are common attitudes, common standards and patterns of behaviour, common approaches and assumptions. This goes surprisingly wide and deep. It cuts across other mental patterns, such as those of religion, or politics or class. [p. 16]

Westerners also make rigid distinctions between human and nonhuman forms of life as well as between living and nonliving things in ways which many other cultures do not. For example, trees, stones, physical landmarks, and even winds and storms may be treated as living beings in many non-Western cultures. Such differences in attitudes toward science make it difficult for Western-trained researchers to "make sense" of (or to explain in scientific terms) the unfamiliar phenomena they study, as well as to ask questions which make any sense at all to their subjects. Reo Fortune encountered such differences in a conversation about food in Dobuan gardens. His informant, Kinosi, had told him that yams are persons. Puzzled over whether Kinosi believed this literally or was using a metaphor, he later questioned another informant, Alo.

> "Kinosi said in the garden that yams are persons. How is this?"
> "Yams are persons," said Alo—"what else? Like women they give birth to children. As my grandmother gave birth to children, among them, my mother, as she gave birth to me and as my daughter will bear children . . . such also is the way of yams."
> "But," I said, "how is it yams are persons? Do persons stay still always?"
> Alo had his counter-statement.
> "At night they come forth from the earth and roam about. For this reason, if we approach a garden at night we tread very quietly. We do not dig the harvest when the sun is low in the morning . . . We wait until the sun has mounted. Then we know they are back. If we dug in the early morning . . . Nothing would be there."
> I enquired if the vine and the root tubers walked about at nights entire.
> "No! The vines remain. You may see them steadfast any night in the garden. The tubers alone emerge from the ground and walk the bush tracks in the night."
> . . . It will be apparent from these various statements that the yams are treated as highly personal beings . . . The Dobuan will class yams with his own people as personal beings, but he excludes white men. In fact, he has indeed the more friendly feeling for the yams. [*Sorcerers of Dobu*, 1963, pp. 107–109]

THE IMPACT OF DISCIPLINARY TRAINING

Personal theories include the mindset provided by the discipline in which a research is grounded. Scholars trained in particular disciplines or in dominant traditions of such disciplines commonly formulate questions reflecting the categories and assumptions current in those fields. Such training predisposes researchers to examine phenomena from certain perspectives and to ignore others. Disciplinary training also may affect the initial constructs or analytic frames with which a researcher begins work and can affect the conclusions reached or explanations given for the existence of particular phenomena. In anthropology, for example, explanations for acculturative phenomena are frequently based upon conflict theory, a pervasive perspective also used by sociologists. Such influences often remain implicit, except where individual researcher orientations and overtly discrepant data force them to the surface.

SUMMARY

The personal life experiences, cultural ideologies, disciplinary training, philosophical commitments, and issues and problems identified by significant others that so clearly affect goals and questions operate far more subtly on choices of research design. We feel that all ethnographers, regardless of their disciplinary grounding, actually approach even the most concrete, empirical description with a set of implicit questions that structure and schedule their investigations. Because these affect the course of research and preselect the aspects of the setting which the research will deem important to observe, they should not remain hidden. To ignore them is to "write the researcher out" of the story being told and to present, as a consequence, an incomplete portrait of the group under study.

We refer to these influences as informal, personal, and tacit theory, and we call attention to them because to the extent that they are not made explicit, they can become a significant source of distortion in research. They can lead researchers *not* to ask questions or to gloss over ideas and concepts not usually considered in a given discipline. They also can predispose researchers unconsciously to interpret data in accordance with traditional or accepted constructions in the discipline rather than permitting the data to suggest new or novel interpretations. Below are a series of questions that facilitate unearthing these sources of distortion.

— How do the researcher's personal experiences contribute to an interest in this topic?

— What ideologies are involved in the research purpose and what are the researcher's personal and cultural preferences among these ideologies?

— What elements of the researcher's personal and professional philosophies are relevant to the investigation?

— Are the theoretical perspectives the researcher has chosen congruent with the researcher's personal life experiences, cultural ideologies, philosophical and ethical commitments?

— Do they match with the ideas of significant others, including mentors, colleagues, and students and friends, in both lay and scholarly communities?

— How may these philosophies bias the researcher's perceptions and interpretations of phenomena related to the topic?

— About what aspects of the study is the researcher most enthusiastic?

—In which aspects of the study is the researcher least interested? To what extent could these enthusiasms and interests lead the researcher to distort presentation of the data or give an imbalanced account or interpretation of the data?

Having addressed the impact of tacit, informal, and personal theory on a research project, we now move to a discussion of formal, or scientific levels of theory.

Formal Theory

A discussion of formal theory must begin with the disciplines in which such theories developed. These represent divergent perspectives on the world; they also affect approaches to inquiry. Theoretical perspectives are interrelated sets of assumptions, concepts, and propositions that constitute a view of the world. Turner (1978) identifies four general theoretical perspectives predominant in sociology: functionalism, conflict theory, interactionism, and exchange theory. Related to these are four perspectives in anthropology discussed by Kaplan & Manners (1972): evolutionism, functionalism, historical reconstruction, and cultural ecology. Likewise, most psychologists use one of four underlying perspectives: behaviorism, cognitive structuralism, interactionism, or psychodynamic theory (Dagenais, 1972).

Sometimes theoretical perspectives consist of tight, or nested, statements or propositions. Frequently, however, they are little more than conceptual frameworks or typologies. Their significance derives primarily from their influence on the way social scientists perceive and interpret the empirical world. While we have grouped these perspectives according to the disciplines which most often use them, none is exclusively the province of a single discipline. For example, functionalism implicitly underlies the analysis of all social scientists in that it is designed to determine how things work or fit together. It is analogous to systems theory.

In addition, there are some anthropologists who consider themselves "behaviorists," as for example, Marvin Harris, whose primary interest is observable behavior, rather than meanings attributed to it by observers or participants. There also are examples in psychology of historical reconstruction, such as Erik Erikson's analyses of the lives of Martin Luther (1962) and Mohandas Gandhi (1969).

Social theorists have adapted Kuhn's analysis (1970) of theoretical paradigms in the natural sciences to describe the current ferment among predominant theoretical perspectives in the various social sciences. (See Tuthill & Ashton, 1988, for examples from educational research.) Kuhn suggests that disciplinary perspectives constitute intellectual cultures which dictate the directions of research. These cultures remain stable, and "normal science" continues, as long as their theories adequately explain the phenomena of interest to the group. However, when the data or phenomena of interest no longer fit or are explained by prevailing theories, they are replaced by different, emergent perspectives. The ideological and intellectual conflict generated by the dislodging of entrenched scholarly cultures has been likened to warfare. In educational research, the traditional structural–functional, behaviorist, and conflict frameworks are increasingly replaced by emergent paradigms which build upon them, such as systems theory, symbolic interactionism, social exchange theory, and critical theory. In turn, these have been modified by feminist, poststructural, and postmodern perspectives.

Table 5.1 presents some of the most common theoretical models used in social science research, their major premises, and their origins. It is easy to see that how researchers approach a particular human phenomenon and even the type of questions which they considered interesting or legitimate would be affected dramatically by the perspective they hold. Later in this chapter, we will examine the different slants which each theoretical perspective might give on one specific research topic.

As our table indicates, many of the theoretical models of the social sciences either borrow directly from the natural sciences, especially physics, or use analogies drawn from them. Others, like critical and conflict theory, are reactions to the perceived inadequacies of earlier models. All are rooted in a particular historical context and reflect cultural biases current at the time. Critical theory, for example, developed in Europe after World War I, when it became clear to many intellectuals of both left and right that the conditions which fighting World War I was supposed to eliminate were still present. This led social scientists to despair about the efficacy of current thinking to solve social problems. Criticial theory has experienced a resurgence in America in the 1970s and 1980s in the wake of disillusionment over the failure of the social experiments of the

TABLE 5.1

Major Theoretical Perspectives in the Social Sciences

	Functionalism	Conflict theory	Symbolic interactionism and ethnomethodology	Critical theory	Ethnoscience or cognitive anthropology	Exchange theory	Psychodynamic theory	Behaviorism
Focus	Analysis of social and cultural systems.	Expansion of functionalism; emphasis on conflict and change rather than upon order and maintenance.	Elimination of the subject–object dichotomy. Integration of self and society. Analysis of the constructed nature of social meaning and reality.	Individual response to social, political, and economic oppression; inadequacy of current social theory to improve human condition; differential construction and distribution of knowledge.	Production of the cognitive maps or rules which govern behavior and beliefs of groups of individuals.	The how and why of human decision making.	Human personality development and its psychological and cultural determinants.	Identifying causal basis of behavior.
Assumptions	1. All social systems are composed of identifiable, interconnected components. 2. These components are structures and institutions. 3. Each social system, like each biological system, must carry out certain functions to survive. 4. The components of each social system carry out these	1. All social systems are composed of identifiable and interconnected structures. 2. Economic organization, especially the ownership of property, determines the rest of society. 3. While the basic categories and analysis of functionalism are accepted, traditional functional-	1. Meaning is constructed through social interaction. 2. Individuals act on the basis of meanings they perceive. 3. Meanings change in the course of interaction because of different perceptions held by the actors. 4. Thus, reality is not a prior *given*; it is based upon interpretations and it is *constructed*	1. Analytic basis of functionalism and conflict theory as well as methods of symbolic interactionism are used. 2. However, conventional social theory is a bankrupt construction of ruling elites whose purpose is to perpetuate patterns of oppression and misery. 3. Humans are oppressed	1. Each group of individuals has a unique system for perceiving and organizing phenomena in the material world. 2. This cognitive system constitutes culture. 3. Individuals use this cognitive system to generate "culturally appropriate" behavior. 4. Most cultural knowledge is reflected in lan-	1. While humans are not totally rational and do not always maximize their profits, they do seek some reward in their social transactions. 2. They calculate these rewards in terms of costs and benefits. 3. Even though they do not have perfect access to information, they usually are	1. Human behavior and personality development are greatly influenced by early social and cultural influences, particularly relationships with parents and siblings. 2. Overt behavior is a manifestation of specific personality characteristics or traits. 3. Certain constellations of these	1. The world is linear, rational, time-bounded and controllable. 2. All human behavior can be defined as a response to identifiable prior stimuli. 3. The direction of behavior can be modified and its consequences predicted in accordance with the degree to which preceding causes can be

survival functions.
5. Each component thus contributes to the overall health and order of the system.
6. Homeostasis is normal; disorder and deviance are pathological.

alism fails to explain the dynamism of social systems.
4. Inherent in social organizations are contradictions which cause their opposite. Hence, conflict is inherent.
5. Systems are not necessarily at their healthiest in a static equilibrium.
6. Conflict and change are normal forces within social systems and contribute to their health and adaptation.
7. Conflict is manifested in bipolar opposition. It is designed to resolve dualisms.
8. Inequality of resource distribution is the major source of contradiction, hence conflict in society.

during interaction between and among individual actors.
5. Reality is not *fixed*, but changes according to the actors and the context.

because power is hidden or disguised in language practices, communication patterns and information flow defined and dominated by ruling elites.
4. Social life operates at multiple levels of meaning; knowledge and understanding of meaning is stratified and differentially distributed.
5. Men and women are essentially unfree, inhabiting a world filled with contradictions and asymmetrical patterns of power and privilege.

guage.
5. If the concepts and rules for this system can be elicited and described, their behavior can be predicted.

aware of some alternatives regarding their decisions.
4. The alternatives have varying costs and benefits.
5. Humans make decisions balancing those costs and benefits.
6. They compete with one another to make profits in their decision making.
7. Humans are differentiated in prestige and power in terms of their relative access to commodities, including information.
8. Competition also causes differentiation as some humans make better decisions than others.
9. People exhibit behaviors as

traits are recognizable as "ideal types" or labels which characterize individuals or cultures.
4. Identification of the personality type which characterizes an individual or culture facilitates prediction of future behavior.

identified and controlled.

(*continues*)

TABLE 5.1
(*Continued*)

	Functionalism	Conflict theory	Symbolic interactionism and ethnomethodology	Critical theory	Ethnoscience or cognitive anthropology	Exchange theory	Psychodynamic theory	Behaviorism
		9. Conflict is dialectical; it creates new sets of opposing interests to resolve.				long as they are profitable or rewarding. They stop when the cost is too high. 10. Institutionalized networks or exchange not only serve the needs of individuals, but shape and constrain the development of social systems.		
Major concepts	System, functions, goals, latent and manifest functions, adaptation, integration, institution and structure, norms, values, cultural rules, social equilibrium and order.	Uses the same concepts as functionalism, with the addition of others including legitimacy, consciousness, domination, coercion, subjugation, contradiction, dialectic, correspondence, ideology, strain, deviance, change and adaptation.	Self, self-concept, mind, symbols, meaning, interaction, role, actor, role taking, role expectations, construction of reality, discourse, scripts, texts, communication.	Resistance, human agency, oppression, hegemony, domination, subordination, subjectivity, political economy, consciousness (false and true), stratification of power by race, class and gender, deconstruction.	Cultural knowledge, cognitive processes, cognitive models, and cognitive maps.	Cost, benefit, rationality, fair exchange, rewards, norms of reciprocity, satiation, deprivation, shared values, oppositional values, legitimating values, power, prestige, privilege.	Id, Ego, Superego, culture and personality, neurosis, psychosis, anxiety, adolescence, transference, rationalization, dependence.	Individual differences, stimulus, response, conditioning, experimentation, statistical controls, probability, error, bias, sampling, testing.

Major questions and topics for investigation							
1. What are the categories of the social world? 2. How do the characteristics of actors influence the patterns of social organization? 3. What structures and institutions constitute a given social system? 4. How are they interrelated? 5. How do they work to maintain social order?	1. What are the sources and consequences of conflict in social systems? 2. How do conflicting groups organize and mobilize? 3. Where does power reside and how is it exercised? 4. What are the sources of societal inequality? 5. How do social systems transform themselves?	1. What meanings—both overt and covert—do humans attach to behavior patterns and objects in their world? 2. How do varying interpretations of meaning, expectations, and motivations affect human behavior? 3. How does the process of constructing meaning take place? 4. What symbols and rituals do humans create to structure their interaction?	1. What are the sources of inequality and oppression in society? 2. What is the experience of individuals within social organizations? 3. To what degree and how can humans achieve autonomy in the context of societal oppression? 4. How are research and oppression linked? 5. What roles do researchers and subjects play vis-a-vis each other? 6. What patterns of language use, communication and interaction do people use to oppress one another? 7. How are positive and negative meanings and identities constructed?	1. What parts of the material world are important for people? 2. How is cultural knowledge organized? 3. How does language reflect the cognitive processes of individual human beings? 4. What behavior is expected and appropriate?	1. What social, material, or psychological factors do individuals define as costly or beneficial? 2. How do individuals calculate costs and benefits in human interaction? 3. What criteria do individuals use to determine value? 4. How do individuals acquire information needed to make decisions?	1. What are the sources of personality differentiation? 2. Do specific cultures "push" development of specific personality types? 3. What traits characterize human personalities and how are they arrayed or clustered? 4. What consequences do varying personality types have for social organization and cultural patterns?	1. What actually caused a given effect to occur? 2. To what extent can sources of "noise" or variation be controlled or explained? 3. How can human behavior and motivation be explained and controlled?

(continues)

131

TABLE 5.1
(*Continued*)

	Functionalism	Conflict theory	Symbolic interactionism and ethnomethodology	Critical theory	Ethnoscience or cognitive anthropology	Exchange theory	Psychodynamic theory	Behaviorism
Levels of analysis	The macro level: groups, collectivities and their interrelationships.	Same as functionalism.	Micro-level observation of individuals in interaction with others.	Macro and micro; integration of individual interaction with macro-level social analysis. Meaning in interaction, text, and text items.	Speech samples from individuals and their cultural frame of reference or cognitive map; cultural categories and the organizing principles underlying them.	Face-to-face interaction.	Individuals and their immediate family in clinical interviews.	Individual living organisms in a controlled laboratory or quasi-laboratory context.
Goals	*Identification* of system components; *Description* of how systems work; *Analysis* of how order and equilibrium are maintained.	A more realistic portrayal of social reality, one which includes an explanation of change, social cleavages, and conflict.	To unmask sources of oppression; promote understanding of causes and consequences of oppression; encourage human agency or individual participation in liberation.	Understanding patterns of and patterns for behavior and belief of human groups.	Introduction of individual human motivation and agency into analysis of social systems; synthesis of individual psychological needs for material and emotional satisfaction with societal needs for social integration and solidarity. Examination of the genesis of privilege and power.	Linking behavior and belief to early familial influences on personality development.	To develop laws for predicting human behavior and responses.

Critique	Too static; focus on order maintenance justifies the status quo, obviating concern with conflict or change, which come to be regarded as aberrations. Teleological: Implying system *purpose* in needs and requisites for survival. Tautological: The cause of a structure is the need it fulfills.	No definition of what constitutes conflict. Cannot agree if the consequences of conflict are positive or negative. Cannot resolve the question of order: How can a society constantly in conflict create order and stability?	Remains at the micro level; seeks no connections to external, social structural variables.	Lacks objectivity. Can lead to reductionism and nihilism.	Philosophically idealistic. Lacks a behavioral dimension; analyzes only what people say they do, or their language patterns, without testing them against what they actually do.	Reproductionist and simplistic; linear causal and stimulus-response analysis inadequate to explain complex social phenomena. Does not respond to questions of how free and rational humans really are. Too theoretical; concepts like cost, benefit, and value are not measurable or quantifiable.	Ignores social structural variables; tends toward ethnocentrism, defining "Them" in terms of "Us." Excessive emphasis on early childhood influences and development.	Simplistic model of linear causality; in attempting to create laboratory-like purity, a false not replicable world in the laboratory is created.
Contributors	T. Parsons, C. Levi-Strauss, A. R. Radcliffe-Browne, B. Malinowski, R. Merton, E. Shils, E. Durkheim	K. Marx, G. Simmel, R. Dahrendorf, L. Coser	H. Blumer, G. H. Mead, R. Park, C. Cooley, R. Turner, E. Goffman, M. Kuhn, H. Garfinkel, A. Cicourel, H. Becker, J. Dewey	T. Adorno, M. Horkheimer, H. Marcuse, H. Gadamer, M. Foucault, J. Habermas, (in education: H. Giroux, M. Apple, P. Freire, M. Fine, L. Weis, P. Wexler, P. McLaren, J. Dewey, I. Illich)	W. Goodenough, J. Hansen, C. Frake, S. Tyler, J. Spradley, E. Jacob	A. Smith, J. S. Mill, J. Frazer, B. Malinowski, B. F. Skinner, G. Homans, P. Blau	S. Freud, C. Jung, R. Benedict, M. Mead, E. Erickson	B. F. Skinner, G. S. Hall, E. L. Thorndike

1960s to eliminate poverty and inequality. It probably also is fair to say that many theoretical frames have European origins and that in crossing the Atlantic they have been altered somewhat from their original premises.

SUBSTANTIVE THEORY

Substantive theories, the simplest form of scientific theory, are interrelated propositions or concepts which create explanations for the existence of phenomena lodged in particular aspects of populations, settings, or times. They are restricted to features of populations, settings, and times that can be identified concretely (Glaser & Strauss, 1967). Theories developed to explain formal learning and teaching in school settings (e.g., Smith & Geoffrey, 1968; Lave, 1988; Tharp & Gallimore, 1988; Vygotsky, 1962; Wertsch, 1985)—a major concern of educational researchers, including educational ethnographers—are substantive in nature. In sociology, substantive theory addresses such empirical areas as race relations, sex-role socialization, juvenile delinquency, or family relationships. Comparable theory in anthropology focuses upon things such as peasant society, kinship organizations, urban society, folk religions, or colonialism.

Most ethnographers restrict their use of theory to empirical statements or generalizations that shape initial research questions, formulate conclusions, or facilitate comparisons between several ethnographic products. However, in the course of their studies, other researchers have developed typologies or categorical systems (e.g., Henry, 1960, classroom behavior; Hilger, 1966, and Whiting, Child, & Lambert, 1966, patterns of child rearing; McNeil, 1988a,b, defensive responses of teachers to imposition of school reforms) that may be regarded by subsequent scholars as substantive theory. Such typologies or systems constitute theories when they include a careful explication of how the components, categories, or concepts are connected or interrelated.

MIDDLE-RANGE THEORY

Middle-range theory as envisioned by Merton (1967) is termed formal theory by Glaser & Strauss (1967) and Denzin (1978). It is somewhat more abstracted from specific populations and settings than is substantive theory. It addresses general areas of human experience, makes statements which apply to this kind of experience in a variety of settings, and often utilizes an explicit empirical data base as its foundation. Middle-range theories usually developed from multiple comparisons, wherein similar phenomena have been observed repeatedly under the same circumstances or where observed relationships seem to hold true regardless of the population, time, or setting. For example, social scientists have generated substantive theories about relationships involving the social roles of "mother-in-law" and "stepchild." Observing that these relationships usually are fraught with tension, substantive theories explain how individual societies manage these tensions by establishing ritual patterns of joking, teasing, or social avoidance. Subsequently, comparative studies of kinship have generated middle-range theories which predict and explain the dynamics of these relationships across cultures. For sociologists, middle-range theories include those that address topics such as reference groups, social mobility, role conflict, socialization, deviance, stigma, and alienation.

Anthropologists also develop middle-range theory. Kaplan and Manners call this level of theory "empirical generalizations," referring to "relationships which hold under specified conditions irrespective of time and place" (1972, p. 13). Empirical generalizations (the term used by anthropologists for middle-range theory) include theories of ideology, social structure, technoeconomics, cultural change, and personality development.

Psychologists such as Piaget, Bandura, Vygotsky, and Erik Erikson have developed middle-range theories of cognition and learning, social learning, and development of children and adults (Hilgard & Bower, 1966). Although few educational ethnographers systematically test or generate middle-range theory, many researchers draw from this level of theory to maintain a conceptual focus throughout the research process. Ethnographies may be designed to verify such a theory by examining potential negative cases, and comparative ethnography can be used to refine middle-range and formal theory (Glaser & Strauss, 1967).

"GRAND THEORY"

Many scholars have tried to develop so-called "grand theory," or comprehensive and nonprobabilistic (predictive, not ruled by chance) explanations of large and complex categories of phenomena such as Newton's and Einstein's theories explaining the relationships among matter, energy, and motion, or Darwin's and Mendel's explanations and predictions about change and development among living organisms. Theories constructed to address issues of this scale have been called "grand theories" or theoretical paradigms (Kuhn, 1970). They tend to consist of systems of tightly interrelated propositions or statements made up of abstract concepts.

Like natural scientists, social scientists have attempted to generate grand theories which comprehensively explain all of human behavior. Among these have been Social Darwinism, which used as analogies Darwin's hierarchical classifications of living things and notions of "survival of the fittest" to explain differences between classes and societies of human beings; Marxism, which explained the behavior of human groups and social institutions in terms of their relationships to the economic bases of society; Toynbee's advocacy of historical law to explain political events; Benedict's concept of cultural configurations which sought to explain differences among cultures and to integrate individual and cultural levels of analysis; and Parson's and Malinowski's theories of social systems, which used the implicit metaphor of the human body, or biological system, to explain the organization, interdependence, and functioning of social systems. In psychology, both the stimulus–response formulation of behaviorism and psychodynamic theories have attempted to provide comprehensive—though quite different—explanations for the behavior and motivations of individual human beings. "Grand theory" in the social sciences has, however, tended to argue from analogies from the natural sciences rather than from the empirical grounding achieved by natural scientists; for this reason, it has lacked the predictive value achieved by theory in the natural sciences (Beck, 1949; Homans, 1967).

Despite the appeal which social scientists feel for the emulation of the natural sciences, social scientists have grown discouraged with their attempts to create human "laws." The nature of human phenomena has proven to be too slippery, unpredictable, and elusive. Thus, instead of attempting the impossible, current social scientists have devoted their efforts to the use and development of more modest middle-range and substantive theories. These, while still designed to explain abstract categories of human behavior, are more limited in scope than grand theories. One current and promising exception is the application to human phenomena of chaos theory, which attempts to explain the operation of apparently random systems and to discover the underlying order in seemingly random patterns of behavior in the natural universe (Dobbert & Kurth-Schai, 1992; Gleick, 1987).

One of the most intractable problems which social scientists have faced with regard to development of grand theory is the unruliness of human behavior; people just do not engage in predictable, orderly patterns of interaction and belief. However, scientists are beginning to discover that the physical universe also is chaotic, or disorderly and unpredictable, within limits. Chaos in the physical universe means that phenomena are organized into recurring patterns or cycles, within which behavior or events occur randomly. These patterns seem to govern phenomena as disparate as the weather and heartbeats. Scientists also are discovering that chaos may serve a regulatory function. In some natural systems, such as the beating of the human heart, chaos acts as a stimulant, shaking them up to avoid patterns which are too stable and stultifying. In other cases, introducing chaos seems to resynchronize oscillating electrical or radio signals which have become unsynchronized (Langreth, 1991). This approach may well fit more closely to the kinds of phenomena observed regularly by social scientists than previously employed static and predictive models. Dobbert & Kurth-Schai (1992) suggest that applications of chaos theory may facilitate explanations of behavior in animal social systems, including those of human beings, which heretofore have been dismissed as unpredictable, merely random, or irrational.

How Scholars Use Theory in the Research Process

Our contention, formulated from the arguments of many scholars (e.g., Denzin, 1978; Glaser & Strauss, 1967; Kaplan & Manners, 1972; Turner, 1978) and confirmed by our own research experience, is that research designs are improved radically—in applicability and generalizability, in credibility and validity, and in precision and reliability—by explicit attention to the influence of theory throughout the design and implementation process. The remainder of this chapter addresses the question of how scholars may use theory at each of following seven stages of research activity:

1. Formulation of purpose and research question
2. Choice of overall research design
3. Choice of research participants and settings
4. Definition and enactment of researcher role
5. Choice of data collection techniques
6. Development of data analysis strategies
7. Presentation, intepretation, and application of findings

FORMULATION OF THE RESEARCH PURPOSE AND QUESTION

Established theories, such as those addressing cultural assimilation, social alienation, and patterns of deviance, can be used to generate a research question. For example, Sindell (1974) developed specific research questions in his study of the socialization of Mistassini Cree children from factors identified as important in Bandura's social learning theory (1977). Spindler's examination (1974b) of the impact of the school on attitudes toward urbanization among inhabitants of a rural German village drew explicitly from assimilation theory. Much contemporary research on adolescent alienation from school draws on the critical theoretical constructs of hegemony, symbolic violence, and the political context of knowledge and meaning (Apple, 1986; Fine, 1987; Fine & Zane, 1989; Giroux & Simon, 1989; Roman, 1988; Weis, 1990). Researchers also may design questions to amplify, to refine, or to disconfirm or verify established theories. This use of theory is described in Glaser & Strauss (1967); it commonly draws upon substantive or formal levels of theory and may be approached as a rigorous test of an existing theory or as an exploratory inquiry into whether given phenomena may be explained by a new theory. Strauss did this in his work on death and dying; he identified death as a social *process* rather than a discrete event and in so doing modified his initial definitions. Similarly, Holland & Eisenhart (1990) used their study of college-aged women to test theories of work and gender identification which they felt were inapplicable to women because they were developed primarily from research on working-class young men.

Each discipline is associated with specific theoretical models or perspectives. These are organized, as we have depicted in Table 5.1, around a series of questions and concepts which its scholars have developed to describe and predict the course of phenomena in the human universe. These disciplines render some aspects of the universe, and some ways of looking at it, more important than others. They also generate the topics which are of interest and affect the kind of queries which scholars will have when faced with a hitherto unknown situation. Depending upon the discipline into which researchers have been socialized, they might choose to study teachers from the perspective of their motivations (psychology), the relative power they hold within a system or the processes by which they become professionals (sociology), or the wage differentials and opportunity costs which accrue to teaching as a career choice (economics).

Even within a discipline, variation might occur in how a researcher approached a problem, given different theoretical perspectives. In Table 5.2, we demonstrate how different theoretical perspectives would predispose researchers to approach one phenomenon—school dropouts—differently, in terms of both the questions asked and the research designs chosen.

In the course of their own experiences, researchers also may develop hunches about the way things are or why they have occurred. They then seek theories which match with, or elaborate on, their own findings to

TABLE 5.2
Theoretical Influences on a Single Research Problem: How to Study the "At-Risk" Student
or Potential Dropout

Theory	Approach
Functionalism	1. What are the characteristics of the dropout population? 2. What role do dropouts, as a group, play in the social system of the school? 3. To what extent does dropping out serve to remove from schools those students for whom formal schooling is inappropriate or wasteful of public resources?
Conflict theory	1. What are the social class origins of dropouts and at-risk students? 2. To what extent are disadvantaged students overrepresented among dropouts? 3. What structural sources of inequality lead to tension between students and teachers?
Symbolic interaction	1. How do the patterns of interaction between teachers and students lead students to define themselves as failures?
Critical theory	1. What patterns of resistance do students (and teachers) employ to resist the hegemony of the dominant order in schools? 2. What processes operate within the school to push students out?
Ethnoscience or cognitive anthropology	1. How do at-risk students define themselves as students? 2. How congruent are the rules of the school, as they define them, with the notions students have about how they are able to operate in the school world?
Exchange theory	1. What are the costs and benefits of staying in school to the at-risk student? 2. How do at-risk students calculate the decision to drop out?
Psychodynamic theory	1. What personality characteristics and attitudes are most associated with dropping out of school? 2. To what extent do dynamics within the family of origin affect tendencies to drop out of school?
Behaviorism	1. What dropout programs are most effective in reducing dropout rates? 2. What impact do measured intelligence and academic achievement have on tendencies to drop out of school?
Poststructuralism	1. Which students' or other school participants' experiences are ignored by contemporary researchers? 2. How do such students define and structure the school experience?

explain the phenomenon they have chosen for examination. Explanations provided by a theory often serve as a kind of comparative case,
corroborating the researcher's findings. In some cases, however, the researcher's hunches may be contrary to existing theoretical formulations.
In these cases, new research paradigms or alternative theories may be

formulated, existing theories may be modified, or parts of several theories may be incorporated into a more comprehensive explanation. Smith and Geoffrey's classic investigation (1968) of the interaction of teachers and students in classrooms was developed from a problem originally posed by Geoffrey's teaching experiences and formulated using constructs from structural–functionalism, behaviorism, and personality theory. In this case, although the original inquiry used more traditional concepts, emerging constructs forced a reexamination of initial questions and a subsequent further analysis of the data. By the end of the study, the investigators had incorporated relevant aspects of several alternative theories. Such a recursive and reciprocal process led to a more accurate, thorough, and authentic portrayal of the relationships among pupils, teachers, and classroom activities.

Similarly, there has been a shift in dropout research from viewing students as conscious "dropouts" who choose to leave school prematurely, to viewing them as "push outs" who are actively encouraged in their departure by school practices. Such a shift required a shift from person-centered issues in psychology, and a consequent emphasis on the self-esteem, family background, motivation, and intelligence of the student, to structural issues in sociology. These include the bureaucratic organization of schools and the time schedule, the behavior of teachers and staff, the structure of the curriculum, and the general relationship between schools and the structure of opportunity in the larger society (LeCompte & Dworkin, 1988; LeCompte & Dworkin, 1991; see also Fine, 1987, 1991; McLeod, 1987; Tierney, 1991; Weis, 1990).

The following questions address how theory is used to narrow the focus from a general consideration of the global theoretical context to a consideration of specific concepts, constructs, and ideas from the social science disciplines relevant to the study.

— To what extent is the formulation of research goals and questions framed within the context of current theory—substantive or middle range?

— How do scholars from other social sciences or from different branches within a discipline frame the concepts and relationships under consideration?

— What is the theoretical origin of the concepts proposed and the relationships sought?

— Does it attempt a metatheoretical approach, synthesizing aspects of several theories?

— What competing theories are relevant?

— To what extent are the competing theories compatible or mutually exclusive?

— If current theory on the specific topic is inadequate or nonexistent, what alternative current theories, especially at the formal and meta-theoretical levels, are relevant?

— To what extent do compatibilities, dissonances, and contradictions exist between the social science theories explicitly identified as relevant to the topic and other major influences upon the research?

CHOICE OF ETHNOGRAPHIC DESIGN

Ethnography traditionally is associated with a group of theoretical perspectives from sociology and anthropology: structural functionalism, symbolic interactionism, social exchange theory, and conflict theory. Ethnographers such as M. Mead (1928) and Benedict (1934, 1946) also have combined ethnographic methods with individually oriented theoretical perspectives such as psychodynamic theory. More recently, researchers have built upon these traditional foundations, employing critical, feminist, and poststructural approaches to research. Each of these perspectives addresses the interaction of humans together and affects how the ethnographic product—a portrait of some group of people—is constructed. The data required to apply, examine, and refine these major theoretical perspectives are generated in the course of activities required to implement the ethnographic model. How each individual researcher uses the model to develop a more or less holistic depiction of uncontrived group interaction over a period of time, faithfully representing participant views and meanings (including that of the researcher), will vary depending upon the data, or type of depiction, each theoretical frame mandates.

Ethnography frequently has been advocated for studies which apply middle-range theories to complex group processes such as cultural transmission, socialization, acculturation and change, and culture and personality. Ethnography emphasizes the discovery of shared beliefs, practices, artifacts, folk knowledge, and behaviors, as well as highlights the social mechanisms that facilitate these processes. When combined with concepts like social role and norm used by the sociological symbolic interactionists, it acquires a structural framework for exploring the social construction of meaning. As such, it provides a way to generate concrete empirical data to test these theoretically derived constructs.

There are some creative adaptations to these uses of theory in ethnography which combine micro, or individual, and macro, or group, levels of analysis. Social learning theory, described above as guiding Sindell's ethnographic research (1974), is most commonly associated with experimental designs and focused on the activities of individual learners. However, Sharp & Green's (1975) application of theories of social class differences, which was developed principally by survey analysts at the group level of analysis, was grafted onto an ethnographic model to raise new questions and concerns about how individuals learn and accept their place in the system of social class stratification. Techniques for collaboration in applied research (Partridge, 1987; Schensul & Schensul, 1992) have been combined with perspectives from critical theory by a whole generation of so-called "critical ethnographers" (Anderson, 1989; Carspecken & Apple, 1992; Gitlin & Smyth, 1989; Lather, 1986; Quantz, 1992) to facilitate research which is "openly ideological" (Lather, 1986). Its purpose is not only to expose conditions of asymmetry or inequality in society, but, in the interests of social transformation and human liberation, also to confront both those who live under oppressive conditions and those who perpetuate situations of subordination.

Notwithstanding these uses of grand and middle-range theories, the most salient kinds of theory for ethnography are substantive constructs. Educational ethnographers, for example, have been most concerned with developing and applying theories of educational change, schooling, race relations, and instructional organization. Ethnographic design is especially suited to this level of theory construction. The collection of empirical data which generate complete descriptions of events, interactions, and activities leads logically and immediately into the development or application of categories and relationships that allow interpretation of that data. Even if it is merely implicit in many descriptive studies of cultural scenes and groups, it is the interpretation itself which allows readers to grasp correctly what the investigator wants to communicate. In this sense, the products of ethnographic design are tied inextricably to theory. They are incomprehensible without the integrating and interpretive functions of the theory that informs them.

CHOICE OF RESEARCH PARTICIPANTS AND SETTINGS

Deciding who or what to study requires that the researcher first determine which sources can provide data relevant to the research goals, where these sources can be found, and how they should be selected (see Chapter Three). The theories which inform a study determine which elements—animate, inanimate, objects, or people—in the empirical world constitute the researcher's populations or data sources. Populations do not need to be people; however, most often the populations studied by social scientists are human ones or their productions. The places they can be found constitute the research site. Populations are chosen on the basis of their theoretical significance or their relevance to the theory that informs the research question. If time is significant, designated units of time may form a universe; if settings are significant, categories of setting must be delineated. Whatever the population or populations are determined to be, their categories must be identified and refined into specific selection units that facilitate data reduction and processing (see Chapters Six, Seven, and Eight). Through this process, the salience of theoretical categories and properties to empirical units is reexamined, allowing for refinement, modification, and reassessment of theoretical constructs.

The levels of theory used—grand or global theoretical perspectives, middle-range theory, substantive theory, or tacit hunches—establish parameters for designating populations and selection procedures. Selection procedures should reflect the scope inherent to the theory used. Broad theories, such as socialization theories, require selecting from a wide range of people who currently are experiencing the direct effects of socialization, such as children in general or adults in acculturative situations or in role-acquisition settings. On the other hand, emergent or more specific theories, such as those involving the effects of schooling, may require more limited populations. In general, social scientists can be criticized for too narrowly restricting their studies of learning to complex urban populations and to formal settings (cf., e.g., Hansen, 1979; Studstill, 1979). Studies of teaching and learning which are not situated either in formal schools in urban settings, whether in the United States or Western Europe or the Third World, often have not been considered to involve teaching and learning! Some notable recent exceptions include the work of Lave (1988) and Millroy (1990), as well as that of a group of cognitive anthropologists, Cole, Gay, Glick, & Sharp (1971), Gallimore *et al.* (1974), Gay & Cole (1967), Millroy, 1990; and Moll and Greenberg (1990), who have studied learning in nonschool, and often non-Western, settings.

The content of a theory and its stage of development—that is, whether it is in the beginning stages of conceptualization, is ready for modification and refinement, or is sufficiently well-established that it may be subjected to verification—mandate different strategies for selecting or sampling. Before a researcher can use probabilistic strategies efficiently to establish generality across large populations, the theory being tested must be operational. This means that the constructs it identifies or explains must be well defined and observable in some fashion and the population in which the theory is to be tested must have been identified and described. During the earlier phases of theory development, a more effective strategy may be to use nonprobabilistic means of selection such as extreme-case selection or network selection (see Chapter Three). As the concepts designated by a theory become more concretely operationalized and as the relationships postulated by a theory are more precisely formulated, the theory becomes more amenable to research designs using probabilistic sampling.

Using theory development as a guide in choosing sampling or selection procedures, however, depends on creative judgment. Probabilistic strategies have been used productively through all phases of theory work. Likewise, astute case selection can illuminate the gaps or suggest applications of even the most well-verified theory. An example cited above, Sindell's (1974) use of Bandura's social learning theory (1977), illustrates this point. Probabilistic sampling was used throughout the development of Bandura's social learning theory. Nevertheless, Sindell used a single case study, a group of Mistassini Cree children who attended a denominational boarding school, to test the theory because it provides a unique and contrasting context for examining the processes outlined by Bandura's theory.

More important to choices of sampling or selection strategies are the purposes for and subject matter of a theory. Nomothetic theories—those intended to represent general laws of human behavior—require verification by comprehensive selection or probabilistic means to establish their universality. Idiographic theories, on the other hand, are designed to explain events in a particular historical sequence or behaviors and beliefs of groups and individuals within specific cultural contexts. They are grounded in the selection of relevant instances. For example, Durkheim's theory of suicide (1951) explains the low incidence of suicide in Spain during a designated time period; it is an idiographic theory intended to account for variation in behavior among certain people within their unique historical and cultural frameworks. On the other hand, McClelland (1961) presents his theory of achievement motivation as a universal human response to competition; it is a nomothetic theory intended to explain behavior across historical periods and cultural contexts.

Definitions and Enactment of Researcher Roles

The influence of theory on the other six facets of research activity—goal setting, designing, selecting participants and contexts, data collecting, analyzing, and interpreting—is direct and apparent. In contrast, ascertaining the effect of theories or theoretical orientations on roles assumed by researchers (see Chapter Four) has been more difficult. This is because the influences of positivism led researchers to ignore, assume away, experimentally control, or obscure even the most obvious theoretical influences and biases. Forced to maintain the detachment of an objective observer, researchers tried to have as little impact on the phenomena under study as possible. When interaction with subjects, and consequent influence on them by the researcher, could not be avoided, its direction had to be monitored, described as part of the research data, and considered a weakness. Despite the limitations and inappropriateness of the natural science model for much human research, many scholars still attempt to observe and measure phenomena as if no researcher were present. They transform subjects of research into objects of study—not to be tampered with, touched, or even prevented from doing harm to themselves. Data records are believe to be unaffected by whomever construct them, and the theories constructed from them are deemed neutral and unreflexive. Adherents to the natural science model do not consider it necessary to ascertain who created their theories for what reasons and under what conditions, or what the implications of their application might be.

However, as Tranel (1981) has noted, the Heisenberg uncertainty principle in physics made this conception of the objectivity and value of neutrality in natural science obsolete in the 1920s. The uncertainty principle demonstrates that the act of measuring or observing affects the action of whatever is being observed or measured. Thus, physicists can know either the velocity of a subatomic particle or its location, but not both. What the researcher wants to know—his or her *stance* toward the phenomenon observed—therefore determines the information which will be obtained. The uncertainty principle challenged the notion that observers could be completely detached or objective; it required that even physicists account for their measuring or observing activity in representing accurately the actions of the phenomena they examine. Tranel argued that measurement and observer effects created by social scientists in their various researcher roles are even more significant than those in physics, because the examined phenomena are animate, self-conscious human beings with whom researchers must interact in order to observe and measure.

Perhaps because of this misapplication of the natural science model to social science research, the issue of researcher role has been relegated to methodological or design decisions rather than being viewed as a theoretical problem. In the past, few social scientists discussed the relationship between theory and researcher role. Those who did generally were concerned with how alternative roles provide investigators with new or creative theoretical insights (e.g., Erickson, 1973; Wax, 1971), how researchers examining sociocultural belief systems could use the comparison between the alternative systems presented by their informants and that of their own culture to create a third theory of human behavior and belief from the interactive impact of the first two (e.g., Campbell, 1979), or how theory informs the investigator's choice from the range of roles available.

Applied social scientists, so-called critical ethnographers, and many other researchers of a Marxist, poststructural, or feminist persuasion have challenged this model, especially as it permitted a "cafeteria" conception of the researcher role: the idea that researchers can choose among roles available within the researcher setting. They focus, rather, on the constraints of theory on researcher role, indicating that researchers may *not* be capable of choosing theories which exist outside the limited field of vision which culturally imposed meanings or their position in the structure of domination imposes.

Historical tradition also impedes the consideration by researchers of both the reflexivity of relationships in the field and the responsibility which researchers have for the preconceptions they bring with them to the field. The problem is that the sociocultural theoretical perspectives which traditionally informed ethnography and much qualitative research—functionalism or evolutionism—focused on explication of broad, abstract social phenomena. They provided little guidance for the intimacy of day-to-day interaction in the field. However, theories that focus on interpersonal interaction are more directly relevant to the conduct of personal relationships in the field. These include social exchange theory, symbolic interaction, psychodynamic theory (which anticipates, with its concept of transference, interaction between the client subject and the therapist researcher), and critical, feminist, and poststructural perspectives which explore relationships of domination and subordination inherent in social structures, including relationships between researcher and researched. Denzin (1978), for example, views methods within the framework of symbolic interaction; his analysis of research activity as a social production symbolically negotiated between researcher and participant provides valuable insight into both the processes and the products of scholarly inquiry. Finally, substantive or middle-range theoretical systems which directly inform the interaction of human beings, such as reference group theory, role conflict theory, and theories of the family or of formal instruction, exert more influence on how researchers act in the field than do abstract formulations, such as theories of folk religions or technoeconomics.

Researcher Stance versus Researcher Persona

We feel that a distinction needs to be made between theoretical *stance*, or how the researcher views subjects and subject-generated data, and actual conduct in the field. In the past, these were treated as if they could be separated. The rsearcher could assume a *persona* in the field which facilitated elicitation of data, and that persona could be shed upon return to the "real world." While most experienced fieldworkers realize in practice the futility of maintaining life in such a "double exposure" (Roman, 1992; see also Shaffir & Stebbins, 1991), the theoretical implication of the researcher's *standpoint* (Hartsock, 1983) vis-a-vis the race, class, national origin, sexual orientation, and gender affiliations of the researched also are increasingly becoming clear. Equally clear are the race, class, and gender biases inherent in both the conventionally objective roles mandated for researchers and the conventional theoretical explanations for data put forth by the research establishment. By contrast, critics of so-called normal science have found that what we have taken as given in science often is a product of cultural myth and metaphor. It often obscures in bias more than it elucidates [see Harding & Hintikka's 1983 collection of essays elaborating on this point; also Eisenhart & Holland's 1988 discussion of the ways in which class-based analysis of resistance developed by male researchers studying male adolescents (e.g., Willis, 1977) failed to explain the career patterns of young women].

CHOICE OF DATA COLLECTION STRATEGIES

The data researchers collect (see Chapter Six) depend upon the way those researchers view the world. A researcher's standpoint (Hartsock, 1983) is constituted by both the researcher's place in the political economy and his or her self-conscious and active participation (according to Hartsock), or lack of it, in the degree of oppression experienced by the people studied. This, as well as personal philosophies and theoretical perspectives, dictates perceptual categories and the kinds of questions posed. A researcher's social science discipline also affects the kind of data considered to be relevant as well as the data collection strategies chosen; disciplinary biases may eliminate some kinds of data while mandating others. Even when researchers formulate comparable research questions and problems, different world views, philosophical assumptions, and theoretical perspectives may result in different choices of data to address the same or similar questions. Such data may differ in the levels of analysis or scale of measurement used; they also may be derived from different operational definitions. Similar substantive or empirical questions thus can be addressed differently, depending both upon the researcher's disciplinary training and identification and upon the theoretical frameworks being used. Data collection strategies also are informed by theory; the techniques chosen must match the constructs in the theory so that the data collected answer the questions posed in the study.

Although ethnographers in the past have been predisposed to choose data collection strategies that avoid enumeration and standardized instrumentation, the literature in educational ethnography (e.g., LeCompte, 1978; Spindler, 1982a; Maxwell, Bashook, & Sandlow, 1986; Deyhle, 1989; Dobbert & Kurth-Schai, 1992) reflects a more eclectic use of quantitative data collection stategies. To some extent, cultural anthropologists' and field sociologists' predispositions to choose observation and interviewing as their primary data collection strategies reflect common theoretical perspectives in these disciplines. Major frameworks such as structural functionalism and symbolic interactionism focus upon group behavior and interaction in natural settings; these phenomena are most accessible through direct observation. Ethnographers do use techniques other than participant observation, however. Methodologists such as Maxwell *et al.* (1986), Pelto & Pelto (1978), Goetz & LeCompte (1984), and Patton (1980) have advocated the incorporation of data collection strategies such as survey analysis and other components of alternative research models into ethnographic designs. This is because ethnographers have begun to engage in studies that transcend descriptive analysis and, as such, mandate a wider range of techniques to ensure reliability and validity of the research results.

Constructs drawn from formal and substantive theory commonly used by ethnographers also dictate constraints upon data collection strategies. Acculturation, socialization, and schooling are abstract constructs most readily operationalized in natural, ongoing behavioral transactions. They are most directly accessible through observation. However, as ethnographers become increasingly concerned with the enhancement of construct validity—the extent to which abstractions are meaningful and shared across times, settings, and populations—they have become more concerned with supporting constructs through multiple data collection strategies. The most recent view of theory is that, if it is valid, it should be amenable to substantiation through a variety of data collection strategies, not restricted to particular ways of obtaining data. Although many theories develop primarily through the use of a single approach to data collection, they are generally enriched by broadening the data collection base.

DEVELOPMENT OF DATA ANALYSIS STRATEGIES

The general theoretical perspective informing the research establishes broad parameters governing how units of analysis are defined (Goetz & Hansen, 1974). For example, structural functionalism requires a focus upon groups and or social structures and the relationships among them, whereas symbolic interactionism mandates examination of the interaction among individuals. The narrower or more concrete the theory being applied or generated, the more precisely the units of analysis must be defined. A broad theoretical framework like symbolic interactionism requires only that the data reflect exchanges among individuals. Such exchanges may be observed in ongoing social interactions, may be reported by informants or respondents, or may be analyzed in social documents such as plays or stories. More focused theories, such as Gearing's (1973, 1975) and Pitman, Eisikovitz, & Dobbert's (1989) emergent theories of cultural transmission, set more precise and exact limits on the relevant units. Gearing's work, which designates social exchange as a major construct, illustrates that not all social exchanges involve cultural transmission, only those exhibiting the characteristics denoted by the particular theory used. Pitman *et al.* (1989) employ a strongly functional systems-analytic approach which requires extreme precision in identification, categorization, and coding of data. This facilitates complex mathematical manipulations which unearth hitherto unnoticed patterns in the data.

At the most mundane level, units of analysis can be borrowed from existing research schemes. Goetz (1976a) chose Lofland's (1971) scheme because it was convenient, it fit the assumptions of the structural functionalism and symbolic interactionism that informed her initial research questions, and it helped her to address the questions raised in the study. Similarly, LeCompte (1975, 1978) used a modification of Barker, Gump, Friesen & Willems's concept of the behavioral episode (1970) in her study of teacher behavior because it provided a convenient way to divide the data. It defined clearly the beginnings and endings of segments in what otherwise would have been an undifferentiated stream of behavior. As a construct drawn from the formal theoretical level, it was congruent with the substantive theory she was refining.

Compared to its influence on designating analytic units, the effect of theory on analytic processes is more subtle. As discussed in Chapter Seven, theories are generated, refined, and verified through the cognitive processes of categorizing and relating. Even the most descriptive research entails portions of the art and skills of this theorizing process. The cognitive operations that form the basis of analytic strategies are differentially relevant to a research study, depending upon the state of development or refinement of the theory informing the research. Typically, emergent theories are grounded in data more effectively by using flexible and adaptable analytic strategies like analytic induction, constant comparison, and typological analysis. Enumerative techniques are often more appropriate for assessing the extent to which well-established theories account for phenomena across time, place, and circumstances. Nevertheless, creative reexamination of formal theories can be fruitful, as for example, when theories of social mobility, alienation, or stigmatization are tested by inductive analysis of life history data and personal narratives (Anderson & Herr, 1991; Harrington & Gumpert, 1981; Tierney, 1991; Tierney & McLaughlin, 1992). Similarly, emergent theories like Philip's social participation construct (1972) have been clarified and elaborated by Erickson & Mohatt (1982) through use of enumerative tactics.

PRESENTATION, INTERPRETATION, AND APPLICATION OF FINDINGS

Some traditional ethnographies read like travelogs: They describe how the investigator entered the site, what the investigator saw occurring at the site, and how he or she exited from the site. They also may provide an account of the experiences, pleasant and otherwise, acquired in the process (see also Shaffer & Stebbins, 1991, for examples). Although only the rare, inadequate study lacks a real conclusion, some ethnographic reports fail to address all four components critical to concluding a study: (1) presentation of analyzed raw data in a form accessible to readers, (2) interpretation of the raw data, (3) integration of those interpretations or meanings into a more general conceptual or theoretical framework, and (4) a statement of the significance and applications of the study's results (see Chapters Seven and Nine).

The most salient use of theory at the conclusion of a research project is to provide a framework for interpreting the meaning of what a researcher has discovered or established. This framework indicates how results are built upon a foundation of categorized data, elaborated by the relationships discovered among categories, and placed in context by integration with and application to previous studies. Each of these phases must lead inevitably to the next in order for the study to possess a tightly organized statement of results supported by data. The major responsibility of the ethnographer is to demonstrate that changes in the initial research goals and questions or anticipated design are theoretically sound.

Beyond that, the write-up itself becomes a theory-informed act, because it is at that point that raw data encounter theory-driven interpretation. Wolcott states, "it is in the write-up, rather than the fieldwork, that the materials become ethnographic" (1988, p. 199). More important, it is in the write-up that the critical ethnography or feminist study becomes critical or feminist. The author is challenged to determine whose story(ies) need to be told, how they should be presented, and to whom. Thus, the write-up becomes an act with political consequences, which in such cases are framed in the discourse of postmodernism. This discourse has raised yet unresolved controversy over the form of ethnographic writing and forms the core of the postmodern approach to narrative and research (Clifford & Marcus, 1986; Geertz, 1988; Hess, 1989; Marcus & Fischer, 1986; Said, 1978). The debate is informed by and often uses the techniques of literary criticism; it holds the writer of ethnographic or qualitative narrative accountable for answers to the following questions:

—By what right does the author speak for those studied?

—How many of the multiple voices or stories which could have been embedded in the setting have been recovered and recounted?

—Are the stories told or presented in ways which those studied feel are authentic and accurate?

—Have the tellers been rendered capable (or sufficiently empowered) to tell their story, or is the story told a recounting of false consciousness?

—What role did the author play in the construction of the story?

The nature of the theory and its comprehensiveness also may influence generalizability and comparability of a study or the level of application a researcher claims for his or her findings. In some rare cases where grand theory and related perspectives are used, universal applications may be claimed, as when causal relationships among variables are posited with no exceptions. More commonly, researchers in the social sciences use substantive and middle-range theories to seek probabilistic applications where relationships may be expected to obtain in certain cases under given circumstances. In these situations, results may be generalizable if they portray phenomena in similar or related situations or provide helpful comparisons or contrasts with the phenomena under study (Polkinghorne, 1991).

Construction and Purpose of the Literature Review

The literature review is dreaded by many scholars. It often becomes a desperate search for a few confirmatory studies which can be cited in support of the legitimacy of one's research questions, appropriateness of design, and validity of conclusions. However, this approach is inadequate because it does not permit researchers to do justice to work which has preceded their own, show how the new study integrates with old ones, or indicate directions to which their work might point. In fact, the literature review is critical to a study because it is the place where investigators explain to the reader the theoretical underpinnings of the study. It makes explicit the impact of theory in every stage of the study, from formulation of the initial problem and selection of the population through data collection and analysis to interpretation. In so doing, investigators provide a description of their own biases as well as an "advance organizer" as to how the study site and population were viewed and how the data will be interpreted. Later, during the course of the study, the literature review becomes the reference point for retaining or changing the focus of the study.

Novice scholars also are plagued by where to place the literature review in a study and when it should be done. Conventional science practice dating from the 1950s dictates that reviews should be completed prior to beginning any other research activities and placed near the beginning of the report. They include a brief update following data analysis and interpretation to assure that nothing new has occurred during the course of the study. In dissertations such reviews constitute the sacred third chapter, a usage few students dare to challenge.

Even during the 1950s these linear, compartmentalized, and mechanistic conventions were breached by more experienced, confident scholars or by the occasional creative newcomer. Different scholars review literature at different phases during research. Some review material broadly at first, leaving a more focused search for the end of data analysis when emergent patterns provide guidance. This is typical practice for anthropologists, who prepare for fieldwork by reading generally about a group and its culture, knowing that during data collection they are often cut off from libraries and other resources. Only after collecting data and returning from the field may they recognize what conceptual or even empirical material is relevant to the analysis. This approach has led some scholars to advocate leaving the literature review to the end of a study. Other researchers integrate the literature review throughout the study, working back and forth between the literature and other research tasks. Finally some continue to follow conventional practice of beginning the study with a full review.

Placement of literature in a report also has come to vary. Book publishers have begun to pull theoretical material from the sacrosanct third chapter in dissertations, placing material wherever it belonged throughout the text. Although the convention for journal articles continues to place a literature review by itself at the beginning of a report, conventions for research reported in books are more eclectic. Material is cited, reviewed, and criticized where it is relevant to the development of the study.

Our position on the conduct and placement of the literature review is that these decisions should be made by researchers individually. What is appropriate depends on the kinds of questions being posed, the approach to research being constructed, the data being collected and analyzed, and the working styles and circumstances of the investigator. For the career scholar, reviews may never really end, as long as interest in the topic persists. Further, placement of literature reviews in reports depends on the media selected for the report, the audience to whom the report is directed, and the skill and judgment of the author and editor.

THE LITERATURE REVIEW AS ARGUMENT

The literature review can be conceived of as an argument—a debate between the investigator and the audience—in which statements or propositions first are made by the researcher in the form of assertions that a particular problem is interesting, worth investigating by means of specific methods, and amenable to interpretation by the theories suggested by the author. In support of those propositions, reference is made to other studies which have addressed similar or related issues, both those which confirmed the hunches of the researcher and those which did not. These references are used as *evidence,* just as evidence is mustered in a court case, to justify the researcher's activity. They are located by scrupulous library research. The arguments in the review of literature should be tightly constructed so that it can (1) convince the reader of the relevance and interest of the questions and the adequacy and appropriateness of the choice of population and research design, (2) anticipate and justify the results, and (3) where possible, support the interpretation of data and the conclusions reached. When readers are finished with the review of the literature, they should be convinced that the particular topic could be studied in no more profitable manner than the one proposed by the author.

KINDS OF EVIDENCE

The evidence needed in a literature review generally consists of references to three kinds of documents:

1. Empirical or data-based studies which have explored the same or similar phenomena
2. Comparative analyses of several empirical studies of the same or similar phenomena
3. Theoretical or speculative analyses addressing the phenomena under consideration, but lacking an empirical base

A fourth kind of document frequently finds its way into the literature review but probably has limited utility. These are normative, or hortatory works, advocating the adoption of a particular program or pattern of behavior. Examples include the multitude of articles describing how "effective" school administrators should act or what schools should do to eliminate dropouts. These works are quite numerous in educational literature and often can be identified by the frequent use of the conditional verbs "should" "ought to," and "must." They *prescribe*, rather than *describe*, and as such, are *arguments*. They limited in their utility as *evidence*.

Basically, there are three components to the literature review: a substantive review, a theoretical review, and a methodological review. The substantive review compiles references to all the prior empirical work which has been done in the area of the researcher's investigatory problem. It summarizes the results, or the state of knowledge, of all extant studies done to date. The methodological review examines how all prior studies were done. Having done the substantive and methodological review, a researcher can argue convincingly that the topic he or she wants to address has not been done by anybody else, or, if the topic actually has been studied, that the methods proposed for this study are different. The theoretical review looks at how the results of studies in the topic area were interpreted, what theoretical frames were used to inform the study, and what implications were drawn. Sometimes, two researchers may collect exactly the same substantive data but come up with completely different results because their interpretations were different. The theoretical review permits the researcher to see if the theoretical tack proposed in his or her study is unique. Taken all together, the substantive, methodological, and theoretical review permit the researcher to rule out all studies which have already been done and to convince an audience that the proposed study not only is the only logical direction to proceed, but has not been done before, in that way, or with that particular spin.

Literature reviews are constructed analytically, in much the same way that data are analyzed. The process of constructing a literature review branches and is recursive like the process of data analysis. Researchers use the same theorizing processes of matching, comparing, contrasting studies and theories, and constructing domains that they use when they are working with chunks of data to construct categories and constructs. In this case, however, the researcher matches theories, studies, and evidence with the specific questions, methods, and conclusions relevant to the study at hand. The researcher constructing a literature review looks for the following things:

1. Studies, analytic works, or theoretical statements which address the same population, question, and/or setting as the given study and arrive at the *same* conclusions.

2. Studies, analytic works, or theoretical statements which address

the same population, question, and/or setting but arrive at *different* conclusions.

3. Studies, analytic works, or theoretical statements which address similar, related, or very different populations, questions, or settings, but which raise new questions or shed new light upon conventional ways of looking at the population, setting, or question under study.

Sometimes no similar studies can be found, despite searches through the literature in several related disciplines. In this case, the researcher can rejoice in the knowledge that he or she has made a unique contribution to the field.

Construction of a literature review begins with an annotated bibliography which can be used throughout the course of the study. As new questions emerge in the course of data collection and analysis, new and related literature is sought to illuminate concepts and enhance the researcher's understanding. As new data and constructs are elaborated, so also is the literature review added to and elaborated. These additions are, in fact, part of the data analysis and should be documented carefully and included in it. In this way, changes in the direction and focus of the study are mapped, recorded, and explained in convincing fashion to future readers of the research report.

We often have encountered students who feel that they must ignore any insights or ideas which emerged in the course of data collection and which diverged from their original research questions, simply because they were not anticipated in the original design. Similarly, they feel that they cannot use theoretical models which become relevant, but which were not included in their literature review—the infamous "first three chapters" of the dissertation. These beliefs result from unduly rigid adherence to experimental design and are quite inappropriate for qualitative research, especially ethnography. At least for ethnographic studies, the literature review differs substantially from experimental studies. It is not considered complete until the last word of the study is written.

We now list some questions about the relationship of theory to ethnographic design the researcher should consider.

—How does the researcher's theoretical perspective facilitate the reconstruction of the cultural scene, process, or group being studied?

—How does this perspective illuminate or explain social interaction in natural settings?

—Does this perspective ignore or include participant constructs and concepts?

—Is this perspective compatible with the holistic emphasis inherent in ethnographic design?

—To what extent may ethnographic design contribute to the verification, refinement, or generations of formal theory relevant to the research's topic?

—Do the constructs inherent in theory identified as relevant to the topic help to explain or illuminate data provided with an ethnographic design?

—What research models have predominated in the development of substantive theories relevant to the researcher's questions?

—What contributions does ethnographic design make to the advance of these substantive theories?

—To what extent are the premises and assumptions of these substantive theories compatible with those of ethnographic design?

Summary

Clear conceptualization of research design and activity is crucial to the legitimacy of individual research reports, to the development of lines of inquiry, to the training of competent researchers, and to the communication among scholars that produces any science. Like other sets of instructions and guidelines, however, clear conceptualizations limit research activity as well as enhance it. As suggested earlier in this chapter and as we will demonstrate throughout the text, the research process is composed of interactive decisions and tasks. Some investigators stumble upon an interesting group or event and formulate their designs to match this fortuitous occurrence. Other researchers discover an intriguing instrument or technique for data collection and compose a problem its use would illuminate. The order in which decisions are made, as a consequence, may be somewhat variable and idiosyncratic.

Research decisions are further complicated by being remade, revised, or even rejected during the course of a research project or perhaps years later when an investigator returns to an unmined collection of data. (See Spinder & Spinder, 1992, for a description of how films of fieldwork done years ago suddenly could be framed in an entirely new light.) Such changes in design decisions usually are scholars' self-corrections of suddenly perceived errors. Lewis Thomas, in his account of a lifetime spent in medical research (1983), accords to human error the valuable experience that leads to advances in scientific research. He emphasizes that errors and their recognition by scientists are a powerful source of motivation for further activity as well as a significant means for eliminating false and misleading possibilities. In this chapter we have identified sources of theoretical bias and predisposition as well as uses of theory that are explicit and clearly defined. In discussing these influences on research design, we have sought to promote more self-conscious, reasoned, "error-recognizing" applications of theory to research activity. Like formulations of research activity, use of theory can either strengthen or weaken a study. The goal of most social science research is to produce valid theory; on the other hand, studies are regarded as more credible if they are guided by theory. We hope that this chapter will help ethnographers and qualitative researchers both to produce valid theory and to use theory competently in the generation and execution of their studies.

C H A P T E R   S I X

Data Collection Strategies

Qualitative researchers, including ethnographers, deal with *empirical* data, or potentially verifiable information obtained from the environment and accessed via human senses. Sources and types of data are limited only by the creativity and energy of the researcher.

> In anthropology you usually cannot specify in advance what it will be important to pay attention to . . . One must be open to the data, to the possibility that very small clues will prove to be critical and that accident will provide pivotal insights. You go out, ready at least to do natural history as the three Bateson brothers [did] . . . with their butterfly nets and collecting boxes. [Bateson, 1985, p. 203]

Data, then, are any kind of information which researchers can identify and accumulate to facilitate answers to their queries. A hallmark of qualitative and ethnographic research is eclecticism. The complexity and variability of human life in its natural habitat mandates that those who study it must collect rich and diverse data on whatever they study.

The most common categories of data collection used by ethnographic and qualitative researchers are observation, interviewing, researcher-designed instruments, and content analysis of human artifacts. Each of these may be subdivided into more specific strategies. Participant observation and the varieties of nonparticipant observation—stream-of-behavior chronicles, proxemics and kinesics, and interaction analysis protocols—are different ways of collecting data through observation. Key informant interviewing and life histories are variants of interviewing; researcher-designed instruments include confirmation surveys, participant-construct instruments, and projective techniques. Content analysis of human artifacts includes collection of archival and demographic material as well as analysis of physical traces.

Such lists of methods for data collection preferred by qualitative researchers and ethnographers are useful for considering the array of possible methods for obtaining desired data. They may obscure, however, the process that ethnographers develop when they are in the field. Depending on the purpose of the research and the conceptual framework assumed (see Chapter Five), ethnographers anticipate relying on observation, interviewing, artifact collection, or some combination of these. Once they have identified sources of data, entered the field, begun data collection, and started preliminary analysis, they review their initial choice of methods. They then adjust, expand, modify, or restrict their choices on the basis of information acquired during the mapping phase of fieldwork (see Chapter Four). Ethnographers may discover that the information originally sought through observation or interviewing is available only in documents. Phenomena initially investigated through observation may be verified or substantiated through unanticipated interviews or questionnaires. Data that surface in reviewing documents may suggest a new focus for observation or unexpected topics for interviews. Finally, as ethnographers negotiate initial relationships with participants and develop appropriate researcher roles (see Chapter Four), they discover other possibilities for and limitations to acquiring data.

Choosing methods for data collection means considering available alternatives and continually reexamining and modifying decisions. Only after they have left the field are ethnographers and qualitative researchers able to specify all the strategies they actually used for a study. Even then, many continue to seek data relevant to the site or group from archives, media resources, relationships maintained with field participants, and other sources discovered during data analysis and further reexamination of data.

In their seminal work on ethnographic research techniques, Pelto & Pelto (1978) distinguish two categories of research methods: *interactive* and *noninteractive*. The former are methods for collecting data involving interaction between researcher and participant; as a result, they may produce reactions from participants affecting the data collected. Unobtrusive and other less reactive techniques (Webb, Campbell, Schwartz, & Sechrest, 1966), which necessitate little or no interaction between investigator and participant, comprise the second category.

Interactive Methods

The distinction between interactive and noninteractive methods is useful for discussing choices and their consequences. However, in practice the amount of interaction between researcher and participants varies along a continuum. Even within a single observation or interview, researchers move back and forth between passive-to-active participation and passive-to-active observation. To an extent, then, all qualitative and ethnographic methods of collecting data are interactive.

INTERVIEWS AND SURVEYS

The term *survey* is borrowed from engineering; a survey maps out and describes a piece of land. In the social sciences, surveys map out and describe the characteristics and boundaries of groups of people, bodies of information or research, or collections of documents and artifacts. We discuss a survey of research literature in Chapter Five. In our discussion of unobtrusive measures we will talk about surveys of documents and artifacts. We are concerned here with surveys of people. A survey of people distributed to potential respondents for them to answer unsupervised by the researcher is a questionnaire; one administered face-to-face by the researcher is an interview, whether formal and structured or informal and unstructured.

The term *survey research* often is used in sociology and political science; it refers to collecting information from a large group of people, usually selected probabilistically, to be representative of a whole population. Survey research may be conducted by mailed questionnaires or collected by single interviewers or interviewer teams.

Interviews and questionnaires are a conversation, albeit a systematic one. Because these methods are based on human dialogue, their use requires knowledge of "voice" and context.

A Question of Voice

Voice is the interpretation usually associated with the perspective of a particular individual or group. In any research setting, there are many ways to tell the story of events, both past and present. Each participant, including the researcher, comes to a project with a different set of background experiences, beliefs, and values, and each interprets what happens in a different way. This creates multiple voices and cross-cutting, often conflicting, discourses. In the past, researchers assumed that there was one *objective* reality that they recognize, discover, and describe. *Objective reality*, whether in the physical or in the human sciences, was the *researchers' interpretations* of what they saw. The interpretations of experience given by the people studied were labeled subjective; local explanations for phenomena were dismissed as myth, folk tales, pagan delusions, or mistaken beliefs. However, as more and more researchers studied the same phenomena and generated different descriptions of what they saw, this perspective has come to seem simplistic and even arrogant.

A classic example of differences in interpretation is the description of adolescent life in Samoa by Margaret Mead (1928) and Derek Freeman (1983). The differences in portrayal can be attributed to history, or difference in the time periods when the studies were carried out. More critical is the different research goals these researchers had for examining "their people" and their data. They talked to different groups and collected different kinds of data. Even though the differences in portrayal could have been caused by any of these factors, the discrepancies were treated by scholars as differences of objective fact and led to accusations of poor scholarship. Which researcher had, indeed, discovered the truth about Samoa?

An alternative is to view both portrayals as legitimate and to explore the causes for the discrepancies. Mead admitted that the Samoa data—her first fieldwork—had flaws. Because she was herself a young girl, she associated with girls in the community who were her own age. They told her what she wanted to hear, and she also was told by the elders what was appropriate for a girl her age to be told. She also sought data on Samoa corroborating the theories of her mentor, Franz Boas.

Freeman, by contrast, examined a wide range of data, including government statistics on crime and deviant behavior—data Mead did not use. As a sociobiologist, he sought data supporting biological explanations for human behavior. Both depictions are *real*, but neither constitutes the whole picture.

Contemporary researchers believe that the beliefs and interpretations of those studied are just as important as, even if wildly different from, those of the researcher. Furthermore, there are many "stories" told by the people being studied; their perspectives depend on their relationship to each other and to the phenomenon being studied. Each story represents reality to the teller. How to portray all of these realities is a challenge of contemporary research. Clifford & Marcus's (1986) discussion of alternative ways to describe cultures, Geertz's critique of several contemporary ethnographies (1988), David Hess's article on ways to write an ethnography (1989), and Tobin's (1989) research on three preschools in three different cultures all address this issue.

Meanings and Mutual Understandings

Surveys, whether they use interviews or questionnaires, provide material for baseline, process, and values data. Such information has limitations, however, because self-reports of behavior elicited through a survey sometimes are inaccurate indicators of actual behavior (see Dean & Whyte, 1958, for sources of respondent bias and distortion). However, self-reports are useful for assessing how individuals make judgments about people and events, and they do register what people think they do or what they think is socially acceptable to do, especially when they are corroborated by observational data. Self-reports are reliable and valid when interviewers and respondents, as well as coders and other assessors of protocols or data, share common or consistent assumptions about what protocols and instrument items mean and how they are structured (cf., e.g., Phillips, 1971; Mehan, 1976). Although discussing protocol design with respondents may be unfeasible, interviewers should use questions that make sense to respondents and that elicit the data required. Demonstrating such equivalence of meaning between researcher and respondent is difficult in itself (e.g., Gay & Cole, 1967; Modiano, 1973; Mischler, 1986); these problems are highlighted in interdisciplinary research where shared meanings among researchers operating from different disciplines must be established (Petrie, 1976). Thus, the early fieldwork, and the shagging around we described in Chapter Four, is necessary as a prelude to instrument construction (Pelto & Pelto, 1978). The more formalized methods we now discuss are based upon information first gathered through less formal and more unstructured observations, an examination of existing literature, or pilot studies.

Kinds of Surveys

Qualitative researchers use a variety of surveys. The three we discuss are participant-construct surveys, confirmation surveys, and projective surveys.

Participant-construct surveys. One category of data collection commonly used by ethnographers to facilitate backgrounding and development of common understandings between researcher and those being studied involves participant-construct surveys. These are used to measure the strength of feeling people have about phenomena or to elicit the categories into which people classify items in their social and physical worlds. Participant-construct instruments help researchers identify the set of "agreed upons" that structure the life of each research participant. These consist of the categories of knowledge deemed important by the group, the canons of discrimination used to sort items into categories, the cognitive or social processes that develop as a function of the way variables are seen to relate to one another (Kimball, 1965), and the components of their participants' worlds and the constructs by which these worlds are structured. Surveys using participant-construct instruments thus provide material for both process and values data (for a more detailed discussion of participant-construct surveys, see Spradley, 1979; Weller & Romney, 1988).

One of the most efficient techniques ethnographers use to assure equivalence in meaning and interpretation with their participants is modeled on procedures used by linguists. These social scientists first obtain from their informants lexical and other items of vocabulary and then ask informants to sort the items into like, unlike, and related categories. Pearson (1982, 1986) and Burger (1991) used this technique to develop a system for classifying the belief structures behind the strategies two teachers used in their classrooms, identifying both in terms of the rationales teachers gave for actions and the relative importance they assigned to each action. Enumerative listing is another example of such elicitation used by ethnographers. Participants are asked to tell the investigator all the members of a particular category of things. In community studies, a researcher might request that participants enumerate all the types of birds found in the area, all the kinds of food eaten by community people, or all the gift-exchanging occasions throughout the calendar year. Bowen (1954) details how she learned the language of the Tiv, being forced to learn the words for all the plants in the area before she was taught what were to her more relevant phrases involving where to eat, where to go to the bathroom, and the names of people in the community. More relevant to educational settings was LeCompte's (1980) request that kindergarten children tell her all of the things they thought they and their teachers could do in kindergarten. From their responses, a typology of children's perceptions of student and teacher roles was developed. Fetterman (1979) used photographs of familiar neighborhood sites and settings to elicit how adolescent informants categorized their own community.

Such techniques can be developed further by asking participants to sort and arrange given sets of items to discover the boundaries of categories. Through conversations with respondents, investigators elicit the parameters of categories and the canons of discrimination used to determine them. Sorting and arranging techniques customarily are reserved for physical items, but they can form the basis for sociograms, where participants sort and arrange names of their associates along any number of dimensions. For example, teachers may sort children according to their popularity, to their desirability as students (Feshbach, 1969; Silberman, 1971), to their ascribed intelligence (Rist, 1970), or by the degree to which they are considered "at risk" (Richardson, Casanova, Placier, & Guilfoyle, 1989) or "ready for school" (Eisenhart & Graue, 1990). Goetz (1976b) used this procedure with third graders, identifying child-designated and defined categories of good and bad students. In a less structured approach, teachers may be asked to group children into whatever categories they believe exist in a class and to explain what those groups are and how they are defined. Once the background work of establishing common categories, definitions, and constructs has been done, other kinds of surveys can be undertaken. These include confirmation instruments and projective devices.

Confirmation surveys. Structured interviews or questionnaires verifying the applicability of key informant and other data to the overall study group are confirmation surveys. Their purpose is to assess the extent to which participants hold similar beliefs, share specific constructs, or exhibit comparable behaviors. For example, confirmation surveys are mandated in educational research where an investigation involves large numbers of participants, whether teachers or students, who cannot be examined individually. Because confirmation surveys use formal instrumentation that can easily be stored for later examination and use by other investigators, they facilitate replication of studies and comparison of results with other, larger groups (for detailed discussions of confirmation surveys, see Colson, 1954, and Gordon, 1975). Thus, they are used with a variety of sampling procedures (see Chapter Three) to improve representativeness.

In her analysis of differential teaching patterns among urban schools serving different racial and socioeconomic groups, Leacock (1969) used confirmation surveys to establish concurrent validity of her observations in classrooms. LeCompte (1978, 1980) used a similar technique to ascertain whether students recognized normative messages teachers claimed to use. Ogbu (1974) sampled more widely than Leacock and LeCompte in his interviews with teachers, parents, students, and other community participants to demonstrate the existence of common attitudes toward and beliefs about education in a lower-class, ethnically mixed urban neighborhood. Similarly, Deyhle (1989, 1991) used confirmation surveys to assess whether the reasons for dropping out and the attitudes toward school that she found in her intensive study of Navajo adolescents obtained more widely in the community of native American youth she studied.

Projective surveys. When it is impossible to have individuals react to the actual stimulus or context under study, indirect or *projective techniques* may be substituted. (For detailed discussions of projective strategies, see Anastasi, 1982, Chapter 19; Lindzey, 1961.) Photographs, drawings, or games often can elicit people's opinions or reactions or enable the researcher to determine patterns of social interaction unobservable in the natural setting. Clinicians, for example, use doll play with children to elicit descriptions of events taking place in the home. LeCompte (1980) was faced with the difficulty of asking 4- and 5-year-old children to imagine what kindergarten would be like before they had attended school. She used photographs of typical classroom situations as stimuli for what otherwise would have been a task too abstract for children of that age to perform. Tobin (1989) used a videotape of a typical day in preschools in the United States, China, and Japan to stimulate discussion among participants from those three countries about appropriate patterns of child rearing and child behavior.

Pelto & Pelto (1978) discuss the use of games, naturally occurring and contrived, as projective techniques designed to elicit interaction styles among groups of people. Spindler (1973, 1974a) used abstract drawings of familiar rural and urban scenes and activities to assess the school's role in the transition of a German village from rural context to urban community. (See Collier, 1973, for an extended discussion of using concrete visual stimuli for responses.)

More familiar to many researchers is the use of vague or indirect stimuli to elicit statements about people's values or images of themselves. Spindler & Spindler (1958) used the Rorschach technique to develop hypotheses about the relationship between personality types and acculturation to white society among the Wisconsin Menominee. Educational ethnographers more often use participant-constructed abstractions such as the Draw-a-Man [sic] test. Hostetler and Huntington (1971) used this technique to examine subcultural differences in the influence of curriculum in Amish and mainstream schools. It also was used by Minuchin, Biber, Shapiro, & Zimiles (1969) to assess differences in the effect of classroom environment and authority structure on the self-concept and level of social and emotional maturity of elementary schoolchildren in New York City.

Yet another technique involves the elicitation of narratives from respondents that flow unstructured or uninterrupted by the researcher. Eliciting narrative requires that the researcher relinquish control over the direction of the interview and attend to the asymmetrical relationship of power between interviewer and interviewee. This almost therapeutic approach means that respondents tell their stories in their terms, defining their own high and low points and their own beginnings and endings, without cues or directive questions from the interviewer (Mishler, 1986).

Kinds of Interviews

Interviews depend on face-to-face questioning of participants and eliciting data from them (Brenner, Brown, & Canter, 1985; Douglas, 1985; Siedman, 1991). They share an advantage over less obtrusive measures like questionnaires because researchers guide the revelation of information: Through elicitation and personal interaction, the investigator is better able to obtain data addressing the questions asked in the study. However, interviews can be more reactive or obtrusive, and respondents, deliberately or unconsciously, may supply false or misleading data. These distortions can be ameliorated by corroborating information obtained through interviews by other forms of data collection, including observations. Two specialized kinds of interviews contribute to developing sufficient understanding of the context of research so that communication between the researcher and those studied is facilitated. These are key-informant interviews and career- or life-history interviews.

Key-informant interviewing. Key informants are individuals who possess special knowledge, status, or communicative skills and who are willing to share that knowledge and skill with the researcher (Zelditch, 1962). They frequently are chosen because they have access—in time, space, or perspective—to observations denied the ethnographer (for detailed presentations of key-informant interviewing, see Freilich, 1970; Kelley, 1978; Spradley, 1979.) They may be long-time residents of a community, participants in key community institutions, or individuals knowledgeable of cultural ideals. They often are atypical individuals and should be chosen with care so as to ensure that representativeness among a group of key informants is achieved. (See Adler & Adler, 1987, and Dean *et al.*, 1967, for a discussion of common types of informants.)

Key informants have been used in a variety of ways in educational ethnography. Deyhle (1991) used information from all members of the Navajo extended family with whom she lived to document Navajo child-rearing philosophy and the range of responses Navajo youth have to school and the job market. Tobin *et al.* (1989) asked the teachers they observed in their study of preschool classrooms in Japan, China, and the United States to react to videotaped vignettes from their own classrooms as well as from the other two countries. These reactions formed a major source of cultural data for the study. Carroll (1977) developed his discussion of participant constructs in the domains of work and play by interviewing children as he and they observed ongoing classroom activities. Jackson (1968) used interviews with the students he studied as a means to corroborate his own observations of classroom exchanges. In her study of communication patterns between surgical nurses and their patients, Kirby (1982) depended on the departmental housekeeper to provide a view of nurse–patient relationships held by nonnursing hospital staff.

Key informants play other roles as well. Projects involving close collagial relationships between researchers and key informants may actually become collaborations. Such research partnerships have a lengthy history in ethnography (e.g., Malinowski, 1935; Whyte, 1955) and are becoming more common in education (Florio & Walsh, 1981; Nihlen, 1991; Reyes & Laliberty, 1992; Schensul *et al.*, 1981; Tobin *et al.*, 1989). Smith & Geoffrey's (1968) analysis of the behavior of a classroom teacher and his rationale for his actions provides a model emulated in research for years. Gitlin & Smyth (1989) include a theoretical and conceptual framework for collaborative evaluation with teachers presented in a report of their own fieldwork. Data collected from key informants may add material to baseline data otherwise inaccessible to the ethnographer because of time constraints in a study. Because key informants often are reflective individuals, they may contribute insights to process variables not evident to the investigator. Finally, key informants may sensitize researchers to value dilemmas within the culture and to the implications of their findings.

Career histories. Anthropologists use the term *life-history interviewing* to refer to the elicitation of the life narratives of participants, which then are used to formulate questions or inferences about the culture of a people (for detailed discussions of life-history interviewing, see Dollard, 1935; Whyte, 1984; Faraday & Plummer, 1979; Langness & Frank, 1981; Watson & Watson-Franke, 1985). Use of life histories has been rare in educational research (for exceptions, see Aisenberg & Harrington, 1988; Boardman *et al.*, 1987; Bogdan & Taylor, 1982; King, 1991; Melrose, 1989, and Shaw, 1930). However, career histories, or narrative accounts of individuals' professional lives, are useful for determining how people in similar circumstances respond to settings, events, or innovations (Evetts, 1989; Ball & Goodson, 1985; Goodson, 1980–1981; Goodson & Walker, 1991; Sikes, Measor, & Woods, 1985; Risenborough, 1988; Wolcott, 1973).

One element of Wolcott's (1973) study of an elementary school principal is the participant's account of his career to the time when the researcher entered the field. Scheppler (1980) likewise gathered a career history from the state-level curriculum supervisor whose professional role she documented and analyzed. A variation on this method was developed by Fuchs (1969), who used intermittent interviewing to follow the emerging career histories of novice teachers in inner-city school settings. Career histories may be used to assess differences in life and training experiences as they affect teachers' roles (e.g., Newman, 1979, 1980; Tabachnick, Zeichner, Adler, Densmore, & Egan, 1982) or to predict which teachers are most amenable to participating in innovative programs. They can supply significant baseline data and provide a source for inferences about value contrasts in school settings.

More recently, biographies and career or life histories have been used to document the experiences of minorities or exceptional individuals (Lightfoot, 1988). Researchers seek personal narratives and life histories to illuminate how people, particularly those from oppressed groups, construct their identities over time (e.g., Anderson & Herr, 1991; Bateson, 1989; Fine, 1991; Herr, 1991; Tierney, 1991; Tierney & McLaughlin, 1992). Anderson & Herr (1991), for example, use student career histories to trace the "identity work" among minority individuals in an elite, white preparatory high school. They document aspects of personality and culture that minority students incorporate into their identity as well as those they discarded or found too difficult or painful to accept.

DEVELOPING INTERVIEWS AND SURVEYS

Researchers constructing interviews find available an overwhelming array of instructions, suggestions, protocol frames, and prescriptions. Within this massive literature, contradictions abound. For each proscription on format or question structure pronounced by one researcher, other investigators suggest alternative uses for the same technique. Many of the prescriptive—and proscriptive—guidelines reflect differing world views, philosophical assumptions, and values held by social scientists. They also represent protocols used for differing purposes and research questions, compatible with varying theoretical frameworks and research models, and applicable to disparate research settings, participants, and situations. Consequently, researchers are best served by seeking and following guidelines for interview construction consistent with the goals, assumptions, and designs of their research projects. The following discussion of methods for conceptualizing, building, and conducting interviews is a synthesis of approaches to interviewing advocated by qualitative researchers; the emphasis on alternatives is intended to convey how situation-specific interviewing is.

CATEGORIZING INTERVIEWS AND SURVEYS

Interviews and surveys are most commonly categorized on the basis of (1) the type of person being questioned or the roles that they occupy, and (2) the structure and administration of the interview. For example, Marshall & Rossman (1989) distinguish among "in-depth interviewing" (p. 82), "ethnographic interviewing" (p. 92, from Spradley, 1979), "elite interviewing" (p. 94), and "life-history interviewing" (p. 96). This categorization mixes methods of interviewing, types of respondent, and purposes of interviews. Additional categories are the "long interview" (McCracken, 1988), the "focus group interview" (Krueger, 1988; Morgan,

1988; Stewart & Shamdasani, 1990), and the "critical interview." Other writers discuss interviews with children (Fine & Sandstrom, 1988; Rich, 1968), women (Warren, 1988), or the institutionalized and handicapped (Dworkin, 1992).

Categorizing interviews by who a respondent is may be confusing. Respondents, whether they are minor children, members of an exotic culture or a political elite, or the mentally handicapped, deserve procedures which treat them with utmost respect, are well organized, take into account their personal characteristics, and honor the world view to which they adhere. More useful to the preparation and conduct of interviews and surveys are categorizations based on the purpose or structure of the interview.

Denzin (1978) differentiates three forms of interviews according to their degree of structure: the scheduled standardized interview, the non-scheduled standardized interview, and the nonstandardized interview. The scheduled standardized interview is an orally administered questionnaire. All respondents are asked the same questions in the same order; if probes are anticipated, they too are standardized. This format is useful in situations when administration must be constant for all respondents and when results must be readily enumerated. The nonscheduled standardized interview is a variant of the first format; the same questions and probes are used for all respondents, but the order in which they are posed may be changed according to how individuals react. Again, results can be readily enumerated, but the flexibility in question order allows the interviewer to be more natural and responsive. Some researchers refer to Denzin's nonstandardized interview as an interview guide, in which general questions to be addressed and specific information desired by the researcher are anticipated but may be addressed during the interview informally in whatever order or context they happen to arise.

Patton's (1990b) categorization of interviews includes (1) the informal conversational interview, (2) the general interview guide, and (3) the standardized open-ended interview. The first is an interview so well embedded within a conversation that the respondent may be unaware of being questioned. The general interview guide is a set of issues, developed before the interview takes place, that the interviewer wants to discuss with the respondent. These issues may be addressed at any time in the conversation; the guide is a checklist to assure that all relevant topics are covered for each respondent. The standardized open-ended interview is far more structured than these. It is a set of questions worded and arranged so that each respondent is interviewed the same way (Patton, 1980, p. 198). It is similar to Denzin's standardized interviews, scheduled and nonscheduled.

In addition to differences in structure, interviews and surveys vary along other dimensions. The kind of information sought, the phrasing of questions, the sequencing of questions and the ordering of topics addressed, logistics such as anticipated length and number of interviews, and desired interviewer–respondent interaction all affect the content and delivery of interview protocols.

The Content of Questions

The data researchers collect in interviews can be categorized in different ways. In this section we summarize several approaches to categorizing information.

Babbie (1973, pp. 138–139) divides the information researchers seek into four groups on the basis of how variables are measured. The first group of variables are *nominal* measures, such as sex, political affiliation, college major, or race. These are the measures which distinguish the categories comprising a given variable. The data sought on each respondent represent mutually exclusive choices; a person is considered male or female, Republican or Democrat, depending on the categories preordained by the researcher. The second group are *ordinal* variables such as social class, alienation, and attitudes toward school. These reflect a rank ordering among the categories comprising a variable. They are usually assessed by numbers on scales (for example, Likert-type scales such as strongly agree, agree, neutral, disagree, strongly disagree or categories such as upper class, upper-middle class, middle class, upper-lower class, lower class). While the numbers these categories represent indicate a relative distance or quantity distinguishing one respondent from another, they indicate neither *how much* respondents differ nor whether the differences between adjoining categories are equal. A third kind of variable is measured in *intervals*. This involves using real, rather than relative, positions to differentiate categories of a given variable. Although the distances between the numbered categories of these variables are numerically equivalent, the scale has no upper and lower boundaries. A common interval measure is the Farenheit temperature scale. For example, although the difference between 70 and 80 degrees and 50 and 60 degrees on a Farenheit scale is the same, zero on the Farenheit scale is not an end. The fourth group of variables are measured on *ratio* scales. Ratio measurements have all the characteristics of interval measurements, but they also have a true zero. Ratio measurements include age, height, weight, and length of residence in a city. Not only do they have a zero point at which no quantity of the variable exists, but they are multiplicative, in that all designated intervals measure the same quantity. For example, on the Kelvin temperature scale, 40 degrees Kelvin is twice as hot as 20 degrees Kelvin, and a human being 3 feet tall is half the height of someone 6 feet tall.

Zelditch (1962) suggests another system for organizing data. He identifies three information types: frequency distributions, incidents and histories, and institutionalized norms and statuses. He advocates intensive, nonstandardized informant interviewing as the most efficient and efficacious format for obtaining data on institutionalized norms and statuses and as an adequate format for obtaining data on incidents and histories. Systematically sampled, standardized interviews, on the other hand, are favored for the acquisition of data to be arrayed in frequency distributions. This is the kind of data that can be conceptualized using Babbie's system discussed in the preceding section. Zelditch's system thus provides a rationale for choice of overall interview format.

Other investigators have proposed typologies of questions intended to elicit differing data. Patton (1990b) categorizes data by kinds of questions researchers ask to elicit them. They include (1) experience and behavior questions that elicit *what respondents do or have done,* (2) opinion and value questions that elicit *how respondents think* about their behaviors and experiences, (3) feeling questions that elicit *how respondents react emotionally to or feel about* their experiences and opinions, (4) knowledge questions that elicit *what respondents know* about their worlds, (5) sensory questions that elicit respondents' descriptions of *what and how they see, hear, touch, taste, and smell* in the world around them, and (6) background and demographic questions that elicit *respondents' descriptions of themselves.* Patton suggests that researchers vary these cells by framing questions by dimensions of time: past, present, and future. For example, respondents can be asked to report how they respond emotionally to an experience in the present, how they responded in the past, or how they expect to respond in the future.

Spradley's typology (1979) of question content, intended to generate the categories into which respondents divide their cultures, overlaps with several of Patton's cells. Spradley separates researchers' questions into three groups: (1) descriptive questions, eliciting a respondent's representation or depiction of some aspect of the culture or world; (2) structural questions, substantiating or generating the constructs respondents use to depict their worlds; and (3) contrast questions, eliciting the meanings respondents attach to and the relationships they perceive among the varying constructs they use. Spradley elaborates researcher tactics for acquiring what Schatzman & Strauss (1973) assert is the goal of qualitative interviews—acquisition of data representing participant meanings.

Schatzman and Strauss depict the interview as designed to reveal how participants conceive of their worlds and how they explain these conceptions.

Like Patton (1990b) and Spradley (1979), Schatzman and Strauss offer a typology of questions. Their system differs from these first two, however, in that it addresses both the kind of data elicited and the form of question used. Schatzman and Strauss divide questions into five groups: (1) reportorial questions eliciting a respondent's knowledge of factors in a social situation, usually preceded by interrogatives such as who, what, when, where, and how, (2) devil's advocate questions eliciting what respondents view as controversial, (3) hypothetical questions encouraging respondent speculation about alternative occurrences (cf. Patton, 1990b, for role-play and simulation questions), (4) posing-the-ideal questions eliciting respondent's values, and (5) propositional questions eliciting or verifying respondent interpretations. Schatzman and Strauss's system overlaps those proposed by Patton and Spradley. Each framework, nevertheless, offers a variant perspective toward data and the worlds represented by those data. Table 6.1 compares these typologies.

These typologies, both individually and in combination, provide alternatives for matching an interview format more precisely with the purposes intended in research questions. They alert researchers to aspects of topics or research settings that otherwise may be overlooked, and they facilitate construction of a balanced interview.

A final kind of data is mentioned by Lofland (1971). He advises investigators to consider not only the content of what is elicited and volunteered in an interview, but also the content of what is evaded and ignored or left unsaid. In many cases, omissions reveal significant social data.

Scripting

The second dimension of interview construction, scripting, is how individual questions are structured and sequenced (Schatzman & Strauss, 1973). Once researchers have decided what to elicit from respondents and what questions will be required to elicit the desired data, they develop a script to guide the interview. Script formats vary in structure and standardization (Denzin, 1978). Some are improvisations while others are predesigned protocols. Some researchers use their scripts only to rehearse an interview; others use them while conducting the interviews. Scripts also differ in how questions are worded, how probes are handled, and how interview statements and questions are organized and sequenced.

Regardless of how they are scripted, interview questions should be clearly meaningful to the respondent. In their guidelines for designing

TABLE 6.1
A Summary of Data Types and Categories

Reference	Data type
Babbie (1973)	1. Nominal 2. Ordinal 3. Interval 4. Ratio
Zelditch (1962)	1. Frequency distributions (use systematic samples; standardized format for these data) 2. Incidents and histories (use intensive, nonstandardized interviews for these data) 3. Institutionalized norms and statuses (use intensive, nonstandardized interviews for these data)
Patton (1990)	1. Experience/behavior 2. Knowledge of subject 3. Opinion/value 4. Sensory description 5. Feeling 6. Background/demographic
Spradley (1979)	1. Descriptive (of subject, culture, or world) 2. Structural (of constructs organizing that world) 3. Contrast (of meanings informing that world)
Schatzman & Strauss (1973)	1. Reportorial (of subject world—who, what, when, where, how) 2. Posing the ideal (to elicit values) 3. Devil's advocate (what subject sees as controversial) 4. Propositional (to verify subject's interpretations) 5. Hypothetical (speculation about alternatives)
Lofland (1971)	All that is evaded, ignored, and left unsaid, plus: 1. Acts 2. Activities 3. Meanings 4. Participation 5. Relationships 6. Settings

interviews, Patton (1990b) and Lofland (1971) caution investigators to avoid the use of leading questions—queries worded so as to reveal what the interviewer believes is a preferable answer. This is useful advice. Nevertheless, a well-worded, leading question can contain a deliberate assumption or overstatement, provoking a complex or elaborate response which otherwise would be missed.

The format of a question determines its response. For example, some questions elicit "yes" or "no" responses when more descriptive detail is desired. A political analyst asking, "Are you familiar with the candidates in the upcoming school board election?" might get the answer, "Yes, Mrs. Jones and Dr. Washington are my next-door neighbors." More useful information would be produced by asking respondents to identify the candidates and their platforms. Pelto & Pelto (1978) advocate both open and closed questions, depending on what data are needed and the form their analysis takes. For enumerative purposes, closed questions are more efficient and effective. For qualitative analysis, open questions are preferable. Pelto and Pelto also contrast questions for clarity and ambiguity. Although the clarity and specificity they endorse are preferable in most situations, ambiguity can serve significant research purposes. During the exploratory phases of a study, for example, ethnographers may rely on deliberate ambiguity to elicit variation in respondent answers or to detect respondent meanings and interpretations without the risk of cuing the informant.

Patton's (1980) guidelines for question wording suggest that researchers use open-ended, nondichotomous questions, although these questions do require later holistic coding. Patton also recommends relying on questions that involve only a single idea, rather than double-barreled questions. For example, the question, "How often do you go to movies and concerts?" may confuse the respondent, who does not know which activity to enumerate—movies, concerts, or both. Like ambiguous questions, however, judiciously posed multiple questions can serve exploratory purposes, allowing respondents to indicate which of several ideas they prefer to address.

Patton emphasizes that questions preceded by the interrogative "why" generally are ineffective. They are ambiguous, they make assumptions, and are too abstract to elicit concrete data. They may produce only socially acceptable answers: "Why did you become a teacher?" "Because I loved children. . . ." These are sound arguments; questions preceded by "why" often reflect inadequate preparation by the researcher. Nevertheless, under certain conditions, "why" questions can serve researcher purposes well. For example, investigators studying cause-and-effect relationships in many social situations might neglect a fruitful data source if they failed to ask participants for their explanations of why certain effects occur. Just such a question was posed at the end of Harrington & Gumpert's (1981) life-history interviews with negative prediction defiers. Respondents speculated about why they, rather than their siblings and socioeconomic peers, were so occupationally successful. These answers revealed many of the respondents' underlying assumptions about how their worlds operated; they suggested conditions and processes that the investigators had not yet considered as relevant to negative prediction defiers.

Guidelines and handbooks for how to word questions purposefully and effectively are plentiful. Even though intended for instructional rather than research purposes, many of these manuals for question design (e.g., Sanders, 1966; Hunkins, 1972; Carin & Sund, 1978; Sudman & Bradburn, 1989; Bradburn & Sudman, 1988) are based on principles applicable across dialogues: research interviews, counseling sessions, or classroom exchanges. Nevertheless, researchers should keep paramount their own research questions and the nature of the groups they are studying. If they attend only to formulaic prescriptions or proscriptions for the wording of questions, they may choose inadequate options or fail to consider useful alternatives.

Ordering

Interview scripts and questionnaires are ordered. Ordering is the arranging, organizing, and sequencing of questions and statements to communicate to the respondent the researcher's intent and direction. Lofland & Lofland (1984) emphasize that interviews are conducted more smoothly when prefaced by a brief statement of research purpose, by assurances of protection of respondent identity, and by an outline of how the interaction is expected to proceed. Careful sequencing facilitates completeness and comprehensiveness of responses while deflecting repetitiveness or respondent, and interviewer, fatigue and boredom. Considerations in ordering include the following: (1) complexity of the topic or question format, (2) similarity of topic to that addressed by preceding and subsequent questions, (3) temporality, or sequencing across time, (4) interest level of the questions, and (5) sensitivity or threat value.

Researchers should organize their scripts topically so that questions addressing the same topic or culminating in a major idea are grouped together. If the research question involves the social and professional interactions teachers have, all questions about interaction with students should be grouped together, separate from questions about parents or other teachers. Questions on each topic should be ordered by complexity, beginning with the simplest eliciting the most familiar information. However, researchers may ignore questions on the script already addressed by respondents, fortuitously out of sequence, or allow time during the interview for respondents to volunteer an elaboration on an earlier reply.

Researchers disagree about the placement of demographic questions—age, gender, place of residence, income and education levels, religious affiliation, ethnicity, and similar material. Patton (1990b) advocates spreading them throughout an interview or leaving them for the conclusion because he finds them less interesting than other questions. Other investigators begin interviews with demographic questions because they are readily addressed and ease the respondent into more difficult replies. Most researchers reserve questions that are complex, controversial, or difficult for middle or later periods in an interview when rapport has been established and the respondent's interest has been aroused. Patton, for example, suggests that sequences should begin with descriptive, present-oriented questions and build to more complex issues of emotion, belief, and explanation. Babbie (1973, p. 150), however, recommends that researchers using self-administered surveys or questionnaires should put the most interesting questions first.

Researchers who want a chronology of life events should provide respondents with a framework and then let them relate their memories and intentions in any order. Researchers should be alert to the fact that temporal order can arouse sensitive issues. In the past, researchers asked about marital status before asking about a respondent's children to avoid casting doubt upon the legitimacy of her offspring. However, ordering might be different if the population under study included a high proportion of single parents. If the study were of unmarried teenaged mothers, any questions about marital status might be embarrassing or irrelevant.

One might ask, for example, "Do you have any children?" and "Have you ever been married?" rather than "How many children do you have?" and "Are you married?" The former questions leave respondents more leeway to frame their stories within their own categories and definitions, unprompted by cues from the researcher. Sensitivity to the contextual and cultural meaning of answers also is important; answers to "Do you have any children?" could include:

Yes, I had hard pregnancies with all three.

Yes, we adopted our daughter.

No, all of my children died in the war.

No, my husband and I couldn't have any children, but we raised the children of my deceased sister and three neighborhood kids who were abandoned.

No, we are in the Foster Parent Program and only keep the kids for a few months to a year.

All of these answers leave the researcher to determine whether or not the people queried have children or do not have children, a decision depending on the purposes and definitions of the research question. These responses are more informative than those identifying the number of sons and daughters an individual has. Similarly, asking if a person has ever been married permits the respondent to discuss everything from marriage and divorce to semipermanent cohabiting, widowhood, and extended natural or fictive families.

Bridges, transitions, and clarifications are like a glue, holding an interview together. Patton, for example, recommends that the researcher provide cues or explanations for shifts in interview focus and topic so that respondents can adapt their thinking to the new direction. Lofland & Lofland (1971) also agree that effective interviews depend on effective probing. Schatzman & Strauss (1973) and Patton (1990b) advocate using probes for elaboration and explanation, clarification, and completion of detail. Patton suggests that Schatzman and Strauss's reportorial question—asking for who, what, when, where, and how—is useful for anticipating probes during the conduct of an interview (cf. Cicourel, 1964, p. 99, for possible disruptive effects of probing).

Once a questionnaire or interview is designed, it should be tested and practiced (Pelto & Pelto, 1978). Researchers can do initial troubleshooting by reading their questionnaires aloud or trying them out on friends. Further work usually is necessary however. Pilot administration of scripts on comparable respondents is helpful. These trials allow researchers to adjust to the variations that respondents offer in their answers. When this is impossible, reasonable alternatives can be substituted. For example, Harrington & Gumpert (1981) completed their trial runs of life-history scripts by testing the script on themselves and among people they hired to be interviewers. In addition, having experienced the respondent role sensitized the interviewers to nuances of meaning and affect that might otherwise have been missed.

CONDUCTING INTERVIEWS AND SURVEYS

As investigators choose the topics to be addressed and develop the questions intended to introduce the topics, they simultaneously plan and experiment with the general logistics that frame an interview session.

Logistics of Administering Interviews Effectively

Schatzman & Strauss (1973) identify five conditions affecting the outcome of interviews: (1) duration, or how long a session lasts, (2) number, or how many separate sessions are required to complete the interview process, (3) setting, or location for the interview, (4) identity of individuals involved, or who the interviewers and respondents are and how many are present at a session, and (5) respondent styles, or ways of communicating characteristics of the group to be interviewed.

Deciding how long an interview should be depends on several factors. These include the amount of data required, the time and rapport necessary to obtain the data, the interest of respondents in reporting the data, the time and attention reasonably expected of both interviewer and respondent, and the number of respondents required by the research plan. Some research designs specify a series of interviews to be conducted following key events or over a relevant period of time; in other cases, multiple interviews are conducted to provide breaks in what would otherwise be too lengthy an interview.

Bradburn (1983) believes that the interview setting affects respondent reaction. Life-history interviews and surveys addressing intimate or controversial issues often are conducted in respondents' homes or offices or in locations respondents designate to be more comfortable. On the other hand, scheduled standardized interviews frequently are conducted at a uniform location to equalize setting effects across respondents.

The number of interviewers present at a single session rarely exceeds two; larger numbers may pose difficulties in establishing rapport with respondents. Financial resources limit most projects to a single interviewer for each session. The Harrington & Gumpert (1981) life-history investigation cited previously used teams of two interviewers. The decision was originally made to assure gender–race matches between interviewers and respondent; matching interviewer–respondent characteristics is a common tactic for enhancing rapport. The design required blacks and whites and men and women to be interviewed. Dual-team interviewers increased the likelihood of both the respondent's sex and race being matched by one or the other individual on the team. Because most of these interviews lasted over 4 hours, interviewers had difficulty maintaining their concentration. To avoid fatigue, the paired interviewers alternated questioning; they also served to stimulate appropriate probes for one another's questions. Respondents, on the other hand, became so involved in reconstructing their life experiences that they rarely expressed any weariness.

When time and researcher resources are limited, respondents may be grouped for single sessions. Lofland & Lofland (1984), for example, notes that some data are more productively elicited from several individuals at once. Schatzman & Strauss (1973) recommend this method for discovering variation in people's responses and for revealing significant controversies among naturally bounded groups. Group interviews were used in the evaluation of an integrated program for gifted students. Evaluators wanted to determine how teachers, parents, and administrators viewed the program. Finding it impossible to survey or interview individually the large student population, they developed a youth poll, asking groups of students to respond to specific, often controversial, aspects of their educational experiences. Group interaction in this case elicited responses far more candid and explicit than would have been obtained had the adolescents been interviewed individually by an adult or surveyed with an impersonal paper-and-pencil questionnaire (Giles, Compton, & Ferrell, 1982; Ferrell & Compton, 1986).

Interviewer Style

A common factor affecting all five conditions identified by Schatzman and Strauss is the kind of interaction interviewers seek to establish with respondents. Interactive modes vary from the semihostile adversarial exchanges common in courtrooms and police investigations, to the emotionally neutral but cognitively intricate dialogue of classic Socratic debate, to the empathic exploration of personal trauma found in psychotherapy. Any of these modes is adaptable to research interviews; given appropriate research goals and design, any of them can be the preferred mode. Most qualitative researchers, however, prefer to conduct interviews in the conversational style of everyday interaction (Schatzman & Strauss, 1973; Denzin, 1978). Lofland (1971) emphasizes that this mode communicates empathy, encouragement, and understanding. Schatzman and Strauss argue that it also allows respondents to feel that what they are saying is acceptable and significant. Patton (1980, 1990b) notes that an everyday conversational style permits interviewers to respond neutrally without risking the loss of rapport. The conversational model, familiar and comfortable to all respondents, is most likely to elicit the trust, confidence, and ease among respondents necessary for yielding elaborate, subtle, and valid data.

Cicourel (1964) cautions that the rapport of ordinary friendship increases the idiosyncracy of interviews and poses difficulties for establishing reliability and certain kinds of validity. Spradley (1979, pp. 56–57) emphasizes the differences between friendly conversations and interviews. Interviews, unlike most friendly conversations, have a script, an agenda, and a purpose set by the researcher. They also require greater clarification and attention to details than conversations among friends, who presumably share "inside information" not accessible in the researcher–participant relationship.

Patton (1990b) cautions interviewers to be sure that they talk less than the respondent. An interview transcript dominated by interviewer remarks indicates a poorly trained or insensitive questioner. More important, it supplies less data than the interview is intended to elicit. To enhance skill and dexterity in minimizing their own talk, many interviewers practice as we have advocated previously. In most cases, the cues needed to answer a question or probe can be streamlined or collapsed into far fewer words than initially seemed possible.

Examples of Interview Transcripts

To illustrate some of the characteristics of interviews, we next present two examples. The transcripts are unstructured interviews. Both elicit information from the students about their perceptions of teachers and their experiences in school. Both transcripts show the range of questions qualitative researchers can ask: experience, opinion, and feeling questions; hypothetical questions; and propositional questions. Many of these focus on the institutionalized norms that Zelditch (1962) believes are best elicited through nonstandardized interviews. Nancy's interview illustrates an example of an introduction; it is preceded by a brief statement of purpose, respondent protection, and researcher intent; these are supplemented by occasional statements marking shifts in topic.

Both interviews were recorded on cassette tape recorders, devices familiar to and often used by both respondents. Both were conducted in private settings; Steven's interview took place in the researcher's house, where he often had music lessons, and Nancy's was conducted in a conference room close to the children's classroom. These quiet settings assured better recording quality.

Nancy's interview was conducted as part of an ethnographic study of a third-grade classroom (Goetz, 1976b); it confirmed patterns discovered during participant observation and explored new constructs. The purpose of the interview was to explore concepts used by children in their daily conversations: good students and bad students, good teachers and bad teachers, teaching and learning. Data collected from participant observation had suggested that children's meanings for their activities were different from the meanings assumed by their teacher. Nancy's transcript, for example, emphasizes the children's values for right answers, for finishing work speedily, and for self-expression that were sometimes congruent but other times discordant with teacher goals. Nancy was one of the more articulate students in this class. She also was a key informant.

Steven's interview[1] was part of a study of gifted violin students; its purpose was to trace the decision points and key events leading young students to persist in their studies and become professional musicians. Previous research had emphasized the influence of musical giftedness on future success; this study explored the influence of role models as well as motivational, social, and structural issues. Steven had just decided to return to Europe without receiving his Master's degree; both he and his teacher agreed that his objectives for study in the United States had been met.

These transcripts demonstrate the contrast between procedures used with young children and those used with adults. For example, presupposition questions, based on assumed, unarticulated conditions, are complex.

---

[1] Steven's interview is part of an ongoing study by LeCompte whose results are as yet unpublished.

They are hard for young children to follow. Breaking a presupposition question into its components and asking children about each component separately resolves this difficulty. Children's responses also are less linear than those of adults; they require opportunities to return to a topic and address it from a different perspective. The adaptations required to interview children may be more dramatic than those used for other groups of respondents, but they do show how interviews should be tailored to the respondent and made specific to the situation. Constructing a productive interview script is partly science and partly art. Researchers should consider the use of standard prescriptions and proscriptions for assessing who is to be interviewed for which purpose. In addition, researchers should be careful to record the respondent's exact words and usages. If researchers paraphrase, they may mask, distort, or substitute connotations intended or assumed by respondents and thus misrepresent the data. In general, respondents should be recorded *verbatim*, and paraphrasing should be used only when transcription is impossible (Lofland & Lofland, 1984; Pelto & Pelto, 1978).

Both interviews have weaknesses. Steven's interview begins awkwardly; in a previous attempt, the tape recorder had malfunctioned halfway through the interview. Because the researcher had relied on the machine rather than taking notes, the session had to be rescheduled. Many issues already had been discussed and Steven was reluctant to repeat what he had previously detailed. The interviewer also failed, in this second attempt, to discuss the purpose of the interview or how the respondent's privacy would be protected.

Nancy's interview was an early attempt at interviewing by a novice researcher. It lacks clear descriptive questions at the beginning, such as, "What are some of the things you do in school?" "What do you do by yourself?" "What do you do with other children?" "What do you learn in school?" "What does Ms. Berelson teach you in school?" These questions elicit from children easily recalled material providing them with stimuli for problems on opinions and feelings. Such questions might have prevented some repetitiveness, redundant sequencing, and incongruous material.

The interviews begin below and continue for several pages.

Preissle: You know that I'm writing a book about third graders. The book is for people who are going to be teachers and for other people who care about children. Your answers to the questions I'm going to ask will help these folks understand third graders better. No one will hear this tape except you and me. In the book, all the children will be disguised so no one will know which answers are yours. We'll take about 20 minutes probably, but Ms. Berelson will let us have as much time as we need. Do you want to ask me about any of this before we start?

Nancy: [Shakes her head.]

Preissle: Would you go to school if you didn't have to?

Nancy: Sometimes I would go to school when I was in the mood, and the other times—when I wasn't, when I wanted to go horseback riding or something like that—I wouldn't. But sometimes when I felt I was in the mood to go, I would.

Preissle: Do you like school?

Nancy: Sort of, sometimes.

Preissle: What are some of the things you like about school?

Nancy: Well, sometimes I like school because we have extra recess or art or something like that, and other times—when we have to go to music—I don't like it because I don't like music.

Preissle: What are some other things you don't like about school?

Nancy: When we have a whole lot of work—like we have English, spelling, and handwriting, all kinds of stuff like that in the morning and stuff. Then we have about 42 problems in math, like we did that one time.

Preissle: If you didn't go to school, what would you miss?

Nancy: Sometimes—like if there was laws and stuff that we don't have to go to school and they changed things around—then I might miss art one day and something [else] the next day and something like that, and I wouldn't even know what day we're supposed to have them on.

Preissle: What do you think you'd miss the most about school?

Nancy: Well, the most thing I would miss would be work, I guess.

Preissle: What kind of work?

Nancy: [shrugging] I don't know. Any kind of work. Some play work and some hard work.

Preissle: What would you miss out on learning?

Nancy: Like if we was just starting to do division, but we've already did it—if we was starting to learn it that one day when I was, when I missed school because I didn't want to go or something—then I wouldn't know how to do it when I came back, and if they was stingy and stuff, they wouldn't help me. Then I would probably get all of my answers wrong if we had a test.

Preissle: What are some of the other things you learn in school?

Nancy: We learn where the commas and apostrophes [go] and all kinds of stuff in English and [we] learn how to spell new words and know what they mean in spelling and all kinds of stuff.

Preissle: Are those things important to you?

Nancy: Yes. Because—like if you grew up and didn't go to school and you had your kids to go—and if they asked you something, then you wouldn't know, and you couldn't tell them, and then they would probably get it wrong.

Preissle: So you are saying that partly you learn things to help your own children?

Nancy: Yes. Like my dad, he didn't go to school sometimes. And my brother—he's in ninth grade now—when he asks my dad something, Dad don't know and neither does my grandma cause they had different kinds of school, and my dad only went to sixth grade, I think; that's where my uncle was and [inaudible] my dad.

Preissle: Do these things have any use to you right now?

Nancy: Yes. You've got to learn them cause you got to know all kinds of stuff.

Preissle: What do you use it for?

Nancy: Using it for learning.

Preissle: We've talked about what you learn in school. What kinds of things do you learn at home?

Nancy: Well, at home you learn how to cook, and at school you don't learn that until you're in seventh grade, until you're in home ec. Learn stuff like cleaning up a house, how to ride horses, and stuff like that.

Preissle: Are those things important to you?

Nancy: Yes. And you learn how to fix a garden so you'll have some food.

Preissle: Have you been learning to garden?

Nancy: Yes. I help my grandma a lot every year just about—when she has one.

Preissle: Do you know when you are learning something?

Nancy: Yes.

Preissle: What does it feel like?

Nancy: It feels good.

Preissle: What's happening inside of you when you are learning?

Nancy: Thinking and stuff, and I guess I'm happy cause I'm learning it.

Preissle: How do you know when you have learned something?

Nancy: Well, you know when you learned something is when you can think it again and know it again. Like, if it was your first day of school and you was just trying and trying to learn, and finally you learned it. You go home, and the next day your teacher asks you what it was about or something, and then you can answer her.

Preissle: So you can do it over?

Nancy: Yes.

Preissle: Are you a good student?

Nancy: Yes. I get straight A's and B's on my report card. Haven't ever had a C or D or anything over [sic] a C; [I] haven't even had a C.

Preissle: What else do you have to do to be a good student?

Nancy: You have to know things and learn them sort of fast like.

Preissle: So that the kids who can learn faster than the other kids have a better chance of being good students?

Nancy: Yes, cause then they'll know it more.

Preissle: How do good students treat the other kids?

Nancy: Nice. They try to help them. They don't just say, "Get away from me. I don't want to learn [sic] this," or nothing like that.

Preissle: How do good students treat their teachers?

Nancy: Nice. And, like, if you're a good student, then you have to be a good sport and stuff.

Preissle: What do you mean, be a good sport?

Nancy: Being a good sport is—like if both, like if there is two teams, and one team won, they just don't get out and say, "Ha-ha, you lost," and stuff like that. You have to be good and stuff.

Preissle: What do bad students do?

Nancy: To be a bad student . . . the way you can find out is that if you keep on doing it. You know, you walk up to a good student and say, "Don't hang around me." You're always bad and all kinds of stuff. You'd lose and stuff like that. That's a bad student, like that.

Preissle: What does a bad student do in the classroom?

Nancy: Well, when you're not supposed to talk, he . . . sometimes, sometimes they talk, and they laugh and giggle, and when—like Chuck, one time he was goofing off, and the teacher told him not to—he kept on doing it so he got punished. And stuff like that.

Preissle: So you feel he was being a bad student then?

Nancy: Yes, cause he wasn't minding.

Preissle: What are some things children in the class do that you like?

Nancy: Oh boy, . . . that I like? When they don't sass the teacher and do stuff that the teacher don't say . . . says not to do.

Preissle: So you don't like it when children disobey?

Nancy: Right. Cause I haven't did that ever—ever since kindergarten, and I've been in first grade twice, even.

Preissle: What are some other things you like about school?

Nancy: In school some more things I like is going to the library and when you get to visit other classes. Like up in Benton School, where I was before, well, the thing that I liked about that is that this year I would be changing rooms. I'd be going to a different class to be reading, and you don't start that down here until you're in sixth grade, I think.

Preissle: You'd have a separate teacher for reading? You'd like that?

Nancy: Yes. Because you don't have the same teacher all the time, and you get to know both teachers—know their names and stuff quicker, and you get to do it quicker, too.

Preissle: What are some other things you enjoy doing with other children?

Nancy: Especially going to someone else's house, cause down here I can't. And up in Benton my best friend moved to Kentucky, and I ain't got much friends now—except for here in school.

Preissle: You don't live close to any other children?

Nancy: No. The closest friend that I have is 10 miles away. There's about two or three [children] who live in the same house about a mile away. But [I] can't go down there cause Grandma won't let me cause it's on Fuller Road. And, well, there's lots of woods by it, and there could be some people who go horseback riding that can come out and get us and stuff—cause one time we went down to a creek to swim, you know, and we heard something coming up behind us. We just took off.

Preissle: What are some of the things children do here at school that you don't like?

Nancy: When they come up to you, and you got an answer in your mind, and you're just ready to write it down—and here comes some-one—and they start bugging you and talking to you and stuff; and then, when you get to . . . get to go to work, you forget the answer, and you can't get it anymore; and you have to go up and bug the teacher about it.

Preissle: What do you mean by bugging you?

Nancy: Like Jim, he always asks me how to do this and help him, and he tries to get me to tell him answers and stuff like that. And just sometimes, when I'm not in the mood to talk, people just keep on talking to me; and then if I tell them to be quiet and they keep on doing it, then I have to talk real loud, and the teacher gets after me.

Preissle: What things do you do in class that make you feel good?

Nancy: When I get to go up in front of the class and get to tell them stuff and get it out of my mind and tell other people. Like if there's somebody chasing me at night and I didn't tell no one, then I'd get scared, and I'd think they'd come after me; and if I told someone else, they could help me. In the morning, I told the teacher about the bump on my head, and that made me proud because I got to tell her about it; and one day, you know, she seen it, and she started asking me questions—I might not be in the mood to talk.

Preissle: What things happen in class that make you feel bad?

Nancy: Like one time, if you was outside, you did something bad to someone, you know; and then they came up to you and you came up to them one day—you tried to apologize, and they just wouldn't let you apologize; then they wouldn't play with you anymore, and you might not have any friends.

Preissle: Has that ever happened to you?

Nancy: Well, one time me and this girl named Marsha . . . she, well, we liked each other, you know; and I did something she didn't like, and she did something I didn't like. So then we wasn't friends for about a month or so; and this other girl [a child living nearby] she can only play with this one girl, and that one girl can only have one person playing with her. I have no friends except playing with my brother and sister.

Preissle: That made you feel bad?

Nancy: The only other things I could do is go up to the main road and get a cherry soda or something . . .

Preissle: What do children do that Ms. Berelson doesn't like?

Nancy: Well, when they don't do the things that she likes. When they're bad, and I guess when they just don't do stuff she likes. When they don't mind her and when they sort of, like, sass her and stuff like that. When they bother her. And they keep on going up there [to the teacher's desk] and asking her questions and all kinds of stuff like that.

Preissle: She doesn't like people to ask her questions?

Nancy: Yes, but, you know. Like if they've just been up there, and they did one problem, and then all of a sudden they come just right back up in line with one another—then go back to their seat, and then come right back up with another one. And they keep on coming back up and asking them [questions].

Preissle: You said she liked people to be quiet. Does that mean she doesn't want children to talk to each other?

Nancy: Not really. She don't like them to talk to each other sometimes because she thinks that they're telling them the answer. And they can talk to each other, I guess.

Preissle: She doesn't mind if children are talking normally to each other?

Nancy: No, she don't mind that—but if they're talking loud and all kinds of stuff like that . . .

Preissle: How can you tell when Ms. Berelson is pleased?

Nancy: Cause she is nice. Like sometimes you know when you come in [in the morning], and she talks real happy and stuff. Then you can tell. But if she don't . . . like, if someone was doing something real bad, she wouldn't talk real happy.

Preissle: What does she look like when she's real happy?

Nancy: Well, she has something like a smile on her face.

Preissle: What does her voice sound like when she's happy?

Nancy: [impatiently] It sounds like she's happy. It sounds surprised like and stuff like that.

Preissle: Does she use any special words when she's happy?

Nancy: Yes. She says "well" real happy-like, and sometimes she says good morning, and stuff like that.

Preissle: Can you tell when she's not happy?

Nancy: Sort of and sort of not.

Preissle: Tell me about "sort of."

Nancy: When you can tell she's not happy, she don't say good morning or she don't say "well" real happy, you know. She just starts saying, "Take out your spelling books," or something like that.

Preissle: You said "sort of and sort of not." So you mean that you're not sure when she's unhappy?

Nancy: Yes.

Preissle: What does Ms. Berelson do that you especially like?

Nancy: When she's happy, and when she lets you be in the front of the line. Like if you're quiet and stuff, and she says, you know—and other people's [sic] talking and stuff—and then she lets you go line up first, something like that.

Preissle: Is there anything she does that you don't like?

Nancy: Not really. Sometimes, you know, when she gets mad at me and stuff—and I don't do nothing, but she thinks I do, but I don't. I tell her I don't, but she still thinks I do. Stuff like that.

Preissle: So she won't change her mind?

Nancy: Yes.

Preissle: Should she stop doing that kind of thing?

Nancy: I don't know, I guess. If really I did do it, I don't think she should change her mind. But if I was honest and everything, then I think she should change her mind . . .

Preissle: What makes someone a bad teacher?

Nancy: Bad teachers . . . they act bad. When they talk to the kids, they sound mean and bad, but when they talk to other teachers, they sound like they're happy. Like when they talk to the principal, they're happy and all kinds of stuff like that. But when they talk to the children . . . she . . . I guess she just didn't talk to them the way she should have.

Preissle: So she treated the children differently than she treated other people?

Nancy: [Nods]

Preissle: You've done such a nice job today, telling me all these things. I just have one last question, but it's kind of hard. You told me earlier what learning is; what is teaching?

Nancy: Teaching means that you are learning something.

Presissle: Can a teacher be a learner?

Nancy: Yes. Because my teacher last year, she was just a first-grade teacher, you know. And this other teacher had a baby, and she couldn't teach that year. So my first-grade teacher had to be a second-grade teacher, and she was still my teacher, and she was learning the same thing that we was. She was learning that at the same time.

Preissle: Do you have any questions for me?

Nancy: Yes. How did you feel when you was in school?

Preissle: I was always so scared of everything. I guess I liked school. I liked to read; I really just liked to read.

Nancy: Was that your best subject?

Preissle: My best subject up to second grade was math.

Nancy: I wish I was better in math.

Preissle: I was always scared of people yelling at me. I hardly ever did anything that made people yell at me, but the few times that they did, I was so frightened that I cried for hours. I was very timid, shy, and just a . . .

Nancy: That's what I do at home. Sometimes my grandma starts yelling at me when I don't even do nothing—when my little sister does it—she keeps on, keeps on, keeps on, so I just start to cry.

Preissle: I guess that's the way I was, Nancy; I was just afraid all the time that something was going to happen. So I don't think I liked school as much as some of the other children did.

Nancy: Well, neither did my stepmom. All the time she'd act like she had a fever and stuff. She'd stick a thermometer in her mouth and then put a match under it.

Preissle: So she wouldn't have to go to school?

Nancy: Yes, but her mom always said that she . . . it was too high. She would have died if it was that high. [End of tape]

Steven's Interview

ML: When you and I were talking the other day before the tape recorder finked out on us, you had said that you started in public schools and started when you were about 8 years old, and that that was the customary time for kids to begin in Europe. And that you're, most of your experience has been in public schools. Your training and stuff like that. What happened, how did you continue studying after you got started? How did it all work out?

SR: Well, after I started in school and the teacher, after about 6 months, he would come to my house and then I'd have a longer lesson for about an hour. That went on for a couple of years, and then it was suggested that I go to London for my lessons. And they have like a Saturday morning school at the conservatories, which is just for kids from about 13 through 18, before they go to college. And so I auditioned and I won a scholarship and so I used to go up every Saturday morning to London on the train, which was quite an ordeal for a 12-year-old.

ML: How long did it take you to get there?

SR: On the train it's about an hour from my home, and I had to cross London on the subway and it was quite tough because you had to get up at like 6:30 in the morning, on Saturday, and get down to the train station and then I wouldn't be back until 4:00, 3:00 in the afternoon.

ML: So that took up every Saturday?

SR: Yea, that was every Saturday.

ML: From the time you were 12 years old?

SR: From when I was 12 till I think till 16. I moved colleges because I—the first place I went to was the Royal College of Music. I was studying with that kind of tough teacher who is a real dragon called Mrs. Amidon and at age 13 I didn't really want to become a violinist. I mean I don't see many kids who have made up their minds by 13 that they want to play the violin. And one day she asked me, "What do you want to do?" and I said "Well, I think I want to become a race driver or something" and she was horrified and threw me out of the class because she said "I only teach people who are going to become violinists" which I thought at 13 was a bit tough. So she threw me out. And then I transferred to the Royal Academy which was where I went as a—you know, when I left school. And I went there every Saturday morning from then on. So I was doing it for a few years.

ML: So you started with the dragon lady, Mrs. Amidon, when you were about 12. Then how old were you when you switched over to the Royal Academy?

SR: I was probably 14.

ML: 14. Did going away every Saturday and being a violinist make you feel different from the other kids? Or . . .

SR: Yes. I think it did, I mean I was always aware of it at school, that I was doing something different. Because I didn't go to public musical schools, they didn't have very strong music departments, so there was no orchestra and things like that. It was always that I did all these things on a Saturday when other kids were . . .

ML: Playing soccer?

SR: Yea. And I was traveling up to London. I didn't enjoy it very much but it certainly gave me a good education.

ML: What kind of a community did you grow up in?

SR: Um very ordinary, kind of middle-class. It was um . . .

ML: Not too far out of London?

SR: No, it's about 40 miles from London. So it was easy both to get to London, but it also had its own identity as a town. It was a very busy, kind of musical town. There were lots of orchestras and things going on there.

ML: But not in the schools?

SR: But not in the schools. These were like community . . . not in my school. What they did was they'd get all the kids together from all of the schools during the holidays and you'd have musicals three times a year—Christmas, Easter, and summer. And that was where I really got most of my musical training.

ML: So it was by going to London and then by this teacher who taught you from the time you were 8?

SR: Yes. And then the Youth Orchestras. There was a big system of— there were five youth orchestras and you kind of worked your way up starting in a string orchestra like the young kids like 10 to 12, and then you moved up. Then there was a youth orchestra which was for kids from, well you could be 18 to 24 really. And I got into that rather early—I think I was about 15 when I got into that. So that was where I got most of my education.

ML: Who sponsors those youth orchestras?

SR: They're run by the local educational authority [similar to local school districts in the United States] for the area where I lived in.

ML: I see, so in America, this stuff is often in the school itself . . .

SR: Yes.

ML: . . . and in England it's . . .

SR: Yes. Well, a lot of it's in the school but there was a—I think there was a feeling that it would be good for kids from all over the area to get together at some state rather than just have it in the school where it could only reach a certain standard. You could get all the best people from all the schools together three times a year and have an even better musical experience.

ML: Your town had a lot of musical opportunities. Is anybody in your family musical?

SR: Yea, well my father directed all this.

ML: Oh, I see. [laughs] You didn't have a chance!

SR: He was a music advisor for Hampshire which is the county I live in. So he was in charge of all of that. He conducted the youth orchestra.

ML: Is he a violinist?

SR: Yes, he was. He was a violinist and pianist at the Royal Academy.

ML: Is anybody else . . . what other people encouraged you in your family or outside of your family besides your teachers?

SR: It mostly came from my family. My mother was a singer so it was always there—from the earliest time I can remember. There was music all the time in my house. But they never pushed me. I went, when I decided to take up the violin, it was my decision. And the teacher came to the school—and before that they hadn't pressured me at all to take up an instrument. I think they realized it was going to happen sometime, that I would just, you know, better wait for me to do it than to push me.

ML: How come you chose the violin?

SR: I really think it was just because it was the first thing that was offered to me. I, I, I really don't know. I've never had any talent with anything else. I've tried, I've played a bit of piano and what else did I try, I tried cello. I was terrible, really. But the violin, I just seemed to click with that.

ML: You know why Laura Hunter ended up with the saxophone?

SR: No.

ML: She was the only kid in her school who was big enough to carry the saxophone around and so it had nothing to do with any interest or talent of her own.

SR: I think often it's just, with young kids it's just if you're offered it and you see it as just another something to interest you, you're not really, I don't think little kids are interested in whether it's a clarinet or a violin; it's just something new to play with.

ML: The experiences that you've had with your family—is there any-body—do you have any brothers and sisters? Are they also musical?

SR: Yes. I have a sister who's two years younger than me and she hasn't gone into music at all. She's studying biology in the University. But she's very musical as well. She had more, I'd say more of a typical, you know, encounter with music. She would play cello for 6 months and then give it up and then she did the piano and gave that up. She ended up with the trumpet and she played that pretty successfully for about 5 or 6 years and then she gave that up so . . .

ML: Why did you stick with it? Why did you decide at age 13 not to be a race driver and to continue with the Royal Academy?

SR: Yeah, you know, I don't know really. I think I was interested in the fact that I could actually, I could see some kind of progress in what I was doing with the violin, I guess. I didn't find it very difficult to begin with, but it all seemed to be going pretty well and it was a novelty I think. I mean I enjoyed it, it wasn't all plain sailing, I mean I gave up three or four times in those years. You know, there was something else that interested me and I would give it up for a week or so and get the cold treatment from my parents and then after a week I'd be back playing again.

ML: What were some of the tangents that took you off besides race car driving?

SR: I don't, I think it was the practicing. I had a big, I always had a bit of a problem with practicing and I would never want to put in the time to practice. But my parents, they kind of worked out schedules for me like we went one time with the 5-day-a-week plan that I'd have to practice 5 days a week and I would not practice on the day of my lesson and I'd be allowed 1 day off completely where I didn't have to practice. And that worked for a while. I quite liked that. But I think that was it. Then when I got into, when I was older, I think about 15 or 16, I got into drama at school in a big way and I didn't want to play violin at all, I wanted to direct, direct plays. That was another thing that was pulling me away from music. But it was always—I was still doing it all the time. When I wanted to be doing these other things I was still playing the violin.

ML: It sounds as though your parents rather early on helped you structure playing the violin in an—as if it were a job. The 5-day-a-week thing—did it work that way or am I just making an inference?

SR: No, they tried to make it structured and they would say, "OK, so this week you need to practice, so you need to practice 30 minutes every day." They would put that kind of—I mean it wasn't strict—they didn't like lock me in the study and say "practice the violin," but they structured it so that I could, you know, so it was happening the same time every day. And that's how I managed to keep going.

ML: The teacher that you moved then to, did you continue then to commute from Hampshire to London? After when you went to the Royal Academy and you started studying with . . .

SR: Actually what happened was, when this lady threw me out of the class, I was very unhappy because she was a bully basically, she would shout and scream at me every week and tell me that I was a bad boy and a bad violinist. It really got me down. And I was the only boy in this class, all the others were little girls who did exactly as they were told and along came this, this boy who wouldn't do as he was told. So I left and then I went to the Academy. But I didn't study violin there,

I just took orchestra and theory and all those classes. And I studied violin with a teacher who was at the Academy and also lived quite close to where I lived. So I studied with her and she was the total opposite. She was a 70-year-old lady, about five foot two, very very sweet and gentle. Quite a change after this screaming woman.

ML: You brought up something that interests me and that is the different experience that boys and girls have starting with musical instruments. Did you find that the fact that you're a boy made a difference in the kind of experiences you had?

SR: Yes. I think so. I often felt embarrassed that I played the violin because I didn't think it was a very kind of boyish thing to do. I mean I was always aware that playing sports and stuff like that, that I always had to be careful that I didn't want to get trampled on, didn't want to get my hands caught in stuff. I wasn't very kind of proud of the fact that I played the violin. And then when I got to the college I found that with this teacher, it was the little girls got on a lot better than I did. It's like a nightmare. It was . . .

ML: This was the dragon lady?

SR: Yea.

ML: When you got to the Royal Academy did you find that some of this embarrassment or different treatment began to fade away or have you been sort of fighting with that all your life?

SR: No, no, I found that it was much better. The Academy has, it seemed to me much more normal, the kids who went there were much more normal and easy going. At the college it was very much the kind of child prodigy, pushy parent kind of scene, which I didn't like at all. At the Academy they just seemed like regular kids who happened to be in music and they had a much better time and kids were fun to be with—it was more like school. So I began to kind of relax there, I think, to what I was doing. And then after a couple of years there I went to the intermediate school, which meant going, taking an afternoon off school and going up on Monday. And I took all my lessons then. Which was great because you actually saw then, the people who were in college, adults, so you felt like you were crossing over from being a teenager to this free college kind of scene. Which was good. And it also got me out into London, and I thought it was good to go to a city when you're that age. And I'd kind of do it by stages, I would like, if I had an hour off one day so I'd go to the end of the street. Then after that I'd run to the other side and down into London. And by the end I was going all over London on my own, at 15 or 16 years old. So it was a good experience.

ML: That's about the same age that Mr. Lorenescu [Steven's teacher] was when he lived in London for a year. He had to go to babysit with his cousins at the British Museum. He would take them down there because he wasn't old enough to go any other place. When you mentioned that the kids at the Academy seemed more normal to you, what does that mean? What does normal mean to you?

SR: They didn't seem to be totally involved in music. They seemed to have other interests. The kids at the Academy, I mean at the college, it seemed that all they did was—they seemed very precious and kind of fragile, you couldn't push these kids around, they were all impeccably dressed and their parents were running around with them holding their violin and taking them to class and you know, it was really weird. At the Academy they were kids, they looked just like regular kids I saw at school everyday.

ML: Umhum . . . Were they less talented?

SR: Yes, I would say they probably were less talented. They seemed older, there were a lot of kids at the college who were 9 or 10 and they went there on Saturday with their parents, who were just, the parents would literally just sit there in the canteen or outside the lesson all day. They'd sit with their kids and then they'd shunt them to the next place. But the kids at the Academy had been put on a train, you know, and told to go and do it themselves.

ML: It sounds as though you really appreciated the experience of learning independence early, and also being treated just like an ordinary kid.

SR: Yes. I think it helped me kind of, I suppose come to terms with playing the violin and just doing something a bit different, but realizing that ordinary people go and play the violin just as much as ordinary kids went and did whatever else they did on Saturday.

ML: So you started at the Academy when you were about 15?

SR: Yes, 16, I think . . .

ML: What happened then? What was the next step in your education?

SR: Then I got into the Academy full-time as a student. I won an entrance scholarship to there. So I went there for the 4 years before I came here . . .

ML: When you come out of the Academy, do you have a diploma or a degree in the same way we do? Or is it a conserv- . . .

SR: You have a diploma in violin. And then, that's after 3 years and then after the fourth year is a, you stay on usually and they have a recital to play, to play in which is quite difficult. I got like a pass but I didn't get the distinction, like Diedre has that one. So I didn't get half that, but most people stay in for 4 years.

ML: What does that prepare you to do? The distinction or the kind of diploma that you got?

SR: It doesn't really prepare you for a lot because it just allows you to study for another year. And I think probably to achieve your best playing, I think. Because you haven't got so many of the other pressures on you that you have had for the other 3 years—all the classes. You just concentrate on your violin. It doesn't really prepare you for a lot. I mean, the Academy is a kind of dinosaur really. You know I found this more when I left the place, that they only prepare you for like, if you were going to be a soloist or you were destined for some kind of great career that they didn't really realize that everybody in that place was going to end up in an orchestra probably, and only a handful would ever achieve what they were preparing you for.

ML: And yet you said that one of the things that was neat for you was when you came as a younger person and you saw the grown-ups, and it sort of showed you the way to go. What way were they showing you to go?

SR: Well, I think they were just showing you what could be achieved.

ML: In terms of technical playing?

SR: Yea, the standards that you could achieve there. I mean, I'm not saying that everybody who was at the Academy was no good, I mean there were some very talented people there and you could see that. And they were almost on display there. That gave you, it was an eye opener.

Summary

In his classic survey of research methods in sociology, Denzin (1978) proposes six criteria to assess interview transcripts: (1) communication of meaning, (2) expression of respondent interest, (3) clarity of question and response, (4) precision of interviewer intention, (5) integration of intent within interviewer questions, and (6) interviewer management of potential respondent fabrication.

Novice researchers can balance the rigor of these criteria with Lofland's suggestion that constructing an effective interview is like solving a puzzle. Investigators play with the pieces, collect as many as possible, and organize them in alternative patterns; then they use answers obtained in trial administrations of their plans as their major outlining guide.

PARTICIPATION OBSERVATION

Participant observation is the primary data collection technique used by ethnographers. Participant observers live as much as possible with the individuals they are investigating, trying to blend in and taking part in their daily activities. Participant observers watch what people do, listen to what people say, and interact with participants. Ethnographers become learners, so as to be socialized by participants into the group under investigation (Burnett, 1974b). This stance, of a child, novice, or student, is familiar to most people. All human groups socialize, or teach, new members of their group. Ethnographers and other qualitative researchers take advantage of this ordinary human practice to acquire knowledge about the group they are studying (Wolcott, 1988).

As we noted in Chapter Two, some researchers define participant observation as an overall research design (e.g., Bogdan, 1972; Jacobs, 1970; Jorgensen, 1989); here, however, we discuss it as a method of collecting data. It is a method relying on watching, listening, asking questions, and collecting things. What is perceived and collected is recorded; we present means of recording later in this chapter.

Participant observation is usually combined with other means of gathering data—surveys and interviews in their various forms, artifact and document collection, as well as more structured kinds of observation. Sometimes these methods are so enmeshed in one another that researchers cannot say where the interview leaves off and the participant observing begins.

Placed together, all of these activities are time consuming. Participant observation studies are usually planned over a unit of time defined by the group studied as a cycle of some collection of events. Research among subsistence or agriculture societies customarily follows the seasons of the year until a full cycle of activities has been observed. In industrial and postindustrial societies cycles are less often dependent on the weather. For example, school studies in the United States may last 9 months, following students from the beginning to the end of tenure at one grade level. Studies of student teachers, in contrast, may be much shorter, running only for the 10- or 16-week term that the novices are practicing in schools.

Participant observers elicit from people their definitions of reality and the organizing constructs of their world. Because people express these ideas in language, ethnographers must learn the argot, dialects, and other linguistic variations used by participants. For example, researchers studying children and teenagers in schools become familiar with and imperturbable toward current juvenile work usage and behavior (see Campbell, 1984; Fine, 1987; McLaren, 1980; McLeod, 1987; Roman, 1988; Weis, 1990). Similarly, school ethnographers recognize the tendency for teacher talk to center around descriptions of what is socially acceptable, rather than what teachers actually do (Ginsburg, 1989; Keddie, 1971). They also collect the stories, anecdotes, and myths which people created to express their dominant concerns—material found in the daily round of gossip in the teachers' lounge or among student groups—in the hallways, the bathrooms, or around the school entrance at the beginning and end of the school day. These can tell an ethnographer much about the themes critical to teachers, parents, and children; they indicate what is important and unimportant, how people view each other, and how they evaluate their participation in groups and programs.

One problem researchers encounter is that participant reports of activities and beliefs may not match their observed behavior. Participant observation is a check, enabling the researcher to verify that individuals are doing what they (and the researcher) believe they are doing. For example, curriculum evaluators use participant observation to determine whether people are processing information or reacting to a curricular innovation in the manner intended. What they find is that participants respond to innovations in a variety of unintended ways (cf. e.g., Corwin, 1973; Deyhle, 1989, 1992; Grant, 1989; Puckett, 1989; Smith & Carpenter, 1972; Smith & Schumacher, 1972; Whitford, 1986). In their classic ethnography of the development of an innovative elementary school, Smith & Keith (1971) document how the implementation of innovations differs from intended designs. Their study stands as an exemplar of discontinuities between the goals and objectives of educational reform and the means available to achieve these ends.

More recently, Grant (1989) and Puckett (1989) used ethnohistorical studies, combining participant observation with historical material to trace the interaction of innovative practice with social policy and material, demographic, and political events. Grant examined the impact of changing demographic composition, federal educational legislation and court mandates, and innovative practice on teachers, administrators, and students in one high school. Puckett linked the successes, failures, and longevity of the Foxfire projects of Elliot Wiggington to changes in context, personnel, and resources, as well as to changes in Wiggington's personality. Deyhle's study (1986, 1989, 1992) of dropout prevention programs illustrates how prejudice and racism can be denied verbally but enacted and perpetuated in classroom and extracurricular activities, hiring practices, disbursal of funds, and differential treatment of Anglo-Mormon and Indian students and their parents.

VARIATIONS IN PARTICIPANT OBSERVATION

Participant observation is varied by combining it with other research methods and by involving different people in observation. In some cases, participants may collaborate with participant observers (e.g., Smith & Geoffrey, 1968), reviewing the day's production of field notes to correct researcher misperceptions and misinterpretations. Some researchers (e.g., Carroll, 1977; Gitlin & Smyth, 1989; Romagnano, 1991) are partners with participants, keeping dual accounts of their own observations alongside participant comments. More commonly, ethnographers request reactions to working analyses or processed material from selected informants (e.g., Wolcott, 1973).

Traditionally, participant observation as practiced by anthropologists and sociologists has been defined in terms of its nonjudgmental stance in acquiring data to depict social groups and cultural scenes authentically. Since the 1970s, however, it has been adopted by educational evaluators to study how and the extent to which innovations are implemented. Ethnographic evaluation has been useful in assessing long-term success or failure of innovations as well as documenting the processes of change (Center for New Schools, 1972; Fetterman & Pitman, 1986; Grant, 1989).

Participant observation and interviewing also have been combined in different ways with questionnaires and other standardized instruments. Deal (1975) did this in a comparative evaluation of two alternative high schools in which organizational success and failure depended on the resolution of authority problems. Richberg's evaluation (1976) of a Follow-Through Program in a Choctaw Indian community identifies comparable obstructions to effective program implementation, deriving from conflicting authority jurisdictions. Trend (1979) demonstrates how resolving discrepancies between participant observation data and conventionally quantified outcome measures in an evaluation of a federal housing program for low-income families contributed to a more comprehensive explanation for problems arising in such programs.

A number of researchers have organized groups of participant observers to collect similar data. Some ethnographers have developed observational frames that provide focus for what they observe and record; these can be used by other researchers. Several researchers have even developed schema for data collection in ethnographic research in education; their objective is to facilitate comparison of studies across research sites (Ogbu, 1988; Dobbert & Kurth-Schai, 1992; Pitman et al., 1989).

In evaluation studies, LaBelle, Moll, & Weisner (1979) have proposed a research strategy for collecting data to produce valid and reliable information on program effects. In applying participant observation to evaluation, other investigators (e.g., Burns, 1975; Center for New Schools, 1976; Everhart, 1976; Herriott, 1977) have identified areas of discrepant-value orientations, patterns of social interaction, and methods for conflict resolution among program participants, program developers and evaluators, and policy makers that obstruct achievement of program objectives. Some of these factors have been formulated for examination and assessment across multiple sites. (See Pitman & Maxwell, 1992, for a discussion of multisite ethnographic and qualitative evaluations.)

GUIDELINES FOR DIRECTING OBSERVATION

The framework that follows summarizes what participant observers watch for and listen to and indicates how they organize their activities. It synthesizes the observational grids used by anthropologists and field sociologists; categories of focus overlap because the data they reflect can be interpreted in many ways.

1. *Who* is in the group or scene? How many people are there, and what are their kinds, identities, and relevant characteristics? How is membership in the group or scene acquired?
2. *What* is happening here? What are the people in the group or scene doing and saying to one another?
   a. What behaviors are repetitive, and which occur irregularly? In what events, activities, or routines are participants engaged? What resources are used in these activities, and how are they allocated? How are activities organized, labeled, explained, and justified? What differing social contexts can be identified?
   b. How do the people in the group behave toward one another? What is the nature of this participation and interaction? How are the people connected or related to one another? What statuses and roles are evident in this interaction? Who makes what decisions for whom? How do the people organize themselves for interactions?
   c. What is the content of participant's conversations? What subjects are common, and which are rare? What stories, anecdotes, and homilies do they exchange? What verbal and nonverbal languages do they use for communication? What beliefs do the content of their conversations demonstrate? What formats do the conversations follow? What processes do they reflect? Who talks and who listens?
3. *Where* is the group or scene located? What physical settings and environments form their contexts? What natural resources are evident, and what technologies are created or used? How does the group allocate and use space and physical objects? What is consumed, and what is produced? What sights, sounds, smells, tastes, and textures are found in the contexts that the group uses?
4. *When* does the group meet and interact? How often are these meetings, and how lengthy are they? How does the group conceptualize, use, and distribute time? How do participants view the past, present, and future?

5. *How* are the identified elements connected or interrelated, either from the participants' point of view or from the researcher's perspective? How is stability maintained? How does change originate, and how is it managed? How are the identified elements organized? What rules, norms, or mores govern this social organization? How is power conceptualized and distributed? How is this group related to other groups, organizations, or institutions?

6. *Why* does the group operate as it does? What meanings do participants attribute to what they do? What is the group's history? What goals are articulated in the group? What symbols, traditions, values, and world views can be found in the group?

No participant observer can address all of these questions, even in the examination of a single group scene. However, the preceding framework does indicate major areas of observational focus. Researchers unfamiliar with ethnography and qualitative research often express dismay at the prospect of attempting to record everything happening in a social situation, cultural scene, or institutional group. Likewise, novice ethnographers express frustration at their inability to get it all down. However, neither recording everything nor getting it all down are attainable goals for participant observers. The interactive stream is too complex and too subtle to be captured completely, even by a team of observers.

Most participant observers accept the more achievable goal of recording phenomena salient to the topic they have defined, documenting what they have omitted and why. Wolcott (1982), for example, differentiates between what does and does not require recording and describing; he draws on Goodenough's formulation (1976) of culture as a construct validly attributed to a group by an ethnographer, using relevant and accurate data. Participant observers use their long-term field residence to assure ample opportunity to observe and record salient data and make sound decisions about what to exclude and include.

These decisions depend on a number of factors: the research topic, the theoretical and conceptual frameworks informing a study, the data that begin to emerge as the participant observer interacts in the daily flow of events and activities, and the intuitive reactions and hunches that participant observers experience as all of these factors come together. The diversity of such factors across research sites creates the variety among ethnographies. Nevertheless, commonalities also occur.

Some of the similarities and many of the differences across social scenes are evident in the next section, where we present an account from a participant observation study. It illustrates data addressing many of the questions posed in the guidelines presented previously in the chapter.

EXAMPLE OF PARTICIPANT OBSERVATION

These notes were taken during an 8-year study of Navajo adolescence and schooling; they represent what the ethnographer, Donna Deyhle, wrote as her first distillation from raw field notes (see section on field notes at the end of this chapter) or scratch notes taken immediately after the event. They include Deyhle's description of the event and, in brackets, some of the thoughts and comments she had during the event. This transcript also illustrates some of the difficulties in recording events when many things are happening, rapidly, all at once.

Earlier notes describe a fight that had broken out between a Navajo and an Anglo student. Police were called to the school. The Navajo student went to jail, and the Anglo student was released to his parents. Navajos demanded a meeting to discuss the situation with school officials; 75 parents, students, and members of the community gathered at the community center, along with the school district and the tribal lawyer, the superintendent, the high school principals, several teachers, and the local sheriff. The meeting began at 7:30 PM. Deyhle noted in her field notes that tempers were running high.

CONCERNED PARENTS MEETING: 2-18-87
AFTER RACIAL FIGHTS AT THE SCHOOL

J.S. [president of the parent association] It kind of hurts to hear this information. The parents hurt over this. The parents have come to me with the problem, when kids come home and say they have been thrown around, they can't concentrate on their work. It hurts. Word gets around that the Indians are having an uprising. No. It is not true. We want our kids to go to school and do well. They are far behind. We want them to do well in academics. I hope we can talk about this. It gets worse every time we talk. I hear the police came into school and took him away. This is not fair, to knock around youth. If this is happening in school, I want to know about it.

J.S. sat down and J. H. [principal of high school where fight occurred] stood up, glanced at notes on yellow pad, cleared throat. Let me express very strongly that there are a lot of things that cannot occur in a school for students to succeed. One thing is that they must feel safe. One of our goals is that it be a safe place. A week ago, following a school dance, a group of Anglos and Navajos got into a fight. They have a history of not getting along. The following week there was a fight in the school, only one blow. I didn't talk to the Anglo boy because the police did.

The Navajo student accused of the fight interrupted. "You have a problem. The Anglo started it. He was picking on a little kid and was told to stop. Then he fought me."

The principal shook his head in disagreement. Several Navajo students yelled out that Anglo students are always picking on and making fun of Navajos. The principal, still standing, responded.

This is the first time I have heard this. I didn't know the Indian students were being picked on.

A Navajo senior from the front row stood and faced the principal. We are never asked. I was not asked. I never get anything from Anglos.

[It is clear that Indians don't feel that either school officials or Anglos in general will listen to them. POWERLESS!!] Her mother asked, "Why is it so hard for the kids to go to you with their problems?" This brought several comments from parents about Indian youth and the judicial system. A mother sitting next to me leaned over and whispered, "That juvenile detention place. It's an Indian institution. My son grew up in there!" The young woman persisted. I don't like the way Whites treat Indians. Why do you believe what the Anglo students say only? It's one side in this case. Can you guarantee that they won't continue?

The Navajo crowd clapped. The principal responded. "We can talk about it. No, I can't guarantee. That's what you have to do as an individual. You have to take it." Murmurs of discontent around the room. The principal continued. Rumors of a fight were all around the school on Thursday so I called the police. There was no fight that day. Because of the tension we invited the police in to investigate. On Friday there was a fight. Both students were taken in and charged.

The tribal lawyer stood and asked the principal, "Is it true that the Anglo student was not charged and the Navajo was?" The principal said "Yes" [very softly]. Again the crowd muttered disapproval. "_____ [the cop] tried to get me to fight him," shouted the Navajo youth involved in the fight. "He said, 'Come and fight me.' They told me not to step a foot in the school. Not to ever come back." The principal then made a speech defending the police.

There was a pause for translation into Navajo. The principal urged parents to come to him with their problems. If you feel your kids have been made fun of you should come up to the school. You must come up to the school. We will do everything we can to help you. If I can't help, you can go to the superintendent and say, "That crazy principal can't help us." That is the avenue we have in the district. We will do everything to help.

At this point the superintendent stood and moved to the front of the room, standing by the principal. Some talk ensued about the need for a Navajo liaison person—a proposal supported by the parents.

J.S.: It is a problem when we have an aide who is an Anglo. That doesn't understand Indian kids.

Navajo county official: We will talk it over with the Indian school board. We also need to reevaluate the police officers' role in this.

Home Liaison Person: There is a great, great miscommunication between the school and parents. That person [the policeman] is not bilingual. A new person needs to be hired. That is what I want to say. I know.

Superintendent: I want to say two things. We expect a lot of our principals, but not to be policemen. We don't expect them to do that. We have a good relationship with the police so we turn problems over to the police. And the school gives up jurisdiction. Second, the world is a great place. I hope that the students we turn out have great opportunities. _____ and _____ high school are good schools, not perfect schools. They are better than the other schools in the area.

An elderly Navajo woman brought the discussion back to discrimination. Why is it so hard for us to understand that we have this problem? It has been this way for years. I think the problem is that we have the police treating people differently. So you see, the policeman is the problem.

Other similar comments followed. My boy is handicapped. Anglo boys threatened to kill him in P. E. I have no gas or car to go up to the high school to talk to that principal. I won't send my boy to school so he can be killed," said one mother. A father said, "I hear that the Indian students go to the office and Anglos make fun of them [and say] that they stink. And it's my understanding that when Indians try to excel and do good, they get pushed around for it. We Navajos like to praise you when you do good. We don't like to beat up others." Another mother said, "I used to go to that high school. I bear tragedy with the students now. The higher I went, the greater pressure I got. So I left and went to the BIA school to graduate." Then an elderly medicine man spoke. We are just telling stories about each other now. We who were in the incident should be up front talking. When my kids were in school, it was the same. And we are still trying to solve this problem. These kids who were talking tonight were in elementary school when my kids had this problem in high school. And I think the kids who are in elementary school now will also have this problem.

We need to talk about it. Each time we talk about it the problem continues.

The meeting ended shortly before midnight. The school officials left quickly; many of the Navajo parents and students continued to talk in small groups. I sat with the family of the accused Navajo student. His mother-in-law, who had gone to school with the vice principal 20 years ago, complained that she should have told him, "You know what it is like for the high school kids. You used to do the same things the kids are doing now against Indians. You remember when you put the pins in my seat? All the things you used to do to Indians? It is still going on here and now. You did it, and now your kids are doing it."

Charges were dropped against the Navajo youth, but he wasn't allowed to return to school. "They told me I was 18 so I could not go to high school anymore. I was told to go to adult education and finish."

SUMMARY

One concern most participant observers have is balancing the two activities, participating and observing. Everyone in the course of everyday events, after all, observes and participates with other people. The intensity and concentration people bring to these behaviors vary from little to much. Most people find that the two are related. Concentrating on observation reduces the ability to participate well; participating fully in events can interfere with the scope and depth of observation. Despite this connection, the involvement with each is not negatively related. For example, a skilled observer may be using maximum participation to elicit rich data, which will be recorded, as Deyhle did, at a later time.

Although we distinguish nonparticipant observation from participant observation and discuss it separately in the chapter, we emphasize here that these are matters of degree, not of kind. We distinguish the two on the basis of the predominant role taken by the researcher. A researcher who assumes a recognized role—often one inherent to the group under study—and who plays out that role fully is a participant observer. A nonparticipant observer, as we describe in the next section of this chapter, is a researcher whose only position in a group is to document and record events. However, despite making these distinctions, we also emphasize that most researchers in the field move back and forth between these two stances, as indicated in Fig. 6.1.

The data collection methods discussed thus far require, directly or indirectly, the researcher's physical proximity and interaction with study

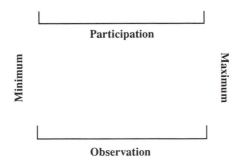

Figure 6.1 Dimensions of participation in observational research.

participants. By contrast, noninteractive strategies for collecting qualitative data allow researchers to gather material with minimal exchange between them and participants of a study. The two methods discussed below, nonparticipant observation and artifact collection, are less reactive or obtrusive than interactive strategies (Webb *et al.*, 1966) because the researcher is less likely to influence participant responses. On the other hand, noninteractive methods may prevent investigators from locating the data they need to identify the objects or processes they find or to address initial themes and questions. Furthermore, in the absence of "feedback from the field" or participants, these methods may suffer from validity problems. They provide little indication of whether researchers and participants shared definitions and interpretations of observed events.

Noninteractive Methods

NONPARTICIPANT OBSERVATION

Collecting data through nonparticipant observation differs from participant observation in several ways (Gold, 1958; Pelto & Pelto, 1978). First, nonparticipant observation requires a detached, neutral, and unobtrusive observer. Researchers assume this stance by positioning themselves on the margins of social events or by withdrawing from the site, leaving audio or videotape machines to record the data. The researcher's objective shifts from a central concern for participant meaning to a focus on participant behaviors. The behaviors do include what people say and how they say it, but nonparticipant observers avoid interrupting to seek clarification—a procedure integral to more interactive methods. Although participant meaning may be inferred from records of what is done and said, meaning is less directly accessible than it is through the preceding interactive strategies. However, derived or inferred meanings can be triangulated with data obtained through more direct procedures, thus providing means for their validation and verification.

Second, nonparticipant observation rarely is used as the initial, exploratory method in addressing problems, topics, and settings; it is more appropriate for refinement and verification stages of the research process. When used in nonparticipant observation, the general categories providing initial focus for participant observation are narrowed, focused, and abstracted. Nonparticipant observation is a derivative technique, introduced after more generative strategies have indicated which interactions are salient for recording. Barker & Wright's narrative (1951) of one child's day is the exception to the general practice of using nonparticipant observation as one technique within a triangulated research design (e.g., Gearing & Epstein, 1982) or as a method of refining or verifying patterns generated in an earlier study (e.g., LeCompte, 1975, 1978).

Third, nonparticipant observation is used when researchers require comprehensive, detailed, and representative accounts of individuals' behaviors. It requires observers to concentrate on a complete and accurate recording of sensory data. Social exchange with participants in a scene is distracting and leads to distortions and omissions in the record. The researcher seeks to capture the interaction occurring when no external observer is present. Consequently, nonparticipant observers seek minimal involvement in whatever they are recording. They position themselves and their recording equipment in a location as unobtrusively as possible. The challenge is to fade into a scene while remaining separate from it. Although participant observers depend on long-term incorporation into social interaction to reduce reactivity, nonparticipant observers rely for concealment on manipulating space and physical objects. When this is difficult, researchers may conduct their studies in two phases: a participative phase to develop rapport, elicit constructs, and produce protocols and instruments, and a nonparticipative phase to record details.

Nonparticipant observation requires researchers to make a series of recursive decisions. The units of analysis usually are specified prior to collection of data; the means of recording observations are chosen for appropriateness to the identified units; strategies for selecting or sampling recorded units are chosen; and trials or pilot studies are used to refine techniques. Complete nonparticipant observation exists, of course, only where the observer views the behavior of others via hidden cameras and recorders or from behind one-way mirrors. By contrast, participant observation is involved, intimate, and reflexive; researchers study themselves as well as other participants in a social setting. However, regardless of their stance, researchers always are given some role and status whenever they become observers. In conducting studies in school settings, for example, investigators necessarily interact with teachers and students, if only nonverbally. This need not be a liability: It simply means that the estimated consequences of being a participant must be noted in the research report. In the remainder of this section, we describe three forms of nonparticipant observation commonly used by educational ethnographers: stream-of-behavior chronicles, analysis of proxemics and kinesics, and interaction analysis.

STREAM-OF-BEHAVIOR CHRONICLES

Recording and analyzing streams of behaviors in narrative chronicles, delineated by Barker (1963), requires accurate, minute-by-minute accounts of what a participant does and says. These may be filmed, taped, or recorded by hand on the spot. Barker & Wright's exhaustive and minute account (1951) of each action during a day in the life of a 7-year-old boy may be the most extreme example of this strategy. Cognitive anthropologists (e.g., Holland & Quinn, 1987) and sociolinguists (e.g., Manning, 1987; Moerman, 1988) also use chronicles of verbal and nonverbal behavior. Stream-of-behavior chronicles are used in microethnography (Erickson, 1992; Gee, Michaels, & O'Connor, 1992) to produce videotaped recordings of behavior streams as a data base. Erickson and his colleagues (Erickson & Shultz, 1982; Erickson & Mohatt, 1982), Mehan (1978, 1979), and Shultz & Florio (1979) are educational ethnographers who have used selective videorecording in microethnography.

Researchers sample across participants, events, and settings to collect chronicles pertinent to their themes and questions. For example, Peshkin (1972) sampled for stream-of-behavior narratives in his study of the effects of schooling on children in a traditional African culture. Patterns of behavior among children were compared across six cultures by Whiting & Whiting (1975) and Whiting & Edwards (1988), who analyzed behavior streams sampled from children in these cultures. Goetz (1976a,b) developed a taxonomy of classroom behavior among third graders, based on stream-of-behavior narratives intermittently sampled from her participants. LeCompte (1975, 1978), on the other hand, took continual stream-of-behavior records in her comparative analysis of the normative behaviors of four elementary schoolteachers (see subsequent example).

These methods help nonparticipant observers to delineate categories of activities, study the use of time and motion, and map movement and the physical environment. Stream-of-behavior chronicles generate process data for investigations of how materials are manipulated or what styles teachers use. However, Pelto & Pelto (1978) qualify the use of data collected through stream-of-behavior chronicles to situations where researchers can validate their interpretations only through participant observation, key-informant interviewing, or surveys. Similarly, Mishler (1986) and Smith & Brock (1970) note the philosophical biases of observational and recording strategies and units of analysis neither meaningful to nor shared by the research participants.

PROXEMICS AND KINESICS

These approaches are concerned with social uses of space and with bodily movement. Proxemics is the study of how people use space (Hall, 1974; Forston, 1975; Scherer, 1974, 1975); kinesics is the study of how people move (Birdwhistell, 1970; Prost, 1975). Educational ethnographers informally incorporate observational records of movement and space use with other narratives (e.g., Rist, 1970; Goetz, 1976b; Larkins & Oldham, 1976). Shultz & Florio (1979), however, focused on an analysis of classroom space in investigating the development of social competence among primary-level students. Guilmet (1978, 1979), Mohatt & Erickson (1981), Vogt (1985), and Tharp (1989) use kinesic analysis in their comparisons of differing behavior styles of native American, native Hawaiian, and white children and of differential teacher reactions to such styles. Aiello & Jones (1971) and Scherer (1974) have conducted similar comparisons across race and socioeconomic class of children's use of space. Proxemics and kinesics are useful when investigations focus on use of classroom space or patterns of teacher–student interaction (e.g., Leviz-Pilz, 1982). Proxemics, kinesics, and stream-of-behavior and language studies all are facilitated by the use of audio and videotaping equipment.

INTERACTION ANALYSIS PROTOCOLS

Nonparticipant observation also includes a variety of interaction analysis protocols. (For detailed discussions of interaction analysis protocols, see Bales, 1950; Medley & Mitzel, 1963; Rosenshine & Furst, 1973; Evertson & Green, 1986.) These range in structure from informal sociograms devised on the spot by the observer to standardized behavioral rating systems such as that developed by Flanders (1970). The focus of these methods for collecting data is record how participants interact with each other. The protocols are based on operationally defined interactional categories. Phenomena not matching these a priori constructs are excluded. Educational ethnographers tend to reject Flanders-like systems, despite their reliability and generalizability, because such systems record only a few, narrowly defined categories of behavior and because they rarely match emerging patterns of concern. More frequently, investigators devise their own protocols, based on early observations in the field. For example, Borman (1978) coded group participation according to numbers of individuals involved when she examined patterns of social control across differentially structured classroom environments. Although most such analyses focus on student–student or teacher–student interaction patterns, comparable examinations of interaction styles among and between groups of teachers, administrators, curriculum developers, and policy makers contribute both process data and values data to investigations of the broader educational milieu (cf., e.g., Bellack, Kleibard, Hyman, & Smith, 1966; Hymes, 1967; Peterson, Wilkinson, & Hallinan, 1984; Sinclair & Coulthard, 1975).

CODING NONPARTICIPANT OBSERVATIONS

Counting or enumerating items requires that the items be defined and located within the data records. This process is coding. Items to be counted can be defined prior to, during, or after data collection; they can be defined by the participants, by the researcher, or by the researcher and participants together. These frequency counts require limited, precise, and concrete analytic units. They also require that the researcher have noted all possible instances of the unit while recording the data. Otherwise the count may be distorted by selective perception or notation. Although researchers can code their observations qualitatively and holistically, they also ask valid and reliable frequency counts with the questions, "How many?" "How often?" or "How much?" Such questions require units that are clearly and unequivocally countable (cf. Johnson & Johnson, 1990).

   This means recording data when they occur, whether the data are naturally occurring behaviors or categories of action abstracted from a more complex behavior stream. Counting data from reconstructed accounts made after the event risk distortion from memory loss. These accounts are too selective for the enumerative purposes of nonparticipant observation. As one Smithsonian archaeological study indicated, people participating in a dig cannot remember 1 hour after observation whether they saw three human skulls or ten, some potsherds or none at all, a collection of human bones or a mixture of animal and human remains (Fowke, 1910).

   Films, still photographs, and audio and videotapes provide accurate and retrievable records to code for frequency counts. Field notes and observational protocols are also used. However the data are recorded, field tests are required for a nonparticipant observation protocol or design. Its effectiveness and validity may depend upon tailoring it to the natural setting in ways that could not be anticipated during planning phases.

EXAMPLE FROM A NONPARTICIPANT OBSERVATION STUDY

In the next chapter we discuss how to construct categories for coding. Here we display an example of field note data coded for enumerative analysis. The excerpts shown in Table 6.2 represent two of the four fourth-grade classrooms LeCompte studied in her 1975 nonparticipant observation study of teacher behavior. They are of handwritten transcripts and focus on what the teachers said. They were coded to reflect activity segments, time allocations, and frequency of specific types of verbal behavior. Both classrooms were in a large city in the Southwest; the students were from middle- to lower-middle-income families.

The first excerpt, from predominantly Hispanic Valley School, includes instructional activities at the beginning of the day after initial rituals of dispensing with coats, taking attendance, collecting lunch money, and warm-up discussions about events of the preceding evening and early morning.

The second excerpt, from predominantly Anglo Heights School, covers events in the afternoon, a time when the teacher occasionally departed from the daily schedule she wrote on the blackboard each morning. Although the Valley School teacher had arranged her room around learning centers and followed no particular schedule for instructional activities, students in Heights School sat in neat rows faced away from the teacher's desk. Classroom organization reflected the principal's predilection for structure and order, and the teacher followed a standard schedule each day.

In both cases, the researcher sat somewhere in the back of the room, usually at a student desk out of the flow of classroom traffic. Observational time was devoted to recording by hand as rapidly as possible whatever the teacher said. Ground rules established at the beginning of each 3-month observation period specified that, while in the classroom, the researcher would respond to direct questions from students but would refrain from any instructional activity. Insofar as it was possible, she tried to become part of the furniture.

In addition to recording classroom talk, the observer noted the time of day every 5 minutes or whenever an activity shifted. Preliminary categories for classroom activities and teacher talk had been developed during

TABLE 6.2
Two Elementary Schools: A Field Note Excerpt[a]

Valley School

Pat, the teacher, is sitting on a student's desk at the front of the room. The students' desks are haphazardly scattered throughout the room; four girls have pushed theirs together in a row diagonally across the room; some are clustered in twos and others are by themselves. There is no teacher desk immediately visible; it is obscured in the corner behind boxes of materials and a motorcycle engine.

9:06		T2A	(T2A) "OK, now let's start." (Todd comes up and gives her a nickel.) "OK, now here's our new word for the day. What is it?" (She writes it on the board.) "Bazaar." (She writes *bizarre* and *bazaar* on the board, explains the differences. Goes through sentences using *bizarre* to illustrate bizarre things [italics added].)
	Discussion		
9:10		T2A	(T2A) "OK, I would like you to pay attention. We've had some problems with money. What's a dollar sign?" (Children shout the answer. She explains how to read numbers as money.) "Now, I want you to pretend you just bought a house. Now, you gotta be careful because houses cost lots of money." (Writes $2856000 on the board. Larry volunteers the decimal placement.) "Darn, I couldn't fool you. Let's see if I can fool this young man." (Does another. He gets it right.) "Who wants a more expensive house—Bernie?" (Does another.) "Let's see, I haven't heard from some of these girls. Aila, that's what I spent at the grocery store." (Does another.)
	Explication		
9:15			"Decimal points are very important when we are writing money numbers." (She demonstrates how to add with decimals by using money numbers. She adds them wrong so that the children can correct them, calling out corrections from the classroom.) "One way to help yourself, people, is to make sure all your dots line up. (R1A) All right, boys and girls, when you get your answers, be sure to put decimal points in."
9:30		R1A	
		T2A	(T2A) "OK, everybody, a pencil and a paper. We're going to do some problems." (Comes over to me and tells me that it is not what she had planned to do but that it was a good introduction to decimals and that they needed the practice in this.)
	Getting organized		
		A6	(A6) "Remember two things. It's very important if you want a hundred—dollar signs and decimal points. (T3C) I'll give you 15 minutes to do these. (T2A) OK, are we ready to start? (W1B) When we finish this, work on contracts—your math contracts. If you don't have one, we'll have a conference and make up one for you. OK, here we go . . ."
		T3C	
		T2A	
9:26		W1B	
9:30			

(continues)

TABLE 6.2
(*Continued*)

9:34	Seatwork	R2G	(She starts writing addition problems on the board. The children are all copying and adding.) "It's 15 problems in 20 minutes." (She explains to three children how to add them.) (R2G) "Mike, do your own." (She continues writing problems on board.)
			(She goes over to the reading area and starts reading over her plan for the day. It is the first time I have seen her with a lesson plan.)

Heights School

The children are coming in from recess. They file quietly to their seats. Some straggle in late. Sara, the teacher, is standing at the front of the room.

1:50		T2A	(T2A) "Each one of you get a piece of scrap paper and we'll
		T2B	add up the total scores" (on a team math-quiz). "Whoever got the least number wrong is the winner. Ready? (T2B) C'mon, hurry up, you are too late" (to children who are straggling in from the drinking fountain). "In one column put 0, then 5, 0, 3" (she reads off the number-wrong scores).
		T3A	(A few children are still entering.) "OK? Now, add. Next
		R2G	column? (T3A) People who came in late, put your heads down. Don't bug us. (R2C) Mr. Campbell, don't get up, just put your head down." (She reads the list of numbers.) "Add each column and hush." (Kids say, "I've got it.") "Wait, wait a minute." (She calls on students to give answers.) "You
		A3B	know who brought down Eddy's team? The captain of the
		A4	team. (A4) Eddy, you missed 21. (A3B) And Leslie, 15.
		A3B	(A3B) I threw out Daniel's and David Sanchez's and
		A4	Timmie's and Janet's papers because they would have pulled the scores down so much." (She reads the scores of each kid.) (A4) "Eddy, you missed 21. That means you really need practice. Your team had more 100s but you brought
		A4	it down. (A4) *YOU* are the one." (She continues reading scores.) "Mike Campbell, great! 100! I was real proud of the ones who got 100 and minus one, but there were some who pulled it down—that's how averages go." (She goes back to
		A4	her desk at the back of the room.) (A4) (Reads off the names of those whose papers she threw out.) "Nobody in fourth grade should take so long. We are going to start on 7s next
		T2A	week and you were way behind the limit." (T2A)
	Seatwork	W1B	"Now, finish your *Weekly Reader* while I (W1B) finish cutting up paper for your art work." (She goes to get some paper. Stops to help two kids with words from *Weekly Reader*.
	Getting organized	R1A	They ask what they should do with their papers.) (R1A) "Hang on to them. Hold on to your papers. Just before we go I'll collect them."

TABLE 6.2
(*Continued*)

2:00	Seatwork	R1B	Dale is counting boys and girls for figuring out how much paper to cut. He gets the count wrong. Brenda volunteers, "There are 15 boys and 15 girls." (R1B) "Thank you, Brenda, will you let him do it?"
	Getting organized	T2A T2E T2E T3C	(T2A) "OK, let me see the hands of everybody who is through (T2E) with *all* the spelling. That means B, C, and D. How many are not through? Four. (T2E) Let me see how many have not finished arithmetic? That was page 134 . . . (T3C)
	T2A	T2E	I guess I didn't give you enough time. (T2E) How many people in Ventures [reading group] have finished? How about your Building Vocabulary? Let's see, I'll give you art today and give you time to do them on Monday." (The kids sigh with relief. Not many people had finished things and they are glad that they get to do art.)
2:05		T1C R1A	"Let's all clean up our desks . . . How many want to do art? (T1C) Get the desks cleaned (R1A) off like we are going
	R1A		home. Ricky, get two chairs and put them in the front. Not desks; chairs." (The children are cleaning their desks. She's at the back at her desk.) "OK, get out pencils, crayons, glue, and scissors. Kenneth, will you get the record player? I'll
2:10		R1A	give the directions and play the Bill Cosby record Leslie brought. (R1A) Now listen carefully because boys will be doing something different from the girls." (There's some problem finding the record-player extension cord. She gets
		R1B	it set up. [R1B] David Lastin does not have supplies. She lectures him on the need for getting them.) "Your mother got a list of what you were supposed to have, why didn't she get them for you?" (She lost it, or forgot where it was.)
		R1A R2G	"Well, you go tell her you have (R1A) to have them and don't you come here telling me you (R2G) don't have
	R2G		crayons and scissors in fourth grade!"
			"I thought this time we'd do some free art—we've always done the same thing. The boys will make an insect or animal (gives examples) and the girls will make a flower pot with flowers. You can use crepe paper, whatever you want. OK." (She explains what they are to do again.) "What the boys are doing is to use a yellow background and black paper, the girls will have a blue background and you can use any kind of color for the flower." (She hands out paper to kids
		R1A	and tells them to cut it in half and share it.) (R1A) "I don't want you to use books, I want you to do your own work. I don't care if the circles aren't circles and the squares aren't
2:20			square. The boys may start. The girls, I still have to cut some things." (She goes to cut paper.)

---

a From LeCompte (1975).

fieldwork completed prior to this study. The brackets denoting beginnings and endings of activities as well as codes for specific types of verbal behavior were added in the initial stages of analysis after data collection was complete.

These data were used to enumerate teacher talk and to determine which norms individual teachers stressed. These included time orientations, good grades, working hard, problem solving, and cleanliness. Teachers were compared across a variety of behavioral dimensions, including consistency among what they said they did, what their students said they did, and what the observer recorded that they did.

The transcript illustrates several characteristics of nonparticipant observation. It provides sufficient contextual material for the reader to visualize the classroom and interpret the teachers' shifts in topics. It records conversation in sufficient detail that topical units can be abstracted from the behavior stream. These data can be divided into acts, events, and activities (Lofland, 1971), which can be analyzed separately prior to reassembly into a broader analysis of teacher behavior as a whole. The category codes were deductively applied; that is, they were researcher-developed constructs imposed on the stream of behavior, not definitions elicited from the teachers in the study. LeCompte made inferences about the culture of the school based on her observations and subsequent enumeration, but the study was not a phenomenological one—the voice heard is that of the researcher, not the teachers.

The limitations of the data reflect what necessarily was a low-budget, if traditional, approach to data collection. Field notes were recorded in a ring-bound notebook on regular notebook paper; wide left-hand margins were retained for comments and coding. The notebook pages were xeroxed for analysis so that the original data file could be left intact, but they were not otherwise transcribed. No audio or video recording equipment was used to support the field notes. Teacher talk was recorded as comprehensively and accurately as the researchers' ability to take dictation permitted. Although the adequacy of this technique was corroborated by piloting with several other observers, the lack of a supplementary recording device meant that some sentences inevitably were missed.

Because some teachers talk more or speak more rapidly than others, their speech is more difficult to transcribe. Consequently the omissions may have been distributed differentially. Such issues are less salient for studies in which data are used to generate constructs or to create typologies. However, where counting is required, the lack of backup is a more serious methodological issue. Dependence on a single transcriber is complicated by observer fatigue and writer's cramp. Anthropologists compensate for occasional omissions with long duration in the field. Lecompte spent 3 months in each classroom, and both the sheer volume of field notes generated and the amount of time spent reduced the bias attributable to random omissions. It also meant that systematic differences among teachers that emerged during the study, such as Sara's greater emphasis on grades and sex-role conformity, were documented by repeated observation.

Differential focus, a problem in all observational research, is an issue in nonparticipant observation because of the lack of participant feedback, which otherwise alerts the researcher to alternative topics and themes. Unlike interviews, in which the researcher has to concentrate only on the respondent's answers, classrooms present a multitude of stimuli, many of which are interdependent. An isolated transcription of teacher talk, for example, loses meaning if the activities of children who elicited the talk are omitted. The researcher faces a dilemma of selection: How much of the classroom context can be left out without destroying the meaning of interactions? And, conversely, how much context can be included without precipitating loss of teacher data while context is being recorded? This problem is reduced by the ebbs and flows in social interaction; contextual information can be recorded during times when the teacher is silent.

The logistics of relationships with participants pose a third consideration. Nonparticipant observation may require a time lapse between observation of an interesting behavior and an opportunity to discuss it with the participant. Immediacy may be lost and meaning forgotten; constant after-the-fact questions from the researcher may be viewed as irritating or intrusive. Another factor is spatial; the observer must be close enough to hear the participants, but not so close as to impede normal behavior. Some researchers solve this problem by fitting participants with wireless microphones, but such a tactic was not possible in the LeCompte study. Distances comfortable for some individuals are uncomfortable for others. One teacher wanted LeCompte right at her desk; another placed the observer's desk by the back door. Over time, participant reaction to observer location may change. For example, LeCompte almost was asked to leave one classroom; the teacher initially had placed her in a corner behind the teacher's desk, but after 2 weeks felt as if the observer were always "looking over her shoulder." She never mentioned her discomfort to LeCompte, but she became so nervous that she complained to the principal. Only the intervention of the principal, who mediated an alternative seating arrangement, made continuation of the study possible. After that incident, LeCompte made sure that her location changed regularly. This served to improve rapport with the teachers as well as to provide an opportunity to view the classroom from a variety of vantage points.

In the preceding pages, we have discussed noninteractive methods for recording immediate behavior and speech of human participants. In the following section, we discuss data generated by collecting things and records made and used by human beings or by locating records about participants made by other people.

ARTIFACT COLLECTION

In addition to what they say and how they behave, human beings make and use things. The resulting artifacts constitute data indicating people's sensations, experiences, and knowledge and which connote opinions, values, and feelings. Artifacts include symbolic materials such as writing and signs and nonsymbolic materials such as tools and furnishings. Their existence transforms ethnographers into voracious and inveterate collectors (Spindler & Spindler, 1992). Artifacts provide evidence for the topics and questions ethnographers address because they are material manifestations of cultural beliefs and behaviors. Once accumulated, they provide resources for longitudinal comparisons; reexamining them long after they were collected sheds new light on old observations and sometimes generates entirely new lines of inquiry (Spindler & Spindler, 1992). The methods historians use to study written artifacts produced in the past and that archaeologists use to examine objects created by ancient peoples have been adapted by educational ethnographers to investigate present-day groups. In educational research, the collection and analysis of text-books, teacher-made games and teaching aides, curriculum guides, memos, enrollment records, minutes of meetings, student personnel records, student and teacher handbooks, student classroom products, lesson plans and other teacher files, correspondence, government documents, and such researcher-stimulated materials as teacher diaries, logs, and recollections provide invaluable resources for baseline, process, and values data.

Artifacts can be categorized in many different ways. Two kinds of artifacts require special collection efforts by ethnographers, and we give them particular attention. First are artifacts obtained from archives and demographic data banks. Second are artifacts obtained by following connections among series of nonsymbolic materials, physical trace collection. Discussion of these two categories of artifacts is followed by guidelines for collecting any kind of artifact. The section concludes with two examples of educational artifacts.

ARCHIVAL MATERIAL AND DEMOGRAPHIC
DATA BANKS

Artifacts include archival materials and data banks. Often called "second-ary analysis," analysis of these kinds of materials can be both substantively valuable and an economical way for researchers to expend scarce research resources. Ethnographers often use their preliminary mapping activities (described earlier in Chapter Four) to discover the range of written and symbolic records kept by or on participants in a social group. (For detailed discussions of archival and demographic collection, see Pitt, 1972; Webb *et al.*, 1966, Chapters 3 and 4.) Official demographic material reveals characteristics of the group under investigation that provide a framework for baseline data. Much of this material can be obtained easily through government census documents.

Sources such as attendance records and minutes of a citizen advisory board were analyzed by Mercurio (1979) in assessing community partici-pation in educational decision making, specified as an objective by one of the projects in the Experimental Schools Program. These data substan-tiated information from surveys, interviews, and participant observation. Mercurio concluded that community involvement in this instance was nonrepresentative and generally ineffective, but useful in providing an outlet for the concerns of influential community members. Lee's analysis (1955) of teachers' manuals and guides used in high school home eco-nomics programs is a provocative statement about the discrepancies be-tween program objectives and the means advocated to implement such programs. Similarly, content analysis of textbooks can delineate social and philosophical biases in curricular goals (Anyon, 1983; Zeigler & Peak, 1970; Fitzgerald, 1979). The examination of data (called "field note records" by Sanjek, as described earlier in this chapter) drawn from school enrollment records, documents of community action groups, stu-dent personnel files, school board meeting minutes, and school annual reports strengthened many of the conclusions reported by Ogbu (1974) in the study cited above. Deyhle's (1986, 1989, 1992) study of Navajo adolescence also utilized such field note records: student grades; student discipline, transfer, health, and attendance records; student classwork and diaries, yearbooks, published court records involving the school dis-trict; textbooks, curriculum guides, and course syllabuses; community newspapers, health and employment statistics, and historical records; state and county analyses of demographic change, land use, and migra-tion patterns; and records of consumption and expenditure from the community grocery store.

PHYSICAL TRACE COLLECTION

Among the least obtrusive of the noninteractive data collection methods is the collection of physical traces, the erosion and accretion of nonsymbolic artifacts and natural objects used by people in groups. (For a detailed discussion of physical trace collection, see Webb *et al.*, 1966, Chapter 2.) This also is the method most neglected by educational ethnographers, despite its potential for generating valuable process and baseline data.

Qualitative curriculum evaluators may examine such factors as what equipment is used the most—and thus requires the most repair, according to school records—and what equipment is ignored. What materials remain in teachers' closets, covered with dust, months after they were to be used? Who has access to equipment and supplies? Problems of access may explain why planned innovations fail to materialize. Evaluators also can examine what is discarded and what is retained. Occasionally, this garbage-dump strategy adapted from archeologists can result in educational gains. The 1967 Woodlawn Experimental School Project (LeCompte, 1969) discovered that low attendance patterns were related both to school grounds that children and parents regarded as unsafe because they were littered with broken glass and to the existence of street gangs whose members harrassed children on their way to school. Attendance figures rose when increased police surveillance curtailed gang activity and local merchants were persuaded to sell soft drinks in cans rather than in breakable bottles.

GUIDELINES FOR ARTIFACT COLLECTION

Collection and examination of artifacts in qualitative research involve four activities: locating artifacts, identifying the material, analyzing it, and evaluating it. These activities are discussed here as discrete processes, but in field situations they are more often reflexive. Evaluating a collection of materials for selection biases, for example, leads investigators to search for omissions, thus reinitiating the process.

First, the more familiar researchers are with the groups and settings they study, the more likely they are to anticipate the artifacts to be found. Nevertheless, much material is discovered only after investigators have initiated field residence. As mentioned previously, many artifacts are located during the systematic mapping phase of a research study. Other materials are discovered during later stages of participant observation. Questions about artifact production and use also are added to informant and other survey interviews to locate inaccessible or otherwise undiscovered materials. In addition to locating participant artifacts, ethnographers may solicit the production of materials—summaries by school administrators of their central responsibilities, organizational charts from management staff of personnel distribution, diaries of daily events from classroom teachers, and stories or pictures of home life from students. Finally, ethnographers search for gaps in artifact collections; what is not available or not used can be as meaningful as what is.

Second, after artifacts have been located, they are identified. This requires placing the material in retrievable form. Documents are duplicated; other artifacts are photographed, filmed, or taped. This collection is then organized so that the records are easily accessible for further manipulation.

Identification begins with descriptions of material. These are formulated in concrete, sensory terms—color, size, shape, use. Researchers then sort artifacts by class and category and compare their attributes. How many of these are there? How is an object similar to or different from other materials in the same category? Is an artifact disposable or reusable? Within the history of those who use or produce it, what are the object's precursors or successors? Can reliable frequency distributions of numbers, productions, or uses of the artifacts be constructed?

The third activity is analysis of an artifact (cf. Altheide, 1987). Who produced it? For whom was it made? When and where was it constructed? Under what circumstances and for what purpose was it produced? If material and equipment were produced elsewhere, how did participants in the group acquire them?

Most significant is the use of an artifact. Who uses it, and how is its use allocated? Who cannot or does not use it? Is it used by individuals or by a group? How many people use it? Is it read, manipulated, or displayed? Where and in how many different locations is it used? Under what circumstances and for what purposes is the artifact used? Is it used in different ways by different people? What meaning does the artifact have for the users? Does it have different meanings for different kinds of users?

Fourth, examination and analysis of artifacts allow researchers to interpret and evaluate them. Manifest and latent meanings that participants attribute to them are posited as well as meanings for research analysis. Symbolic materials reveal more subtle or pervasive meanings within the cultural or group context than do nonsymbolic artifacts (see Hughes, 1964; Kaestle, 1988, and Anderson, 1989, for meanings sought by historians in documentary evidence). However, some articles which have little symbolic use for one group are fraught with symbolic meaning when appropriated by another. An example is the adoption of work boots and outdoor clothing—more suitable for mountaineering and heavy construction work—by college students wishing to set themselves apart from prep school standards of dress. Finally, researchers evaluate their artifact collections for what is represented. Selection biases are identified and addressed (see Carr, 1961, for similar selection effects in historical research design). Artifacts are assessed for authenticity and for participant distortion or falsification. Evidence derived from this material is then triangulated with data collected from observations and interviews to facilitate interpretation. This final process requires researchers to review their artifacts within the context from which they were abstracted.

EXAMPLES OF ETHNOGRAPHIC ARTIFACTS

Artifacts may be personal or public; they may be made by the participants in the study or obtained from other sources and used by them. The first artifact example below is a public one, a handout received at the International Conference on Curriculum-Teaching-Assessment for the 21st Century by the principal of an intermediate school studied by LeCompte. The researcher was studying how various approaches to school reform trickle down to classroom teachers. The researcher had wondered why teachers' opinions about empowerment differed markedly from those of the district superintendent, who initially was the researcher's primary source of information about definitions of empowerment. The handout helped to clarify matters, because it came from the principal, who defined empowerment differently from the superintendent.

The second artifact example is a personal one. The following abstract consists of four entries from a researcher-solicited diary kept by Katherine

Berelson, the teacher of the third-grade classroom studied by Goetz (1976a,b). She had agreed to maintain a log throughout the ethnographer's field residence. This was to be a record of whatever she considered to be important in the classroom and of her reactions to such occurrences. Although the intended audience was the ethnographer, the log was kept privately until after the end of the school year when it was added to the artifact files. Ms. Berelson wrote comments in the diary two or three times each week over the research period.

Monday, March 4   Jude and I talked a lot today, especially about her feeling in regard to defending Greenville [the county seat and site of the school district central offices] and the secrecy of the work. She mentioned that this summer I might like to read her notes to see some particular actions or mannerisms I have. I wonder what that means?
Art went better although [the art teacher] is still wasting much of the children's time. They made St. Patrick's Day banners. I gave them the choice of taking them home or up [sic] in the room. All but five took them home.   Ann—At indoor recess is not turning the [jump] rope fairly, and it was she who would cry all the time. I reminded that to her [sic], and she looked down and knew exactly what I was talking about.   Extra outside recess because they came back from [separate] music [instruction] so well.   ([This was] written on Tuesday. [I] don't remember more.)

Tuesday, March 5   A.M. Not enough work. Too many are rushing through their work, only to play and roam around. It gets me up tight. There must be something wrong if *so* many are finished. Also many did not finish yesterday's work, so I kept them in at recess for 5 minutes. I must increase the work load.   Chuck—during sharing [time] Chuck began a story about how he hit Gail [his cousin] at home and she cried. I stopped him in the middle, just by saying that I cannot let him tell stories to make others feel funny. I think he knew. Although he had had a hard day—homework not finished—principal kept him in the lunchroom, I made him go to the end of the lunch line for hitting Doris (he said Dick told him to do it—then he teared up). I spoke with him afterwards, and he understood. I told him I'd like to hear his other stories tomorrow. He smiled.

Wednesday, March 6   My carpool unhappiness seemed to set a damper on a perfectly beautiful day today. All day I was out of sorts. I feel out of patience with the children and that gets me upset. I know it is not their fault, but at the same time I get so exasperated when they are so slow to grasp something, i.e., parts of speech and correct grammar words. I couldn't get to all the reading groups and that got me upset (even though I had 25 minutes of music first) especially since Jude was following someone in the top group who met for about 10 rushed minutes).   I'm suddenly feeling very defensive of my teaching and techniques. After Jude mentioned that later in the summer we would talk about some "mannerisms" of mine, I'm concerned that I must be doing something wrong. What? And there seems little hope of finding it out before the year is up. I'm feeling more and more in a fishbowl. Today I was uncertain about the Earth's rotation, and I asked Jude if she could explain it. She did, and very calmly and clear [sic]. The children didn't react one way or the other, yet I suddenly was impressed with the distinct, different teaching styles. I'm so much more louder [sic]. Now with warm weather, the children are less and less concerned with work. I've been trying to capture them back by ad-libbing or hamming it up. It works, they become more alive and interested, yet I'm so loud (especially in contrast to Jude; I noticed this today).   I'm suddenly feeling that I need some reinforcement. This long period of "nothing" is beginning to get on my nerves. I'm now at a blank about what happened today. Let me think.   I started the day by reminding [the children] I wanted good work, not rushed, and many took heed. John, Gail, Doris, Carl, and Linda all told me personally that they were aware they had been doing this and would try otherwise. I'm very sure many others took note.   I filled the morning with work. They were mostly in their seats, yet I'm wondering if there is any more concrete learning going on, just because they are quiet. I doubt it, I know much of it was busy work—handwriting three times, English A and B [exercises in the language arts textbook]—when just one would tell me if they understood.   Recess—rather pleasant. Many boys playing sock ball [a version of kickball]. They are slowly learning teamwork. [The other third grade teacher's] room joined in. The boys [are] so afraid. Only the brave ones came to watch and then I could invite them in.   Math—O.K. review [of] × [multiplication] facts. Most everyone very involved in learning. Carl doing exceptionally well for him. The sixth graders came [to tutor] for the last time, the children were sorry to hear. They all want to work with them.   Science—The discussion on Mars led us to review Earth's rotation and seasons. Many are excited.   Geography–Art—They worked more diligently than I planned. I passed out report cards, and Carl—[was] concerned about [his] low math [grade]. We talked of his rushing through [the work] and he promised to go slower, to try. Gail wanted to know what the numbers meant [grades on report cards in numbers, not letters].   Nancy asked if with her A's was she on honor roll. I told her we didn't have it but she would if we did. Dick asked about F in Spelling. I reminded him he didn't get any perfect scores. He knew. Later he said he probably would not be able to go out [at home] for a whole week.   Chuck [was] concerned about a grade from the previous [marking] period. I told him he was much better in Reading even though he got a D. It was just hard for him. He kept saying that he did better in all areas except spelling and reading.

Thursday, March 7   A pretty good day. For some reason the morning went very smoothly. [I] was able to have long working periods with each reading group. Jack kept disturbing me. He had copied a poem and wanted to show me.   Carl was very conscientious today. [He] often came [to me] to be sure he was doing the work correctly. I guess the report card had some influence.   Many minor instances of sore eyes, legs, fingers, etc. I have to laugh at it all. I took a long time to finally get down to work. Math—good review on facts. [I] taught odd and even numbers—confusing at first. [They] worked a review page.   Creative writing [was] circus story and description. [It] went over rather well. [We were] interrupted by recess (a long one). Jude and I talked because she said today was the first time [she had seen me] threaten to move a child in [to] the hall. I laughed after what I said in this journal yesterday about needing reinforcement. Our conversation during recess was a good airing and clarification of feelings and attitudes. I feel much better about the whole situation. I just hope that it doesn't force Jude to get into a position that she really doesn't want to work in.   [We] clarified [that] no negative comment [was intended] the other day. [It] just was [the] suggestion that there may be other objectives to my teaching hidden in my behavior—since I had suggested two (there are more is what she meant by comment).

Because this diary was written for the ethnographer, it must be assessed as a document of what the participant believed the researcher wanted. Nevertheless, it also reflects what the teacher considered to be important; effects of the ethnographer on the classroom situation, including the same uneasiness at being observed that LeCompte noted in her work; the teacher's intentions for various instructional activities; and her interpretations of interactions with and among the children. As a record of teacher concerns and perceptions, the diary was triangulated with other data—observations, interviews, and teacher records kept for the school—to discover and substantiate the content of teacher meanings and values (Goetz 1976a,b).

RECORDING QUALITATIVE DATA

To the traditional educational researcher, accustomed to a variety of instruments, rating scales, and tests, the data collection methods used by ethnographers and other qualitative scholars may seem absurdly simple. The primary tools of the ethnographer are eyes and ears and other sensory abilities, augmented by a collection of mechanical aids such as computers, video and audio tape recorders, and still and motion picture cameras.

The material recorded includes what investigators observe themselves, what they can induce participants to record, and what they and participants draw, photograph, tape record, film, or video tape. These create a data bank of field notes, formal and informal interviews, questionnaires, written records, newspapers, memos, diaries, letters, recollections and reminiscences, myths, and folk tales, as well as more standardized instruments for recording values and perceptions such as projective devices. In this section we discuss two ways of recording observations, interviews, and documentation of material collected. These are field notes and mechanical equipment.

FIELD NOTES

The data collected by participant observers, nonparticipant observers, and some interviewers are recorded as field notes. Field notes, written accounts made on the spot or as soon as possible after their occurrence, represent the interactions and activities of the researcher and the people studied (Bogdan & Biklen, 1992; Bond, 1990; Burgess, 1982, 1984; Sanjek, 1990; Spradley, 1980; Webb, 1926; Whyte, 1984; Williams, 1967). Field notes have been characterized and classified in different ways.

Kinds of Field Notes

Clifford (1990) describes three kinds of field note. Inscription is the notation made in the midst of interaction and participation. These may be quick jottings of key words and symbols or just a momentary self-prompt to remember something (the mental notes Lofland & Lofland, 1984, discuss). The record resulting from inscription may be written fragments, the researcher's memory, or any other reminder of what occurred. The second kind of field note, transcription, is very different. Transcription is writing something down as it occurs, recording as much as possible as exactly as possible. To accomplish this, the researcher is fully observing and recording; participation is minimal, limited to occasional questions or nonverbal acknowledgments. Transcription is creating a text from what the observer is perceiving, from responses to questions, or from dictated narratives. Description, the third kind of field note, occurs out of the flow of activity, sometimes even out of the field. Description is forming a comprehensible account of whatever has been observed. Descriptions are built on inscriptions and transcriptions, but all three constitute field notes.

Unfortunately, only the products of transcription and description have received much attention in the literature, probably because inscription, which includes what Ottenberg (1990) calls headnotes, has been considered too subjective for rigorous scientific discussion or presentation. Thus field notes have not been seen as legitimate until they are written down or expanded from minimal jottings. However, many researchers rely on headnotes—their recollections and interpretations of events, experiences, and impressions—augmenting whatever is transcribed and described. These become crucial when data are lost (e.g., Srinivas, 1976), although such losses can be minimized by frequent duplication of materials.

Another way to classify field notes is Sanjek's (1990) "vocabulary for field notes": scratch notes; field notes proper; field note records and texts; journals and diaries; letters, reports, and papers; and tape transcripts. Field notes usually begin with scratch notes, fragmented phrases, words, and other symbols intended to help an observer recall what happened. Scratch notes are whatever is written of Clifford's inscriptions (cf. Lofland & Lofland's, 1984, jotted notes).

From scratch notes researchers produce field notes proper—what Clifford labels descriptions and the Loflands call full field notes. These are the core of ethnographic and much qualitative data. They are a chronological account of what has occurred, rendered as completely as possible. They include documentation of observations and records of formal and conversational interviews.

Field note records are collections of materials collected from the group studied: documents solicited from participants or otherwise available from or about the group. They are the questionnaires and the public and private documents we discuss as artifacts in this chapter. They may include household censuses and other demographic data, court records, genealogies, health and nutrition records, maps, food purchases and consumer patterns, and bureaucratic forms and memos.

Sanjek includes in field note records what he calls texts. He equates these with Clifford's transcriptions, word-for-word replications of narratives spoken by an informant or precise recordings of the conversations between the ethnographer and an informant. Texts are created by linguists to preserve the language of a people or by ethnographers to record life histories, myths, jokes and stories, rituals, spells, or recipes. Some ethnographers solicit texts created by literate informants, who record field notes from their own observations and experiences. One example is the excerpt from Ms. Berelson's journal, presented earlier in this chapter. The precisely rendered record of events we discuss as made by nonparticipant observers can also be viewed as a text or transcription.

Journals and diaries are accounts of fieldwork from the researcher's own experiences and perspectives. Some are indexes, chronologies, and comments on the field notes proper. These may include a running record of inferences, hunches, and ideas to be pursued in data collection. Others are personal and private accounts of what the ethnographer makes of what is happening, including positive and negative reactions to people, places, and events encountered.

Letters, reports, and papers the ethnographer writes from the field to personal friends and family or to colleagues and professional groups are part of the field material. They represent an initial distillation of headnotes and notes into more comprehensive renditions of the cultural scenes experienced by the researcher.

Finally, some ethnographers include among their field notes audio tapes and transcriptions from them of dictated field notes and other texts. Because the time required to transcribe these records may exceed the time spent in the field, they are used less often than other kinds of notations.

Keeping field notes is personal and idiosyncratic (Jackson, 1990). Some researchers preserve their notes for use by others; some treat them as if they were the most private of personal documents (see examples in Sanjek, 1990). In the following section we present guidelines for keeping field notes that we and others have found productive. We offer these with a qualification: The best way for any fieldworker to keep field notes is the way that best preserves that individual's observations and interpretations. We believe that everyone's best way is different from everyone else's (cf. Ely, 1991).

Guidelines for Note Taking

The format, structure, and focus of ethnographic field notes vary with the research problem and design, the skills and styles of individual ethnographers, the social role taken by the researcher within the group, and the way people react as a consequence of that social role (Griffiths, 1985; Johnson, 1975). However, all fieldworkers make similar decisions about note taking. They decide how often to take notes, where the notes are to be taken, how to record the notes, what kinds of notes to record, and how detailed to make the notes.

Although continuous recording of all possible events observed is appealing to compulsive beginners, this is usually helpful only at the start of an exploratory study. Even in those circumstances, experienced fieldworkers like Bogdan (1989) suggest alternatives. Bogdan recommends beginning with short periods of observation and recording no more than an hour's interaction. This keeps scenes and events new, fresh, even strange over a longer period of time, and it keeps fieldworkers' concentration intense and their awareness sharp. Shorter, more frequent, and regularly scheduled note taking is effective for many fieldworkers. Boredom and exhaustion, natural responses to prolonged engagement in many activities, produce thin records. This is a more serious problem when researchers are studying routinized, familiar events. Most classroom ethnographers, for example, have nodded off more than once before learning to pace themselves. Pacing, learning how often and for how long to take notes, is crucial to keeping useful records.

When and where notes are taken depends on who is being studied for what reasons. Some records can be made on the spot; others have to be reconstructed. Some can be publicly written, but others require privacy. Across sites fieldworkers experiment with different ways of addressing these issues.

Any record is better than no record at all. Otherwise, the different kinds of records, such as those we describe in the previous section, have different values for the fieldworker. Likewise, how notations are recorded differs, and here the preferences and habits of the researcher are most pertinent. In the past most records were longhand accounts kept on a variety of materials: miscellaneous slips of paper, file cards, stenographic pads, ring-bound notebooks, handwritten bound books, typescripts, or bundles of computer printout. Since the availability of personal computers and laptops, more researchers are keeping notes on word processors. As these become smaller and less obtrusive, they are more useful for making records on the spot in the midst of activity. In this case what researchers seek to achieve is balance between what is efficient and workable and what is least intrusive to participants and their activities.

The usefulness of field notes increases if they include when and where the note was made, who was present, and what circumstances obtained. Glesne & Peshkin (1992) add other practical advice: Use only one side of a piece of paper, leave wide margins, create a personal shorthand system, write full accounts of observations before relating them to anyone, read notes regularly, and include in notes even casual encounters with participants and relevant others. To these we add a last admonition: Mark participants' quoted material differently from what is paraphrased of their words.

Sanjek (1990) places in the category of diaries and journals those field notes that record observations on and interpretations of the activities of observing and interviewing. These may be as simple as time lines for the descriptive notes. More complex are methodological journals documenting the researcher's journey through the investigation. This is a record of thinking, decisions, actions, and feelings about the research. It includes the alternatives for decisions and the rationales for choices. It contains the researcher's speculations about the influence of others on the investigation. These are invaluable resources for writing accounts of how the research was designed and conducted. They refresh fieldworkers' memories when reflecting on material for later interpretation and synthesis. If shared with others, they assist efforts at replication and comparison.

Finally, most guides to field notes distinguish between two categories of notations. The first category, comprising the bulk of observational and interview data, consists of low-inference descriptors. They include verbatim accounts of what people say as well as narratives of behavior and activity (Lofland & Lofland, 1984; Pelto & Pelto, 1978; Schatzman & Strauss, 1973). Low-inference narratives provide ethnographers with basic observational data; they are phrased as concretely and precisely as possible. This is the material excerpted, analyzed, and presented as evidence to substantiate inferred categories of analysis (Wolcott, 1975).

For example, "The house was middle-sized and shabby," assumes too much. A low-inference description would assume less and say more. "The structure was about 1500 feet square, made of cracked wood siding and painted gray. About half the paint had peeled off. The red asphalt shingle roof had a hole in it near the front door, and all the screens were torn."

The second category of notation is any combination of high-inference interpretive comments. An example is, "The house was run down and abandoned." High-inference descriptors vary according to the analytic scheme researchers choose. They include the names researchers assign to what they think they see or perceive to be happening. They are derived from researchers' theoretical frameworks, disciplinary backgrounds, and cultural perspectives.

High-inference notations are the building blocks of analysis, interpretation, and theory generation (see Chapter Seven). Called theoretical memos by Glaser & Strauss (1967) and field reports by Sanjek (1990), they are records made in the field, prefiguring and speculating on the meaning of what is occurring.

As they acquire various roles during the investigation, many of the interpretive notes researchers take are based on their perceptions of and empathy with their participants. Janes (1961) discusses the differential data to which he had access as his role underwent progressive redefinition during 8 months of fieldwork in a small midwestern town. Everhart (1977), whose field residence extended over 2 years in a junior high school, documents changes in his sensitivity to data as a function of participants' redefinition of his role. Interpretive comments can be added, deleted, or modified in the running account of a study, but the record of who did what under which circumstances should be as accurate and concrete as possible (Wax, 1971).

MECHANICAL RECORDING

Ethnographers and qualitative researchers use a variety of mechanical devices to record data and preserve it intact (Erickson & Wilson, 1982; Jackson, 1987). They must decide what is going to be recorded and who is going to record it. Audio and video equipment indiscriminately record whatever is occurring within their purview. Transcription, coding, and analysis are imperative to render material usable. Using mechanical recorders increases analysis time because researchers may observe events while recording and then repeatedly reobserve them while processing, coding, and analyzing data later (Erickson, 1992). Consequently, the use of mechanical equipment for exploration or general observation can hinder the research. We recommend deciding what to record before recording it. This is more efficient when a focus has been selected.

The second decision is who is going to do the recording? The researcher? A research assistant? A participant? A professional, like a photographer? Each choice has strengths and weaknesses. Usually the researcher records the data. It is less expensive than hiring others, and control remains in the investigator's hands. However, it takes time and energy away from participation. Some studies have been enriched by involving participants in recording data, independently of or cooperatively with the researcher. This generates records made from the participants' perspectives and may resolve some issues of cost and focus. Because so much recording equipment is available and familiar to participants, skill is less an issue than it once was. Some adults and children may be more skilled in the technical use of recording equipment than are their investigators. In the remainder of this section we discuss equipment in two categories, aids to recording sound material and aids to recording visual or audiovisual material.

Sound Recording

People have made sound recordings of what they value in their cultures for as long as recording equipment has been available. Archives of material collected over the years from singers and musicians, storytellers, and the speech of dying language groups are increasingly available for study. Through the middle of the century researchers lugged around their field sites the tape-recording equipment accessible to them, cumbersome, expensive, and fragile. In the following we discuss what equipment with which features may be used, first, to record data and, second, to transcribe the recordings.

Cost, ease of transport and handling, and quality are no longer issues for most qualitative researchers. Cassette tape recorders and microcassette recorders are inexpensive, convenient, and sturdy. The equipment is so widely used among the general population of industrial and postindustrial communities that obtrusiveness and reactivity are no longer the issues they once were. The equipment can be so small it is unnoticeable, and people are accustomed to it. There are, of course, exceptions to this, and researchers use their discretion in discovering the familiarity and ease of participants with such equipment. However, sound equipment is so ubiquitous that the dangers of misuse and overuse are greater than the possibility of underuse.

The kind of equipment selected depends on the purpose of the recording, who is being recorded, and the circumstances under which the record is made. In addition to selecting from cassettes or microcassettes, researchers can use internal or external microphones or battery-operated or electrical equipment. They can choose from tapes of different lengths and qualities. Remote microphones can be attached to participants to record their conversations as they move through their daily activities. Researchers should explore advantages and disadvantages to each of these choices before making decisions.

Once the material has been taped, researchers then consider what to transcribe and how to transcribe it. Transcription equipment varies from expensive machines controlling the speed at which a tape is played to simple on-and-off foot pedals for ordinary tape machines which cost less than a package of tapes. Researchers disagree about hiring out transcription. Some see it as essential to efficient time management. Others see it as too costly, as putting the identity of their respondents at risk, or as depriving themselves of the knowledge of the data that transcribing provides. This decision may become less problematic with the inexpensive availability of speaker-independent voice recognition systems—systems permitting a computer to transcribe voices of any kind.

How much of the tape collection to transcribe is a key decision. Full transcription usually requires several hours of transcribing time for each hour of tape. Some researchers expect all tapes to be transcribed in complete detail. The detail itself can vary—what is detailed transcription for a linguist may overwhelm another scholar. Partial transcriptions also vary from detailed renderings of selected portions of tape to topical characterizations of all of the tape. In either case transforming spoken material to written material requires the transcriber to edit. Although pauses and other verbal and nonverbal clues from a tape provide some guidance, punctuating and organizing dialogue is an art. Most transcribers try to achieve a balance between faithfulness to the spoken word and ease of readability for the written word.

The kind of transcription selected depends on the kind of analysis intended and the purposes the analysis serves. Timing can be another influence. Preliminary analyses begun in early phases of research can be based on listening to tapes, with more definitive and thorough study postponed until transcriptions are available.

Visual and Audiovisual Recording

Visual records of what people do are captured by photography, motion pictures, and videotapes. Like audio equipment, this technology is widely available, used routinely in their private lives by participants and researchers alike.

Photography can be used by researchers to take inventory of artifacts, settings, and activities (Banta & Hinsley, 1986; Collier & Collier, 1986; Walker & Wiedel, 1985). Photographs provide a record of who partici- pants are and what they look like, invaluable for prompting scholars' memories once they have left a field site. Pictures taken by participants with regular or Polaroid℗ cameras in color or black-and-white film pro- vide evidence of what they deem important in their lives and how they view these phenomena. Photography, like other visual records, can pro- vide data for analysis, can document the research process itself, and can form a report of the study (English, 1988). Photographic essays are representations of visual themes and patterns that researchers formulate in analysis (e.g., Wieder, 1988).

At one time motion pictures, on 16 or 8 mm film, were the only way fieldworkers could preserve the moving, audiovisual world. This tradition has been so productive in documenting the lives of diverse peoples that a subdiscipline of cultural anthropology, enthnographic film, has devel- oped around it (Bellman & Jules-Rosette, 1977; Heider, 1976; Hockings, 1975). Unfortunately the cost and complexity of the equipment has re- stricted its use to well-funded and well-trained scholars and, compared to the other technologies we discussed, its flexibility is limited by its lack of familiarity to participants. We note its use here to acknowledge a tradition in fieldwork that has been transformed and revitalized by video- tape recording.

Videotape recording, although not yet as accessible as audio tape recording, has become a routine way that middle- and upper-class individ- uals around the world document their lives. The equipment is common in schools and other institutions where it is used for instruction and evaluation. Videocameras or more mobile camcorders are used in ways similar to audio tape recording, photography, and motion picture re- cording (Albrecht, 1985). They have many of the same features and limitations. However, transcribing videotape is far more complicated and time consuming than creating a written record of what is on an audio tape. This may be affected by advances in computer technology, which already allow the input and output of audiovisual material and full- motion animation.

SUMMARY

Mehan (1979) argues for observational techniques that record as much as possible and preserve to the greatest extent the raw data, so that the veracity of conclusions may be confirmed by other researchers. Video and audio tape recorders and still- and moving-picture cameras are standard equipment in the collection of ethnographic and qualitative data. How- ever, these technologies have disadvantages. Although cameras and recorders register much that a researcher could forget or ignore and consequently may increase the reliability of a study, they both preserve all data in uncodified and unclassified form and record only that data chosen by the researcher to be preserved. They are an abstraction, on one hand; on the other hand, they may preserve too much data. Use of these aids neither eliminates bias nor hastens the research.

Field notes and handwritten records are less complete than mechanically produced records. They reflect the interests of the researcher, and they represent data preselected; consequently, they are less amenable to accurate enumerative coding than are films, tapes, and photographs. However, documenting observations in field notes can be less reactive than mechanical recording strategies, eliciting less contrived behavior from participants and functioning more discreetly in sensitive settings. Field notes may generate more flexible data than mechanical records because they may be coded informally during data collection and used to generate categories and constructs about phenomena at the moment they are observed; they also can be divided and rearranged readily for analysis.

Recorders, cameras, and computers are tools created by human beings to enhance their perceptions of the world. For those unfamiliar with them, they are more complicated than pencil and paper. We recommend all these aids to preserving observations and other data. However, whichever means of recording data is chosen, researchers should select only what they can use well. Complex, sensitive cameras and comparable equipment may interfere with data collection unless they are used by skilled practitioners. Novices are served better by simpler devices that provide the data required, albeit in a less artistic or sophisticated manner.

THE ETHNOGRAPHER AS METHODOLOGICAL OMNIVORE

Noninteractive strategies for data collection possess several advantages for ethnographic researchers. Many types of data are collected or generated in raw form and consequently may be amenable to reanalysis by either the collector or other researchers. Such reprocessing may be used to establish reliability coefficients or to generate new constructs and hypotheses. Noninteractive strategies are more replicable than interactive strategies because observer effects are controlled more easily. On the other hand, access to the records and written materials comprising much of this data may be contingent on rapport between researcher and participants. In those cases, the type, amount, and quality of data may depend as much on the special characteristics of the researcher as on data from more interactive and obtrusive methods. In these situations, the special role of the researcher should be delineated clearly.

Unfortunately, the very richness of data drawn from archives or from stream-of-behavior chronicles can be a disadvantage. The cross-cultural data collected in 1954 on child rearing in six countries, first published as separate ethnographies (Whiting, 1963), remain unexhausted (Whiting & Edwards, 1988; Whiting & Whiting, 1975). Overcollection of unselected data threatens both noninteractive and interactive methods of data collection. At issue are decisions on the appropriateness of given data to the original research question, the suitability of the analytic strategies propsed for their reduction, and the larger purposes to which the study is directed. Such decisions determine which data are relevant and facilitate production of the final report.

As methodological omnivores, known for using many methods of collecting data (Werner & Schoepfle, 1987), most qualitative researchers depend on interactive methods for data collection. Field notes, interview transcripts, and other interactive documentation preserve not only participant data but also a record of how researchers interact with groups. Other investigators seeking to reanalyze this material, stored in data banks like the Human Relations Area Files, can assess the influence of the data gatherer because it is integral to the data themselves. Detailed information about how ethnographers negotiated relationships with participants also facilitates the design of studies intended as comparisons with original investigations. Subsequent researchers can seek similar roles in the new study sites.

More importantly, interactive methods provide ethnographers with the data crucial to authentic cultural reconstruction. These involve first-hand encounters as a novice member of a group, intimate experiences with the social and physical environments of participants, and opportunities to discover the perceptions, meanings, and interpretations of others. Interactive methods permit investigators to substantiate their perceptions and interpretations of participants by posing questions about them and using them in daily interaction, and they provide the lengthy association that allows analysis of latent and implicit functions and processes in group life. Because this material is so complex and diverse, most ethnographers present it in a series of reports, each focusing on different aspects of social scenes and cultures.

These reports can be produced only after data have been sifted, selected, abstracted, and synthesized. The analyses converting raw data to a finished report are time consuming; many researchers believe that analysis is as arduous a task as fieldwork. In Chapters Seven and Eight, we provide detailed descriptions of the methods qualitative researchers and ethnographers use to analyze and interpret data and produce their final documents.

CHAPTER SEVEN

Analysis and Interpretation of Qualitative Data

The preceding six chapters address concerns raised in the initial phases of an ethnographic or qualitative study. In the prefieldwork or first stage, preliminary research questions and theoretical frameworks are considered, and a study is formulated. The second stage encompasses the first days in the field; its agonies have been documented amply by numerous investigators (Powdermaker, 1966; Bowen, 1954; Wax, 1971; Chagnon, 1974; Mead, 1972). In it, the ethnographer decides who or what can serve as data sources and how cooperation from those data sources can be obtained. Techniques for collecting data are chosen, and methods for data storage and retrieval are established. The third stage of the project is devoted to what many people think is the real work—collecting data. However, we, and most experienced fieldworkers, do not agree. This chapter is devoted to the stage at which an ethnographic study becomes an ethnography—analysis of data (Wolcott, 1988). Miles and Huberman nicely describe the dilemma of the ethnographer facing a mountain of brand-new (and unanalyzed) data:

> A chronic problem of qualitative research is that it is done chiefly with words, not with numbers. Words are fatter than numbers and usually have multiple meanings. This makes them harder to move around and work with. Worse still, most words are meaningless unless you look backward or forward to *other* words . . . Numbers, by contrast, are usually less ambiguous and may be processed with more economy . . . Small wonder, then, that most researchers prefer working with numbers alone, or getting the words they collect translated into numbers as quickly as possible . . . [However] converting words into numbers, then tossing away the words gets a researcher into all kinds of mischief . . . Focusing solely on numbers shifts our attention from substance to arithmetic, and thereby throws out the whole notion of qualitativeness;

234

one would have done better to have started with numbers in the first place. [1984, p. 54–55]

Because our focus is on substance, not arithmetic, we devote this chapter to analysis, not coding, and to eliciting meaning from data, not converting it to computable formulae.

Beginning the Analysis

Data collection in any study usually ends because time, energy, funds, and forbearance have been exhausted rather than because the sources of information have been depleted. It is only after an ethnographer stops collecting data and the romance of fieldwork ends that the real work of data analysis and interpretation begins.

INITIATING ANALYSIS

The basic goal of ethnography is to create a vivid reconstruction of the culture studied. This requires researchers first to separate, for analytic purposes, any empirical meanings they have assigned to behavior and belief from meanings assigned to the same behaviors and beliefs by their participants. Researcher-constructed descriptions of reality may be quite different from the meanings that participants use to construct their reality (see Chapters One and Two). These differences need to be made explicit. Researchers should also identify any subjective components in their descriptions that derive from their biases or philosophical leanings (see Chapter Five). With these goals in mind, the ethnographer is ready to begin the data analytic phase of the research project.

Data analysis should begin with a review of the proposal or plans with which the work began. A student of ours has called this process "tidying up" (Romagnano, 1991), and he spent a month doing it after he concluded his fieldwork. His guilt at having "wasted" so much time filing papers, making neat stacks of tapes, putting interviews in order, and organizing documents and artifacts before he began data analysis was considerably assuaged when we assured him that he had been engaged in a time-honored and necessary component of the research project.

One of his most important tasks was to relocate the original research question. Most research projects wander from the original question, but the original questions, as well as subsequent iterations, must not be lost entirely. They shaped the initial inquiry and must be addressed, either to lay them aside with good reasons made explicit in the final report or to indicate in detail how they changed and were necessarily modified. A review of the original research proposal also reacquaints the researcher with the varied audiences for whom the study originally was intended and permits their needs and interests to be addressed as analysis proceeds.

The second step involves scanning. This means rereading the data. It is a process analogous to the mapping procedures used in the first stages of data collection (see Chapter Four). Rereading differs in that it has two purposes: One is to check the data for completeness, and the second is to reacquaint the researcher with territory previously covered, this time with the wisdom of hindsight. Investigators who postpone analysis until data collection is complete should scan their records before leaving the field, so that critical gaps left accidentally in the collecting or recording of data may be remedied. Fieldworkers may become so familiar with certain events that they neglect to document them thoroughly. They then are faced with inadequate evidence to substantiate assertions about aspects of behavior. Siskind (1973) found herself in such a predicament with the agricultural practices of the Amazonian women. She acknowledged the gap in her data, indicating that it had occurred somewhat deliberately. She had avoided observing in the gardens because she could not endure the heat and hard labor that participant observation would have entailed.

An inventory for completeness includes noting events for which descriptions were postponed and then forgotten and relocating pieces of data misplaced and, with luck, not lost. The initial scan should include the complete set of raw data gathered to that time.

The second purpose for scanning the raw data is to wander through the record, jotting notes and observations as the reading progresses. The notes serve to isolate the initially most striking, if not ultimately most important, aspects of the data. The guides used for note taking are intuitive. They also are informed, consciously and unconsciously, by several factors: the metatheories inherent in the researcher's personal training and background; the explicit theoretical frameworks, if any, with which the study was initiated; and constructs made explicit by the participants of the study.

The investigator asks questions of the data just as questions are asked of informants; these questions generate additional questions, insights, and puzzles to discuss with other investigators and to ponder alone. Data analysis retraces many of the phases of data collection. The notes taken while scanning constitute the beginning stages of organizing, abstracting, integrating, and synthesizing, which ultimately permit investigators to tell others what they have seen. The notes are developed into a primitive outline or system of classifications into which data are sorted initially.

The outline begins with a search for regularities—things that happen frequently with groups of people. Patterns and regularities then are transformed into categories into which subsequent items are sorted. These categories or patterns are discovered from the data. They emerge in a rather systematic, if not totally conscious, application of the processes of theorizing outlined later in this chapter.

EMERGING PATTERNS

Once a researcher has established the categories within which the data are organized and has sorted all bits of data into relevant categories, the portrayal of a complex whole phenomenon begins to emerge. The process is analogous to assembling a jigsaw puzzle. The edge pieces are located first and assembled to provide a frame of reference. Then attention is devoted to those more striking aspects of the puzzle picture that can be identified readily from the mass of puzzle pieces and assembled separately. Next, having stolen some surreptitious glances at the picture on the box, the puzzle worker places the assembled parts in their general position within the frame and, finally, locates and adds the connecting pieces until no holes remain. Thus, analysis can be viewed as a staged process by which a whole phenomenon is divided into its components and then reassembled under various new rubrics. The creativity of ethnographic analysis, however, lies in the uniqueness of the data, or parts, and in the singularity of reconstructed cultures, or pictures.

The researcher first establishes broad outlines of the phenomenon studied. These may derive from an actual examination of the data, as Becker (1986) recommends writing first from memory and later checking material against the data. The next step is to assemble chunks of data, fitting those pieces together so that they are a coherent whole. A helpful organizing device here is a written summary of what has been found so far. Such a summary tells a basic story much as an investigative reporter writes an article. It informs the reader where the study took place, who was studied, how the study was done, and why it was initiated (Pelto & Pelto, 1978). It also summarizes, in narrative form, the major events and issues discovered in the course of investigation. Writing such a summary helps the researcher to withdraw from minute details and look for the larger picture that emerges. It facilitates what Guba (1978) calls convergence: figuring out what fits together, either because the investigator believes they should or because the participants say that they do. The next step is to begin the time-consuming and laborious process of pulling apart field notes, matching, comparing, and contrasting, which constitutes the heart of analysis. The standard analytic strategies discussed later in this chapter or variants of them can then be used to process the material until it yields the patterns sought.

THE PECULIAR NATURE OF ETHNOGRAPHIC ANALYSIS

The analysis stage of ethnographic and qualitative research probably feels more foreign to researchers from other traditions than any other part of the research. Differences in the timing of analysis and its integration with other research tasks in particular differentiate qualitative from experimental research and the positivistic tradition. Qualitative researchers analyze data throughout the study rather than relegating analysis to a period following data collection. Because of this, analysis is linked with choices of theoretical frameworks, selection strategies, and data collection methods. Many of the strategies ethnographers and other qualitative researchers use depend on feedback from the field; this redefines research questions as the researcher gains deepened understanding of the culture under study and learns the meanings participants attach to things. Much of this information is neither known nor salient to ethnographers before they begin to ask questions. Because ethnographers emphasize meaning as defined by participants, they cannot choose all the data collection methods necessary for a study in advance of fieldwork. In other words, their data collection and analysis techniques are inextricably linked because the ethnographer may not know what questions to ask until initial impressions and perceptions have been analyzed and tentative conclusions have been formulated.

To clarify the interdependence of these processes, we have divided this chapter into three sections. The first section presents the common conceptual techniques that ethnographers use to analyze data. These include theorizing, sequential selection strategies, and general analytic procedures. Theorizing consists of all the modes of thinking upon which analysis is built: perceiving, comparing, contrasting, aggregating and ordering, establishing linkages and relationships, and speculating. Sequential selection strategies are formal operations designed to integrate data analysis with data collection: negative-case selection, discrepant-case selection, theoretical sampling, and selection of theories relevant to various stages of the research (see Chapter Three, Table 3.2). General analytic procedures are systematized means of manipulating data and constructs derived from data throughout the research process.

The second section of the chapter illustrates how these processes are chosen and combined to build an ethnographic analysis. The emphasis is on how raw data are handled, processed, and manipulated to generate constructs and discover patterns. The task is illustrated by a detailed outline of LeCompte's learning-to-work research (1975, 1978), which provides a concrete instance of one investigator's use and development of the analytic processes described in the first section.

LeCompte's example is elaborated in the third section of the chapter, interpreting and integrating results of ethnographic research. Researchers interpret their findings through any combination of four processes: theoretical consolidation, theoretical application, using metaphors and analogies, and synthesis. These are described and discussed. The first two are illustrated with a detailed account of how they were used in LeCompte's studies (1975, 1978, 1981). Throughout this section, we stress the interplay of interpretation and integration with analytic processes and procedures, all in the service of constructing a viable description of cultural phenomena.

Conceptual Techniques for Qualitative Analysis

During initial stages of analysis ethnographers decide how to retrieve the data, what to do with it, and what it all means. This task of tidying up usually is neglected in textbooks on research methods. As a result, many researchers find their initial confrontation with a mountain of undigested data—drawers of field notes, notebooks full of interviews, and boxes of protocols, photographs, instruments, and other memorabilia—to be so depressing that they are reluctant to memorialize the experience in print. One researcher complained that his team of investigators had generated over 25,000 pages of classroom protocols alone. Situations such as this support the claims of Wax (1971) and Wolcott (1975) that effective analysis requires at least double the time expended on collection of data.

THEORIZING

Theorizing is the cognitive process of discovering or manipulating abstract categories and the relationships among those categories. It consists of playing with data and ideas. Data analysis depends on theorizing; it is the fundamental tool of any researcher. It is used to develop or confirm explanations for how and why things happen as they do (Kaplan, 1964; Zetterberg, 1966; Glaser & Strauss, 1967). Many investigators have difficulty describing what they do when they are theorizing, but the intellectual tasks are similar to everyday cognitive activities. Formally, the tasks of theorizing are perceiving, comparing, contrasting, aggregating, ordering, establishing linkages and relationships, and speculating. Although theorizing is a process used by researchers, theorizing uses the same thought processes people use in everyday behavior. As they process information, people notice the phenomena around them; they differentiate those phenomena by comparing and contrasting them with past experiences, a set of values, or some predetermined attributes. They select those to which they wish to attend, and they plan their activities accordingly. They change plans when activities cannot be executed as anticipated and must be modified. In other words, at a mundane level, theorizing consists of inquisitive behavior—a process of collecting information, abstracting, comparing events, applying past experiences, solving problems, and building ideas—and is merely normal human cognitive processing (Bruner, Goodnow, & Austin, 1956). When it is formalized and systematized, however, it constitutes research, empirical or speculative. Each of the tasks involved in theorizing is subsumed in the next. Although they may vary in importance, they are used in some degree at each step of the research process.

Perception

Ethnographers address the issue of perception somewhat differently from investigators using other research designs. Experimental and quasiexperimental researchers attend only to variables they designate a priori as the focus of the study or which they specified in advance of data collection. Other factors are considered, post hoc, when unexpected results obtain. By contrast, ethnographers consider everything to have potential importance, at least in the initial stages of the research. This is because ethnographers seek to examine the complexity of phenomena within their naturally occurring contexts. Consequently, all the factors composing or influencing the phenomena are noteworthy.

Most ethnographers begin by recording everything of interest within their purview that their perceptual abilities allow. They try to "make things strange" (Erickson, 1977) by adopting a studied naivete that allows them to view each aspect of the phenomena as if it were new and unfamiliar and, hence, potentially significant. For example, in initial fieldwork to determine the values teachers emphasized most in their instruction, LeCompte (1975, 1978) simply recorded everything teachers said. Similarly, when creating an inventory of students' classroom behavior, Goetz (1976a,b) made no initial attempts to sort student actions; she merely recorded each behavior as it occurred. Initial data crunching requires that the recordings be successively narrowed, dividing up the stream of behavior until legitimate analytic units emerge. This requires formal and informal scanning and coding of preliminary data gathered during mapping phases. It is the ethnographer's first step in data analysis.

Discovering or establishing units of analysis constitutes one of the primary tasks in processing ethnographic data. The ethnographer's challenge is to choose divisions that retain their natural integrity while providing sufficient focus for observation. Once discovered, analytic units serve a dual function in the research process. First, they are perceptual divisions that guide collection of data. Sometimes, these correspond to the population units discussed in Chapter Three. Second, they are the means for reducing raw data to divisions manageable for manipulation.

In the initial or constructive phases of ethnographic data analysis, conceptual categories embedded in the social phenomena are discovered. This may, in fact, be all the researcher intended to do. However, such a procedure is insufficient for studies whose goal is to enumerate the relative distribution of units within the conceptual categories. Narrative field notes, such as those collected only to identify the activities within an elementary school classroom (e.g., Goetz, 1976b), are inadequate for enumerating such units as verbal behavior. This is because the unit of analysis used to structure the field notes is the construct "activity" (Lofland, 1971). Although some verbal behaviors might indeed be categorized as activities, not all would be. In studies whose objective is creating comprehensive taxonomies, relative distributions are unimportant; an activity is significant even if it occurs only once. On the other hand, a researcher who wants to to establish relative distributions requires frequency counts, and those require initial categorization and an inventory of all possible units. Only then can a coding or counting procedure delineating the relative distribution of specific items in relation to others be done (e.g., Jackson & Lahaderne, 1967; Kounin, 1970; LeCompte, 1978; 1980).

Choosing and defining units of analysis become particularly crucial when the research includes a number of field sites. Comparative researchers have been hampered by the tendency of investigators to proceed idiosyncratically, studying whatever interests them without specifying the perceptual and analytic units which guide their data collection and analysis. Results become idiosyncratic insofar as researchers fail to establish systematic data collection across several field sites or where they ignore fieldwork guidelines established in advance. However, specifying what is to be studied in advance reduces the danger of producing noncomparable data (e.g., Whiting *et al.*, 1966; Cassell, 1978). Where this is impossible, researchers can use collaborative efforts, such as frequent team meetings to negotiate agreement on perceptual and analytic units (e.g., Becker *et al.*, 1961; Becker *et al.*, 1968).

Comparing, Contrasting, Aggregating, and Ordering

The tasks of comparing, contrasting, aggregating, and ordering dominate fieldwork. With them, researchers begin to establish classificatory schemes for organizing data. They constitute the processes by which an ethnographer first begins to build a baseline description of the culture under study. The first step is categorization of the data. Categorization requires ethnographers to describe what they observe and to divide observed phenomena into units. The first categories to emerge from the data generally are those that occur most frequently. Properties of a category are discovered by listing how all units are alike and how they differ systematically from units outside the category. Core properties are then used to develop an abstract definition of the category. The description in Chapter Eight of qualitative data analysis programs illustrates some structured ways these categories may be developed.

Ethnographers then move to the second step of categorization, indicating how units are like and unlike each other. They do this by massing and scanning data in a systematic content analysis, in which the guiding questions asked are, "Which things are like each other?" "Which things go together, and which do not?" Aspects of similarity and difference may be attributed to phenomena both by investigators and by the participants in a study. These bases for differentiation and sorting are used by ethnographers to define how units are used and what their significance is. They may include spatial, physical, temporal, functional, compositional, philosophical, semantic, grammatical, or social dimensions. The rules or canons for discrimination the ethnographer uses are not haphazard, but are guided by certain semantic rules for aggregating single units or items. One type of differentiation and sorting creates *domains* (Spradley, 1979) based on the type of semantic relationships listed in Table 7.1.

The next step in categorization, or creating a domain analysis, is to determine which of the described items are associated with each other and thus may be aggregated into groups. This requires identifying those properties and attributes that the data units of a particular category share. Categories or groups of data may be generated directly from inspection of the data, or they may be established in advance of data collection for their a priori relevance to the overall research question. An example of this process is described next.

Personal integrating is a category developed by Goetz (1976a) in her examination of students' classroom behaviors. By comparing incidents of personal integrating, Goetz generated a definition: Personal integrating consists of those strategies students use to relate their own experiences or ideas in some manner to an environmental cue. The following field

TABLE 7.1
Semantic Relationships for Spradley's Domain Analysis[a]

Relationship	Form
Strict inclusion	X is a kind of Y
Spatial	X is a place in Y; X is a part of Y
Cause–effect	X is a result of Y; X is a cause of Y
Rationale	X is a reason for doing Y
Location for action	X is a place for doing Y
Function	X is used for Y
Means–end	X is a way to do Y
Sequence	X is a step or stage in Y
Attribution	X is a characteristic of Y

[a] From Spradley (1979).

note excerpts (Goetz, 1976a, p. 4b) are examples of incidents grouped in this category.

[First Day of Notes]   When George proudly announced, during sharing time, that his stepfather was going to adopt him legally, it appeared, from the group's responses, that nearly everyone else was also adopted, related to an adoptee, or considering being adopted.

[Another Day]   Ms. Berelson was showing a film on reptiles. Afterwards, she began charting a taxonomy of the animal kingdom on the chalkboard, intending to use the reptiles as exemplars in discussing the entire frame. They began the session by classifying various animals, and Ms. Berelson questioned the students specifically on the differences between reptiles and amphibians. She pointed out the similarities between amphibian young with their gills and fish. Someone wondered if fish had blood, which evidently prompted another child to ask, "What is a tick?"

There followed a long series of anecdotes from the group, each about some experience with ticks: ticks on dogs and where such insects were most likely to be picked up, ticks in human hair and how to get rid of them, and ticks on uncles who died of Rocky Mountain Spotted Fever. They were interspersed with "How many legs do ticks have?"; "Why does gasoline kill ticks?"; "Can ticks get into your brain?"

Ms. Berelson, having long since lost her intended focus: "I don't know. I've already told you all I know about ticks."

Some properties differentially shared among data units can be used to order subcategories or to create a categorized hierarchy. As displayed in Table 7.2, the construct personal integrating has several such subcategories.

Alternatively, properties that vary across categories may suggest distributions of frequencies. Properties shared with units belonging to other categories also may be used to develop *taxonomies*, or the linkages and relationships discussed in the next section.

Taxonomies are much like the domains described previously, but they differ in that they demonstrate the relationships among all the terms or items in the domain and show how each is related to the domain as a whole (Spradley, 1979, p. 137). Table 7.2 is an example of such a taxonomic category; it was developed by sorting data into like and unlike groups. Another is displayed in Fig. 7.1; it was generated by a Korean student who used Spradley's form of analysis to determine why foreign students had so much difficulty with their business school classes in marketing.

Another way to compare, contrast, and order chunks of data can be found in the elicitation interviews of linguists, like those discussed in Chapter Six. These exemplify the process used more generally by ethnographers to generate and refine constructs and categories as well as to depict the meanings attributed to items as they are described by study participants. One of these, explicated by Mischler (1986), divides a narra-

TABLE 7.2
Categories of Personal Integration[a]

1. Modeling

2. Demonstrating (a process, movement, etc.)

3. Anecdoting (about . . .)
   a. One's own experiences
   b. The experiences of someone in primary group
   c. Vicarious experiences

4. Commenting
   a. Labeling
   b. Translating
   c. Summarizing
   d. Observing/evaluating
   e. Comparing/contrasting

5. Solitary verbalizing/self-reciting/eureckaing

[a] From Goetz (1976a, p. 41).

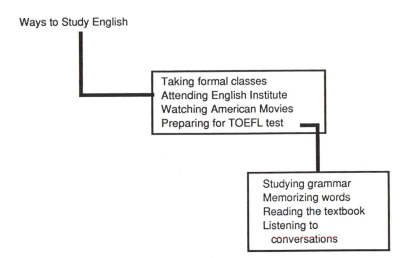

Figure 7.1 A taxonomic analysis: Ways to study English (Jo, 1991, p. 6).

tive text into *narrative clauses*. These are clauses or units of text that cannot be moved or relocated anywhere else in the text without a change in their meaning. They are sentences or fragments about which one could say, "And what happens next?" Table 7.3 displays the categories into which Mischler sorts narrative clauses found in interview narratives. Mischler suggests that the analysis requires the researcher to identify all the narrative clauses within the text, then pull them from the narrative itself and re-order them to form a coherent and temporally ordered story. Then,

TABLE 7.3
A Typology of Narrative Clauses[a]

Clause	Description
Abstract statements	The narrator begins by summarizing the story.
Orientation statements	Time, place, and persons are identified.
Complicated actions	Statements which describe what actually happened.
Results or resolution	Statements which describe the result of the action.
Coda	Returns the speaker to the present situation.
Evaluation statements	Tell how the narrator felt about what was happening, dramatize the action, or compare the actual event judgmentally with others which did or did not occur.

[a] From Mischler (1986).

rather than the functional analysis employed by Spradley, Mischler establishes a *referential,* or *content* domain using textual analysis. The questions he addresses to a text are as follows:

1. What is the sequence of events or the temporal ordering of the material?
2. What is narrative, germane to the story being told, and what is "just talk"?
3. What function does the nonnarrative "just talk" perform?
4. What do the acts of a character mean from the point of view of their significance for subsequent courses of action?

Having established the content of the story, the next step is to figure out what it means. This is done by identifying *themes* within the story, which are built from examination of recurrent patterns of *coherence relations* found within the text. Coherence relations establish a connection between an utterance and some part of the preceding discourse; they can be recurrent patterns of complicating actions, evaluations, orientations (such as who is the narrator with most often, and why?), or moves (such as what things most frequently change the course of action?). Themes may be established deductively, using frames from the researcher, narrator, or other literature; or they may be established inductively, so that they have what Mischler calls *local coherence* within the narrative under consideration. The process results in a story reconstructed from the original text narrative, linking its various parts and making coherent relationships which might not have been clear in the original iteration. Reconstructing a story is similar to the elicitation of stories from nonnarrative data, a more functional analysis we discuss next.

Establishing Linkages and Relationships

Once items have been identified, raw data may be reduced to quantifiable form by scanning, listing, coding, and scoring. Linkages then may be established by simple comparing and contrasting, by identifying underlying associations, by inference, or by statistical manipulation. All are guided by both implicit and explicit theoretical assumptions. The latter derive from whatever theoretical framework structures the research project; the former come, as mentioned earlier, from the perferences, culture, and training of the researcher.

Discovering connections and confirming relationships among individual as well as classes of constructs involve establishing the time order among incidents and making inferences as to how incidents are associated, covary, or cause one another to occur. In closely controlled studies, potential causes are specified in advance; the treatment, or a series of independent variables, are assumed to be prior causes or at least important covariates. Because ethnographers usually cannot specify, in advance, the genesis of events, they engage in detective work, following hunches, looking for and ruling out negative cases, and chasing down all suggested causes of the events being studied. To guide this procedure, they ask questions of participants and check alternative groupings and ordering of specific events by triangulating with alternative data sources (see Chapter One). Ethnographers proceed both inductively, to generate statements of relationships, and deductively, to test working statements of relationships in the field while developing a theory or hypothesis that is grounded in data.

For example, LeCompte's (1974) learning-to-work research explored the extent to which normative messages emphasized by teachers were recognized by their students. Analysis of field note data from one classroom revealed a heavy emphasis on cleanliness. The teacher vacuumed the classroom twice daily with a battery-powered vacuum cleaner; students could not leave in the afternoon until they washed their desks. And the teacher frequently referred to personal hygiene when reprimanding students. Repetition of actions such as these led to an hypothesis that the norm of cleanliness was very important to that teacher. In her interviews, she made statements such as, "The children feel better when they work in a nice clean classroom" and "Children who come to school looking like that [with a soiled shirt] you just can't expect to do the same kind of work as the others." Students echoed their teacher's sentiments almost verbatim. LeCompte was able to link constructs created by aggregating like statements made by the teacher to similar constructs evident in classroom observations and student interviews.

Speculation

A fourth component of theorizing requires speculating and making inferences. It is the basis of hypothesizing and involves the informed guesswork that permits scientists to eliminate rival hypotheses and to posit or to predict the existence of relationships or constructs to be explored. Just as children play with puzzles or blocks to fit them together and create larger toys, so the processes described previously allow the investigator to create chunks of data from smaller bits, fit pieces together, and build larger and related constructs. The last component of theorizing, speculation, involves playing with ideas probabilistically. With it, the investigator can go beyond the data and make guesses about what will happen in the future, based upon what has been learned in the past about constructs and linkages among them as well as on comparisons between that knowledge and what presently is known about the same phenomena.

These guesses convey the confidence with which the relationships found or explanations developed can be asserted to occur in the future or describe which relationships occur with greater than chance frequency. Researchers from more positivistic traditions use speculation and inference in hypothesis generation differently from ethnographers; they also integrate these processes into studies at different times. In highly deductive, verificative studies, researchers avoid making inferences explaining the phenomena under study until data collection is complete. In fact, the preferred structure for research reports reinforces these differences: positivistic researchers reserve separate sections in their manuscripts for statements of the hypotheses, description of the sample and data collection procedures, and presentation of data analysis strategies. Because the raison d'etre for the research is testing or verification of an hypothesis, they also may use post hoc inference and speculation to argue why the research was significant.

For ethnographers, inference and speculation are integral components of the research design and are used throughout generative and inductive studies, the stock-in-trade of ethnographers. Ongoing processes of hypothesis formulation constitute the basic tool for data analysis. Thus, ethnographers formulate and systematically test successive hypotheses throughout the research project, generating and verifying successive explanations, both mundane and theoretical, for the behavior exhibited and attitudes held by the people under study.

This process is well documented by Geer (1964) for the investigation she and her colleagues conducted of undergraduates at a midwestern university (Becker *et al.*, 1968). Reviewing her field notes from the early phases of the field residence, she notes the formulation of working hypotheses that guided further data collection and analysis. She had observed that the entering freshmen had little knowledge of college academic scheduling or of the variety of available extracurricular activities. While their group interaction indicated little or no interest in collegiate athletics, in "cultural advantages," or in religion, learning social niceties and etiquette appeared to be significant to these students. Throughout the field residence, hypotheses such as these were refined, modified, rejected, or confirmed. Geer found, for example, that the lack of interest in athletics was an anomaly associated with only one group of entering freshmen. The limited number of extracurricular interests she observed led Geer eventually to hypothesize that undergraduates focused seriously on academic coursework and that their lives revolved around grades earned in these courses.

Deyhle's research on Navajo and Ute dropouts shows the same thematic evolution. She began with conventional explanations for why students dropped out of school, testing them against explanations which Navajo young people gave her (Deyhle, 1989). She then tested what school personnel told her about attitudes of Navajo parents and students and found that these did not correspond to what she observed and heard among those parents and young people in the Navajo community. This led her to generate a theory of culturally generated miscommunication which was linked to maintenance of existing power structures in the community and had little to do with what Navajos believed about the value of schooling (Deyhle, 1991). Her current research (Deyhle, 1992) examines the relationship between Anglo perceptions of the local job market and economy and the perpetuation of Navajos in the lowest-paying sectors of the labor force. This has permitted her to hypothesize that, given a limited pool of desirable jobs, Anglos construct a belief system about economic opportunities which paints as appropriate jobs for Navajos only those which Anglos do not want. To be defined as ambitious and successful, Navajos must leave, even though the same is not true of Anglo children. Navajos who might compete for Anglo jobs are forced out of the community so that Anglo young people have a chance to remain in the area, close to their extended families. In this way, Anglo hegemony is perpetuated.

Summary

Theorizing, then, is a formulized and structured method for playing with ideas and data. Researchers generate problems for study during the course of a project and decide how data can be used, whether to discover concepts and propositions or to confirm concepts and propositions. The thought processes, or theorizing, by which an ethnographer analyzes data involve mixing, matching, comparing, fitting together, linking, and constructing hierarchies analogous to games children play with simple toys, such as puzzles, strings of beads, blocks, tinkertoys, and Lego sets. Researchers differ in their activities in that the criteria used for sorting and matching are neither so simple nor so concrete as size, shape, and color. Research constructs are far more complex and abstract than a house of blocks. They also may be poorly constructed initially and, like the unsatisfactory house of blocks, need to be smashed a time or two before a firmly grounded, well-integrated structure emerges.

A difficulty with separating discussions of data collection and data analysis, such as we have done in this text, is that they may be perceived as distinct procedures. In ethnography, they are not; they are as inter-active and interdependent as child's play and children's toys. The inter-connections are particularly apparent when ethnographers use any of a set of analytic procedures that Zelditch (1962) calls sequential sampling and that we prefer to label sequential selection. (See Chapter Three for distinctions between sampling and selecting.) Sequential selection strategies use the generic processes of theorizing to combine or subdivide data in different ways for theory construction.

SEQUENTIAL SELECTION STRATEGIES

Sequential selection is different from choosing original populations for a study. It is open ended and exploratory and is used to establish new sets of phenomena to examine as the research study unfolds. Sequential selection strategies include negative-case selection, discrepant-case selection, theoretical sampling, and selection and comparison of cases testing theoretical implications.

In sequential sampling, persons, events, artifacts, or other phenomena of interest are further defined and examined. For example, in LeCompte's work (1975, 1978) on classroom socialization, the population under study ostensibly consisted of four classrooms. However, those classrooms included 4 teachers and about 125 children. These subjects in turn were engaged in hundreds of discrete activities and generated thousands of individual sentences and verbal episodes, of which approximately 3129 proved germane to the study. Thus, what appeared to be a study with a very small number of participants proved to be composed of many much larger subpopulations, although the subpopulations derived from decomposition of the larger whole. The size of the group selected is dependent upon the number of units required to generate and refine an abstract concept or postulate. Selection continues only until the researcher is certain that no new instances that modify the construct will emerge (Zelditch, 1962).

Most forms of sequential selection are designed to facilitate emergent constructs and theories and to eliminate rival constructs, theories, and hypotheses. Whereas most probabilistic samples and criterion-based selections are defined, designated, and obtained during initial phases of research activity, sequential selection begins only after sufficient data have been collected to initiate the analysis. Although sequential selection is associated with qualitative designs in which data collection and data analysis proceed simultaneously and mutually influence each other, it also can be used with other research models.

Negative-Case Selection

The most common form of sequential selection is negative-case selection. A negative case of a concept or postulate is an exception to the emergent rule, a case that refutes or disconfirms a construct. It functions like a null hypothesis. Researchers establish the universality of emergent constructs by a deliberate search for instances that contradict it. Negative cases allow researchers to establish the parameters or distribution of a construct. Negative-case selection also provides examples that indicate the degree of applicability of a construct and the conditions or circumstances under which it can be expected to obtain. Miles & Huberman (1984) emphasize that finding exceptions to hard-won patterns is challenging for analysts. We concur, but we also believe that overattachment to patterns can be avoided by this very method. Searching for negative cases as the pattern is developing makes the researcher conscious of pattern limitations and permits incorporating these very limitations into explanations and interpretations.

For example, a school ethnographer may find that high school students are expected to interact freely among themselves only in five kinds of situations. To refine this emergent construct of peer interaction, the researcher deliberately searches for exceptions to the developing pattern. Such exceptions allow the typology of permissible interactive situations to exclude whatever circumstances appear in the negative instances obtained. When additional negative cases indicate no further new circumstances, selection ceases.

Discrepant-Case Selection

A procedure related to and sometimes indistinguishable from negative-case selection is discrepant-case selection. Researchers may or may not designate them as different activities; Miles & Huberman (1984), for example, combine the searches for negative cases and discrepant cases into a search for outliers, the label used by statisticians for elements lying beyond the pattern of a curve.

When they are differentiated, the discrepant case is considered to be an instance that modifies, refines, or elaborates a construct. Whereas the negative case is the exception to the emergent rule, the discrepant case is a variant of the emergent rule. A discrepant case requires that a construct be modified to some degree. Using discrepant-case selection, the researcher searches for all pertinent instances for which the emerging construct cannot account. These are not contradictions or exceptions to the pattern, like negative cases; they are cases that fail to fit the emergent construct exactly.

For example, a search for discrepant cases for the five kinds of permissible peer interactive situations among high school students may result in identifying a sixth category, collapsing two categories into one, or eliminating a category.

Negative- and discrepant-case selection are guided by common-sense assumptions, by empirical or participant concerns, by evaluative or normative expectations, or by explicit theoretical and conceptual frameworks used semideductively. They are most commonly used, however, when researchers wish to generate new theory about some topic from data collected for that purpose. Under those circumstances, negative- and discrepant-case selection are frequently combined with the search for positive instances of a construct. This process is called theoretical sampling.

Theoretical Sampling

Theoretical sampling (Glaser & Strauss, 1967) is the development or construction of a theory to match the data. During fieldwork or data collection, theoretical sampling guides collection of successive data sets, and each pattern found in a set generates the next question to be explored. Answers to successive questions constitute alternative explanations to be discarded or tested, verified, and installed into the mosaic of patterns the researcher is assembling.

The researcher begins with the selection of several incidents, events, or chunks of data that may be compared and contrasted. They are chosen for their relevance to the theoretical domain designated for study. During the early phases of data collection and analysis, these chunks are chosen for similarity. During later phases, they are chosen to highlight differences. Glaser and Strauss suggest that minimization to maximization of differences aids the generation of theory. Similarities permit the identification of a category, the delineation of attributes of a category, and the specification of conditions under which categories are found. Differences among chosen instances permit elaboration of category attributes, identification of variations in categories, and qualification of categories.

In the peer interaction example cited previously, a researcher using theoretical sampling would frame the phenomenon more broadly. The goal might be a theory explaining adolescent peer interaction. Although the researcher might begin with data collected in a school setting, the theory eventually would require the maximization of differences created by collecting examples of interaction in such diverse environments as shopping centers, community social centers, or automobile race tracks. An ultimate goal of the theory might be a typology of the circumstances under which teenagers interact, unfettered by adult supervision. This might be similar to the school-specific typology suggested previously, but its theoretical framework would provide it with a wider scope.

Theory Implications Selection

Campbell (1979) has suggested a sequential sampling strategy to reduce biases in analysis or increase the confidence placed in research results (cf. Miles & Huberman, 1984, on eliminating rival explanations). This procedure, called theory implications selection, is most useful at the midpoint of fieldwork.

Campbell (1979) suggests that theoretical implication selection involves the specification of the implications of a theory, the search for data or cases to test those implications, and the appraisal of the theory on the basis of whether its implications hold true for the selected data. This strategy is particularly useful in situations when two or more theories are legitimate competitors for explanation of some phenomena. For each theory, the researcher identifies implications. Campbell suggests that researchers should construct a running score of hits and misses for the implications of each alternative theory. The theory with the most frequent hits should be the most convincing.

Researchers can increase the level of confidence with which they present their explanations by triangulation with independent sources of information during the data collection phase. They separately and successively test given explanations of a phenomenon by means of what Rosenblatt calls a "relentless tracking down of theoretical implications" coupled with a quick move into error correction processes (1981, p. 216). For example, if adolescents interact with each other in hierarchically arranged cliques, then they arrange their daily school schedules to maximize association with clique members (Cusick, 1973). The researcher seeks data to determine whether such an implication is true. Although only one implication is given here, a theory of adolescent clique interaction would have other implications for which cases could be sought.

We now turn to a second and more comprehensive set of standard analytic procedures. We include these five analytic procedures because they share with general research designs the assumptive modes discussed in Chapter Two: inductive to deductive, generative to verificative, constructive to enumerative, and subjective to objective (see Fig. 2.2). The positions of the strategies on the continua in Fig. 2.2 are descriptive rather than prescriptive and reflect the usages generally accorded the strategies in the research literature. We indicate that strategies are associated with particular sets of assumptions, as indicated by the solid lines in Fig. 2.2, and we note these cases in the discussion below.

GENERAL ANALYTIC PROCEDURES

The five strategies described next are analytic induction, constant comparison, typological analysis, enumeration, and standardized observational protocols. Analytic induction and constant comparison were specifically designed as inductive techniques for the generation of theory. Most standardized observational protocols provide deductive frameworks by which enumeration data may be organized to test or verify propositions. Typological and enumerative analysis can be adapted for varying purposes. They also are used throughout the entire research project. Typological analysis is particularly flexible because categories in a typology can be added, subtracted, or retained depending on their relevance to the data collected. Enumeration can only be used after data are categorized with sufficient clarity to allow items to be counted.

These strategies illustrate the variety of techniques available to researchers conducting naturalistic research. They are neither exhaustive nor exclusive alternatives within a comprehensive research design. All may be used within a given study. Their purpose is to facilitate the researcher's construction of innovative ways to examine the commonplace.

Accompanying the discussion of these strategies are two excerpts from field note narratives recorded in school situations. They illustrate an actual application of each of the strategies. These particular episodes exemplify the nature of most field note narratives: They are descriptive accounts at a low level of inference reflecting commonplace, everyday activity.

Analytic Induction

Qualitative researchers usually begin analysis with a form of analytic induction. This strategy involves scanning the data for categories of phenomena and for relationships among such categories, developing working typologies and hypotheses on an examination of initial cases, and then modifying and refining them on the basis of subsequent cases (Znaniecki, 1934; Robinson, 1951). Negative instances, or phenomena that do not fit the initial function, are consciously sought to expand, adapt, or restrict the original construct. In its most extreme application, analytic induction is intended to provide universal rather than probabilistic explanation: That is, *all* cases are to be explained, not merely some distribution of cases.

Table 7.4 provides an example of analytic induction. A researcher scanning the field note narrative in Table 7.4 might first identify the category gaming and one of its attributes, in this instance, rule setting. Subsequent data would be scanned for additional exemplars both of gaming and of rule setting. To use analytic induction on this field note excerpt, the researcher would then develop typologies of both categories, gaming and rule setting. Simultaneously, instances of interaction among the children would be examined to discover relationships between gaming and rule setting. These relationships would be translated into working hypotheses to be refined continuously until all instances of relationships

TABLE 7.4
Recess: An Example of Analytic Induction

1:20   Bill carries one of the basketballs into the multipurpose room (a room which functions
       as a lunchroom, gymnasium, and auditorium), hands it to David, and joins the
       group at the basketball hoop (Howard, Nancy, Linda, and Jack) that already has
       a ball. Bill throws, misses the basket, and tosses the ball to Linda. There is a brief
       discussion between Linda and the others regarding second chances to throw the
       ball.

1:25   Linda makes a basket and tosses the ball to Nancy. Linda and Bill engage in a 5-
       second mock battle at the end of the line of players. Bill shoots again and just
       barely misses. He drops the ball and goes running after it. Upon returning, he
       tries again, only to miss. He catches the ball twice for Jack, a consistently good
       shot, who makes both baskets. Bill misses another toss, makes two good ones, and
       fails the third try. He runs over to me with assurances that he lost the ball earlier
       only because his foot slipped. Linda sends the ball backwards through the hoop,
       and everyone giggles. Nancy has deserted them now for the group at the jump
       rope.

[a] Derived from an ethnographic study of a third-grade classroom in the midwestern U.S.
(Goetz, 1976b). All named individuals are students. The 10-minute sequence is an observation of an indoor recess period.

between gaming and rule setting in this social context could be satisfacto-
rily explained.

Analytic induction is used exclusively in generative research. Although it has been used principally to construct concepts, ideas, and
themes, it may be adapted for enumeration. In the example above, the
strategy could be applied by imposing external observer categories on
the behavior stream and then counting the number of incidents in each
category. In the early phases of analysis, it also may be used to identify
subjective participant constructs; however, this application may be limited
in those cases where the researcher uses the techniques to identify relationships which obtain across many participants. The strategy is particularly useful because it does not require a particular kind of analytic unit.

The classic instance of analytic induction is Lindesmith's analysis
(1947, 1968) of narcotics addicts, which sought to account for differential
addiction to opiates. Using a series of negative cases to revise explanations, Lindesmith derived an interrelated set of propositions predicting
the circumstances leading to addiction. More recently, Mehan has demonstrated the use of analytic induction as an alternative approach to studying
classroom interaction in his analysis of a multiethnic inner-city school.
He incorporated this strategy into a research design he labels constitutive
ethnography (1979).

Constant Comparison

Devised by Glaser & Strauss (1967), this strategy combines inductive category coding with a simultaneous comparison of all social incidents observed and coded. This means that as social phenomena are recorded and classified, they also are compared across categories. Thus the discovery of relationships, or hypothesis generation, begins with the analysis of initial observations, undergoes continuous refinement throughout the data collection and analysis process, and continuously feeds back into the process of category coding. As events are constantly compared with previous events, new typological dimensions as well as new relationships may be discovered.

The constant comparative method shares with analytic induction its focus on identifying categories and on generating statements of relationships. Constant comparison might also direct a researcher to the categories of gaming and rule setting identified in the first field note example (see Table 7.4). However, these categories would be processed differently. Rule setting, for example, would be examined across all of the instances in which it occurred, not just in gaming contexts and not only as conducted by students. All interactions observed in the school would be scanned for rule setting, and instances would be compared and contrasted so theoretical statements about institutional rule setting could be developed. In this sense, then, the constant comparative method may be regarded as a supplement to analytic induction.

Glaser & Strauss (1967) describe constant comparison as an inductive procedure, devised to assist in generating social theory. Although participant constructs may be used in its preliminary phases, the relationships so developed are defined objectively. Typically, the constant comparative method is used as a constructive rather than as an enumerative procedure. Like analytic induction, this technique is flexible; it does not require the use of any particular unit of analysis.

Glaser & Strauss's own application of constant comparison appears most clearly in their examination of the institutional treatment of death (1965, 1968). A theory predicting reactions to death was developed by comparing the responses of dying patients and all participants involved with them in a hospital setting. Carroll used the strategy to assess the significance of work and play domains for predicting student and teacher behavior (1975). A modification of the constant comparative method was used by Smith & Pohland (1976) in the evaluation of a computer-assisted instructional project. In her study of the relationship of gender and deviance among schoolchildren, Davis (1984) uses constant comparison to generate theory about how males and females differ in rule breaking. She uses the metaphor of script to demonstrate how the intersection of social and cultural forces with personal history and experience results in gendered reactions to power.

Typological Analysis

Typological analysis involves dividing everything observed into groups or categories on the basis of some canon for disaggregating the whole phenomenon under study. Such typologies may be devised from a theoretical framework or set of propositions or from common-sense or mundane perceptions of reality. Becker *et al.* (1968) developed the latter, an atheoretical framework for analyzing field note data in their investigation of undergraduate university students. Data were divided into mundane categories that roughly correspond to how people from Western European cultures classify their experiences. These categories—the type of event, the time of occurrence, the participants involved, the reaction of participants, and the physical setting—were then subdivided and the resulting units were scanned for patterned relationships. Cusick used the same system in his analysis of student interaction in a high school setting (1973).

A mundane analytic system also might be used on the field note excerpt in Table 7.4. In it, the physical setting of the school's multipurpose room would be noted. Indoor recess as a type of classroom event would be formulated. The names and statuses of the individuals involved, including the researcher, might be coded. Time of occurrence in both clock time and school unit time would be noted. Reactions of participants might be identified according to any one of a number of emergent categories, including student cooperation, student decision making, or leadership juggling. Using other coded field narratives from the same setting, a cross-coding system indicating relationships among the various categories could be developed. The researcher might, for example, wish to cross-code classroom events with the participant reaction labeled student decision making to discover which events involve the most student autonomy.

Although intended primarily to construct the reality of a particular research site, such typologies may be developed by one researcher and then borrowed by another. Used in this way, they provide consistency in data collection throughout the field site residence and may be adapted for enumerative purposes (Lofland, 1971; Lofland and Lofland, 1984; Ogbu, 1988; Erickson, 1992; Dobbert & Kurth-Schai, 1992). Despite the bias inherent in using typologies or analytic frames developed for other purposes, they may be applied readily in the discovery of participant-designated categories and relationships. Because these analytic frameworks serve descriptive as well as generative purposes, they may be more flexible than strategies like analytic induction and constant comparison.

They have been applied in this manner by anthropologists (e.g., Whiting, 1963). On the other hand, the use of these typologies requires that researchers use whatever units of analysis are intrinsic to their construction, and in that sense they are less flexible than analytic induction and constant comparison. Certain elaborated typologies, such as Henry's cross-cultural outline of education (1960), for example, have been designed deliberately to compensate for observer perceptual and cultural biases (cf., e.g., Hilger, 1966; Whiting *et al.*, 1966).

Lofland (1971) advances a second category of typological analysis. His scheme is related to standard structural functionalist social theory (i.e., Radcliffe-Brown, 1965; Merton, 1967). In Lofland's work, social phenomena are assumed to be divisible into one of six categories: acts, activities, meanings, participation, relationships, and settings. Observations are initially sorted into one of these six basic categories, and typologies are built within the categories. Observations then are scanned for patterned regularities among categories, which may form the basis for casual or consequential explanations.

The field note excerpt displayed in Table 7.4 was coded using one of Lofland's categories, acts. This procedure resulted in an identification and classification of student behaviors into more or less abstract categories such as attention seeking, social reciprocity, and conflict resolution as well as physical activities like dribbling and tossing a basketball. Cross-coding a typology of student acts with a comparable typology of teacher acts provided an empirical data base for generating hypotheses about the ways in which teacher behaviors are related to student behaviors.

Goetz's analysis (1976a,b) of student behavior in a third-grade classroom is one application of Lofland's typological system. Such applications do require a compatibility between the research problem posed and the theoretical perspective that informs the strategy. If the categories sought or discovered in the research site match the categories described in the borrowed classification scheme, typologies such as Lofland's may be used inductively for both descriptive and generative purposes and for analyzing either objective or subjective data. Because of the abstractness of the social categories, Lofland's strategy is primarily constructive; it lacks the precision required for enumerative purposes (Denzin, 1978). In addition, both atheoretical typologies and theoretical typologies such as Lofland's impose units of analysis upon the data.

Enumeration

Data analysis strategies that use frequency counts require a precise identification of phenomena or categories of phenomena and a consistency in data collection techniques. In ethnographic research, such strategies are generally of two types. First, enumerative systems may be used for data quality control or as a supplement to descriptive data. For these purposes, enumeration functions to provide supportive evidence for the existence and validity of research categories and hypotheses and comes after such categories and hypotheses have been developed in the study at hand. It operates within the ethnographic study as a corroborative minisurvey of certain phenomena and is conducted according to the rules of survey analysis (Denzin, 1978). Ogbu's examination of educational orientations in a multiethnic California neighborhood (1974) includes quantified data pertinent to schooling, for example, family composition, family socioeconomic characteristics, ethnic composition of the client population, community unemployment rates, and educational levels attained by students' parents and grandparents.

McCall's data quality control index (1969) uses frequency counts as a strategy for coding field note data to evaluate each observation for possible contamination. This method is particularly aimed at reducing or controlling for the reactive effects of the observer's presence, possible distortions in the observer's perceptions and interpretations of events, and biased selectivity within an observed record of events. In their ethnography of medical student culture, Becker *et al.* (1961) used a variety of frequency count techniques to substantiate the validity of their conclusions. As with minisurveys, data quality control systems are generally subordinate to some primary technique of data analysis. Unlike most minisurveys whose purpose is to generate additional data to address substantive questions, data quality controls serve as checks for the reliability and validity of the principal data collection techniques. Table 7.5 provides an example of research whose enumerative coding categories first were developed in a pilot study which used analytic induction and constant comparison; the categories then were applied for the actual research to a setting similar to the one in which the pilot study was executed. A typology of norm-related teacher verbal behavior was developed first; that typology was then used deductively to code the transcripts of teacher talk. The primary unit of analysis was a verbal episode; other units included specific categories of activity as might be delineated with Lofland's typology (LeCompte, 1975).

Enumeration of data such as that found in both Tables 7.4 and 7.5 might be used to supplement primarily constructive techniques. Sociometric information might be developed: In Table 7.4, it would be possible to count the contacts each child has had with each other child. Translated into frequency counts, the patterns of actual child-to-child contacts provide comparisons with both sociometric survey instruments and nonenumerative observations (cf., e.g., Glascock, 1976). Among the patterns of

TABLE 7.5
The Day Begins: Excerpt from a Field Note Narrative[a]

(Children are playing outside the classroom; a few are standing on the porch. The teacher arrives.)

8:55			"Come in, girls first." (There's some messing around before
8:57			they line up.) (They come in and move toward their
		T2A	seats.)(T2A) "Mrs. Smith is ready to start."(She's sitting on
	Getting	R1A	the desk in the front of the room.) (R1A) "Mrs. Smith is
	settled	R2B	waiting." (R2B) "I like the way Bernie is sitting down, and
		R1A	Atocha." (R1A) "Please, people, do not throw snowballs at
		R4B	one another." (R4B) "There isn't enough snow on the
			ground and you pick up rocks with it. If we have a lot of
		R4A	snow we'll have a snowball fight, but please don't throw the
			snow when there isn't much . . . " (R4A) "If you go along
		R4B	with me and don't throw now, as soon as there's good stuff
			we'll have a snowball fight." (R4B) "It isn't just that you hurt
			people, but you'll get in trouble too."
		T2A	
9:03		W1B	(T2A) "All right, the girls will go to bake cookies at recess."
			(W1B) "Boys, come back here if you aren't done; if you
		W2B	can't work alone you can go into Mrs. Dvorak's game room."
	Getting	R1A	(W2B) "I expect if you come in here to work I expect you
	organized		to work." (R1A) "I want everybody to bring a nickel by
			Monday." (Is it for the girls' surprise?) "No, it's for
			everybody."

[a] This is derived from an observational study of four fourth-grade classrooms in the southwestern United States (LeCompte, 1975). Teacher talk is recorded in quotations; pupil talk and locational description are enclosed in parentheses.

peer interaction that might emerge are those of an isolate who usually initiates interactions only with class leaders and with adults such as the ethnographer. Similarly, data focusing on teacher talk, as in Table 7.5, could be recoded for counts of teacher–pupil verbal interaction.

Some supplemental enumerative strategies may be used inductively while others serve clearly deductive purposes. They may provide strictly descriptive material, or they may augment attempts to generate, refine, or verify hypotheses. Most are intended for an analysis of objective data although frequency counts of subjective participant constructs are not uncommon. All require explicitly formulated analytic units so that what is countable is clearly designated. These units may be developed on site by the researcher or borrowed from other's schemes.

A second major type of enumerative system consists of an overall analytic strategy whereby field note data are coded into operationally defined categories and frequency counts are made of phenomena in the different categories. As is the case with all enumerative techniques, units of analysis are clearly specified in advance of data collection and are determined by the nature of the coding categories. The example in Table 7.5 illustrates this type of system.

Table 7.5 demonstrates two types of coding. First, classroom activities were classified and delineated within parentheses (see Barker, 1963). Second, certain types of verbal episodes or statements emitted by the teacher were classified according to a coding system. This is represented by the parenthetical numbers and letters within the text and to the left of the brackets. The coding categories were developed inductively both from fieldwork in other settings and from the entire body of field notes generated for this study. They were then applied systematically, as illustrated, to the field notes for enumeration.

The coding categories in Table 7.5 represent teacher talk that reinforces the teacher's authority or establishes rules (R), organizes a time schedule (T), or focuses on tasks or work (W). Although this excerpt does not include all of the coding categories used in the study (see LeCompte, 1975), examination of other coded chronicles determined the distribution of types of teacher talk within specific classroom activities. It also provided a means for distinguishing among management styles of individual teachers. Mrs. Smith, for example, established rules by making reciprocal deals with students (R4A); other teachers simply stated their expectations (R1A) and required students to comply.

Systems such as these are generally concerned with the refinement or verification of categories and hypotheses rather than with the generation of such constructs. They may be devised either deductively from some theoretical basis (e.g., Borman, 1978) or inductively from other ethnographic data. Such systems are used customarily to analyze objective data, although their genesis may involve identification of participant constructs (e.g., Talbert, 1970). LeCompte's comparative analysis (1978) of fourth-grade teachers was based upon frequency counts of verbal and nonverbal instructional behavior and was devised to refine hypotheses about teacher normative messages that had been generated in prior ethnographic classroom study.

Standardized Observational Protocols

A final, much discussed strategy for analyzing observational data is a combination data collection–analysis technique. (See discussion of interaction analysis protocols in Chapter Six.) Sometimes inaccurately termed ethnography, this analysis involves the application of any one of hundreds of standardized observational protocols (cf., e.g., Medley & Mitzel, 1963;

Rosenshine & Furst, 1973; Dunkin & Biddle, 1974). If well done, this strategy requires that initial constructive stages of fieldwork be used to develop enumerative instruments in which units of analysis are precisely specified. Phenomena then are coded during observation into previously designated categories of behavior. Such categories, amenable only to objective data, usually have been carefully operationalized and field tested so as to guarantee adequate levels of reliability and validity. These categories represent selection of very precise aspects of behavior from the general stream of behavior and events and differ from the first four analytic techniques discussed in that they are more often deductive and are designed explicitly for the verification of hypotheses. Such protocols are obviously enumerative rather than constructive. Because of these characteristics, an application of a standardized protocol to the first field note excerpt (see Table 7.4) might produce misleading or inappropriate results. The excerpt represents observer-selected units from the stream of behavior, and protocols require access to the intact stream, whether directly or by transcription. Although the coding system used in Table 7.4 is not a standardized protocol, it could be developed into one by replication in similar settings.

The Flanders system (Amidon & Flanders, 1963; Flanders, 1970) of analyzing teacher–student exchanges is the most publicized of such protocols; its strengths and weaknesses are typical of such instruments (Mehan, 1979). Although generally ignored by ethnographers, standardized observational protocols are widely used, particularly by curriculum developers and evaluators of teacher and administrator performance. Because they are designed to code concrete observed behaviors at a low level of inference and then to enumerate them, they may facilitate the data analysis task in a number of ways. In cases where data have been collected on video or audio tapes or transcribed from such recordings, protocols may be used as either primary or supplementary analytic strategies to enumerate salient categories of interest. Erickson and his associates (e.g., Erickson & Mohatt, 1982; Erickson and Wilson, 1982; Erickson, 1992) have used such protocols, developed from videotapes, extensively to delineate subtle differences in behavior among classrooms in cross-cultural milieus. They developed their protocols, however, after they had achieved familiarity with the field and the phenomena studied.

In instances where long-term residence in the field is planned and where observations are to be collected over a year or more, standardized protocols, prudently chosen to reflect emerging patterns of analysis, may be incorporated into the ethnographer's total array of data collection techniques. Finally, in cases where the overall research design requires limited observational data, the substitution of appropriate standardized protocols for the costlier and more time-consuming alternative of participant observation should be considered seriously.

SUMMARY

Analysis in ethnography is like disaggregation of particles in subatomic physics. Inventories appearing to exhaust the components of given structures often may have been limited by the sophistication or precision of observational or analytic tools. Just as the physicist exhausts the utility of his analytical tools, an ethnographer's final analysis represents an arbitrary stopping point established by the ethnographer's choice of components to be studied, the data collection tools used, or the depth of analysis to be accomplished, because cultural phenomena always can be further analyzed, subdivided, and reconstituted. Some researchers are satisfied if they have broadly outlined the general patterns of belief, behavior, and relationships within a culture. Others cannot rest until the smallest intricacies of observable behavior and audible speech have been dissected. Limits are set only by the predilections and stamina of the individual researcher, constraints of funding, and other exigencies.

Ethnographers also share with subatomic physicists the Heisenbergian dilemma: To obtain information about one aspect of a phenomenon, knowledge of another aspect must be foresworn (Zukav, 1979). In physics, to learn the exact location of a particle within an atom, knowledge of its momentum must be sacrificed, and vice versa. In the ordinary ethnographic project, if tiny details of movement and language are sought, limits on time and resources preclude establishment of larger patterns of thought, ritual, and behavior. These are, of course, decisions made as the units of analysis for a particular study are chosen. However, units of analysis within a given study may vary considerably in scope; similar data also may be aggregated differently given different units of analysis. For example, when seen from the perspective of a specific school campus, interracial conflict may seem to be no great problem. However, if interracial conflict is examined from a perspective that takes entire school districts as the unit of analysis, patterns of conflict may emerge that are serious indeed. The level of aggregation, as well as the unit of analysis, must fit the specific issue under consideration. Further, discovery and interpretation of patterns and ordering principles may, in fact, require examining data from different vantage points or on different scales (see Gleick, 1987; LeCompte 1993). In the next section of the chapter we describe how ethnographers, having hacked and chopped their holistically gathered data into bits, then reassemble it into an intact cultural scene.

Building An Ethnographic Analysis

Generic theorizing processes and the formal analytic procedures discussed above are the conceptual tools ethnographers use to devise their analyses. These tools are variously used and combined as each ethnographer addresses particular research goals, within chosen theoretical frameworks, to study diverse human groups. This section of the chapter examines data analysis as it is undertaken by researchers using a variety of strategies. To illustrate, we provide an extensive example of how the process is executed in practice.

COMBINING STRATEGIES IN A RESEARCH PROJECT

The general analytic procedures discussed above include examples of how individual slices of data are handled within a research project. Below, we describe how a variety of analytic techniques were used throughout a single study. In the study of classroom socialization described earlier, LeCompte (1974) first observed extensively in numerous classrooms, recording teacher behavior in detail. From these preliminary observations, she developed a typology from which was derived both the unit of analysis, the verbal episode, and a general framework of value categories that represented what teachers emphasized. These included a range of valued student behaviors, including not fighting or stealing, working hard, being on time, and demonstrating a desire to learn. The value framework represented the outline or edge pieces of the puzzle analogy described above. Later, when the actual project began, observation of the four study teachers yielded a body of field notes that recorded what the teachers actually said. These notes or transcripts were transformed into units, the verbal episodes, and sorted into categories delineated by the value framework described above.

At this point, both constant comparison and analytic induction were used to clarify which units fit into specific categories. Units that did not fit the original framework were used to create additional categories, such as the value placed upon cleanliness by one teacher. Other categories that the researcher originally thought were important ended up being stressed very little. One of these was an emphasis on the intrinsic rather than the extrinsic value of learning, which was stressed by only one of the four teachers. Thus, some of the pieces of the original value framework did not appear to belong to this puzzle. Rather than being discarded, however, they were used as negative cases to clarify what really did occur in the classrooms. These items also proved important in another phase of the analysis.

An additional step occurred in this stage of analysis. The contents of the original framework were tested to see if they made sense to and matched with the value frameworks of the teachers in the study. This took place in the form of several interviews with each teacher during the fieldwork phase of the study. The teachers were asked what values they wanted to transmit to their students; they also were queried about what the researcher had observed them doing. For example, one child who consistently did perfect or near-perfect work was seldom praised for her efforts. She did not even always receive A's on her perfect papers. This seemed inconsistent with the teacher's claim that she believed in encouraging children to do their best. However, she explained that in this case it was more important that the child not grow to feel she was superior to other children, hence, the dearth of positive feedback. (See Pearson, 1982, for a detailed procedure for reconciling conflicts in value hierarchies held by teachers.)

Data from the teacher interviews were used to modify the value framework; they also facilitated interpreting the distributions for teacher behavior that emerged later. An enumerative procedure was then used, in which the researcher examined the relative frequency of subdivisions within each category. Some categories had many more units in them than others; some subdivisions contained more data instances than others. Subcategories that made more explicit and concise the content and definition of larger categories were created in some cases. For example, one large category called "taking responsibility" actually was composed of two rather different subsets. On the one hand, some teachers defined taking responsibility as following teacher orders. On the other hand, a few teachers defined taking responsibility as students' self-direction and initiative. Although the two were not incompatible, they did have widely different consequences for classroom ambience. Thus, enumeration was used to clarify the original typology.

In the process of matching and cross-matching categories, a pattern began to emerge, particularly when the distributions of behavior for each teacher were examined and compared. First, six categories of verbal episode subsumed more of the episodes recorded than any of the others. Second, distribution of these six categories was relatively similar for each of the four study teachers. As a group, these six types of episodes occurred more than any other set of categories. This seemed particularly puzzling. At the beginning of the study, the researcher had noticed and wondered how to reconcile the apparent differences among the activities, environments, and teaching styles in each of the classrooms. The initial impression of divergence was inconsistent with the uniformity in activities that content analysis of teacher behavior had produced.

Two additional patterns in the analysis provided clues for this puzzle. First, other categories of verbal behavior appeared frequent for some, but not all, of the teachers. Second, those six most frequently occurring categories of verbal behavior formed a coherent emphasis on classroom management and discipline—work, order, timeliness, and conformity to authority. They were labeled the "management core." The other frequently occurring, but not universally shared, categories represented values that individual teachers felt were important: academic achievement, cleanliness, independence, and additional emphasis on discipline and management. These categories were labeled "discretionary" behavior. A Venn diagram (see Fig. 7.2) was used to portray graphically how the shared and nonshared behaviors created surface variance and underlying uniformity in the classrooms.

At this point, manipulation of raw data ceased. The analytic process had produced results. The study then moved into the final stages of the analytic process—integration and interpretation of results. Although the Venn diagram in Fig. 7.2 interested LeCompte's dissertation advisory committee, they viewed it as insufficient for an end product. Her final task was to demonstrate "what it all meant" by integrating her results with those of related studies, showing how her results related to broader theoretical frameworks, and explaining what the study really meant (see

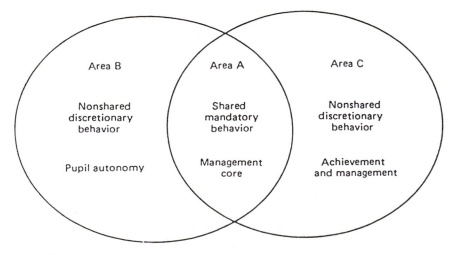

Figure 7.2 Emerging patterns: Three areas of teacher behavior. (From LeCompte, 1975, 1978.)

below). The way ethnographers approach these tasks is discussed in the following pages.

Interpretation of Data and Integration of Findings with Existing Knowledge

The implications of a study tell a reader how the research is useful beyond an intriguing analysis of a unique case. The significance of the study facilitates judgments about how valuable the implications are for circumstances beyond the actual study site. Interpretation of data varies according to the purpose of the study, its conceptual and theoretical frameworks, researcher experience and background, and the nature of the data collected and analyzed.

In this section, we outline first the difficulties investigators often have with interpreting their results and integrating them within broader frameworks. We then describe the conceptual tools used to clarify the meaning of ethnographic studies (cf., e.g., McCutcheon, 1981). To make sense of their description, qualitative researchers apply theory to their data, make interpretations based on metaphors and analogies, and synthesize their results with those of other researchers. Skillful use of these tools not only makes the reported study more vivid and interesting, but also leads to generation of new theory, integrates the current research with macrocultural issues, and makes explicit contextual connections and generalizations that the investigator discovered in the course of the research report.

PROBLEMS WITH INTERPRETING RESULTS

If encountering mountains of data is a daunting enterprise, interpreting results from data may make researchers feel as though they have committed hubris. But if they give up on interpretation and simply describe what they saw, they fail to do justice to their data. By leaving readers to draw their own conclusions, researchers risk misinterpretation. Their results also may be trivialized by readers who are unable to make connections implied, but not made explicit, by the researcher. Qualitative researchers may fail to recognize the implications of a study until sufficient time and distance permit data to be reexamined in less immediate, more dispassionate ways. Researchers may be too close to fieldwork, too immersed in personal relationships and detail, to recognize their most important findings. Although fables circulate of researchers who have built careers from mining and remining their doctoral dissertations, more common are examples of descriptive reports which are followed by more theoretically integrated work. An example is Peter Blau's study of social service agencies. The initial study, *Dynamics of Bureaucracy* (1955), was a comparative depiction of interaction within formal organizations; it contributed significantly to the literature in that area. Blau's major work on social exchange theory, based in part upon data from his earlier study, was published much later (1964). Similarly, LeCompte's study of conflicting constituencies in an inner-city school reform project was reported in 1969. Later material from that study was used to demonstrate how ideologies adopted by funding bureaucracies, rather than specific educational crises, generated proposals for school reform and and associated research (LeCompte, 1970).

In both cases, later work depended on two crucial elements: the existence of an original data bank and sufficient time for reflection. We are not suggesting that all ethnographers wait 3 or 4 years before completing their reports. However, we believe that lapse of time is critical to a researcher's ability to reflect on data. Because the process cannot be hurried, ethnographers must expect their studies to generate several reports at different levels of abstraction. This differs from the process in experimental studies, where different questions require new studies and generation of a new set of data. Ethnographers, by contrast, raise different questions of the *same* data sets, used in different ways. What is critical to the integrity of each report is that the data adequately address the questions raised and that they are used with a level of theory which is appropriate to the data under analysis.

In addition to the ethnographer's need for sufficient reflective time in which to identify the significance of a study, articulating the importance of one's work requires that the researcher develop an existential commitment to a political, ethical, conceptual, or theoretical position. Not only does interpretation require researchers to shift gears and think in new ways, it forces them to take a concrete stand on the significance of what they have been doing for the past months or years. As they discover the conceptual inadequacy of a mere recitation of the bare facts, they must make a daring leap into the murky ambiguity which lies beyond the data.

Although qualitative researchers should avoid wild guesses about meaning and long-shot connections to chunks of data or theory, carefully reasoned arguments that develop inferences and establish connections beyond the limited scope of a study are legitimate goals toward which all researchers strive. The process uses the same concrete procedures of matching and testing categories for interpretation as is used for analysis. However, interpretation involves redesigning old categories, formulating

new relationships by combining elements in novel ways, projecting beyond what actually exists, conjuring up improbable connections and metaphors, and wondering "why not?", "what if?", and "just suppose?"
(Kress, 1982). These are playful modes of thought for serious researchers;
those who have spent years in hard-nosed dissection of phenomena may
find them perilously ambiguous.

The third difficulty investigators have with building an interpretation
is that it *does* require the shift in cognitive style to which we alluded above.
Researchers spend the vast proportion of their intellectual life engaged
in the convergent process of focusing down on a topic. The convergent
thinking that this requires is commonly taught and rewarded in formal
schooling and is a style congenial to many researchers. It facilitates concise
and coherent descriptions of the phenomena observed. Researchers use
convergent thinking both to disaggregate data and to reconstitute them
in new ways. They rarely have difficulty describing results, because competent ethnographers know that what they report was observed and that
what they observed was corroborated by various slices of data that have
been integrated into their overall scenarios. However, interpretation demands a shift into different, more creative and divergent thinking styles,
especially that most complex theorizing process, speculation. Neophyte
researchers may have had little encouragement and less practice in this
type of thinking.

The foreignness of these processes and the riskiness of going beyond
the data into a never-never land of inference may make this stage of a
project truly terrifying. Our intention is to ease this phase and to clarify
its tasks by identifying how it is approached in qualitative study: consol-
idating theory, applying theory, interpreting with metaphors and analysis, and synthesizing results within relevant lines of inquiry.

THEORETICAL CONSOLIDATION

In the first section of this chapter we described processes of theorizing as
well as sequential selection procedures that ground theory development
in the collection of data. These processes and procedures foreshadow the
tools to be used in the final states of the study. In research informed
by an explicit theoretical orientation, researchers begin the interpretive
process by stepping back from the data and assessing whether the data
collected mesh with the initial theoretical framework. This can be done
during the early, preanalysis stage of "tidying up" or it can be done while
data are still being collected. Interpretation thus begins very early in the
research process. Goetz (1976a,b), for example, found that Lofland's
categories for arranging classroom phenomena were quite adequate to

subsume her data (see Chapter Two). Had the categories been incompatible with the data, she would have discarded or modified them. Such choices are crucial to assigning meaning to the data analysis and are explicitly summarized for the reader when results are interpreted.

In a study of the socialization of student teachers, Ginsburg & LeCompte first examined existing theories of career socialization (1980). One theory indicates that career aspirants pattern their professional identities on direct instruction received in training. This structural model (cf. Wrong, 1961) assumes that what is taught is absorbed. The other theory (Bucher & Stellings, 1977) characterizes career aspirants as active negotiators who shape their own experiences. Using these frameworks, Ginsburg and LeCompte created dichotomous categories to classify their participants according to the student teachers' identifications of most salient influences on how they viewed themselves as teachers. However, the actual data did not fit into the dichotomous categories. Neither theory adequately explained how these particular student teachers acquired attitudes and behaviors relevant to their chosen profession. Thus the original theoretical framework had to be modified to include other categories more closely attuned to the data. The modification of theory differentiates ethnography from other research designs (see Chapter One). Because interpretation is grounded in data, results are neither discarded nor discredited if the data fail to support an original hypothesis. Rather, the hypotheses themselves are modified to match the nonconforming data.

Some theories informing studies are less elaborate than those described above. LeCompte had hypothesized in her (1978) four classrooms that learning as an intrinsically valuable activity would be stressed universally, simply because this value is embedded in philosophies of education, teacher training, and general Western European culture. However, data from only one of the four classrooms supported the hypothesis. Discovery of the maldistribution in teacher activities reinforcing this value forced her to reexamine both the data on patterns of classroom activities and environment and the information from the teacher interviews. This led her to formulate a new but related hypothesis: that emphasis on the intrinsic value of learning is unnecessary for the smooth, effective operation of a classroom. Rather, it is an optional behavior that only is emphasized by some, but not all, teachers, after basic requisites for order and task orientation are met.

We have noted that ethnographers often begin the process of interpretation in the earliest stages of data collection. However, they also engage in interpretation in subsequent stages of the process, just as all other researchers do. A second type of interpretation, and one which constitutes the second stage of many studies, involves investigation whose purpose is to generate both descriptions of phenomena and theories to explain them. The latter studies usually begin with data collection and analytic strategies that are theoretically informed, simply because the units of analysis—how the stream of behavior is divided—are themselves derived from explicit or implicit theoretical frameworks. However, they are not initiated under the aegis of an overall explanatory theoretical framework used to subsume anticipated data. The data obtained are used to generate explanations of phenomena because the aim of these studies is to create new structures rather than to build upon existing ones.

This type of research is unsettling to investigators who need the security of structural underpinnings. To many, the process appears to be like a post hoc search for explanations. We do not believe that this is the case. Glaser & Strauss (1967) demonstrate the utility of generating theory that is grounded in data. Such theories constitute the best explanations of phenomena observed. Equally important is the use of the interpretive process to elaborate upon theories that initially framed a study. In the example below, we use LeCompte's four-classroom study (1975) to describe how theory was generated. This study used theory in two ways. First, a substantive theory was generated to explain the actual data. Second, the theory generated was then applied to and integrated with other relevant research (LeCompte, 1981) to widen its scope and demonstrate its generalizability. The explanation of this application is presented in the following section.

LeCompte's data indicated that the reason teachers with divergent teaching styles were so similar in the amount of managerial behaviors they used was lodged within the social construction and purposes of the classrooms. Students lived in a crowded environment (cf. Jackson, 1968); they had specific tasks to complete; only 1 leader, the teacher, was present to assure that the 30 other individuals in the room would comply with what was expected. These conditions were imposed upon teachers by district-wide staffing ratios, school lunch schedules, curriculum guides, and standardized test scores. Teachers had little control over such external constraints. Regardless of their philosophies of teaching, they had to adapt their behaviors accordingly. The core of similar behaviors was a response to similar constraints. The hypothesis generated from this linkage is that certain necessary, rather regimented conditions must occur in any classroom before instruction can proceed. These conditions include order, student attentiveness, and adherence to schedules, none of which can be maintained without conformity to the teacher's authority. LeCompte suggests that these conditions form a substructure constraining whatever teachers do. Despite the obvious and observable variations in teaching styles among the four teachers, LeCompte asserts that as long as schools are organized as the ones she observed were, substantial limitations on popular notions of democracy in the classroom will exist.

LeCompte made the connections between teacher behavior and school organization after long cogitation over how to explain the similarities and divergencies in behavior she had found in the managerial and discretionary areas of teacher behavior. What clarified the connections was her realization that, for the most part, discretionary behavior was oriented toward establishment and recognition of individual differences among students, while the managerial behavior was directed toward group activities, even crowd control. To provide a rationale for the consistency of the managerial core across teachers, LeCompte used Durkheim's (1961) and Dreeben's (1968) interpretations of schooling as a social enterprise developing both secondary relationships and ideals of universalism and citizenship. The managerial core of behavior existed because it was tied to the very nature and purpose of schooling in contemporary society.

At this stage, the first report generated by the research project was complete (LeCompte, 1975, 1978). The researcher had grounded a reasonable explanation for the puzzling phenomenon in the data. The next stage of the interpretation, reported in a later publication (1981), involved larger implications of the same study.

THEORETICAL APPLICATION

Application of theory is the technique used in the second study generated from LeCompte's original 1975 work. It involves a systematic search for studies or analytic frames that fit the data more abstractly or generally. This allows the researcher to locate the universal implications of the idiosyncratic case. Occasionally, such a search produces no good theoretical fit or demonstrates that the data at hand contradict all existing theory. The researcher then must decide whether the data collected or analytic techniques used were faulty and the conclusions drawn incorrect or whether a theoretical or conceptual breakthrough overturning or modifying existing theory has been achieved.

Mead's early work on child rearing in the South Pacific provides an excellent example of research which she felt disconfirmed conventional wisdom. Mead had attempted to study cross-culturally the well-documented phenomenon of adolescent anxiety surrounding sexuality. However, her data indicated that Samoan adolescents, and even young children, did not behave in the same way European and North American children did. In fact, they did not appear to experience any sexual anxiety whatsoever. Mead used this data in combination with data from subsequent studies in the South Pacific and existing data from Europe and the

United States to posit that different cultures had radical differences in their behavior and belief regarding the role of sexuality in child rearing. She hypothesized that these differences appeared to produce dramatic personality differences in adult individuals from different culture areas. Thus, not only were notions of adolescent development greatly modified by Mead's work, but Mead and her immediate colleagues generated a whole study area of the impact of culture on personality development. In a sense, the culture and personality approach to cultural anthropology represented a synthesis of existing theories and emerging theories, ones which drew upon theories well grounded in empirical data as well as those which transcended data and those which were conceptual frames not necessarily associated with data at all.

More mundane is the approach LeCompte took in her study of four classrooms (1975, 1978). She used existing theories and studies as support for explaining the results of her study within a wider, more abstract social context. Theories of social stratification and correlational studies of the relationship between schooling and occupational attainment (see Chapter One) served as background for her research. Using sophisticated statistical techniques, sociologists had established correlations between parent levels of schooling and occupational attainment and those of their children (e.g., Blau & Duncan, 1967; Hadjighasem, 1980; Rosenfeld, 1971; Sewell, Haller, & Portes, 1969). Later studies used neo-Marxism or cultural materialism to suggest that forms of schooling are related to levels of occupational attainment. Vocational and nonacademic schooling are reserved for children from low socioeconomic statuses. Children from higher socioeconomic groups are provided with schooling commensurate with their statuses (Bourdieu & Passeron, 1977; Boudon, 1974; Bowles & Gintis, 1976; Lundgren & Pettersson, 1979). Some researchers looked at the fit between parental orientations, expectations, and formal schooling and suggested that these had a strong impact upon the destiny of their children. Upper-class children, for example, are socialized to be task oriented, to defer gratification, and to accept as legitimate the teacher's authority and the rewards offered by the school. These characteristics are supported in formal schooling and are viewed as contributing to effective scholarship. Lower-class children are socialized in expressive modes of communication and behavior (Bernstein, 1971; Furlong, 1976) and adopt adult social roles and behavior at an earlier age than school authorities deem acceptable (Stinchcombe, 1964; Kahl, 1953; Strodtbeck, 1961; Willis, 1976).

At the time the LeCompte study was done, however, few researchers had examined classroom dynamics to assess whether middle-class culture is reinforced in schools and how such reinforcement occurs. All of these theories offered reasons for the underlying similarities in LeCompte's four classrooms, patterns they shared despite their differences in student clientele, teacher philosophy, and classroom environment. LeCompte's analysis demonstrates that schools do present specific and uniform expectations for behavior to which children are expected to conform. Children who enter school already socialized to those expectations adapt best.

LeCompte then examined the cultural orientations of the dominant minority among her student participants and found that they reward behaviors tangential to, if not actually in conflict with, school culture. These differences are discussed in a later work (1981) suggesting that certain school cultural practices, many of which are more or less immutable given the way public policy and funding dictate how schools are organized, act directly and systematically to disadvantage minority children, in this case, Mexican-Americans. LeCompte suggests that these school practices are shrouded in the guise of promoting equality based upon achievement and merit, thus supporting both overt democratic ideological functions of schooling and covert social stratifying functions. The latter result in unequal outcomes for students with apparently equal initial intellectual potential. Thus, the data collected in LeCompte's study were compared with studies that address school structural issues and their impact at differing levels of analysis. When these were applied to the ethnographic data the study began to achieve greater generalizability.

METAPHOR, SIMILE, AND ANALOGY

Use of these tools requires greater divergence of thought and artistry than the others; they also facilitate the creation of catchy titles for ethnographies. They can be, however, powerful ways to create linkages between seemingly unrelated topics.

Some similes, metaphors, and analogies derive from other social science research. An example is Cox's (1980) interpretation of kindergarten attendance as a rite of passage, using Van Gennep's (1960) formulation of this concept. Van Gennep explained the function of rituals as events confirming growth and change in tribal societies—acknowledgment that an individual's position has shifted. Cox documents four events comparable to those described by Van Gennep. A prekindergarten orientation held in children's homes and a visit to school before classes begin constituted the separation phase of the rite of passage: Individuals are shifting position from child at home to student at school. Two events including parents and younger siblings were held at the end of the year—a trip to the zoo with all four of the kindergarten classes and a ceremonious first lunch in the school cafeteria. This incorporation phase acknowledged the children's new status as students. Its culminating rituals prepared children for working in larger groups and for the most significant crowd control aspect of elementary school life—eating lunch in the cafeteria. Cox argues that kindergarten functions as a transitional phase—children are quasistudents—and that the events described above serve the same purposes for kindergarten children as do the rituals described by Van Gennep. Other analogies between the notion of rites of passage and stages of schooling include Bennett & LeCompte's (1990) application of the concept of liminality to the status of high school students. In an analogy drawn from empirical and descriptive, rather than conceptual, frames, Lutz (1982) compares how both institutions of higher learning and societies such as the tribal Kuikuru of Central Brazil maintain political and social stability. In *Witches and Witchcraft in Modern Organizations,* Lutz integrates data on witch behavior, witch findings, and witch killing in a number of societies with patterns of status, control, and causality in contemporary educational institutions. He suggests that the social dynamics of communication about and interaction with alleged witches are similar to the social dynamics in contemporary organizations for treatment of marginal individuals and are change agents for establishing organizational cohesiveness and for maintaining administrative control. Although Lutz does not imply that university deans engage in sorcery and witchcraft, the analogy clarifies organizational practices by comparison and contrast with quite different social groups. Lutz's analogy is based upon structural functional premises that all societies, be they traditional or contemporary, have specific needs to be fulfilled. The structures evolved to execute these functions vary, but the dynamics that elicit them are similar. In Lutz's tightly argued framework, the analogy becomes plausible. Other analogies between rituals in tribal societies and schooling in urban society include Lesko's (1986, 1988) description of ritualistic practices in parochial schools which act to reinforce gender roles and social solidarity and McLaren's (1986) discussion of rituals of performance in public school classrooms and hallways.

Metaphor is used as an analytic tool in Barnhardt's (1982) report of linguistic interaction between Athabaskan students and their Athabaskan teachers. In the study, she and her associates discovered that concepts such as rhythm, tempo, density, and beat, which structure musical compositions, also can be used to structure the patterns of physical and linguistic interaction in classrooms. She implies that each culture generates patterns of rhythm, tempo, and beat for communication and contact among its members in various social settings and that communication is facilitated when these patterns are shared. Thus, Barnhardt suggests that Athabaskan teachers are successful with their Athabaskan students because they "tune in" effortlessly to culturally appropriate patterns of interaction and communication in ways non-Athabaskan teachers do not. She also compares the Athabaskan teacher's self-chosen role to that of a jazz band conductor, who gets the music started, uses a minimum of signals to support the performance, and blends into the group rather than actually conducting it. This analogy is comparable to Smith & Geoffrey's (1968) account of an Anglo teacher's self-described role as a "ringmaster," who has eyes in the back of his head and maintains tight control over events at all times (see Chapter One).

SYNTHESIS

The example of Mead's work, described above, illustrates how achieving a synthesis that transcends existing theory requires the investigator to pursue ideas in several contexts or from several vantage points before real insights emerge.

Synthesis requires an interdisciplinary or intradisciplinary effort. Researchers integrate data and concepts from multiple research efforts, some of which may appear to be tangential or even contradictory. The investigator's confidence in the results may be difficult to sustain when the new configuration supersedes those of mentors, a disciplinary establishment, cultural beliefs, or conventional wisdom.

Ogbu's (1978) work combines data on occupational attainment from his ethnographic study of low-income residents of "Burgherside" (1974) with studies of ethnic minorities in the United States, Great Britain, New Zealand, India, Japan, and Israel. He examines the status of such minorities in societies with egalitarian cultural ideologies. He reviews different theories for societal inequality, including those involving cultural deprivation, culture conflict, and intellectual and educational deficiency; these theories and the strategies for remediation they generated are examined in the context of social history. The material is used to test Ogbu's hypothesis, related to social stratification theory, that a job ceiling exists within societies for specific minority groups, even though those groups may not appear to be very different from higher-status groups. He also argues that both disadvantaged minorities and higher-status groups respond to remediation in ways that perpetuate inequality rather than overcome it. He argues, as do Hurn (1978), Persell (1977), and LeCompte & Dworkin (1988, 1991), that promoting social equality by altering familial and educational institutions does not work, since both relate only tangentially to the source of the issue—access to economic power.

Similarly, Bowles & Gintis (1976), Karabel & Halsey (1978), and

Carnoy (1972) are controversial not only because they attack dearly held cultural myths about the possibilities for and causes of equality, but also because they document so thoroughly, empirically and theoretically from multiple sources and types of data, that schools cannot transform society, a notion objectionable to both educators and politicians. To construct these syntheses, researchers used the same processes of theorizing described above: perceptual freshness and openness, comparing, contrasting, aggregating and ordering, establishing relationships, and speculation. Thus, the analytic process repeats itself at higher and higher levels of abstraction and generalizability throughout the research process.

Summary

Although organizational form and emphases vary considerably, most ethnographers present the conclusion to their studies in four stages: a summary presentation of data, interpretation of data, integration of findings within broader areas of interest, and applications or significance of the findings.

Summary presentations of data generally are descriptive statements, whether in prose or graphic format, that specify attributes of the phenomena investigated. In some cases these may be organized into categorical models that describe groups of attributes or phenomena. This stage of the conclusion is characterized by concrete descriptors or enumerations that address only the subject under investigation.

Interpretation of data requires that ethnographers specify what the data mean for the questions asked in the study and why particular meanings are salient. Interpretation includes explanatory statements of cause and effect relationships, whether predictive or retrodictive. Here, the researcher notes how categories of phenomena and their attributes are related expirically to one another. In some cases this may be presented in the form of processual models where categories are not only specified, but the relationships among them are defined.

At the integration stage of the conclusions, ethnographers move beyond the immediate subject under investigation and specify how the data relate to broader areas of interest. These may be empirical, as when data are compared or contrasted with comparable data from other studies. They may be theoretical, or they may be placed within the context of normative or policy implications. In educational ethnography, all three areas of integration are attempted by effective ethnographers. Theory generated from data is examined within the context of alternative theories and showed to be sufficiently compelling to challenge, if not to refute, the alternatives. Theory verified by data is likewise examined in its broader context. The nature of the theory also may suggest unanticipated empirical implications and policy applications.

The process of theorizing that guides an ethnographic design becomes particularly salient at the stage of interpreting and integrating data. In predominantly inductive studies, abstractions must be integrated with both data and theory to create a coherent system by which to explain or convey the meaning of the study. In more deductive studies, researchers must demonstrate that the evidence collected and the research design constructed actually prove or disprove the hypotheses developed from their a priori theories. Whether a researcher proceeds from a deductive–verificative or an inductive–generative research design, the mode of theorizing chosen to construct the general argument leading to the conclusions drawn in the study must be applied consistently throughout the integrative stage. The extent to which the research design is tightly defined and credible, the data are dense and comprehensive, and both data and analysis address the original research questions determine the persuasive power of the inferences upon which interpretive statements are based.

In the preceding pages, we have discussed strategies and cognitive processes used by qualitative researchers in analyzing and interpreting their data. We have emphasized how these resemble, and differ from, those used by other researchers. Qualitative research does not use processes of analysis in ways radically different from other forms of research, but it does use analytic processes at different stages of the research process and defines them more broadly than the statistical procedures that form the analysis tasks of more quantitative research.

We also have emphasized that data analysis involves more than simple reporting of fact. Research reports must indicate what the results mean and how they advance a particular line of investigation, add significant portions to a body of knowledge, or modify existing theories or hypotheses. Theorizing, together with the tools of consolidation, application, metaphor and analogy, and synthesis, enables researchers to interpret data and integrate results into the overall corpus of knowledge that constitutes their particular disciplines. In the next chapter we discuss how these processes are supported by use of qualitative analysis programs for personal computers. In explaining how programs are designed to aid data analysis, we illustrate many of the procedures discussed in this chapter.

Personal Computers in
Qualitative Research

Introduction

A common misperception is that introducing a computer into qualitative research rigidifies the procedures and distances the researcher from the data. This is like fearing that introducing scissors results in the dissection of the data and the loss of the researcher's holistic perspective. Computers, like scissors, are tools. In themselves, they have no influence on the research process. Although future programs may enable the researcher to handle qualitative data more comprehensively than would be possible manually, and therefore may change the nature of qualitative analysis, even specialized analysis programs will not prescribe analysis steps or perform tasks not indicated by the researcher. Only what researchers want to do with the data will be done. If anything, computers are more flexible than scissors, index cards, or file folders. They encourage the researcher to become playful and to try multiple ideas on the data, since the mechanical part of the analysis process is no longer cumbersome.

It is often more important to clarify what computers don't do than to describe what they do. Computers cannot yet perform any conceptual functions or recognize the meaning of language. They do not think. Whatever their artificial intelligence capabilities are now, these are only slowly being incorporated into personal application software. Artificial intelligence is most appropriate when computers have to learn from repeated new input how to perform a task with increasing accuracy. Qualitative analysis usually is a one-time process. Even software developed specifically for the analysis of ethnographic data is not meant to *guide* the researcher through this process. The computer waits for the qualitative analyst to decide what task to perform next, then performs that task with great speed and accuracy. In summary, computers cannot analyze; they merely assist in organizing data for interpretation.

On the other hand, computers no longer mangle researchers' data or require memorizing series of keystrokes. Qualitative analysis programs leave the data untouched; they merely add new electronic files as the analysis proceeds. All of them provide menus from which the researcher selects the action the computer is to perform, and most save new work automatically. They are elegant, efficient, and reliable tools.

Although computers don't think for the researcher, they can execute so many other tasks with such efficiency that they liberate researchers previously overwhelmed by the sheer mass of text awaiting analysis. Listed below are some of the tasks computers can perform for researchers. Computers help researchers:

1. Accept, proofread for spelling errors, and store textual and numerical data.

2. Produce numerous copies of raw data and collate or partition original data files. (A *file* is one data document, designated as such by the researcher, and stored, usually on an electronic disk, under a researcher-determined name.)

3. Accept and store the researcher's memos, usually with a reference to the place in the data to which the memo refers.

4. Search for words or phrases in the data text and retrieve text portions where they occur.

5. Automatically attach identification labels to prestructured units of text, such as responses to a questionnaire, and sort the data accordingly.

6. Segment data into researcher-determined or natural language analysis units.

7. Invite preliminary coding of data segments in preparation for development of a classificatory scheme (*codes* are usually the abbreviated names of the categories).

8. Sort and collate data segments (analysis units) into preliminary categories to facilitate their comparison and consequently the refinement of the classificatory scheme, in as many rounds of analysis as needed.

9. Code researcher memos according to the same classificatory scheme.

10. Accept final segmenting and coding of the data, and sort and assemble the data segments according to the established categories in preparation for summarizing and comparing category content.

11. Count the frequency of occurrence of coded segments in each category.

12. Identify data segments coded as relevant simultaneously to two

or more categories in preparation for the discovery of linkages between and among categories.

13. Count the frequency of the co-occurrence of segments in two or more categories.

14. Retrieve coded data segments from subsets of data—females only, for instance, or any other subgroup—in preparation for contrasting with other subsets.

15. Search for and identify segments in the data that appear in a certain (for instance, chronological) sequence.

16. Search for constellations of code appearances within files in preparation for exploring linkages among categories.

17. Display hierarchical or temporal relationships of categories in graphic form.

18. Transfer selected data segments as quotes into the research report.

In this chapter it will become clear how these functions are related to the building of a qualitative analysis. A few can be performed by word processors, a type of software familiar to researchers in the social sciences. Most, however, require specialized software. Software can be divided into two groups: commercially available packages, such as word processors, and programs specifically developed for academic purposes. Commercially available packages are multipurpose programs. They are meant to be used for many different applications in diverse situations. Researchers have been able to adapt data base managers and spreadsheets for organizing their data, for example. Before special analysis programs existed, even word processors were used to replicate the cut-and-paste process that used to be the modus operandi of most analysts. It no longer makes sense to use software that performs the organizing and retrieving tasks required for qualitative analysis in cumbersome, restrictive, or error-prone ways when programs exist that do the same job elegantly and reliably. These specialized programs have been created by scholars and packaged so they could be used by their colleagues. None of them performs the entire array of tasks previously listed. If it did, it would probably be quite unwieldy. However, only rarely must all these tasks be performed in a single research project. Researchers can choose from the available software packages the one that is most appropriate for their analysis needs.

Researchers today need a good word processor for data entry and storage and a qualitative analysis program. (Macintosh owners need "HyperCard" in addition to an analysis program.) Qualitative analysis programs are inexpensive, and the time saved justifies their cost. Sometimes an additional program for graphic data display may be helpful.

In this chapter we mention commercial general-purpose programs only in passing. Reviews of commercial programs are available in many computer journals, and the personnel in computer stores can be consulted about the features each provides. Our emphasis is on qualitative analysis programs specifically designed for scholarly purposes. The ones for personal computers most frequently used now in the United States are The Ethnograph (MS-DOS), HyperQual (Macintosh), QUALPRO (MS-DOS), and Textbase Alpha (MS-DOS). These software packages are designed for descriptive and interpretive types of qualitative research, such as phenomenological research, case studies, action research, ethnography, or qualitative evaluation. Some place more and others less emphasis on linguistic features of the data; some connect to quantitative procedures, others do not. These programs are most useful for the type of theorizing that requires comparing, contrasting, and aggregating. Higher-level ordering and the establishing of linkages and relationships are more the domain of theory-building research such as Glaser & Strauss's (1967) "grounded theory" construction or Miles & Huberman's (1984) relationship-oriented approach to ethnography. Recently, software has been developed geared to generating theoretical propositions. Being readied for distribution are AQUAD (MS-DOS), HyperSoft (Macintosh), Hyper-RESEARCH (Macintosh), and NUDIST (Macintosh; planned also MS-DOS). ATLAS (MS-DOS) is another program for theory-building analysis. It is not described here in detail, since it was not yet available at the time of this writing.

In this chapter, the functions of programs for qualitative analysis are described according to the tasks listed above. We will indicate which of the programs perform each task. All academic programs are available through their U.S. distributor: Qualitative Research Management, 73-425 Hilltop Road, Desert Hot Springs, CA, 92240, (619) 329-7026. Whenever appropriate, commercially available programs useful to the qualitative researcher are also mentioned.

The 18 tasks from the list compiled earlier are clustered in four groups: data preparation and storage; segmenting, coding, and collating; establishing linkages; and transferal and display.

Data Preparation and Storage

DATA ENTRY

Although some of the data collected by qualitative researchers may be in the form of numbers, most are text. Numerical data can be processed by one of the statistical programs, the description of which is beyond the purpose of this book. If a study includes only a small amount of numerical data, the researcher might consider entering them into a spreadsheet or a data base manager. Sophisticated word processors also often can perform simple calculations such as totals and grand totals. Textual data collected for enumeration, such as the classroom behavior example toward the end of Chapter Six, may be entered in abstracted form into a spreadsheet.

Narrative data from interviews, questionnaires, protocols, field notes, diaries, minutes of meetings, and other records can be entered either into word processors or into data base managers. Macintosh users may consider entering data into "HyperCard," since it connects directly to programs such as HyperQual, HyperSoft, and HyperRESEARCH. There are two kinds of data base managers: structured and free-form. If the data come in natural segments of limited length, such as brief responses to a questionnaire or to an interview conducted according to a script, and if the researcher intends to make these segments the analysis units, a structured data base manager is most appropriate. No preparatory work is needed to later extract all responses to a question; the fields of the data base manager—the compartments into which the data segments were entered—can be retrieved according to their name. Fields are created by the researcher as the data are entered, and each field is named. "Question 1" could name the field, for instance, into which the researcher types first answers, "Question 2" holds second answers, and so forth. Later, the data base manager can retrieve everything across all data sets that is contained in the field "Question 1," and the computer will produce a print-out of all responses.

Most data base managers also allow the researcher to extract responses within a field according to words in the text. This is a useful feature for linguistically oriented qualitative researchers, those interested in the words used by the people studied. The disadvantage of structured data base managers is that they usually have no easy way of changing the boundaries of fields or of working across fields. They should only be used if the qualitative researcher is sure that the analysis units and the classificatory system can be determined in advance of the analysis. Some data base managers also have difficulty printing out long text fields. Some make only a single field available for long text entries. As a class, data base managers were created for the storage and easy retrieval of a pool of brief information pieces to which the user periodically adds new items. A data base becomes more useful the longer information is allowed to accumulate, because bits are easily retrieved, regardless of the size of the accumulation. Data base managers were not designed for the one-time process of data entry and retrieval that is the usual mode of the researcher's work.

Unstructured data base managers accept text in the same way word processors do: Interviews or field notes are entered in a continuous stream. There is little advantage in using a free-form data base manager over a word processor for research. Usually data base managers have more complex search facilities for locating words in the text, which might be useful for the linguistically oriented researcher. Otherwise, the advantage is with the word processor, since data are more easily exported or moved from the word processor into qualitative analysis programs for further organizing. Once data are entered into the data base manager, they must be analyzed there. Segmenting text into analysis units in a free-form data base manager is usually difficult. Although the user may be able to mark blocks of text for printouts, the marking is gone once the task is executed. Furthermore, the marking and printing usually have to be performed one block at a time.

Word processors are most useful for text data entry. Not only are they so common that ethnographers are usually familiar with their operation already, but they also forgive typing errors, a great convenience for researchers who must enter their own data but lack typing skills. Most word processors have spelling checkers that make it possible to correct, in a matter of minutes, all misspelled words after a document has been produced. Qualitative researchers using qualitative analysis programs should make sure, however, to choose a word processor that provides for ASCII conversion. ASCII is a text form that excludes formatting codes, the invisible characters a word processor embeds in the text to create indents, page breaks, underlines, etc. The vocabulary for ASCII conversion differs among word processors; it may be called "export," "printing to disk," "DOS text" or "text only." The researcher should make sure the word processor used can transform its documents into ASCII. If a Macintosh computer is used, it is often advantageous to enter the data into the program called HyperCard. This special word processor accepts text entry on "cards." Although cards are more limited in length than normal files, the inconvenience of having to use additional cards is offset by the convenience of eliminating the data transfer step when using HyperCard-based analysis programs.

Although most qualitative data are text, occasionally the researcher may want to use drawings. HyperQual and other HyperCard-based programs for the Macintosh allow the import of pictures. Still more useful to researchers may be the inclusion of audio and video recordings. Video recordings can show the social use of space and of bodily movements, and they are important to the researcher who studies the interactions of people in an educational environment. NUDIST allows the researcher to enter user-defined analysis units from an audio or video tape, such as the number counter in an audio tape recorder or any other extraneous medium, or manually applied paragraph counts in a paper document such as court records or newspapers, as a reference for collating units similar in content. HyperRESEARCH even provides a direct connection to certain recording machines, so that playback of selected portions of the tape can be achieved as a result of coding the data. Currently only audio–video connections are planned.

DATA STORAGE

Compared with paper files, computers provide not only an easily accessible system, but also the most space-saving storage system. Of course the original data, plus one paper printout of the transcribed data, should always be stored in a safe place. But all working copies can reside in the computer. If a hard disk is used, all data should be backed up on floppy disks so that a computer failure will not make the data inaccessible. If the data are stored on floppy disks, there should always be at least one set of backups.

A few words about files. Usually the raw data come in some kind of unit: one interview transcript, or the field notes from one day at one site. Each of these should be stored in separate files; it is not wise to accumulate many different pieces of data under one file name. Later, when analysis units are extracted from a file, the only indication of the segment's context may be the file name. If a file is too long, locating the context of segments may be difficult or impossible.

In any but the smallest qualitative study, data tend to accumulate at an alarming rate. Early in the process researchers should develop a system for storing data. In MS-DOS systems (IBM computers and IBM compatibles) file names can be up to 8 characters long, plus a 3-character estension—the letters after a period. Periods may not be used in a file name except to indicate the beginning of an extension. File names can be used as a coding system for the identification of files. For instance, field notes can be distinguished from interview transcripts by the extensions .FN and .INT, respectively. The 8 characters preceding the extension can be abbreviations of the name of the interviewee or the observation site. Additional information, such as the chronological order of interviews with the same person or the name of the interviewer in team research, can be encoded in the remaining characters. A file name in a directory thus provides an immediate clue to its content.

If the researcher uses a computer with floppy disk drives only, data files of a similar type should be assembled on one disk so that the disk name can also be created according to content. Most computers now have hard disk drives; copying the analysis program and all data files into the same subdirectory of the hard disk is advantageous. The program thus "knows" where to look for the data and, when using several or all data files for the same operation, the computer will not demand that the disks in the floppy drive be changed continuously. Several programs now require a hard disk: all Macintosh programs, AQUAD, and version 4.0 of The Ethnograph.

RESEARCHER MEMOS

Many researchers who work with qualitative data accumulate a secondary set of data: researcher memos. These memos are, most commonly, notes about analytic ideas such as sudden insights, plans for the next steps, preliminary summaries of developing categories, etc. They are written from the moment the first data are collected and revised and added to over time. Often they become so numerous that it is difficult to keep track of them. They can be entered, of course, into a word processor. A more efficient way of storing them is in a memory-resident note taker. This strategy has two advantages: First, researchers need not save and then retrieve again the document they are working on when these ideas occur. Second, a certain note can be retrieved from a large collection just by remembering and providing a single word contained in the note. In fact, notes containing a common word can be retrieved quickly and reviewed as a batch.

Memory-resident note takers are small commercial programs loaded by the user as the first program every time a computer session begins, or they can be stored on a hard disk and loaded automatically when the computer is switched on. These programs do not appear on the screen, as other programs do, but reside in memory until they are called up. The command with which they are fetched is the hot key, usually an uncommon key combination. This hot key combination is pressed while working in a regular program, such as an analysis package. The current screen disappears, and the note taker's screen appears. The note is entered and, in response to an exit key, the regular screen is restored. The note is saved without a file name, much like free-form data base managers. Programs that have this capacity to be used while other programs are running are called terminate-and-stay-resident (TSR) programs. Common TSR programs are Memory Mate, Sidekick, and Info-Select. Since they usually produce ASCII files, the notes can be imported into other programs and further processed there.

Several qualitative analysis programs have built-in memo-writing abilities (HyperQual, HyperSoft, AQUAD, NUDIST, and version 4.0 of The

Ethnograph). These memos can be attached to segments of text or to categories. They can be retrieved by locating them according to those segments or categories or by searching for words the researcher has added to the memo as titles or key words. This direct connection is advantageous because the context of each memo is automatically supplied. The memos themselves can be treated, in most of the programs, as new data documents—they can be coded and collated according to the codes.

Segmenting, Coding, and Collating

SEGMENTING

Segmenting means dividing data into analysis units. An analysis unit is a text passage understandable in itself, that is, it is large enough to make sense when taken out of context and is defined by the researcher as relevant to the research objective. Segmenting once meant literally carving up the data by cutting paper copies into pieces or by excerpting text passages onto index cards. As a preliminary step, some researchers would underline or color highlight a copy of the data or indicate analysis units in the margins with wavy lines or square brackets.

The nature of an analysis unit differs depending on the research project. In some cases data are already structured, since the researcher has collected the material with a set of conceptual divisions. If brief, specific questions are asked, responses will pertain to one topic. Often, however, the researcher observes a continuous stream of behavior, or in an open-ended interview the respondent tells a story and the interviewer is nondirective. In these cases it is usually difficult to divide the data into discrete units. This must be done, nevertheless, since the human mind cannot deal with all topics contained in the data at once. If there is no crisp break between one topic or theme and the next, the researcher is usually generous about the boundaries of the analysis units and includes more rather than less data. In these cases, boundaries may overlap: The same portions of text may be included toward the end of one segment and the beginning of the next. A researcher's classificatory system may be not just a list of topics, but a hierarchical structure, with general topics branching into more specific ones. This necessitates a form of segmenting in which smaller analysis units are nested in larger ones. Although once researchers had to make several copies of the same text to cut out physically overlapping or nested segments of data, all qualitative analysis programs handle these kinds of segmenting easily.

MARKING ANALYSIS UNITS

When data are entered into structured data base managers, subsequent segmenting is unnecessary; each unit of analysis already resides in a separate field. This means that the initial segmenting remains the same throughout the analysis. While in some research projects this is acceptable, for others it may be a disadvantage, especially when overlapping or nesting is required. Some researchers may prefer the freedom of remaining flexible during the process, with an opportunity to change segment boundaries as the ongoing analysis affords additional insights.

A word processor is more flexible than data base managers, because blocks of text can be highlighted and transferred into another document or window. Before qualitative analysis programs were available, many researchers used this feature to painstakingly assemble all segments relevant to the same category in a secondary document. This method, however, requires as many readings of the text as there are topics or categories in the classificatory system, because one category is assembled at a time. To avoid this problem, a researcher may insert certain words in the text as codes. These codes can then be found with a word search; but this procedure is efficient only if all data are in the same large file. Furthermore, the segmenting must be done while searching, not while coding. Aside from the work involved and the potential for human errors, another disadvantage of word processors is that each time a segment is transferred, its source reference must be added in the secondary document, that is, its file name and perhaps page number.

Today, data can be exported from the word processor into other programs that cut and paste efficiently and without error. Two kinds of software accept files created elsewhere and then manipulate them further: text retrievers and text analysis programs.

Text retrievers are commercial utility programs; they make life easier for the computer user. They find words or phrases when the user needs information but is unsure in which file it is located. The program lists the names of the files containing the word or phrase, usually providing a word count, and displays the content of each file for browsing. Some of these programs have features useful to the linguistically oriented researcher. They retrieve not only entire files, but also give researchers the option to specify natural language units within files, such as paragraphs or sentences. They they find all paragraphs, for instance, that contain the specified word and make them available for on-screen review, as well as assembling them in a new document. AskSam, Magellan, Golden Retriever, and The Text Collector are some current programs that have this facility. FlexText allows the researcher to mark words and phrases found in the text as signifying concepts. When a search for the concept is conducted, it automatically includes all words and phrases assigned to it.

Qualitative analysis programs are one type of academic text analysis programs. The other types consist of analysis programs for traditional, quantitatively oriented content and literary analyses, such as Word-Cruncher, and indexers, such as ZyIndex. For the researcher who is less interested in what words were used than in the meanings expressed, qualitative analysis programs faithfully duplicate the old cut-and-paste process, except it is now the computer that does the cutting and pasting. These programs, of course, do not actually analyze text; they merely reorganize it for interpretation. Working with text analysis programs is not as fast as working with text retrievers because they do not automatize in the same way. Qualitative analysis programs await instructions from the researcher about the portions of the text that are to be considered analysis units. They also require the researcher to construct or develop a classificatory system for the data according to which they will be sorted. Text retrievers go no further than retrieval of individual language units. More about this sorting later; we will first see how segmenting is accomplished by the programs.

MS-DOS Programs

Programs for IBM computers and compatibles mark segment boundaries in two different ways. One way is to have the computer number all lines in a data document and use the numbers as indicators of segment boundaries. The original data documents can always be printed out with these line numbers attached. For instance, the researcher may decide that an analysis unit runs from line 423 to line 456. Because the computer does not recognize sentences, segments extracted from the raw data text include the words preceding and succeeding the relevant sentences on the same line. Two programs that work this way are QUALPRO and The Ethnograph. Figure 8.1 is an example of a segment in the format used by QUALPRO. The first line begins at a question and therefore coincides with the beginning of a sentence. On the last line the text continues; the unit ends with ". . . something like that." In our experience, researchers who work with these programs easily become accustomed to disregarding incomplete sentences at the beginnings or ends of data segments.

The other way of setting segment boundaries is to insert special markers, either visibly (AQUAD uses the ∧ symbol) or invisibly (Textbase Alpha uses the INS key). The INS key in Textbase Alpha may be pressed at any place in the data text. The resulting segments, therefore, contain only the exact sentences the researcher wishes to include.

In addition to this free-form segmenting, Textbase Alpha offers a

```
15   P: Would you go to school if you didn't have to?                    15
16   N: Sometimes I would go to school if I was in the mood, and the     16
17   other times -- when I wasn't, when I wanted to go horseback riding  17
18   or something like that -- I wouldn't.  But sometimes when I felt I  18
19   was in the mood to go, I would.                                     19
20   P: Do you like school?                                             20
21   N: Sort of, sometimes.                                             21
22   P: What are some of the things you like about school?              22
23   N: Well, sometimes I like school because we have extra recess or art 23
24   or something like that.  And other times -- when we have to go to  24
```

Figure 8.1 Data segment with line numbers. (Note the irrelevant sentence fragment at the end.)

function to expedite the analysis of prestructured data, such as open responses to a questionnaire or an interview script. If the beginning line of each response is typed to protrude into the left margin, the program treats each response automatically as a segment. Of course, the unstructured segmenting described above can be done with such data as well and overlayed on the structured segmenting.

In almost all MS-DOS programs the segmenting of text is done in the same working step as the coding of the data segments, much in the same fashion as in precomputer times. We provide illustrations of computer screens that facilitate segmenting and coding in the next section.

Macintosh Programs

HyperQual, HyperRESEARCH, and HyperSoft use facilities provided by HyperCard, a kind of word processing program supplied with or available for all models of Macintosh computers. HyperCard is based on the metaphor of the card and of stacks of cards. Cards belong to stacks. The difference between a file and a card is that cards can be connected to other cards in their stack as well as to cards in other stacks. This facility makes text analysis different in Macintosh analysis programs from the same process in MS-DOS programs. The first difference is that data are not entered into a word processor and then transferred, but typed directly into HyperCard. For the user this is the same as entering data into the analysis program.

A screen into which data are entered in HyperQual would look like Fig. 8.2:

The first entries on top are the researcher's name and the name of the data document. The box on the left is available for notes the researcher makes about the text on the right. The text does not stop in the middle of the sentence; the card is scrollable. This means that the

****

```
Preissle                        Int-Nancy

Notes:                          Data:
```

```
                        ┌──────────────────────────────────────┐
┌──────────────┐        │ P: Would you go to school if you didn't │
│              │        │ have to?                             │
│              │        │ N: Sometimes I would go to school if I was │
│              │        │ in the mood, and the other times -- when I │
│              │        │ wasn't, when I wanted to go horseback │
│              │        │ riding or something like that -- I wouldn't. │
│              │        │ But sometimes when I felt I was in the mood │
│              │        │ to go, I would.                      │
│              │        │ P: Do you like school?               │
│              │        │ N: Sort of, sometimes.               │
│              │        │ P: What are some of the things you like │
│              │        │ about school?                        │
│              │        │ N: Well, sometimes I like school because we │
└──────────────┘        │ have extra recess or art or something like │
                        └──────────────────────────────────────┘
```

****

Figure 8.2   Data entering screen from the software package HyperQual (Macintosh).

remainder of the text can be brought up to the screen with the mouse, showing a windowful of text at a time. The data entry windows in Hyper-Soft and HyperRESEARCH are larger; they take up almost the entire screen.

HyperQual provides two slightly different procedures, one for structured and one for unstructured data. The organization of the data from an open-ended but structured interview or questionnaire can be preserved by entering each answer onto a separate card. As in Textbase Alpha, all responses to the same question can then be assembled without any coding. Unstructured material is entered as a whole on one card; cards hold 30,000 characters, and a new card is made with a click of the mouse when the researcher needs more space. HyperQual invites the researcher to highlight text passages by clicking and dragging with the mouse anywhere to mark them in structured or unstructured data as analysis units. Accordingly, the segments do not contain fragments of sentences. The same segmenting procedure is used in the other Hyper-Card-based programs. In HyperQual, the highlighted chunks need not be coded at the time as is required in MS-DOS programs. NUDIST uses a segmenting procedure similar to the MS-DOS programs: The boundaries of analysis units are indicated by line or paragraph numbers.

CODING TEXT SEGMENTS

Although for clarity of presentation we described segmenting as if it were a separate operation from coding, in practice the two activities usually happen simultaneously. The researcher cannot note where a topic begins and ends without realizing what the topic is. Writing the topic of a segment of text in the margin or adding it electronically is the beginning of coding.

Coding varies depending on whether or not a classificatory system exists when the analysis begins. If the researcher has developed such a system a priori, derived from theories or from the conceptual tools used in other studies, or from the research questions at hand, coding is easy. Each category in the system is named by the researcher to signify its topic. The code is an abbreviation of the category name. It serves the same purpose as the destination tag attached to luggage at the airport; it tells the computer where to send a copy of the segment. As data are scrutinized for portions of text relevant to one of the categories of the scheme, the code is added in some way to each segment. The process is like panning: Analysts know that they are looking for and sift out all but the precious material. Each nugget is then marked for later sorting.

If most or all of the classificatory scheme is still to be developed, the first step is more like surveying: The analyst carefully examines each portion of text, one after the other, and decides whether it has potential significance. Only material obviously irrelevant to the purpose of the study is dismissed. The remainder is divided into analysis units by changes of topic, and each topic is tentatively identified. In descriptive qualitative research this is different from summarizing the content; the topic is what is talked about, not what is said. When theorizing, the researcher tentatively identifies the concept contained in the analysis unit.

Once a number of data documents are worked with, usually the first few collected for the project, a list of topics or concepts is made. They are compared, sometimes clustered, reformulated, and refined, and then tried out on the same and on new data. Researchers repeat this process until definite topics or concepts are defined; the categories have emerged. In practice, both methods of coding are often combined, since the beginnings of a classificatory system may exist but need fleshing out, or the researcher may be interested by serendipitous discoveries.

As the classificatory scheme is refined, the researcher may decide that some categories are too broad and others too narrow. While it was time consuming to reorganize data by hand according to a new scheme, qualitative analysis software accommodates these changes with ease. Many programs have special facilities that support such recoding. Several rounds of tentative coding still take time, but very little compared with manual reorganizing.

Thus far we have treated coding as consisting of assigning one code to each relevant segment of data. This works only when the segment contains a single topic, when it fits in only one category. Often, topics are intertwined, or the words refer to one topic explicitly while another is implied. In these cases, the researcher doing a manual analysis needs enough extra copies of the data so the segment can be cut out more than once and placed in two or several piles. This concurrent coding is also facilitated by the computer, since all that is required is to add another code to the relevant segment.

In the following, to illustrate the principle, we describe work with analysis programs as if only one round of coding were necessary. In practice, two or more rounds are customary to refine the classificatory system.

MS-DOS Programs

All MS-DOS programs combine coding with segmenting: As analysis units are identified, they must also be assigned to tentative or established categories. The coding is done either as a two-step or as a one-step procedure.

QUALPRO and The Ethnograph use the two-step procedure. They both require the actual assignment of codes to be done on paper. The researcher works on a printout of the data made from within the program, not a word processor. When the programs print out data, they show line numbers. The researcher can then use the margins to indicate segment boundaries with square brackets, for instance, and to add code names. A coded data sheet might look like Fig. 8.3.

Figure 8.3 is an example from The Ethnograph. A QUALPRO printout would look much the same, except the line numbers appear on both sides of the text. Once researchers prepare a paper copy of a data file, they enter the codes and their associated line numbers into the computer. QUALPRO instructs the researcher to list them, one to a line, as in Fig. 8.4.

The first four lines are the program's instructions to the user; the last five lines indicating the coding categories have been typed by the researcher. "From Line" and "To Line" refer to the segment boundaries. When all codes for one document have been entered, QUALPRO saves the instructions in an ASCII file. This is a very simple file; experienced computer users can create it in a word processor (where it is easier to edit and save in multiple copies) and then import it into QUALPRO.

Instead of expecting a list, The Ethnograph provides a form into

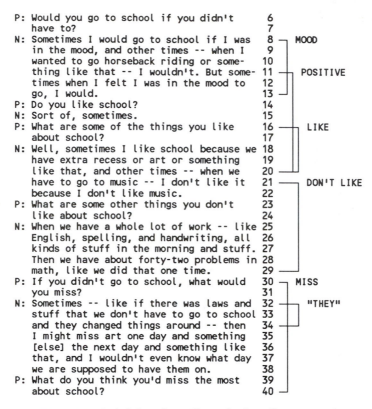

```
P: Would you go to school if you didn't     6
   have to?                                  7
N: Sometimes I would go to school if I was   8 ─┐ MOOD
   in the mood, and other times -- when I    9
   wanted to go horseback riding or some-   10
   thing like that -- I wouldn't. But some- 11 ─┤ POSITIVE
   times when I felt I was in the mood to   12
   go, I would.                             13 ─┘
P: Do you like school?                       14
N: Sort of, sometimes.                       15
P: What are some of the things you like      16 ─┐ LIKE
   about school?                             17
N: Well, sometimes I like school because we  18
   have extra recess or art or something     19
   like that, and other times -- when we     20 ─┘
   have to go to music -- I don't like it    21 ─┐ DON'T LIKE
   because I don't like music.               22
P: What are some other things you don't      23
   like about school?                        24
N: When we have a whole lot of work -- like 25
   English, spelling, and handwriting, all   26
   kinds of stuff in the morning and stuff. 27
   Then we have about forty-two problems in 28
   math, like we did that one time.          29 ─┘
P: If you didn't go to school, what would    30 ─┐ MISS
   you miss?                                 31
N: Sometimes -- like if there was laws and   32 ─┤ "THEY"
   stuff that we don't have to go to school 33
   and they changed things around -- then    34 ─┘
   I might miss art one day and something    35
   [else] the next day and something like    36
   that, and I wouldn't even know what day   37
   we are supposed to have them on.          38
P: What do you think you'd miss the most     39
   about school?                             40 ─┘
```

Figure 8.3   Coded data sheet. (Reproduction of paper copy.)

```
**************************************************************************
The Format: Name of Code, From Line Number, To Line Number

To end coding a block type a period (.) on a line by itself.
To end coding all blocks enter two periods (..) on a line.

>_

MOOD,8,13
POSITIVE,11,20
LIKE,16,20
DON'T LIKE,21,29
MISS,30,40
THEY,32,34

**************************************************************************
```

Figure 8.4   A list of code entries from the software package QUALPRO (MS-DOS). Code name and two numbers appearing on each line indicate the beginning and end of a segment.

which code names and line number are entered (Fig. 8.5). This form is used for all codes that start on the same line, in this case, line 8. Up to 12 codes can be listed that begin on the same line. One code has been entered in the form above. If there is only one code to be attached to a line, the user presses the END key, and a new blank form appears in which the next start line, code, and stop line are entered. The instructions on top of the box tell the user how to move the cursor around in the box or edit.

In QUALPRO codes and line numbers are changed easily by editing the code list in a word processor. This requires that the files be converted from ASCII. The Ethnograph provides an elaborate system of correction and modification, including global delete and global replace, permitting the researcher to delete or replace one code word with another throughout the document.

Textbase Alpha uses the one-step coding procedure. It provides a coding screen that looks similar to those in word processors: The data text fills the screen, and the user moves the cursor around in the text to the place desired. The only major difference is a long thin box across the bottom of the screen. This box is where the code name is entered. The researcher decides where an analysis unit begins, moves the cursor to that location, and presses the INS key; the cursor jumps to that bottom bar. After the code name is typed in, the cursor moves back to where it came from. Now the analyst moves it to the end of the analysis unit, presses the INS key again, and the segment is coded. The text has not changed in any way, and additional codings can be added anywhere. If the researcher wants to see what coding has been done, Textbase Alpha provides two options. Pressing the F2 key toggles to a code list screen that looks much like the code list in QUALPRO; it lists the line numbers and

```
****************************************************************************
                            ENTER CODE WORDS
                  UP-Prev Field  DN-Next Field  F1-Del  F2-Ins
      PREVIOUS START LINE: 0                        END = Go to next Code Set
```

START LINE	CODE WORD	STOP	CODE WORD	STOP	CODE WORD	STOP
8	1- MOOD	13	5-		9-	
	2-		6-		10-	
	3-		7-		11-	
	4-		8-		12-	

```
****************************************************************************
```

Figure 8.5 Code entry "form" from the software package, The Ethnograph (MS-DOS). Code name and two numbers appearing on each line indicate the beginning and end of a segment.

character positions of the cursor associated with each code word. A more elaborate way of seeing the codes is to leave the coding screen, press one of the main menu selections, and see a reproduction of the data text together with the codes and square brackets indicating the segment boundaries. It looks like the coding sheet done by hand, shown above for the two-step coding procedure.

Researchers can also use two-step coding with a program that permits coding on the screen. The work proceeds in the same way. The researcher first prepares a written work sheet, then enters the coding information into the program.

In addition to offering one-step coding, Textbase Alpha makes coding even more efficient. For instance, the program remembers the last code name entered and lets the researcher reuse it with a single keystroke. To make finding a topic easier, Textbase Alpha has a search function that takes the researcher to a chosen word or phrase in the text, much like a word processor. The researcher can then decide whether and how to code the text that surrounds the word.

Like QUALPRO, correcting and modifying the coding is done in the code list in Textbase Alpha, except that no word processor is needed. Adding new codings or changing the code names is easy; changing the boundaries of already coded segments is more complex. No facility is provided for global searching and replacing of codes.

AQUAD supports both two-step and one-step coding. It uses line numbers that can be entered into the computer together with the associated code word. If the researcher prefers on-the-screen coding, the code name and the line number of the segment end are entered immediately to the right of the first line of the segment. Special editing functions, including global substitution, are available in AQUAD for correcting and modifying the coding already done.

Macintosh Programs

In the MS-DOS programs, with the exception of the Windows-based new program MARTIN, segmenting and coding are always done together; assembling coded segments is performed as a separate step. In contrast, HyperCard-based programs may combine coding and assembling, while segmenting can be done separately as a first step. This gives the researcher the opportunity to play with coding by highlighting analysis units with the click-and-drag feature and collating the segments without having to name the topic or concept. HyperQual provides this option. The researcher may use it to decide whether the selected segments are consistent in content and which name to give that content, thus gradually developing a classificatory system.

When ready to code, the researcher enters tags while browsing through the data and highlights segments. Coding is done in HyperQual by clicking on a button called "Tag & Stack" that appears on all data cards, as shown in Fig. 8.6. The portion of text highlighted by the researcher is underlined in this illustration. When the Tag & Stack button is clicked, the researcher responds to questions, entering the code name and thereby creating a new "card." In a simplified version, one of these would look like Fig. 8.7. Additional tags may be added in the field on the left. Later, the stack with coded segments can be filtered so that all cards with the same tag can be placed in a new stack together.

HyperRESEARCH and HyperSoft handle the coding process similarly, except that codes are attached by selecting one from a master code list provided in a separate window. These master code lists are becoming more common; they not only relieve the researcher from memorizing or looking up code names, but also provide an overview of the classificatory system. This makes it more likely that the researcher will apply the system to the data appropriately. Version 4.0 of The Ethnograph is the first MS-DOS program to supply a master code list.

NUDIST's coding is similar to that of MS-DOS programs, using the

```
************************************************************************
Xview T&S Stack Name: "ThirdGr"

Interview No.: 1                  Question No. 6.a

Notes:                            Data:        ▓ Tag and Stack
 ┌─────────────┐  ┌───────────────────────────────────────┐
 │             │  │ P: Do you know when you are learning some- │
 │             │  │ thing?                                │
 │             │  │ N: Yes.                               │
 │             │  │ P: What does it feel like?            │
 │             │  │ N: It feels good.                     │
 │             │  │ P: What's happening inside of you when you │
 │             │  │ are learning?                         │
 │             │  │ N: Thinking and stuff, and I guess I'm │
 │             │  │ happy 'cause I'm learning something.  │
 │             │  │ P: How do you know when you have learned │
 │             │  │ something?                            │
 │             │  │ N: Well, you know when you learned some- │
 │             │  │ thing is when you can think it again and │
 │             │  │ know it again.  Like, if it was your first │
 └─────────────┘  └───────────────────────────────────────┘

 ▓ Dump File   ▓ Tag List

 Card No. 4                       Card ID 8384
************************************************************************
```

Figure 8.6 The marking of a segment in the software package HyperQual (Macintosh).

****

Xview T&S Stack Name: "ThirdGr"

Interview No.: 1   Question No. 6.a

Source Card: 8384   Source: stack "Nancy"

Tags: Exemplar:

```
P: How do you know when you have learned
something?
N: Well you know when you learned some-
thing is when you can think it again and
know it again.
```

Card No. 1   Card ID 6686

****

Figure 8.7   Coding screen from the software package HyperQual (Macintosh). The code ("tag") is entered in the box at the left side.

two-step procedure. Because the program invites the researcher to think of the classifactory system as a hierarchical tree structure, the codes are considered the nodes in that structure. Although they also have a name, they are expressed as a list of numbers signifying their place in the system and are attached in response to written prompts that the program supplies during segmenting.

COLLATING CODED TEXT SEGMENTS

The reason for attaching codes to text segments is to make possible the sorting of the segments into categories. Even if the classifactory scheme is unfinished or still tentative, the content of each category must be explored. Comparing and contrasting is used in descriptive studies to discover whether the content of a given category is homogeneous, whether the category name is appropriate, whether the category makes sense, or whether it is too broad or too narrow. Once the classifactory scheme is established, the content of each category is examined for major themes, unique manifestations of the phenomenon under study, or groupings of the content that become precursors to a typology. If the researcher is developing theoretical propositions, the same cognitive tools are used for two tasks. First, the researcher decides whether the exemplars in the category are indicative of a single concept. If so, the researcher decides what the properties of the category are and what criteria can be used to judge whether a data segment belongs in the category. Finally, if the category content is lacking in substance, the researcher may decide to collect more data for it; this is theoretical sampling (Glaser & Strauss, 1967). Collating text segments by categories, therefore, is one of the most important steps in qualitative analysis.

MS-DOS Programs

In MS-DOS analysis programs, as a rule, the user is asked to provide the name of the code that the program is to find and the names of the files through which to search. Since the researcher usually wants to include all data files of a research project in the search, most programs let the user list all file names once and then call up the list whenever all files are needed.

Once code and file names are entered into the computer, the program collates all data segments associated with the codes. The results can be viewed on the screen (except in Textbase Alpha), printed out on paper, or stored in an ASCII file. Code segments can be printed in two different sequences. In one all segments from one file are presented first, then from the next file, and so forth. In the other, all segments from all files coded with the first code are printed, then all segments from all files coded with the second code, and so forth. The second sequencing is usually preferable. Only Textbase Alpha and version 4.0 of The Ethno-graph have this facility. In the other programs the same effect can be achieved in a more cumbersome way by performing searches for one code at a time.

In addition to displaying or printing the code name and text of all retrieved analysis units, the programs provide information useful to the researcher. All of them let the researcher know where each segment came from—file name and line numbers. Most also mention the co-occurring codes. The Ethnograph even allows the researcher to add context infor-mation from the original data retrieved with each segment, such as the name of the speaker or a comment about the topic. Each segment is separated from the adjacent ones by a full-width line, and for each the context information is provided again.

A single retrieved text segment from QUALPRO looks like Fig. 8.8. At the top of the display the program lists the name of the file from which the segment was taken, then the code it has searched for, and the line

```
*************************************************************************

File IntNancy      Code LIKE found in lines 16 to 20

                    Block 2 (lines 6 - 56)

16        P: What are some of the things you like        16
17           about school?                               17
18        N: Well, sometimes I like school because we    18
19           have extra recess or art or something       19
20           like that, and other times -- when we       20

All the codes in lines 16 - 20 are:
LIKE POSITIVE

*************************************************************************
```

Figure 8.8   Example of a retrieved coded segment from the software package Textbase Alpha (MS-DOS).

numbers for the segment. The line numbers are identical to the ones that run parallel to both sides of the text. The text follows. Blocks are divisions in the text the user can create before the text is imported into QUALPRO; they are useful for structured interviews but are not required. The bottom line lists other codes overlapping this segment—the "co-occurring" codes. In a search print-out, the next segment would now be printed, and so on.

Textbase Alpha's retrieval results look much the same, except that no co-occurring code names are given. The Ethnograph produces similar printouts, but handles the co-occurring codes differently (Fig. 8.9). The word INTNANCY at the top is the file name. In the next line the program lists the name of a co-occurring code: LEARN. The $ symbol allows the user to recognize which lines within the text segment are coded with LEARN, and the $ symbol at line 19 shows where the overlapping coding ends. It began somewhere prior to this segment. This is important when more than one code overlaps; each has its own symbol, automatically selected by the computer. E: stands for external segment. The Sort Code (SC) for which the program searched is "KNOW." It is repeated just above the text to indicate which symbol is assigned to it. In this case it is a #. Note the line of #s in the right margin.

In AQUAD, as in all programs for theory building, collating text segments is viewed not as the final outcome of coding, but as a step toward postulating linkages among categories. The researcher examines the text in one category mainly to check on consistency in coding. Accordingly, the program does not permit entering more than one code at a time in its search procedure; additional searches for the other codes are done whenever needed. Co-occurring codes are not listed in the printout,

```
*********************************************************************

INTNANCY

E: $-LEARN

SC: KNOW

#-KNOW
      : What's happening inside of you when you     16 -# |
      : are learning?                               17  #  |
      : Thinking and stuff, and I guess I'm happy   18  #  |
      : 'cause i'm learning it.                     19  # -$
      : How do you know when you have learned some- 20  #
      : thing?                                      21  #
      : Well, you know when you learned something   22  #
      : is when you can think it again and know it  23  #
      : again.  Like, if it was your first day of   24 -#
------------------------------------------------------------------------

*********************************************************************
```

Figure 8.9   Example of a retrieved coded segment from the software package, The Ethnograph (MS-DOS).

since the program provides special facilities that explore the connections between coding categories.

Macintosh Programs

HyperCard-based Macintosh programs assemble text segments by printing together all the cards onto which text segments with the same code have been pasted. In HyperQual the result looks like Fig. 8.10. Since

```
*********************************************************************

Sometimes I would go to school if I was in the mood, and other times -- when I wanted
to go horseback riding or something like that -- I wouldn't.  But sometimes when I
felt I was in the mood to go, I would.

Tag for above selection = MOOD

***** Above selection from ***** card id 586

----------------------------------------------------------------------

What are some of the things you like about school?
Well, sometimes I like school because we have extra recess or art or something like that

Tag for above selection = LIKE

***** Above selection from ***** card id 587

*********************************************************************
```

Figure 8.10   Examples of retrieved segments from the software package HyperQual (Macintosh).

the assembly of text segments is only an auxiliary and not a main function in HyperRESEARCH, its collating features are not designed with the same thoroughness as those in HyperCard. Whenever the researcher wishes to see the data associated with a coded segment, the reference file name and line and page numbers to that segment are chosen from a reference list (alphabetized according to code names), and the choice of display is selected from the various options in a dialog box. HyperSoft directs the user to the stack on which all data bits that were coded have been stored, and then offers the option of retrieving data segments according to one code or a combination of codes. In NUDIST the collating of data segments is part of the feature that allows the researcher to browse the classificatory system. If a node in this system (all data coded with the same code) is wanted, the program first provides a list of all data documents in which the code occurs, then asks that one be chosen, then shows the text of all appropriate data segments from that document, including the co-occurring codes.

COUNTING OF CODE OCCURRENCES

All MS-DOS programs count how often a particular code occurs. Such counting may not be central to qualitative analysis, but it can be useful to researchers for certain analytic tasks. How often a code occurs in a set of free-flowing interviews, for instance, may indicate the emphasis people place on a topic. In field notes it may signify either that an observed behavior occurs more often than others or that the observation is biased: More attention is paid to one item than to others. Textbase Alpha and The Ethnograph, Version 4.0, allow the researcher to count separately for subgroups of data—according to age groups or to study sites, for instance—and then export the numbers into a statistical program for simple statistical tests. Textbase Alpha makes a table of code counts per file group according to a "selection" variable (see the succeeding section on selective searches), which can be imported into Statistical Package for the Social Sciences (SPSS). For example, if the researcher wishes to know how often three codes occur in files from young people, middle-aged, and older people, Textbase Alpha displays this information in a table; if the numbers in the table are large enough, it may be possible to ascertain whether the differences are statistically significant. With the exception of HyperSoft, Macintosh programs do not offer counting functions, although HyperRESEARCH can add a frequency count when retrieving references to coded segments in specified files.

Establishing Linkages

When qualitative researchers want to illuminate a situation or experience, or when they wish to create a thick description, the text segments extracted from the data are viewed as individual manifestations of that situation or experience, and the categories serve as vessels for interpreting them. The analysis programs have completed their basic job when all relevant data segments are collated according to the categories. However, even the most simple programs offer more than that to the researcher.

Additional functions may enhance categorization, such as the frequency counting mentioned previously. Some, however, are not merely additional, but the core of the program. This is the case for software packages created for establishing linkages among conceptual categories: AQUAD, HyperSoft, HyperRESEARCH, and NUDIST. Here text segments become instances of evidence; the evidence is or is not present in a particular file. The qualitative studies for which these programs are designed, therefore, are not systematic description and illumination, but are for the generation and confirmation of theoretical propositions or hypotheses.

One difference between the two types of programs is the definition of the term *code*. In both cases codes are abbreviations of category names, and categories are the building blocks of an organizing system. However, codes in theory-building programs differ from those in descriptive–interpretive programs like QUALPRO, The Ethnograph, HyperQual, and Textbase Alpha. In theory-building programs, when codes are attached to a segment of text in a data file each code can be viewed as characterizing the entire file. Consequently, a code does not indicate just a topic, such as relationship with father, but the content as well, *poor* relationship with father. Once such a code is attached to a segment of text, it not only points to the place in the file where evidence can be found, but also identifies this file as one from someone with a poor relationship with the father. The program's purpose is to look for codes occurring within a file or across all or a number of files. Thus, an analyst might ask whether the code "poor relationship with father" occurs frequently in files also coded "low self-esteem." If so, there may be a connection between the two characteristics, tentatively formulated as "poor relationship with father" goes together with "low self-esteem." The program can then be instructed to search for disconfirming instances.

"Going together with . . . " is one of the simplest kinds of linkages. Other relationships may involve "if . . . then" sequences, causation, or subordination, as well as the opposites of these linkages (X never goes together with Y, and so forth). It is, of course, the researcher's job to deduce the nature of the relationship. Theory-building analysis programs facilitate this job by providing sophisticated search mechanisms in which two or more codes—file characteristics—can be combined. All of them use Boolean operators (AND, OR, NOT), and some offer many other options. The researcher divides data files into subsets that provide evidence for a regularity that can be postulated as a hypothesis. The more intricate the combination of variables, the more files the researcher needs to find the postulated constellation of characteristics. These programs are not meant for a phenomenological, in-depth analysis of a small number of cases.

Theory-building programs consequently allow the researcher to move away from the raw data, to concentrate on the conceptual notions they contained, and to ponder and visualize these concepts. The classificatory system, used as an organizing tool in descriptive–interpretive studies, is refined and elaborated. Patterns are discovered and complex new categories created from simple ones by establishing relationships, until the system becomes the result of the study. While NUDIST merely expects the researcher to visualize the structure as tree-type hierarchies, ATLAS concentrates on the actual graphic display of the system as a conceptual network.

The preceding description uses the dichotomy descriptive–interpretive and theory-building to highlight the differences between the two types of analysis. In qualitative work, a study rarely is either purely descriptive–interpretive or purely theory-building. Whatever a researcher describes, the description concentrates on patterns found in the data; the conceptual step from isolating patterns to making claims about regularities is small. Such claims can lead to propositions about what goes together with what, and the formulation of hypotheses may, in turn, grow from such propositions. In practice there is no crisp dichotomy between description and theory; it is more realistic to view the matter as a continuum. Any qualitative project may fall anywhere on the line connecting the two poles of that continuum.

Software packages available for qualitative analysis mirror research practice; they were, after all, developed by practitioners. They have always offered functions for theorizing. In the following, we describe these functions from the still descriptively oriented to the more theoretically oriented. We do not, however, intend to convey a preference for theory over description. The research goal determines how theoretical a study is. In some cases the study is a foray into uncharted territory, and the scientific challenge comes from making lucid what previously was obscure. In other cases, previous research has generated hunches about how things may influence each other, and the appropriate strategy is to isolate concepts and explore their linkages. One type of research is neither more difficult nor more respectable than the other. Both require the researcher's full competence in applying the methods chosen; to both the same standards of scientific conduct apply. The reason why we describe the theory-building functions provided by computer software in an advancing order is that computers, because of their mechanical nature, stop being of help where the researcher's task is interpretation. In theory-building research the mechanical tasks include additional searching and sorting, which computers can perform with more accuracy and speed than human beings.

SEARCHING FOR CO-OCCURRING CODES
WITHIN SEGMENTS

All analysis programs allow the researcher to attach more than one code to any segment, to overlap segments, or to nest segments in one another. Therefore, it is easy for the computer to identify the places in the data where codes co-occur in a single segment. The co-occurrence means that the segment belongs to different categories. These co-occurrences are useful to the researcher in more than one way. They may help in modifying and finalizing the classificatory system. By assembling all segments coded with two or more codes, the researcher may discover resemblances in their content and decide that separate categories are unnecessary. On the other hand, the researcher may discover that although the segments belong in different categories there seems to be a conceptual relationship between the categories (perhaps through one or more shared properties of the category). Such an outcome warrants further investigation and can become the beginning of a theoretical notion.

MS-DOS Programs

All MS-DOS programs except Textbase Alpha collate the segments coded with one or more of the same codes, and the next version of Textbase Alpha will have this facility. The process is simple. The user supplies the codes to be searched for and the files to be searched, and the output is much like the one for single codes. In The Ethnograph the researcher may choose to see only those areas of the segments that overlap, or the entire text of both segments, with the overlapping area indicated. Further, several codes can be combined in one search request. The instructions for such searches include the Boolean OR and NOT; The Ethnograph can look for all segments coded either for one category or the other; it can search for segments coded for one or several codes but retrieve them only if they are not also coded with a specified other code. Since all segments relevant to two or more categories are displayed so they can readily be perused, it is easy to discover any commonalities that constitute a link between the categories.

AQUAD distinguishes in its searches between nested segments (in which the inner segment is viewed as a hierarchical subcode of the outer) and the two types of overlaps mentioned for The Ethnograph.

Macintosh Programs

HyperQual sorts all cards in a stack with a certain code, then sorts through the new stack for another code, so that only those cards are left that have both codes. The sorting procedure may continue for additional codes and can be repeated for as many rounds as there are co-occurring codes. HyperRESEARCH has no facility for finding co-occurring codes. HyperSoft, like AQUAD, concentrates on nested codes, since it considers them subcategories. In NUDIST, co-occurring, nested, and overlapping codes are located specifically for the nature of their positions relative to each other, with intersect, union, overlap, inside, and outside search operations.

SELECTIVE SEARCHES: LINKING VARIABLES TO CATEGORIES

Baseline and other sociodemographic characteristics such as gender, age, income group, or other variables, such as years of experience, connection to a school site, or grade level taught, often are of interest to researchers seeking differences or similarities between or among groups of people. These searches can be done for descriptive purposes or to discover regularities. This kind of code search, sorting according to subsets of data, is called a selective search in computer-assisted analysis; only specified data documents are electronically selected for collating segments.

MS-DOS Programs

Textbase Alpha and The Ethnograph let the researcher attach information pertaining to an entire file. Retrieval can later be restricted to files with this information. Only those files are selected for the search to which certain criteria apply. This can be demographic variables like age or gender, but could be anything the researcher chooses as a selection criterion. These criteria can then be combined for a code search. For instance, the researcher may instruct the program to search for segments coded ABC but collate them only for those files where the interviewee's age is less than 35 and the interviewer was John. Such searches are useful only when the researcher is working with a rather large number of data documents.

The selection variables must be entered into the computer before such a search can be conducted. This is not done in a word processor, but in the analysis program itself. First, the researcher identifies the "variables" to be attached to each file. These are called "facesheet variables" in The Ethnograph. Textbase Alpha provides a selection file—a file in which the values for each variable are stored, file by file. The values are the actual information, for instance the number "33" for age in file "Interv-1." The user is prompted to provide the information for each file. The Ethnograph handles the process differently. It first asks the user to make a template that holds the variable names. Entering the variable values is then done like coding files, by filling in blanks in forms on the screen.

Selection variables make the search process quite sophisticated. Both Textbase Alpha and The Ethnograph provide for all kinds of combinations of these variables, and their entry screens take into account the most complex kinds of searches. Therefore, it takes a bit of learning in both programs to understand how to use this facility. Fortunately, the user's manuals for these programs are very detailed and helpful in explaining the process.

While descriptive programs provide selective searches as an additional feature, these kinds of searches are at the heart of theory-building programs. As we explained previously, when a code is attached in a theory-building program, it can be viewed as characterizing the entire file. Therefore, no special facesheet or selection variables are needed. AQUAD, for example, considers selective searches a part of its hypothesis-testing operation. The function is similar to linking categories and is described below.

Macintosh Programs

HyperQual does not perform selective searches. To simulate them, the researcher can search for a code by typing in the names of selected data documents. The remaining Macintosh programs operate like AQUAD (see the preceding explanation).

SEARCHING FOR CO-OCCURRING CODES WITHIN FILES: LINKING CATEGORIES TO CATEGORIES

It is important here to distinguish between searches for codes that co-occur in single data segments and those that co-occur in files. In the second case, the codes are viewed as characteristics of the file—one file standing for one interviewee, for instance, as previously explained. This characteristic is usually called a concept in theory-building programs, even if it is no more than a demographic variable. Each concept is denoted by one category, and each category holds all the text segments found in the data as evidence for the presence of the concept. The concepts are grounded in the data. The purpose of theory-building programs is to discover whether there are linkages among concepts.

Descriptive programs, by their nature, do not provide search functions that locate co-occurring codes in files. In contrast, theory-building programs offer as their major output pointers or references to the files in which a code or a co-occurrence of codes was found.

MS-DOS Programs

AQUAD has two ways of searching for the potential linkages among categories. First, preformulated hypotheses can be used—we would call them speculations or working hypotheses. Second, the researcher may formulate additional hypotheses. This latter requires some programming skill in Turbo Prolog, but the basics of the process are explained in the AQUAD user's manual, and the developer of the program offers individualized assistance. The preformulated hypotheses postulate the co-occurrence of two or three codes, and all the researcher has to do is enter the names of the codes. Some hypotheses explore non-co-occurrence—they provide for the search for negative instances, to establish the degree of confirmation to be derived from the data. This is especially important for the verification process. Additional hypotheses specify the distances within which the co-occurrence must occur to be considered meaningful.

Macintosh Programs

HyperSoft, instead of reformulating search combinations, lets the researcher make up combinations of any codes with the help of the Boolean operators AND, OR, and NOT. This program also lets the user specify the nature of the postulated links between segments within a single data document, as its segments are coded. In addition to segmenting and coding, the researcher may thus enter logical connections as links between coded segments at the time the data are first read and prepared for later searches. Such a link may be "causes" or "caused by." Then a search can be performed for these links between two specified codes.

In HyperRESEARCH the search for co-occurring codes in files is called hypothesis testing, as in AQUAD. The process is conceptualized in this program as constructing a set of rules with Boolean operators. The program not only searches for a co-occurrence of codes, but at the same time considers the consequences if the co-occurrence is established. If it is, then a new code or category is added to the master list of codes. This category contains the references to all the files in which the co-occurrence was found. In effect, a conclusion is drawn: In all files in which this co-occurrence is found the researcher can assume the existence of another factor. For example, if "the mother is critical of the child's body image" and "the relationship between the child and the mother is strained," and "the child is experiencing weight loss," then "there is evidence of mother's influence on child's self-image."

NUDIST uses a similar logic without using the term *hypothesis testing*. In this program, the results of co-occurrence searches are added to the classificatory system as new nodes of its hierarchical tree structure. The references to all text segments that were indexed with the codes used in the search are automatically transferred into the new node, and the text from all of them can be printed together. The rest is left to the interpretation of the researcher. NUDIST's special feature is its provision of more than three Boolean operators. As mentioned earlier, the program can look for codes co-occurring in individual segments. It also includes variations: XOR, segments coded with either one of codes, but not both together; forms of NEAR, which specify the range within which another code has to be found; the inclusion or exclusion in a search of documents that contain a particular code; and the automatic search for codes at a higher level in the tree structure than the specified code.

SEQUENCES

Whenever behavior or other dynamic processes are studied, the chronological sequence of events becomes important. This is often the case in participant and nonparticipant observation and when conversational discourse among people is examined. If properly coded, this dynamic element is revealed in the sequence in which codes are attached in a data text.

MS-DOS Programs

AQUAD has a preformulated sequence hypothesis for two codes. The search specifies that a code must occur in the data with a user-defined distance from (in terms of lines), but prior to, another code. For sequences of three codes or more, the same search must be conducted by pairs, and the researcher can compare the resulting print-outs for each. These printouts are lists in which the file name is given for each data document in which the specified co-occurrence is found, together with reference information about the place or places within the file where it occurs.

Macintosh Programs

NUDIST also offers a ready-made search request for codes occurring in a sequence. It is called the followed-by operator. As in AQUAD, the researcher specifies two codes, indicating which is the first and which is the second. The distance within which the second must follow can be specified not only by the number of lines, but also by the entire document; if the user has prepared the original data documents accordingly, subsections of the document can be used as distance indicators.

TRANSFERAL AND DISPLAY

Whether the kind of analysis is descriptive or theoretical, the results of the analysis program's actions are needed to guide the next analysis steps or for the final research report. Collated text segments for categories can help decide on the appropriateness of the category, selected segments can serve as quotes to illustrate a theme or to exemplify a concept, and search results for co-occurring codes can support the researcher's theoretical propositions. How do these materials get from the computer into the hands of the ethnographer?

First, all programs provide print options at every turn. All programs that use two-step coding print the data with line numbers attached so that the researcher can code the data on paper. The other programs print out results. In the programs for descriptive–interpretive analysis, results are the compilations of coded text segments, sorted according to categories. In the programs for theory-building analysis the results are lists of references to data files, with the option of printing the associated text.

TRANSFER TO A WORD PROCESSOR

In addition to sending electronic material to the printer, all programs allow the researcher to create a file holding new material. Often it is called "print to disk." The user is asked to provide a name for such a new file, and it is stored in the same place in which the program finds the data. Nothing happens on the screen, but the results are secure.

Analysis programs make it unnecessary to retype any pieces of data as quotes to be inserted into the research report. The new results file is saved as an ASCII file. ASCII files can then be imported into most word processors. This saves time, although there is the disadvantage that ASCII files have hard returns at the end of each line (each line is treated as if it were a paragraph). These hard returns can be deleted and replaced with an ordinary space; most word processors can do this with a few keystrokes. Even more efficient are utility programs that specialize in converting ASCII files into popular word processor formats. Once the collated segments or the co-occurrence results are in a word-processor, the researcher can cut and paste relevant portions electronically to the research report using a window or second document, switching between files.

The HyperCard-based Macintosh programs already have their results in HyperCard format. If the researcher is writing the report in another word processor, the material can be transferred with the Clipboard and further processed there.

DIAGRAMS

Aside from the simple frequency matrices mentioned previously, most of the qualitative analysis programs described here do not incorporate graphic displays. The notable exception is HyperSoft, which allows the researcher to represent graphically the results of its retrievals. As a Macintosh HyperCard program, it has access to easy drawing facilities, and it uses these to show results in diagram form. The search results are converted from numbers to fields—rectangles or circles—of differing lengths or sizes on a map; the fields are scaled according to the number of data segments retrieved, divided by the number of cases included in the search. The links between categories can also be graphically represented. They are shown as arrows running from one field to another, having different intensities and thicknesses.

The only MS-DOS analysis program offering similar graphics is ATLAS. Here the graphics are not electronically linked to search results. The researcher uses the graphics capabilities of Microsoft Windows to place onto the screen boxes that represent categories and lines connecting the boxes. The size of the boxes and the thickness of the lines are uniform. However, by placing an arrowhead at one end or at both ends, the user can represent the direction of the lines. Lines can also be named, to specify in abbreviated form the nature of the link between two categories. For instance, "is a" may stand for "X is a type of Y." Graphs created this way let the researcher see as elements of a network the concepts or categories developed from the data.

Although NUDIST represents its set of concepts as a tree-structured system, it does not let users draw that tree or draw it for them. This can be done with ETHNO. Although not assisting in the analysis of text, ETHNO creates complex inverted tree-chart diagrams of the connections the researcher has found in the data. This program is especially suited to the establishment of typologies, the depiction of conceptual connections among words, and the presentation of logical and chronological sequences.

After the researcher has identified the basic logical rules in the data, ETHNO is very easy to use. It works by eliciting from the user two types of information: the elements of the system and the relationship among any newly entered element and all other elements entered previously. Relationship types can be determined by the user and the relationship can be a simple one. For instance, the operator could be "a kind of." If this taxonomic relationship were chosen, the relationships among the software packages described here could be depicted as in Fig. 8.11. ETHNO abbreviates the name of the elements entered. In this case, the elements are software packages. The lines represent the relationships. If the diagram is read from the bottom to the top, the following links emerge: EGR (The Ethnograph) is "a kind of" qualitative analysis program (TAN), which in turn is "a kind of" IBM program, which in turn is "a kind of" microcomputer program. ETHNO (ETH) is not "a kind of" qualitative analysis program (TAN), but it is "a kind of" IBM program, whereas HyperQual (HYQ) is "a kind of" qualitative analysis program and "a kind of" Macintosh program.

ETHNO is especially appropriate for these kinds of taxonomies, but it can accommodate many other types of relationships. While ETHNO currently is the only diagram-creating program developed for researchers, another kind of diagram-drawing program is available commercially: flow-chart designers. Their graphs are similar to the preceding diagram, except all names must be entered in boxes of different shapes, corresponding to the standard symbols used in flow-charting. These programs can be adapted to research projects.

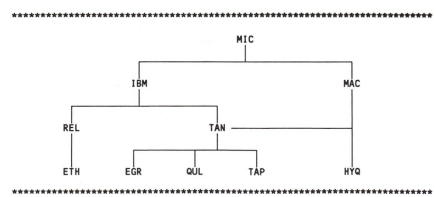

Figure 8.11   A structure created by the software package ETHNO (MS-DOS) according to the printer's output.

Summary

The description of technical features has not done justice to the programs mentioned. Each program has its unique character, in addition to the "mechanics" depicted here. Since they are the creations of individual researchers, they carry their designers' personal imprints. QUALPRO, for example, is the easiest program to learn. It contains all the basic functions described here, but adds to frills, and the user's manual is correspondingly short. A close second in ease of learning is Textbase Alpha, with a similarly short manual. This is one of the first MS-DOS programs to offer on-screen coding, which appeals to researchers who have large amounts of easily codable data. HyperQual also allows coding directly on the screen, but requires more learning, because it uses a special vocabulary, familiar to HyperCard users. The cadillac among the descriptive–interpretive programs is The Ethnograph, and its many features have required a lengthy user's manual. For Version 4.0, the screen succession and manual have been economized, and working with and learning the program should be easier. At the same time, the new features of this program are blurring the differences between descriptive–interpretive and theory-building programs.

The designated theory-building programs were just appearing on the market as this chapter was written. AQUAD stands out through its ability to use not only Boolean operators for searchers, but also a different feature of Boolean algebra, logical minimization. With this mathematial algorithm, the researcher can specify one code as a potential outcome and look for the cause that produced that outcome. The cause is assumed to consist of a number of factors or conditions that contributed to it or had to be absent for it to occur. This cause can be ascertained by exploratorily searching for any constellation of codes appearing in all cases where the outcome is found. HyperRESEARCH is the only program at this time with direct connections to audio and video data media. Like NUDIST, it views the classificatory system as a knowledge base, called an indexing system in NUDIST, and allows the results of searches to become new categories in this knowledge base. HyperSoft places its emphasis on graphic representation of the search results.

By the time this book is published, these descriptions will no longer be accurate. Programmers are eager to please their colleagues by making new, more polished, and more powerful versions of their programs. Textbase Alpha, for instance, is slated for a complete overhaul in 1992. In addition, new programs will be developed. Not all the programs available at this time could be included in this chapter. Some have not been marketed broadly enough; others are very similar to the ones described here; others are not available in English, and others are still in the early development phases. GATOR is a relatively old American program that uses Boolean searches to index and retrieve flexibly definable text segments but does little more. Kwalitan, a theory-building program, was developed in The Netherlands, is quite expensive, and is not yet available in English. MAX is a program much like Textbase Alpha that was developed in Germany, with an English version planned. A Macintosh program not yet on the market is FOP, created at Gothenburg University in Sweden specifically for a type of research called phenomenography (Tesch, 1990).

Although such diversity is needed to provide researchers with appropriate computer assistance no matter what kind of qualitative analysis is chosen, there is also a danger. Programmers are tempted to add more and more features to their packages, especially since researchers pressure them to do so. In the world of computers, however, more is not always better. For instance, the more functions a program provides, the more complex the menus have to be to offer the user the appropriate selections; the more items appear on each menu, the more prompts users have to respond to. With the complexity of the program, the user's manual becomes more voluminous, and the learning time increases. None of the programs described here has become too bulky to be useful. However, unless a special function is needed for a research project, some researchers have begun to opt for the simplicity of the basic functions, as for instance provided in QUALPRO.

The fact that ingenious scholars are thinking of new and sophisticated ways in which the computer can meet special analysis demands is certainly of great advantage to researchers. However, the plurality of programs also imposes the need to become knowledgeable about this type of software. There are few experts who can advise qualitative researchers on the right choice among these programs. While a wrong decision could result merely in frustration, the possibility that researchers may then readjust their research goals to fit the functions of a program acquired by chance creates a serious methodological issue.

The problems described above, however, should not distract from the fact that the computer provides researchers the opportunity to spend more time thinking about the analysis of qualitative data and less time on mechanical tasks. It can make analysis more efficient and more complete. The newer programs make feasible an intricacy of analysis that would have been much too time consuming to expect of any single researcher with limited resources. Although, in principle, computers still cannot do what a human mind and human eyes can do, they can make ethnographers and other qualitative researchers more productive and their professional work decidedly more pleasant.

CHAPTER NINE

Evaluating Qualitative Design

The goal of research is a search for truth. Ever since human beings began studying themselves and their activities, they also have been judging the results of these inquiries. In this chapter we focus on how to judge the value of the claims researchers make about themselves and the world. We explore several questions. What is the connection, if any, between what researchers claim about the world and themselves in it and what they and others experience? How do researchers convince various audiences of the worth and legitimacy of their claims? How do researchers know that these claims match what some consider to be reality, what others see as intersubjective experience, or what the most restrictive critics describe as mere scholarly consensus?

The various approaches to evaluation in the human sciences attest that there are different kinds of truth and that there are different degrees of truth within and across kinds. Further, these kinds and degrees of truth are held differentially for different audiences and constituencies. In the initial section of this chapter we discuss these different audiences and constituencies. Then we turn to the different ways of evaluating—the different assumptions about value and the different philosophies toward research—that methodologists have been proposing for qualitative study. The chapter ends with a comparison of standards for evaluating quantitative research, using conventional notions of reliability and validity, with their counterparts in qualitative and ethnographic study. We begin our consideration of how qualitative research is evaluated by examining the relationship between the evaluation and the evaluator. For whom is a study being evaluated? Who are the people who care about the legitimacy and worth of qualitative research, and what do they want to know?

Our own concerns arise from teaching qualitative research design to those attempting an initial inquiry for a thesis or dissertation, from working in thesis and dissertation examining committees, from consulting with other researchers on issues of design and method, and of course from doing research ourselves in the human sciences. The philosophical, theoretical, and methodological issues underlying evaluation of qualitative studies are also crucial to the topic, and we adddress these in the middle section of the chapter. However, the locus of any investigator's struggles with evaluation occurs on the front lines of research activity, in the midst of ongoing, daily decisions. This is where the philosophies, theories, and methodologies are applied, tested, adopted, adapted, or rejected. The key issue in assessing qualitative studies is how particular researchers struggle to attain value in their endeavors, in the daily decisions they make in posing questions, and in selecting, collecting, analyzing, and interpreting data.

Evaluation for Whom?[1]

A commitment to seeking quality in the human sciences requires responsibility to ourselves as researchers, to the participants we study, to our community of scholars, to the various publics who support or otherwise take an interest in the research, to the traditions that inform the research, and to those who inherit the knowledge generated by the research. Unfortunately, as the examples we discuss at the end of the chapter illustrate, these different constituencies can evoke different, sometimes conflicting choices because their expectations, standards of assessment, and concerns vary. We believe that each of their voices should be considered in any discussion of evaluating qualitative research because these groups legitimize research and decide whether qualitative results are relevant, appropriate, illuminating, and useful.

Among the most important research constituencies are ourselves as scholars, members of the disciplinary traditions each of us represents, other researchers, the participants we study, and the publics who take an interest in our work. Our purpose in the following discussion is to emphasize the variety of obligations and expectations to which we are susceptible as we seek to produce research that is honest, truthful, and valid.

EVALUATION FOR OURSELVES

Two questions that plague most investigators are "Did I get it right?" and "Did I get it all?" They are part of the more basic question, "Have I done a good job here?" Completism is a problem familiar to any researcher,

[1] Our apologies are in order to Robert S. Lynd (1964) and to Derek L. Phillips (1971) for the format of these chapter headings.

qualitative or otherwise. For ethnographers and other qualitative scholars completism is especially troublesome. A commitment to holistic and contextualized research means an obligation to study phenomena as thoroughly, as broadly, and as deeply as time, energy, and resources allow. Qualitative researchers lay claim to portrayals that tell, more or less, the whole story of the research. Simultaneously they know they never get it all; they know they get only pieces, views, and aspects of what they seek to describe. Most qualitative researchers cope with the impossibility of completism by making tradeoffs. They collect as much data, selected with as fine a net, as possible. Then they attempt to discover what the limitations of the material are. They try to discover what they have not considered, sought, or collected and subsequently undertake the difficult task of reporting these limitations, thereby revealing what they know, or only suspect, they may have missed. They reassure themselves that, in the course of a research career, they will return to the omissions.

Getting it all is impossible, but getting it right is tougher. Many qualitative researchers are uneasy with the notion of getting information, much less interpretations, "right." They may make phenomenological, constructivist, or interpretive assumptions about reality. They assume that what they observe and interpret is constructed on the bases of prior experiences, skills, knowledge, and the peculiar layout of the human brain and sensory apparatus. They believe these are not dictated but are developed by each individual in the course of living. Qualitative researchers assume that humans do have choices about the constructions they use and devise, although constructions deeply embedded in cultural and psychological phenomena are difficult to discern. The issue of getting it right hence can be translated as how and when to select standards of assessment, given the limitations of a very slippery reality being perceived by a complex but limited apparatus, the human being (see Rorty, 1985, for a pragmatist's view of reality).

Except perhaps for the solipsist, the notion of a constructed observation and interpretation does not preclude some reality external to the observer. We believe something is "out there" (however many "out theres" there are) and that the obdurate nature of what is out there does not always cooperate with our dearly cherished constructions. Sometimes reality comes and bashes us on the head. Anyone who has been fired from a job or rejected by a lover, let alone confronted with data that do not fit expectations, has faced an "out there" that resists internal constructions. Indeed, often it is these very confrontations that permit humans to learn new constructions and ways of understanding the world and themselves within it.

Letting themselves be challenged in their research by some surprises, pleasant and otherwise, is one way scholars try to connect with the "out there." Surprises add to the credibility of observations and interpretations, but even surprises are constructions. Surprises indicate that scholars are seeing something discrepant with their initial constructions, but still viewable with them. Perhaps they are not just seeing what they expect, but they may just be seeing what they do not expect.

Another source of reassurance for at least "doing it right" even if not "getting it right" is the traditions in the areas researchers study—philosophical, theoretical, and methodological. These are the practices, conventions, and principles of the disciplines and professions scholars study. Self-confidence in the quality of a study is built on practicing research, exploring material, reflecting on data, and comparing these experiences with what the traditions endorse. These traditions are conveyed in books such as this, which is one way of transmitting, maintaining, and changing ways of doing it right.

EVALUATION FOR THE SCHOLARLY TRADITIONS

Claims made by scholars ought to be open to demonstration and ought to be supported by evidence. Few researchers question that premise. What is questioned, argued, and debated is what the evidence ought to be, how the demonstration should be conducted, and what it is that the evidence and demonstration mean (Kvale, 1989; Smith, 1990; Wolcott, 1990). For example, some scholars seek for certainty; they seek assurance that a claim is true, regardless of who the claimer may be and without qualification (for discussions of this view, see Kirk & Miller, 1986; Marshall, 1990). Other researchers settle for confidence instead of certainty (e.g., Brinberg & McGrath, 1985). The assumption here is that nothing is certain; the best that can be achieved is varying degrees of confidence in a claim. The skeptical stance associated traditionally with the scientific method is consistent with choosing confidence over certainty (Phillips, 1990a,b). Another criteria for evaluating research is utility. In this case scholars seek claims useful in furthering theory, additional lines of empirical inquiry, or the development of new questions to pursue (cf. Howe & Eisenhart, 1990).

Researchers choose the standards or criteria they use to assess studies from their scholarly traditions. These standards are no longer dictated, if they ever were, by research design, theoretical framework, or substantive topic. These standards, which we elaborate in the second section of the chapter, are constructed. They are developed, argued, promoted, and sometimes rejected by groups of researchers working in disciplines, subdisciplines, and interdisciplines. It is these groups who constitute the communities of scholars.

EVALUATION FOR A COMMUNITY OF SCHOLARS

Demonstrations accepted as adequate for assuring certainty, confidence, or utility do vary, of course, from one group of scholars to the next. Logic, rhetoric, and approved uses of research methods—methods defined as broadly as "the scientific method" or as narrowly as, for example, Glaser & Strauss's (1967) constant comparative method—are among the kinds of acceptable demonstrations. What constitutes adequate evidence also varies. The quantity, quality, and definitions of data offered as evidence vary across disciplines, professions, and other specialty areas.

For example, our graduate students are frequently disturbed by Glaser and Strauss's statement that "even if some of our evidence is not entirely accurate this will not be too troublesome" (1967, p. 23). This seems like heresy to those who equate scholarship with the verification of data. Read in context, of course, Glaser and Strauss express concern for confidence in accuracy of data and stipulate the necessity for checks on accuracy. They also note the slipperiness of data, emphasizing that facts change, that facts are open to doubt and multiple interpretation, and that facts are only a means to an end. Glaser and Strauss argue that a preoccupation with accurate facts ought not to distract scholars from a focus on other kinds of claims.

This is one of those balancing acts or tradeoffs researchers seek in establishing the worth of a study. To strengthen one part of a study, scholars accept some amount of error, doubt, or uncertainty in another part. One tradeoff qualitative researchers make is to request that their respondents and participants assess observations and interpretations or cross-check descriptions and analysis.

EVALUATION FOR PARTICIPANTS

Scholars vary in their reasons for using member checks on researcher information. Sometimes their purpose is to confirm an observation. Other times they wish to substantiate their interpretations by seeking the agreement of the group under investigation. This creates a consensual validity, authenticating the researcher's material to the degree that participants assent.

However, a difficulty with consensual validity is that it requires a unanimous vote. It is based on the assumption that because objectivity is impossible, the best that can be achieved is intersubjectivity, or on the assumption that humans share similar views and are able to devise joint lines of action in communicating with one another. Validity based on consensus, then, is more than a unanimous vote. Not only must there be no disagreement, but there also must be what Quakers refer to as no qualms; in endorsing the group position, individuals must not qualify their support.

This is difficult to achieve in any situation, let alone something as complex as human research. What most scholars finally accept and report is a ratification from some participants, the qualified approval of others, and the outright refutation and denial of the remaining. However, even should an elusive consensus be achieved, there always remains the issue that group perception may be as wrong as an individual's perception. As Scriven (1972) notes, mob rule does not guarantee confidence, let alone certainty.

Nevertheless, people who are being studied do have a stake in the quality of research results. Their lives are being recorded, and their record becomes "sealed in time" (Holecek, 1983). Researchers thus have an obligation to address the concerns participants express for accuracy, honesty, and truthfulness, despite how these may be diversely interpreted. This same diversity of interpretation occurs when a research study is offered for public assessment.

EVALUATION FOR VARIOUS PUBLICS

A hallmark of the sciences, human and natural, has been that the information and knowledge produced be publicly available and open to all, so that they can be subjected to the broadest possible scrutiny. This stance assumes that public availability of research is the final check on truth, allowing for refutation and correction from the largest audience.

The public is itself diverse. Policy makers who apply research recommendations and implications and funding agencies who support research constitute major portions of any investigator's public. Taxpayers and contributors to private funding agencies compose additional parts of the public. Others who read and apply the results of qualitative design—teachers, parents, consumers, tourists, the intellectually curious—want to know if material is authentic, and they discuss whether interpretations are credible (cf. Ambrose's 1991 account of a historical study purporting to establish General Dwight D. Eisenhower's culpability in the deaths of a million German prisoners of war).

Human scientists in professional areas—education, counseling and psychotherapy, evaluation, business, and so on—have a special responsibility to the public, and this makes their work more likely to be widely disseminated. However, beyond the bounds of academia, the issue of evaluating results becomes a question of truth. How can the public be assured that the research presented is true? Human scientists of the late second millennium have avoided philosophical discussions of truth and falsity. Within academia substituting words like *validity* and *reliability* for the word *truth* sidesteps philosophical issues and excuses researchers from attending to their basic assumptions.

The relationship between validity and truth has been hotly debated (e.g., Guba, 1982; McCutcheon, 1990; Phillips, 1990b). What should be accorded validity or truth in human science research is, of course, a serious issue. We use these terms interchangeably here although we are not convinced that they are or ought to be synonymous. It seems to us that validity is a category of truth. If refers to the kinds of qualified and tentative truths that scientists seek. There are other kinds of truths, of course; but in this chapter our use of truth is restricted to the truth of scientific claims or what scientists have come to call validity.

This kind of qualification and hedging is unacceptable to most publics. They may even hear it as the kind of doublespeak Patton (1990a) finds so troublesome in much current scholarship. The public wants to know whether scientific information is fabricated or real, whether claims are contrived or true. After all, newspapers do report instances of data being invented or falsified. People understand that scientific claims affect policy decisions, distribution of public and private funds and other resources, as well as personal decisions they may make. Although we offer no formula to resolve these concerns, we do believe that research in the human sciences is accorded value by the public that uses it.

SUMMARY

The question this section emphasizes (evaluation for whom?) suggests that assessing the value of a study requires a balance among different approaches and considerations. It is not only impossible, but also undesirable, to apply all of the possibly relevant evaluative standards to a qualitative research study. Standards may be contradictory, and priorities may vary according to such factors as which audience is evaluating the research. We believe that researchers or research teams, collaborative and otherwise, should exercise their own discretion in decisions about which standards to apply, case by case as the study proceeds.

In the following pages we argue that no single approach to evaluation is adequate for assessing qualitative design, much less the human sciences as a whole. The best we can achieve are standards necessary and sufficient, applied case by case. Part of the case-by-case decision depends on the traditions in research that frame a study and inform those conducting the research. In this section we ask, "Evaluation for what?" We discuss the varying meanings that a key concept in evaluation, validity, has across the traditions influencing qualitative and ethnographic design.

Evaluation for What?

As we emphasized in the preceding section, validity is the concept used in the sciences, natural and human, to represent the philosophical and lay notion of truth. In this section of the chapter we examine the various meanings accorded the concept of validity and discuss the implications of these meanings for qualitative and ethnographic research.

WHAT IS VALIDITY?

Like many scientific constructs validity is used by researchers from different traditions to refer to somewhat different things. Because human sciences and scholarship are developed by people across time and space, the constructs on which this endeavor rests also change and develop. Just as people tinker with building better mouse traps, so do they tinker with their abstract concepts and theories.

Commonsensical Validity

Validity is first a term used in everyday language to convey a number of common-sensical meanings. Sometimes people mean accurate when the use the term *valid*. A valid prediction of tomorrow's weather, for example, is one that closely matches what occurs tomorrow. A second common-sensical meaning for the term *valid* is justifiable, warrantable, and hence believable. An example of this usage is an explanation for shooting someone; self-defense can be considered a valid reason for homicide. Other times people mean that something is logically correct when they refer to it as valid; an argument for preserving the rain forests, for example, is valid if the conclusion, preservation, follows the premises, among them that rain forests generate much of the earth's oxygen. Valid is also used as a synonym for sanctioned or authorized. Police officers are accorded a valid reason for breaking and entering private property, otherwise considered illegal, when the action is duly authorized by a judge, who issues the appropriate search warrant. Finally sometimes people mean something is effective, for whatever reasons, when they label it as valid. A valid way to solve a problem in mathematics, for example, may just be one that works; it does the job.

Any of these meanings for valid, or even some combination of them, may be evoked in more technical applications of the term. Scholars sometimes refer to common-sensical meanings when they use "valid"; other times they have a more specific definition in mind. Whatever the denotation intended, however, the connotations remain and should be considered in any applications.

Conventional Validity

Scientific and scholarly meanings for validity have multiplied since the 1970s, along with the diversification in acceptable research designs and methodologies. In the conventional approaches to research in the human sciences that predominated through the 1960s, experimental and quasiexperimental design and sample survey research, for example, validity was associated with accuracy. In this tradition validity is the extent to which scientific findings are correct; it requires determining the extent to which conclusions effectively represent empirical reality and assessing whether constructs devised by researchers accurately represent or measure categories of human experience. Distinctions are commonly drawn between internal validity and external validity. Internal validity is the extent to which scientific observations and measurements are authentic representations of some reality. External validity is the degree to which such representations may be compared legitimately across groups.

Qualitative Validities

Validity for qualitative researchers varies; emergent constructs representing the worth and value of qualitative research are undergoing much argument and debate. Because these constructs may be based on very different philosophical and theoretical assumptions, we refer to them in the plural.

During the twentieth century these assumptions have evolved significantly. Much qualitative research conducted through the middle decades of this century, until the 1970s, presupposed the use of conventional definitions of validity. Few scholars questioned this, and it is reflected in the research methods books of the times (e.g., Bruyn, 1966; Goode & Hatt, 1952; Madge, 1953; Naroll, 1962; Pelto & Pelto, 1978; Zetterberg, 1966; Znaniecki, 1934).

In the 1970s and 1980s, methodologists began to use a metaphorical application of conventional standards of validity and reliability to qualitative and ethnographic design. Researchers such as Denzin (1978), Dobbert (1982), Patton (1980), and we ourselves (LeCompte & Goetz, 1982) explored how this had been and could be done. Our approach was to look at what qualitative researchers do to assure confidence, authenticity, cogency, and soundness in their designs and to present the results convincingly to their publics. In the final section of this chapter we review this metaphorical application of conventional standards to qualitative research.

By the 1980s researchers were struggling with an approach to validity that we see as neologistic, as the substitution of new, unconventional labels for a mix of old and new ideas. A number of methodologists have sought ways to address the issues involved in validity without recourse to the definitions and assumptions of conventional usage (e.g., Guba, 1986; Lincoln, 1986; Smith, 1984). The goal of this neologistic approach is to derive a construct of validity from the special characteristics of qualitative research that would function independently of conventional usage. Lincoln and Guba have proposed various sets of such a usage. They began (Guba 1981, 1986; Guba & Lincoln, 1981; Lincoln & Guba, 1985) with four standards for assessing the rigor of naturalistic study: credibility, or internal validity; fittingness and transferability, or external validity; auditability and dependability, or reliability; and confirmability, or objectivity. We see these standards as similar to the metaphorical usage discussed previously, albeit with different labels. Subsequently (Lincoln, 1986) they discarded the concept of rigor as too positivistic and substituted the notion of trustworthiness. A study can be trusted if it meets these criteria: (1) fairness, the balanced representation of the multiple realities in a situation; (2) ontological authenticity, a fresh "more sophisticated" understanding of something; (3) educative authenticity, a new appreciation of these understandings; (4) catalytic authenticity, courses of action are supported by the inquiry; and (5) tactical authenticity, potential benefit of the inquiry to all concerned. These five criteria have their counterparts in values sought by much conventional research: objectivity, novelty, meaningfulness, applicability, and availability to the public. Conventional, metaphorical, and neologistic approaches to validity continue to fire scholarly debate (e.g., Eisenhart & Howe, 1992). This is, of course, a function of the state of the discipline; new ways of conceptualizing experience depend on and relate to previous concepts, and scholars seek to discover these relationships.

By the 1990s a kind of oppositional stance had emerged. Some qualitative methodologists dismiss concern with reliability and validity by considering them irrelevant: "We don't do reliability and validity." Smith (1984), for example, has taken the position that the philosophical assumptions of interpretive research preclude any common standards for evaluating qualitative studies. This position is not only a rejection of conventional standards but also a rejection of any common criteria for assessing research.

Finally, some methodologists have proposed what we see as a paradigmatic approach to validity. Those who see research as divided by different world views and basic philosophies use Kuhn's (1970) notion of paradigm to separate kinds of research. Smith (1990), for example, suggests that the criterion for the goodness or validity of a study depends on the paradigm of the researcher. For postpositivists a valid study is one that demonstrates objectivity; it is unbiased, open, honest, precise, and receptive to criticism, and it corresponds to some experience of reality. For constructivists a valid study is one that demonstrates solidarity; its results are based on and open to negotiation and dialogue within participant and research communities. For critical theory a valid study demonstrates emancipation; it reveals the distortions and limitations of ideologies, communication patterns, and social structures underlying everyday life. Similarly Lincoln (1990) has proposed sets of criteria she believes represent more comprehensively the constructivist aproach than her previous standards (cf. Lincoln & Guba, 1988, 1990): axiomatic criteria, those reflecting the assumptions of constructivism; action criteria, those evoking responses from readers; rhetorical criteria, those involving the presentation of an inquiry; and application criteria, those eliciting inferences to new contexts.

VALIDITY AND THE RESEARCH PROCESS

How validity is defined and treated may vary according to what researchers do and what tasks they are undertaking in what phase or stage of the research. The question here is "How does validity function across the research act?" In this section we examine how validity may be viewed across the different, albeit overlapping, tasks researchers seek to accomplish during their investigations. We have separated this into eight sections corresponding to different aspects of research activity.

Formulating Goals

Qualitative researchers typically pose many and diverse questions about the problems they wish to study. Part of the task of processing these questions is sorting them according to their match with the research situation, with the people being studied, and with the circumstances of the study. As they formulate goals, investigators consider who the research is for—whose interests are served, ignored, or offended by the direction of the research. For example, Patton (1978) asks about evaluation research, "Who are the stakeholders?" Whose values and world views are promoted by how the goals and purposes of the research are framed and then developed through the research act? How would the communities referred to previously approach the validity of goals and purposes addressed in a project?

Discovering a Research Philosophy

Elsewhere, we (Preissle-Goetz & LeCompte, 1990) have explored differing positions among methodologists toward the philosophical foundations of qualitative research traditions. In brief, some methodologists see a single philosophical foundation, one that contradicts the assumptions of the so-called positivist philosophy of science. Other methodologists regard qualitative research as a label for a loosely connected set of traditions, stemming from several different philosophical positions. The latter is the position we have taken, thus far, in the debate.

However, regardless of the researcher's philosophical tradition, the question of how this affects and should affect assessment of the quality of the research should be considered. We can ask how a realist, an idealist, an existentialist, a pragmatist, or a phenomenologist might develop criteria for validity, for what is workable and justifiable in a piece of research, for example. How do differing positions toward reality, knowledge, and value influence what is considered to be good research? One way to resolve the validity issue in qualitative research is to select a philosophy, derive its guidelines for validity, and apply them to a research study. We are uneasy with this resolution of the issue because it is likely to be easier said than done and because it comes dangerously close to replacing one positivist orthodoxy with a group of neopositivist orthodoxies, each related to a particular philosophy.

Furthermore, this resolution requires an a priori assessment of research that many qualitative researchers would find objectionable because it ignores how theoretical frameworks, overall design, context and participants, researcher experience, and procedures of data collection and analysis also bear on the issue of validity. What we mean here is that more informs a study than the philosophical commitments of its investigator. Philosophical underpinnings are only one source of specifying criteria for validity. If they are the only source, we risk determinism. Consequently although we urge scholars to discover and formulate what their research philosophy is, we believe that it is only one factor contributing to how validity is defined.

Framing Research Conceptually

The theoretical and conceptual perspectives framing a study or emerging from it relate to how validity is defined. A main issue here is the question of fit. Does the conceptual frame with which the researcher begins or ends fit the research situation as viewed by the stakeholders? How does it fit? How does it fail to fit? What is the meaning of the fit and nonfit? What is the level of confidence that various stakeholders have in the conceptual or theoretical frame? Does it make sense, at some level, to all the stakeholders?

An easy solution to the issue of validity of conceptual frame is to search for a near-perfect fit. This can be a trap for qualitative researchers because it can be merely an indication that the investigators have fallen victim to their own preconceptions and ethnocentrism. For example, much revisionist thought in social theory, whether it be revisions of structural functionalism or Marxism, challenges assumptions of earlier thinkers and researchers whose theories had become blinders rather than vision enhancers. While recognizing that these abstractions produce meaning, understanding, and explanation, researchers must always be skeptical of their theoretical frames.

Developing a Research Design

The research model from which a study develops is generally associated with conventions for assuring quality. As we have emphasized previously, the traditions that compose qualitative research include a variety of research designs: ethnography and microethnography, case study, field study, life history, qualitative surveys, and others. The meaning of validity and issues of assessing validity vary according to which ideal-type model the researcher uses to begin developing a design. Several of these traditions, and their associated philosophical, theoretical, and disciplinary roots, have methodological literatures replete with propositions for assessing validity, discussions of the merits of various propositions, and arguments about the correctness of the standards of merit themselves. Investigators unfamiliar with the literature for the traditions they adapt are ignoring a rich source of ideas for addressing validity.

Much of the heat in the discussion of the meaning of validity in qualitative research derives from methodologists' concerns for the sources of assumptions about validity. For example, a major work influencing researchers in the human sciences has been Campbell & Stanley's (1963) set of propositions for assessing the internal and external validity of experimental and quasiexperimental designs (cf. Cook & Campbell, 1979). That little manual was central to the training of several generations of human researchers. What many of these scholars were taught is that propositions for validity or something homologous to it are associated with each of the qualitative design traditions and have been argued and discussed throughout the histories of these traditions. In ethnography, for example, Bronislaw Malinowski regularly reviewed the quality of his material, of his data sources, and of his means of acquiring information (e.g., 1922, 1935, 1967). For qualitative sociologists, Weber (1949) and Dilthey (1988) struggled with the principles for conducting inquiries. Issues of truth and reality are not a monopoly of twentieth-century human sciences. They lie at the heart of all claims about knowledge and develop with processes humans devise to create knowledge.

Selecting Data Sources

Selection of whom or what to study under which circumstances affects various issues of validity. The kinds of evidence colleagues accept as legitimate and adequate may be affected by whether the researcher is studying up (the powerful), studying down (the powerless), or studying across (power parity?). For example, evidence supporting the prevalence of child abuse and wife beating among affluent families may be scrutinized more carefully than similar data from working-class families. In essence, more powerful data may be required for confirmation of patterns among more powerful people, who are better situated than others to suppress or dismiss unwelcome information (cf. examples in Hymes, 1972; Shaffir & Stebbins, 1991; Shaffir, Stebbins & Turowitz, 1980).

Where and when the study has been done is likewise influential. Claims about circumstances difficult to investigate because access is restricted, events are rare, or people are removed in time and space may be accepted more readily than claims about circumstances easily examined. Likewise, if those who are studied are more likely to comment on the researcher's claims, negatively or positively, investigators may take greater care with the merit of such statements.

Experiencing and Directing the Research

The researcher's background experience and role in the investigation are central to how validity is addressed. Among human scientists, historians, if they see themselves as scientists at all, are perhaps most accepting of the notion that who a scholar is affects the quality of the scholar's investigations. This assumption flies in the face of the proposition we have discussed previously that, because scientific studies must be replicable, scientists themselves can be considered interchangeable. Many people take this to mean that who a scholar is ought not to influence the research a scholar does. Increasingly, the interchangeability-of-researchers assumption in its absolute version is being regarded as untenable, philosophically, conceptually, and empirically. There is no research without a researcher, and scholars' choices in their investigations are influenced by who they are (Jackson, 1989; Jagger, 1983; Quantz, 1992; Richardson, 1990; Roman, 1992; Smith, 1987). How these influences are played out in the research act varies, of course.

History teaches that attention to the individual researcher is relevant to validity in qualitative research. What background and training does the researcher bring to the investigation? How carefully, thoroughly, openly, and honestly are researchers known to do their work? Who was responsible for the researcher's training? What reputation has the scholar earned in previous investigations? How might all of these factors influence the current work? What does the researcher report about participation in the research? Are efforts to self-monitor reported somewhere? Introspective and reflective amounts of influence on what is seen and heard contribute to the audience's confidence that the researcher attempted to track these factors. Critics are notoriously disarmed by being anticipated; if researchers identify their own limitations and weaknesses, they may be regarded as more credible than if such factors are ignored.

Collecting Data

A conventional focus for issues of validity has been data collection procedures—how information is gathered, recorded, and stored. The field of psychometrics, for example, is replete with discussions of how accurately and effectively responses to instruments represent the constructs under investigation. When the primary instrument is a human being—the participant observer, interviewer, or investigator—issues both similar and different are raised. Some of these are addressed in the previous section on researcher role and experience. Others revolve around the acts of watching, listening, asking, and collecting things. Researchers ask whether their observations are typical of what customarily occurs. They speculate on how their own attention to who or what is observed influences what is happening. They wonder about the content of respondent answers to questions: What does this answer mean? Is it what the respondent thinks the researcher wants to hear or ought to hear? Is it what the respondent thinks is socially acceptable? Or provocative? Or is the answer a reflective response from deeply held beliefs and ideas?

Data collection procedures raises issues of credibility, authenticity, trustworthiness, and comprehensiveness of information. Most qualitative researchers assume that those they study interpret reality from multiple perspectives for varying purposes. Not only do truths differ from one individual to the next, but also each individual may hold contradictory notions of truth about the world. A task for qualitative researchers, then, is the attempt to reveal participant ideas of reality and truth. Researchers who can demonstrate that their revelations are based on systematic data collection procedures are accorded more credence than those less able to do so. However, as Phillips (1990a) cautions, procedural validity may strengthen the quality of scholar's claim but is insufficient as the sole basis for criteria. In other words, doing something correctly does not guarantee the outcome, as all good cooks, poets, and golfers can attest.

Analyzing Data

Assessing analytic processes in qualitative research is one of the most difficult issues methodologists face. Many analysts have attempted to develop a workable template, which, in some respects, is an impossible task. Qualitative analysis is interpretive, idiosyncratic, and so context dependent as to be infinitely variable. A creative analyst can never be sure that the ending will match the point of view adopted in the beginning. Even midway through an analysis, uncertainty and frustration accompany the unfolding direction.

How do analysts know when their results are authentic, credible, valid? We believe this is one of the costs of working in twentieth-century science, human and natural; it can never be known with complete certainty. However, there are numerous indicators researchers use to build their confidence in analytic procedures and results. These include participant corroboration, theoretical and empirical consistency, rigorous review by peers familiar with similar methods, content, and populations, personal reflection and introspection allowed by the time to distance from the work, and the later contributions of other scholars to the same areas. The demonstrated fit between the analytic procedures used and the questions posed of the group examined is an additional indicator. Another is how self-conscious the researcher has been about the methods developed through the research process. The more aware researchers are of what they are doing, the more they can make public these interpretive, idiosyncratic, and context-dependent approaches. This permits open scrutiny, discussion, and assessment.

SUMMARY

In this section we have sought to explore how complex the question of validity is in qualitative research. We believe that seeking some unitary meaning for validity in qualitative research is a mistake. Making the qualitative approach to validity analogous to that used in quantitative investigations may distort the very features of qualitative design that contribute something special to the human sciences. The risk in such an analog is rigidity, dogmatism, and the stifling of creativity. The value of the current debate on validity and of the various positions toward validity are that they permit empirical investigators to choose among alternatives in building the authenticity, credibility, and usefulness of their endeavors. Each of these alternatives provides essential guidelines for conducting research, assessing research, and training novice researchers. This multiplicity of meanings for and assumptions about validity fosters creativity in qualitative work. As Peshkin cautions, "One needs to take license to do good research" (1989). The trick is knowing the license you are taking.

Evaluation as Conventionally Viewed

Having noted the limitations and dangers of directly applying the tenets of reliability and validity as used in conventional research to qualitative approaches, we do believe that exploring the application metaphorically is useful. Comparing and contrasting standards and practices across traditions is a good way to find the shortcomings in each. If introduced cautiously, it makes a practical heuristic for introducing the assessment of design to novices. Finally, it helps scholars from different perspectives find their commonalities and refine their distinctions. In this final section of the chapter, we consider the constructs of reliability and validity as conventionally defined and explore their implications for qualitative traditions. We apply the tenets of external and internal validity and reliability as they have been used in positivistic research traditions to work done by ethnographers and other researchers using qualitative methods. In so doing, we have translated the tenets for their relevance to researchers in the qualitative, ethnographic, or phenomenological traditions.

Reliability, translated for qualitative endeavors, depends on the resolution of both external and internal design problems (Hansen, 1979). External reliability addresses the issue of whether independent researchers would discover the same phenomena or generate the same constructs in the same or similar settings. Internal reliability refers to the degree to which other researchers, given a set of previously generated constructs, would match them with data in the same way as did the original researcher.

While reliability is concerned with the replicability of scientific findings, conventional validity is concerned with the accuracy of scientific findings. Establishing validity requires demonstrating a match between the conclusions reached and the assumed reality represented; research concepts are expected to reflect adequately some aspect of human experience (Hansen, 1979; Pelto & Pelto, 1978). Internal validity is the match between what is assumed to have occurred and what is represented by the research; external validity is the extent to which this representation applies to other occurrences.

We first examine problems of reliability and how to address them in qualitative studies. We then provide a similar discussion of problems of validity. In certain respects these issues overlap; what threatens reliability in qualitative research also may pose a threat to the validity of a study.

RELIABILITY

Reliability refers to the extent to which studies can be replicated. It assumes that a researcher using the same methods can obtain the same results as those of a prior study. This poses an impossible task for any researcher studying naturalistic behavior or unique phenomena. Claiming reliability for qualitative design is further complicated by the nature of the data and the research process, by conventions in the presentation of findings, and by traditional modes of training researchers.

Limits on Reliability for Qualitative Work

Compared to the stringently controlled designs of laboratory experiments or to the regulated procedures of field experiments, most qualitative designs baffle attempts at replication. The kind of data gathered and the research process itself may preclude the use of those standardized controls so essential in experimental research. Achieving experimental control requires manipulation of phenomena that distorts their natural occurrence. Attempts at rigorous measurement may impede construction of powerful analytic categories if the phenomena observed are prematurely or inappropriately reduced or standardized.

Unique situations cannot be reconstructed precisely because even the most exact replication of research methods may fail to produce identical results. Qualitative research occurs in natural settings and often is undertaken to record processes of change, so replication is only approximated, never achieved. Like Heraclitus, who could not step into the same river twice, researchers can never duplicate exactly a naturally occurring event studied previously. Fuch's study (1966) of a racial incident at an urban elementary school, for example, cannot be replicated exactly because the event cannot be reproduced. Problems of uniqueness and idiosyncracy are bases for the claim that no qualitative study can ever be replicated. However, researchers whose goals are generation, refinement, comparison, and validation of constructs and postulates may not need to replicate situations. Moreover, because human behavior is never static, no study is replicated exactly, regardless of the methods and designs used.

Reliability in qualitative design is also affected by traditions and ideologies in anthropology and field sociology for how a report is presented. A consequence of the debate on whether anthropology is an art (e.g., Clifford, 1986; Evans-Pritchard, 1962; Marcus & Fischer, 1986) or a science (e.g., Harris, 1979; Kaplan & Manners, 1972) has been the custom of presenting the results of an ethnographic study artfully and accessibly. Although this style communicates cultural knowledge persuasively, its very artistry results in idiosyncratic and individualistic presentations. This contrasts with both the experimental and the survey research traditions, where there is substantial familiarity with the analytic and statistical techniques appropriate to particular kinds of data. These are codified in textbooks and are shared across disciplines.[2] Well-established norms also dictate what should be included in research reports, as well as the order in which they should be presented.

The tradition of an artful presentation of results, combined with the strictures imposed by journal-length manuscripts, has resulted in the use of shorthand descriptors for qualitative research design and analytic techniques, meaningful to research peers but deceptive to the uninitiated. Ethnography uses as its primary data collection technique the writing of field notes, but researchers from other traditions may not understand what field notes are. Further, inclusion of lengthy excerpts from these data is often precluded by limitations on manuscript length. Describing research as qualitative or ethnographic fails to convey the multimodality of most such work (Wilson, 1977). In addition to making field notes, researchers may also have used on-site observations, structured and unstructured interviews, projective tests, photographs and videotapes, and survey censuses.

Because qualitative researchers such as ethnographers share a common intellectual heritage in which familiarity with these research techniques is acquired in apprenticeship, they may assume that their audiences know how they collected their data. Ethnographic researchers themselves recognize the necessity for probing beyond journal-length articles to the more complete description of design, data collection, and data analysis located in technical reports and monographs. Some attempts to replicate may require direct communication with the individual who conducted the original research. However, these actions presuppose that the audience reached has similar research training. Researchers untrained in cultural anthropology or field sociology may not exercise such care or even know where to look for further information.

Neither external nor internal reliability, as problems for the credibility of inquiry, pose difficulties unique to ethnographers. However, in the

---

[2] Claims for the systematic codification across disciplines of experimental, statistical, and other quantitative research techniques are not intended to imply either single-solution approaches to design problems or agreement among scholars on either significance of problem or effectiveness of solution. (See Cook & Campbell, 1979, for delineation of diverse issues in quantitative design.) Our treatment of quantitative methods is simplified for contrast with qualitative approaches. We do assert, however, that quantitative strategies have been explicated more widely and systematically than qualitative methods of research, and this factor may actually contribute to the intensity of debate among experimenters, statisticians, and survey analysts.

subsequent discussion we examine these two issues in an ethnographic context and identify how ethnographers have addressed them.

External Reliability

Although no study attains perfect external reliability, the uniqueness or complexity of phenomena and the individualistic and personalistic nature of the ethnographic process make approximating external reliability more difficult for ethnographers than for practitioners of other research models (Hansen, 1979; Pelto & Pelto, 1978). Ethnographers enhance the external reliability of their data by recognizing and handling five problems: researcher status position, informant choices, social situations and conditions, analytic constructs and premises, and methods of data collection and analysis.

Researcher status position. This issue can be phrased, "To what extent are researchers members of the groups being studied and what positions do they hold?" In some ways, no ethnographer can replicate the findings of another because the flow of information depends on the social role held within the group studied and the knowledge deemed appropriate for incumbents of that role to possess (Wax, 1971). Thus, conclusions reached by ethnographers are qualified by the social roles investigators hold within the research site. Other researchers will fail to obtain comparable findings unless they develop corresponding social positions or have research partners who can do so. Although research results generated by ethnographers whose positions were limited in scope may be narrowly applicable, they are nonetheless legitimate. Glaser & Strauss (1967) refer to these individual facets as slices of data that, taken together, contribute to the total picture of group life. Such conclusions delineate facets of reality within a group, other aspects of which may be identified by researchers taking other social positions. For example, McPherson's analysis (1972) of schooling in a small U.S. town is based on her observations when she was an elementary schoolteacher. Her description of schoolchildren represents the relatively narrow perspective of teacher; it can be replicated only by researchers who assume comparable roles. Studies of students in other small U.S. towns, conducted from alternative role positions, are supplemental or comparative studies rather than replicative studies.

The dependence of ethnographic data on the social relationship of researcher with participants requires that research reports clearly identify the researcher's role and status within the group investigated (e.g., Sieber, 1981). In addition to this, some researchers enter settings as nonparticipant observers whose personal relationships with members of the groups are limited; others develop friendships that provide access to special knowledge while limiting access to other information (see Chapter Four).

Informant choices. Closely related to the role the researcher plays is the problem of identifying the informants who provide data. Each individual informant has access to unique and idiosyncratic information. No single informant can provide universal information. The researcher who hopes to replicate a study must contact individuals similar to those who served as informants in previous studies. This problem of reliability is handled most commonly by careful description of those who provide the data. Such characterization includes personal dimensions relevant to the researcher as well as dimensions significant to the informant and others in the group. Consequently, external reliability requires both careful delineation of the kinds of people who served as informants and of how the informants were selected (see Chapter Three).

Social situations and conditions. A third element influencing the content of ethnographic data is the social context within which they are gathered. What informants feel to be appropriate to reveal in some contexts and circumstances may be inappropriate under other conditions. In his study (1974) of education in "Burgherside," Ogbu distinguishes what parents say at school about the education of their children from what they say at home about this education. He quotes extensively from his field notes to demonstrate that this discrepancy was recognized and discussed among the parents themselves. Ogbu's experiences highlight the necessity for ethnographers to specify the social settings where data are collected.

Other social circumstances also affect the nature of information revealed. In their analysis of medical school student culture, Becker *et al.* (1961) differentiate between the data they gathered while alone with participants and what they acquired from participants in groups. Their study demonstrates that what people say and do varies according to others present at the time. Delineation of the physical, social, and interpersonal contexts within which data are gathered permits comparative ethnographies. These contexts are, of course, subject to change over time. What may be a center for informal gathering among one group of high school seniors, for example, may be an anathema to the succeeding class. Descriptions of contexts consequently should include function and structure as well as specification of features.

Analytic constructs and premises. Even if a researcher reconstructs the relationships and duplicates the informants and social contexts of a prior study, replication may remain impossible if the constructs, definitions, or units of analysis informing the original research are too idiosyncratic or poorly delineated. Investigators should identify the assumptions and metatheories underlying choices of terminology and methods of analysis. The culture concept, for example, is defined differently by different researchers. Some use it globally: Linton (1945) defines it as the way of life of a people. Others prefer to define culture more narrowly as observed behavior (e.g., Harris, 1979). Some deny that culture exists independently as an analytic construct; they (e.g., Furlong, 1976; Gearing, 1973, 1975) prefer to examine the minute-by-minute interactions by which shared meanings are negotiated among individuals and small groups. Studies of culture executed under these different definitions vary accordingly.

Definitions for concepts should be clear and sufficiently lacking in idiosyncracy; they should be intelligible to other researchers and, where appropriate, to the participants being investigated. The formulation of concepts varies according to their development in the literature and to their functions in a study's purpose and design. For example, concepts termed operational are defined prior to data collection by how they are to be observed or measured; sensitizing concepts, on the other hand, remain purposely vague and abstract until the researcher has gathered sufficient data to clarify and differentiate their dimensions (Denzin, 1978, pp. 16–17). As we have indicated in Chapter Seven, research reports should indicate which concepts and definitions remained constant throughout the research and which were generated, developed, or refined through data collection, analysis, and interpretation.

Outlining the theoretical premises and defining constructs informing and shaping the research facilitates replication. However, generation of lower-level constructs and terms may create problems for internal as well as external reliability. Unless categories are defined carefully and their theoretical antecedents outlined, the dangers of idiosyncracy and lack of comparability are magnified. Ethnographic practice usually precludes the kind of interobserver reliabilities used in standardized observational studies. To address this problem, ethnographers may use established classificatory schemes (e.g., Henry, 1960; Hilger, 1966; Lofland, 1971; Ogbu, 1988; Pitman et al., 1989; Whiting et al., 1066) because they are well known and easy to administer. However, if relied on unduly, these schemes may result in premature categorization misrepresenting the data or in inadequate standardization and mechanical reduction trivializing the results.

Methods of data collection and analysis. An ideal toward which many ethnographers strive is to present their methods so clearly that other researchers can use the original report as an operating manual by which to replicate the study (e.g., Becker et al., 1968; Heath, 1983; Mehan, 1979; Ogbu, 1974; Smith & Geoffrey, 1968; Wolcott, 1973). Failures to specify methods of data collection and analysis may be related to the aforementioned brevity that journals often require in manuscripts. Pelto

& Pelto (1978) note the regularity with which journal authors fail to report sufficiently their research designs and methodology. To an extent, this is because of the difficulty of explaining in a few sentences the scope and development of ethnographic research techniques.

Some ethnographers erroneously assume that how data are collected and the purpose such information serves in the execution of an ethnography are self-evident to readers and sufficiently standardized across studies to require little or no explanation. However, knowledge of ethnographic techniques is apprehended incompletely and shared unevenly across the disciplines now using them (Burns, 1976; Herriot, 1977; Ianni, 1976; Wolcott, 1971). Until commonly understood labels for these complex techniques are more widely shared, careful descriptions of what has been done must replace the shorthand designations that obstruct reliability.

Follow-up study is impossible without precise identification and thorough description of strategies used to collect data. Similarly, adequate assessment of any ethnographic study requires explicit description of techniques used to acquire data: the varieties of observational and interviewing strategies, the range of noninteractive methods, and the strategies used in amplifying, modifying, and refining data during early stages of analysis while the ethnographer is still in the field. In addition, descriptions should specify how observations were recorded, mechanically or by field notes, how any field notes were composed, *in situ* or post hoc, the circumstances under which interviews were conducted, and how materials from various sources were integrated into the study.

More serious than specification of data collection techniques for both external and internal reliability is the identification of general strategies for analyzing ethnographic data. Simply asserting that analysis has been carefully done is insufficient for establishing the credibility, reliability, and validity of ethnographic efforts. The researcher must clearly identify and fully discuss data analysis processes and provide retrospective accounts of how data were examined and synthesized. Although software programs for qualitative data analysis are not a cure-all for these problems, they do introduce some commonly understood processes for storing, managing, and manipulating qualitative data. Reliability depends on the potential for subsequent researchers to reconstruct original analytic strategies; only those ethnographic accounts that specify these in sufficient detail are replicable, and software programs aid this specification.

Internal Reliability

Problems of internal reliability in ethnographic studies raise the question of whether, within a single study, multiple observers would agree about what happened. This issue is critical when a researcher or research team uses ethnographic or qualitative techniques to study a problem at several research sites (e.g., Cassell, 1978; Corbett, 1984; Herriott, 1977; Herriott & Gross, 1979; Huberman, 1990; Miles & Huberman, 1984; Rist, 1981; Stake & Easley, 1978; Tikunoff *et al.,* 1975; Whiting, 1963). Central to conventional internal reliability is interrater or interobserver reliability. This is one means of determining the extent to which sets of meanings held by multiple observers are congruent enough to describe and arrive at inferences about phenomena in the same way.

Ethnographers, however, rarely use standardized observational protocols, one of the methods permitting quantitative assessment of interrater reliability. Instead, ethnographers ask whether multiple observers agree with each other and with the originator of general constructs on their classifications or on a typology with which to begin categorization. Because they infrequently rate or code phenomena for enumeration, the agreement ethnographers seek is more appropriately designated interobserver reliability. What is sought is agreement on the description or composition of events rather than on the frequency of occurrence of events.

This is a key concern to most ethnographers. Of necessity, a given research site may admit only one or few observers. Without the corroboration of other observers, such investigations may be seen as so idiosyncratic that findings are dismissed. Ethnographers commonly use any of five strategies to reduce threats to internal reliability: low-inference descriptors, multiple researchers, participant researchers, peer examination, and mechanically recorded data.

Low-inference descriptors. Verbatim accounts of participant conversations, descriptions phrased as concretely and precisely as possible from field notes or recordings of observations, and such other raw data as direct quotations from documents are the principal evidence for assessing the worth of an ethnographic report. Wolcott (1975) emphasizes that it is this material that provides reviewers, judges, and other readers with the means for accepting, rejecting, or modifying an investigator's conclusions. Other scholars (e.g., Patton, 1980) stress the significance of reporting any negative or discrepant data as well as providing material that supports conclusions. Ethnographies rich in primary data, what Geertz (1973) calls thick description, provide the reader with multiple examples from field notes. They generally are considered to be the most credible (e.g., Bossert, 1979; Leemon, 1972; Modiano, 1973; Smith & Keith, 1971; Ward, 1971; Wolcott, 1977).

Multiple researchers. The optimum guard against threats to internal reliability in ethnographic studies is the presence of multiple researchers.

In some cases, the members of research teams undergo extensive training; they discuss the meaning of what has been observed during fieldwork until agreement is achieved (e.g., Becker *et al.*, 1961, 1968; Peshkin, 1978; Spindler, 1973). For example, Tikunoff, Berliner, & Rist (1975) conducted intensive 3-week training for their 12 observers to prepare them to obtain comparable descriptive protocols from the 40 elementary classrooms examined in a study of effective reading and mathematics instruction.

Ethnographies based on team observation are a minority, and most involve only two researchers (e.g., Cicourel & Kitsuse, 1963; Hostetler & Huntington, 1971; Whiting, 1963; Eisenhart & Holland 1990; Holland & Eisenhart, 1990). The same constraints of time and money that preclude the use of multiple researcher teams limit the size and scope of teams: Funding is rarely available for more than a single fieldworker. If this is the case, ethnographers depend on other sources of corroboration and confirmation. However, some of the recent federally funded multiple-site research programs have used team researchers (e.g., Cassell, 1978; Wax, 1979); others have used confirmation by short-term observers (e.g., Stake & Easley, 1978); more commonly, each field observer is responsible for an independent site (e.g., Herriott, 1977; Herriott & Gross, 1979). Under this latter circumstance, problems of establishing internal reliability are much the same as for single-site studies.

Participant research assistants. Many researchers enlist the aid of local informants to confirm that what the observer has seen and recorded is being viewed identically or at least consistently by both participants and researcher (Magoon, 1977). Confirmation thus may be sought for various levels of the collection and analysis process: description of events and interactions, interpretation of participant meanings, and explanations for overall structures and processes.

When fieldworkers cannot speak a language fluently, or sometimes do not speak it at all, informants double as translators, eliciting and checking data (Sanjek, 1990). The tradition of depending on a single or a few key informants for corroboration and other services has a lengthy history in cultural anthropology and field sociology (e.g., Powdermaker, 1966; Spindler, 1970; Stocking, 1983; Wax, 1971; Whyte, 1955). However, participant corroboration is rarely a simple matter of agreement with the investigator's observations and interpretations. Although some confirmation is to be expected, negotiation is also inevitable and invaluable. Bloor (1983), Georges & Jones (1980), and Whyte (1984) provide examples and discuss outcomes of what researchers learn when disagreements occur. Although some fieldworkers may still hire their informants and research assistants, more recently participant corroboration has become an integral part of collaborative and action research (see Chapter Four). Because researchers from inside and outside a group are working together, opportunities to confirm what is seen and what it means occur regularly.

Peer examination. Corroboration of findings by researchers working in similar settings proceeds in three ways. First, ethnographers may integrate descriptions and conclusions from other fieldworkers in their presentations (e.g., Borman, 1978; Clement & Harding, 1978; Sieber 1979a,b). Discrepancies between current data and older material are valuable sources for reinterpretation, elaboration, and refinement of explanations (Kaplan & Manners, 1972). Second, findings from studies conducted concurrently at multiple sites, such as those discussed previously, may be analyzed and integrated. Independent generation or confirmation of results supports the reliability of observation and enhances cross-site validity of conclusions (Campbell, 1979). Finally, the publication of results offers material for peer review. Wolcott's admonition (1975) to fieldworkers to include sufficient primary data in published accounts emphasizes the significance of collegial review in the evaluation of ethnographic reports and underscores the need for researchers to provide enough information in their reports for them to be reviewed adequately. The thick description that Geertz (1973) makes central to cultural interpretation allows readers to assess for themselves the extent to which the patterns claimed are evident in the data cited.

Mechanically recorded data. Although equipment that works for one researcher may malfunction for another, use of tape recorders, photographs, or videotape strenghtens the reliability of results. This occurs, however, only if different researchers make sure that the same camera angles are used, similar kinds of participants are selected, and comparable segments of behavior are recorded. Unfortunately, mechanical reliability may mask other, far more serious sources of unreliability.

As we have stressed previously, mechanical recording devices preserve all data, unabstracted. Without selection and integration, they cannot be used. Analysis of such data requires coding or classification; these activities may introduce idiosyncracies that hinder reproduction by other researchers. If several researchers are working on the same data, more sources of variance may be generated unless they train and work together for equivalence in their analysis. Firm adherence to constructs generated and refined is critical. When constructs are revised, those revisions must be as explicit as the original attributes. One safeguard against unreliability is deriving concepts from the theoretical framework informing the study.

It provides an anchor for consistency and a point of departure for elaboration and refinement.

Summary

Qualitative research is a personal endeavor; no investigator does research just like another. The failure to specify precisely what was done in a study may thus create serious problems for any follow-up study. Insufficient design specificity has led to controversy even among ethnographers. Pelto & Pelto (1978) and Kaplan & Manners (1972) identify the highly publicized discrepancy between two ethnographers' studies of the same Mexican village (i.e., Redfield, 1930; Lewis, 1951) as a consequence of the nonequivalence of their research designs. Redfield and Lewis addressed different issues, used different methods and time periods, and elicited responses from different segments of the population. Their studies were conducted from different, unexplicated world views and scientific assumptions. The problem is aggravated by their presentations of results as representative of the belief system and social structure of the village as a whole rather than as deriving from the discrete units they actually investigated.

Lewis's research was not a replication of the study done by Redfield. The two shared little more than the same space, separated by two decades. The questions arising from their different results stem less from reliability issues than from difficulties surrounding validity, our next topic.

VALIDITY

Establishing conventional validity depends on demonstrating that the propositions generated, refined, or tested match what occurs in human life. Matching scientific explanations of the world with agreed-on conditions resolves into two questions. First, do researchers observe and measure what they think they are observing and measuring? This is the problem of internal validity. Solving it credibly is a fundamental requirement in conventional research design (e.g., Campbell & Stanley, 1963; Cook & Campbell, 1979). Second, to what extent are the abstract constructs and postulates generated, refined, or tested by scientific researchers applicable across groups? This is the issue of external validity. It poses special problems for ethnographers because of the nature of their research designs and methods. In this section we discuss contrastive modes for addressing these problems.

As indicated previously, applying reliability to much qualitative work is limited; at best it can only be approximated. However, validity, conventional and otherwise, is a major strength of this approach to inquiry.

This becomes evident when ethnography is compared to survey studies, experimentation, and other quantitative research designs for assessment of internal validity (Crain, 1977; Erickson, 1977; Reichardt & Cook, 1979). Ethnography's claim to high internal validity derives from its data collection and analysis methods (see Chapters Six and Seven) for a comparison of research designs summarized from Denzin, 1978). First, the ethnographer's common practice of living among participants and collecting data for long periods provides opportunities for continual data analysis and comparison to refine constructs; it ensures a match between researcher categories and participant realities. Second, informant interviews, a major ethnographic data source, are phrased in the empirical categories of participants; they are less abstract than many instruments used in other research designs. Third, participant observation, the ethnographer's second key source of data, is conducted in natural settings reflecting the life experiences of participants more accurately than do more contrived or laboratory settings. Finally, ethnographic analysis incorporates a researcher reflection, introspection, and self-monitoring that Erickson (1973) calls disciplined subjectivity, and these expose all phases of the research to continual questioning and reevaluation.

Although internal and external validity are interrelated, they customarily are separated to clarify procedures (e.g., Campbell & Stanley, 1963; Cook & Campbell, 1979). We follow that custom in the succeeding discussion. Among the indicators of conventional scientific credibility—internal and external reliability, internal validity, and external validity—problems of external validity most frequently have been ignored by ethnographers. The problems, goals, and applications of qualitative research affect how issues of external validity are defined and resolved. As we emphasized earlier in this chapter, the credibility of research that is contextual, theoretically eclectic, and comparative is threatened by and grounded in factors different from those affecting experimentation and other forms of quantitative research.

Issues in the validity of ethnographic research, internal as well as external, are addressed by field workers who are aware of these characteristics. The following discussion presents threats to the conventional credibility of ethnographic design and ways they may be remedied.

Internal Validity

Internal validity raises the problem of whether conceptual categories understood to have mutual meanings between the participants and the observer are shared. The threats to conventional internal validity that Campbell & Stanley (1963) and Cook & Campbell (1979) describe as posing difficulties for experimental research are also applicable to ethnographic research, although they present different problems and are resolved differently. These threats include history and maturation, observer effects, selection and regression, mortality, and spurious conclusions.

History and maturation. The extent to which phenomena observed at entry or at other initial occasions are the same as those observed subsequently becomes salient where process and change are the focus of the research project. Unlike the experimenter who uses various methods to hold constant the effects of time, the ethnographer conducts research in natural settings where the clock advances. Changes occurring in the social scene are comparable to what experimenters designate as history; changes involving progressive development in individuals are maturation.

Ethnographers assume that history affects the nature of the data collected and that phenomena rarely remain constant. The ethnographic task is establishing which baseline data remain stable over time and which data change. Such change may be recurrent, progressive, cyclic, or aberrant; sources of change and their operation also should be specified (Appelbaum, 1970; Lofland, 1971). This is facilitated by systematic replication and comparison of baseline data, analogous to the pretest data collected by experimentalists. Researchers also use replication and time-sampling strategies to distinguish relatively stable phenomena from phenomena subject to the varieties of change.

Many of the methods used by ethnographers to allow for the effects of history are applicable in allowing for maturation. Experimental researchers manage these variables through such constraints as designing projects of limited duration and assigning subjects randomly to control and experimental groups. When effects of treatments are being measured, maturation may be regarded as a source of contamination. Experimenters posit a biological or quasibiological model with universal stages of development. Maturation is conceptualized as a universal, normative process, proceeding through well-defined stages. Ethnographers, however, view maturational stages as varying according to cultural norms. Fieldworkers allow for the effects of maturation by discovering the behaviors and norms expected in different sociocultural contexts. They are less concerned with what people may be capable of doing at some developmental stage than with what people at varying stages are expected to do by the older members of their groups.

Maturation and development frequently become the focus of ethnographic studies (e.g., Howard, 1970; Moore, 1973). Leemon (1972) and Burnett (1969) used Van Gennep's model (1960) of passage rites to analyze maturation among students in the United States. Other researchers (e.g., Becker *et al.*, 1961) have reconstructed the maturation process through the perceptions of the participants involved. Constant comparison (Glaser & Strauss, 1967), discrepant-case analysis (Erickson, 1973; Robinson, 1951; Wolcott, 1975; Znaniecki, 1934), and a variety of logico-deductive strategies (e.g., Scriven's modus operandi, 1974) can be used to distinguish maturation influences from other intervening phenomena to identify possible causes, their interactions, and their probable impacts (e.g., Eddy, 1969; Ward, 1971).

Observer effects. Ethnographers qualify the validity of data they collect from informants. First, information is valid even though it represents a single point of view or is shaped by special characteristics of, or relationships with, the researcher. It is valid for those contexts, and it can be replicated if the contexts are made explicit. Such data become problematic only if they are used to represent views beyond those contexts. Second, cultures are composed of members with a variety of points of view; validity for a culture, if it could be achieved, would be some amalgam of opinions. Thus, the ethnographer must search for informants who match the range of variation in the population. Third, many sources of invalidity can be reduced if the researcher spends enough time in the field. Time permits a thorough search for informants who can augment, disconfirm, or corroborate information already gathered. It makes the researcher less visible, and hence less reactive, in the setting so that the normal flow of activities resumes.

Observer effects operate in a number of ways in ethnography. The ethnographer's chief source of data, participant observation, is more fraught with problems of reactivity than any other mode of data collection. In the initial stages of research, informants may dissemble, present an ideal self, or tell the researcher what they think the researcher should, or wants to, hear. Yoors (1967) describes this among gypsies, saying that most of the conventional wisdom about gypsy women's use of fortune telling has been fabricated by them to satisfy and evade curious anthropologists. Participants being observed may act abnormally. LeCompte's fourth graders spent considerable time clowning, acting out, and making wisecracks to provide material for the book they knew she was writing. Finally the teacher begged her to explain to them that it was a serious book, intended to describe how things happen in school, not one for entertainment.

These issues are complicated by the personal relationships, mentioned elsewhere, that develop between informants and researchers. The roles researchers assume affect the information participants supply and thus influence the validity of the data.

Parallel to this problem in observation is the credibility of informant reports in interviewing. Informants may lie, omit relevant data, or misrepresent their claims (Dean & Whyte, 1958). Independent corroboration from multiple informants (e.g., Fuchs, 1969) or other fortuitous observers of the social scene (e.g., Smith & Keith, 1971), sufficient residence in the field to reduce artificial reactions (e.g., Wolcott, 1973), and coding participant responses according to situations expected to elicit contrived responses (e.g., Becker *et al.*, 1961; McCall, 1969) are techniques used by ethnographers to reduce such distortions in the data.

Unusual observer effects, described elsewhere in this book as informal social experiments arranged by the researcher, also threaten the validity of ethnographic studies. Such contrivance may distort data gathered; this may occur when the ethnographer plans and executes some exceptional act to elicit responses from participants. Such strategies may also violate the research ethics of participant consent (cf., e.g., Denzin, 1978; Jorgensen, 1971; Rynkiewich & Spradley, 1976). However, inadvertent faux pas and gaffes committed by the investigator are less controversial than deliberate manipulations and do provide valuable information on norms and sanctions. Here the researcher must establish that it is the act itself that elicits the responses rather than the act as performed by the researcher (Webb *et al.*, 1966).

Finally, ethnographers must demonstrate that, in cases when presentation of participants' perspectives are important, the categories are meaningful to the participants, reflect how participants experience their lives, and are supported by the data. When formal instruments are used, ethnographers attempt to establish the extent to which measures have the same meaning for both researcher and participant (e.g., Goodman, 1957; Spindler, 1973, 1974b). Even when participant-derived constructs are less important, researcher-designated constructs should be grounded in and congruent with the data.

In essence, researchers must guard the instruments they use and the constructs they create from their own ethnocentrisms and perceptual biases. These are conditions inherent in human activity. Although sociocultural theories and analytic models provide ethnographers with perspectives for monitoring themselves as members of both participant groups and the scientific community (Schatzman & Strauss, 1973), biases resulting from academic training may distort data. For example, disciplinary biases may appear, however implicitly, in the categories an investigator chooses as salient for analysis and coding of ethnographic data, regardless of whether participant-derived categories or researcher-designated constructs are used. Researchers with different theoretical backgrounds may focus on different aspects of the data. The strategies discussed previously for enhancing the reliability of analytic constructs and premises and for ensuring the internal reliability of ethnographic studies also contribute to monitoring and managing observer analytic biases; thus, they enhance validity as well. Of these, participant reaction and confirmation, conducted throughout the research, may be most effective in revealing researcher-induced distortions (Wax, 1971).

Selection and regression. In experimental research, investigators control selection and regression effects so that they can claim more confidently that differences between treatment and control groups are caused by the treatment rather than by differences inherent in the groups. Although ethnographers rarely grapple with the problem of isolating treatment effects, they do cope with distortions in their data and conclusions created by selection. Selectivity becomes a serious problem in situations when there are too many participants to gather data from all of them or when the social scene is so complex that observation of all events, activities, and settings is impossible. In these cases researchers must take an adequate inventory (cf., e.g., Schatzman & Strauss, 1973) of subgroups, factions, events, and social scenes in the field site. Without such an inventory, the ethnographer cannot determine if the findings are representative only of certain participants or of particular circumstances. These strategies are as useful for ensuring external validity as they are for ensuring internal validity: If cross-group comparisons are to be credible, then they must be grounded in accurate data from individual groups.

Mortality. How groups change over time as a result of losses and gains in membership poses special difficulties for ethnographers. Although experimental researchers may replace subjects who are lost from their studies, ethnographers assume that the naturalistic approach precludes the interchangeability of human informants and participants. Loss and replacement as they naturally occur become topics of study in themselves. Growth and attrition are assumed to be normal to most groups, so the ethnographic task becomes the identification of their effects. This requires careful attention to baseline data, discussed previously, so that the researcher may compare events and activities occurring over time.

In his study of enculturation, Jocano (1969) examined mobility of young people into and out of a Philippine barrio, as well as the treatment of birth and death, to establish cycles of growth and attrition as defined and interpreted by the community. By studying the spring enrollment of a new child into a third-grade classroom, Goetz (1976b) validated socialization practices and goals observed among students earlier in the school year. Smith & Keith (1971) similarly approached staff attrition and turnover to illuminate the social dynamics of innovation in an elementary school program. In each of these instances, collection of baseline data enabled researchers to analyze the effects of subsequent loss and replacement.

Spurious conclusions. However thoroughly an ethnographer accounts for effects of history and maturation, observer impact, selection and regression, and mortality, relationships posited among phenomena observed nevertheless may be spurious. This problem is analogous to Cook & Campbell's formulation (1979) of statistical conclusion validity. They define this construct as (1) the extent to which a treatment actually caused a predicted effect, and (2) the extent to which presumed phenomena actually covary or are causally related. Statistical conclusion validity alerts experimental researchers to search for spurious relationships and to resist assuming relationships where there may be none or, conversely, assuming relationships to be nonexistent when they may be obscured by an artifact of instrumentation or treatment. These issues are paramount to experimental researchers whose designs customarily preclude laborious post hoc examinations of sources of error except when intuition or insight suggest such errors may exist.

In contrast, ethnographic design mandates what Scriven (1974) calls a modus operandi perspective, in which the geneses of observed data are traced retrospectively. Plausible causes are delineated by examination of data collected during the research and through discussion with informants. Postulating associations among phenomena depends on elimination of alternative explanations (Campbell, 1979). Denzin (1978) sees an adequate support of generalizations as establishing the time order and covariance of constructs and as eliminating rival hypotheses. He rates participant observation as excellent, good, and fair, respectively, on these three factors.

Eliminating rival explanations depends on consideration of factors threatening internal validity. It also requires effective and efficient retrieval systems for ethnographic data and the scrupulous use of corroboratory and alternative sources of data. These serve to support the fieldworker's search for instances that negate tentatively postulated relationships and for evidence that qualifies or disconfirms emergent constructs (Mehan, 1979; Robinson, 1951; Znaniecki, 1934). Although no research design can identify the precise cause of an observed datum, ethnography can specify an array of the most plausible causes and designate from among them the most probable.

Because what many researchers consider as causal may not be so seen by participants, participant explanations of events are one of the central features that ethnographers examine. Although Rist (1970) rejected teachers' explanations for student failure in his 3-year study of a group of elementary schoolchildren, he demonstrated that those students who failed were those expected to fail by the teachers, for whatever reason. In contrast, Smith & Keith (1971) expanded on participant accounts and interpretations to explain the failure of innovation in an elementary school.

Longevity in the research site, presupposed in ethnographic research design, facilitates the search for causes and consequences. If ethnographers have not witnessed personally the antecedents of events, they talk to people who have done so. Thus, data from informants, documents, and other sources may be substituted for eyewitness accounts by the researcher. Similarly, long-term field residence permits identification of the covariance of phenomena in natural settings. Nevertheless, Cook & Campbell's counsel (1979, p. 55) to experimental researchers is applicable as well to ethnographers:

> Estimating the internal validity of a relationship is a deductive process in which the investigator has to systematically think through how each [factor] . . . may have influenced the data . . . In all of this process, the researcher has to be his or her own best critic, trenchantly examining all of the threats he or she can imagine.

For the ethnographer, the process is inductive as well; sources of bias or contamination must be discovered as the study proceeds, rather than waiting for post hoc analyses.

External Validity

In most ethnographic studies, as well as in many quantitative studies, the strictures required for statistical generalization may be difficult to apply. Rules for appropriate sampling improve the generalizability of quantitative studies; ethnographers, however, must address issues differently. We believe that threats to the conventional external validity of ethnographic findings are constituted by whatever obstructs or reduces a study's comparability and translatability.

As we said in Chapter Two, comparability is the degree to which the components of a study, including the units of analysis, concepts generated, population characteristics, and setting, are sufficiently well described and defined that other researchers can use the results to compare to other studies addressing related issues. Establishing the comparability of a study makes it scientifically useful. Translatability is related, but distinct; it is the degree to which the researcher uses theoretical frames, definitions, and research techniques accessible to and understood by other researchers in the same or related disciplines. A study is of little use to other researchers if its theoretical basis or the constructs around which it is organized are so idiosyncratic that they are understood only by the person who did the study. The lack of comparability and translatability reduces the usefulness of a study to interesting cultural salvage.

To establish comparability and translatability, an ethnographer must demonstrate what Wolcott calls the typicality (1973) of a phenomenon—the extent to which it may be compared and contrasted along relevant dimensions with other phenomena. Consequently, external validity depends on identifying and describing characteristics of phenomena salient for comparison with other, similar types. Once the typicality or atypicality of a phenomenon is established, bases for comparison then may be assumed, and results may be translated for applicability across sites and disciplines.

This problem is addressed to an extent by multisite ethnographic designs. The increase in size of selection from one to several enhances a study's generalizability (Campbell, 1979). Rarely, however, can investigators sample their sites from the larger population. Usually multiple sites are chosen nonprobabilistically, using any of the criterion-based selection procedures discussed in Chapter Three. Because sample size is insufficient for confident generalization (Reichardt & Cook, 1979), investigators in multisite studies must address threats to external validity with as much care as do single-site ethnographers. Four factors affect the credibility of a study for such cross-group comparisons: selection effects, setting effects, history effects, and construct effects.

Selection effects. Some constructs cannot be compared across groups because they are specific to a single group or because the researcher mistakenly has chosen groups for which the construct does not occur. This occurs more frequently in those situations in which researcher-designated categories are used. Here, the researcher's initial task is to determine the degree of match between the categories and the experience of the group, culture, or setting under investigation. When this is neglected, the categories may be assumed by the researcher to exist, and invalid comparisons may be drawn. When a researcher is investigating the cross-group occurrence of participant-derived categories this may be less likely to occur because awareness of the participant derivation of the constructs may function as a control for threats to validity. Finally, the discovery that data are absent for the support of a construct may be useful information in itself. In some cases, the ethnographer then may reanalyze the data for contrasts across groups, as Mead (1935) did with her early field data.

The ethnographic obsession with identifying distinct characteristics of groups investigated derives from the significance of this information for comparative purposes. Although characterization may be rendered partially in subjective qualities, quantitatively measured attributes of groups are essential. Socioeconomic statuses, levels of education attained, and racial composition are characteristics of populations readily reported quantitatively. In his ethnographic analysis of the role of the principal, Wolcott (1973) typifies the studied individual by comparing him to the modal category in a nationwide survey of elementary school principals. Goetz (1981b) notes that the cultural broker role assumed by the teachers in her investigation of sex-role enculturation may be dependent on these teachers' relationships to the community serviced by their school. Cusick (1973) limits his explanations for patterns of teacher–student exchange to schools that serve student populations comparable to the groups he examined.

Setting effects. Investigators affect the groups, cultures, and settings they study just by studying them. Constructs generated in one context may not be comparable to others because they are a function of context under investigation rather than of context only. Reactive observer effects, discussed previously as threats to internal validity, are equally serious when cross-group comparisons are conducted. Where the construct is a function of observer–setting interaction, it may be treated as equivalent only for groups being observed similarly, and the interactive dynamics should be identified clearly. Limitations of school ethnographies conducted by participant observers who were also the classroom teachers (e.g., King, 1967; McPherson, 1972; Rosenfeld, 1971; Wolcott, 1967b) stem from the possibility that findings were distorted by observation–setting–interaction effects. Smith & Geoffrey (1968) sought to avoid this problem by collecting observations from two perspectives: teacher and nonparticipant researcher. Wolcott (1974) and King (1974) addressed the issue with retrospective analyses of the dynamics of interactions in their respective settings. Collaborative researchers address this problem by documenting and checking together their perceptions of how they are affecting the site.

Oversaturation of settings is a second facet of this problem. It relates to group history, a third threat to external validity. Groups and cultures attracting continual or intermittent investigation by social scientists can be assumed to be different from groups and cultures with little or no such experiences. Educational researchers are familiar with this problem in school districts adjacent to research centers; research activities become so integrated with ongoing teaching and administration that the population is altered permanently. Caudill (1963) cites Appalachia as a subculture that has experienced cyclic attention from scholars. He claims that mountaineers have developed a cautious, cynical response to researchers and practitioners based on repeated experiences of disappointed expectations. Likewise, Deloria (1969) comments that native Americans have been "cursed" with anthropologists, who invade their privacy, manipulate their lives, distort their experiences, and exploit their condition.

History effects. Cross-group comparison of constructs may be invalid because of the unique historical experiences of groups and cultures. Researchers are cautioned, for example, against comparing slavery in the United States and slavery in Latin America. Nevertheless, careful identification of the differing historical conditions and subsequent discovery of variations in patterns have proved fruitful (e.g., Elkins, 1959).

In his investigation of schooling in a small German village, Spindler (1974a) outlines the community's transformation from rural to urban conditions and the school's introduction of a nationally disseminated curriculum innovation. The comparison of Spindler's findings with Warren's earlier study (1967) of a school in a similar village might identify common urbanization, but would have to take into account variations in school curricula stemming from the 10-year time difference. Failure to consider historical differences between groups may result in the misapplication of constructs and the assumption that phenomena are equivalent across groups.

The opposite assumption, that all group phenomena are unique, is equally misleading. Studstill (1979) notes the ethnocentricity limiting most school studies to organizations in complex technological societies. He attributes this to the unquestioned assumption that native schools in nonliterate societies have little or nothing in common with the bureaucratic organizations predominant in industrial cultures, despite evidence to the contrary (cf., e.g., Hansen, 1979). Studstill suggests that the failure to identify clearly both common and contrastive features of schools in nonliterate and literate societies has led to the attribution of undeserved uniqueness to schools in complex technological societies.

Construct effects. Construct validity is defined by Cook & Campbell (1979) as the extent to which abstract terms, generalizations, or meanings are shared across times, settings, and populations. Definitions and meanings of terms and constructs vary across these dimensions. A second interpretation of construct validity is how effects of observed phenomena are construed. Explanations seen as valid among some groups are discounted by others. Construct validity also refers to the degree to which instructions for and formats of instruments are mutually intelligible to the instrument designer, to the instrument administrator, and the participants to whom the instrument is applied.

As noted previously, the comparability of ethnographic studies may be reduced or obstructed by idiosyncratic use of initial analytic constructs or by generation of constructs so peculiar to a group that they are useless for cross-group examinations. Cook & Campbell (1979) accord threats to the construct validity of instruments used in experimental research sufficient gravity that they discuss the issue independently of internal and external validity. A number of the effects discussed previously affect construct validity. Because a major outcome of ethnographic research is the generation and refinement, through cross-group applications, of constructs, ethnographers consider issues of construct validity as critical to the credibility of their results.

Where disparities are identified, ethnographers report them as attributes of the groups being examined (e.g., Gibson, 1988; Ogbu, 1974; Peshkin, 1991; Smith & Keith, 1971; Wolcott, 1973). This sensitizes other researchers, directing them to examine comparable effects in other groups. In cases where group dimensions require the customizing of instruments or initial analytic constructs (e.g., Modiano, 1973; Spindler, 1973, 1974b)—a common requirement in cross-cultural studies—modifications are included in the presentation of results.

Summary

Among the limitations of applying these conventional standards of validity perfunctorily to qualitative studies is that they involve conflicting and incompatible practices. Multiple observers, for example, resolve some issues of bias but raise other problems for rapport. Crowding too many researchers into a school or a community stresses its members and can alter the setting. We conclude this section on conventional validity with some examples of researchers troubled by trying to address validity in their own work.

A graduate student complained to one of us, "The conceptions of validity I've read don't work for my study. That doesn't mean they don't work for other qualitative studies, but they don't fit the theoretical assumptions I've made." We believe that the student was right. The premises of her study were incompatible with some notions of validity; applying these incompatible approaches would have made a mockery of some of the very things the student was trying to examine.

The issue in this instance was whether to accept group participant confirmation of various themes and patterns in the data as demonstration of their validity. The design of the study was based on radical constructivism, a theoretical perspective that makes problematic the extent to which themes and patterns in social life are shared among individuals. The researcher in this situation was genuinely troubled by being expected to use a validation method, confirmation by the group studied, inconsistent with the study's theoretical premises.

As a second example, a problem posed by a participant at a professional conference raises different issues. The researcher restricted information in reports submitted because the material could have been used to dismiss employees of the agency under study. In this situation contextual data authenticating general patterns were withheld; however, the conflict here was ethical rather than theoretical.

The delicacy of this situation even precluded customary crosschecking of participant versions of the same event. Posing the questions required for such verification would itself have threatened the security of the employees. The researcher was left with only indirect and highly inferential means to confirm patterns that could be only sketched in the final reports.

A final example illustrates yet a different problem with addressing validity. A few years ago a colleague of ours presented some of his research to a group of educational ethnographers. The ethnographers were disgruntled with our colleague's report because it contained little of the thick description their anthropology background had led them to expect of such investigations. Our colleague, an educational sociologist trained in Glaser & Strauss's (1967) tradition of highly analytic qualitative design, was taken aback by the ethnographers' reaction. Here, the difficulty arose from conflicting methodological traditions. The data that the ethnographers expected to see had been collected. However, Glaser and Strauss's approach requires considerable abstraction of information—translation of raw data into more general categories—before presentation and interpretation.

Our discussion of conventional validity, applied metaphorically to ethnography and qualitative design, draws examples of problems and their solutions from several decades of practice. Neither the problems nor their remedies are ours; these have been explored and developed by succeeding generations of qualitative scholars, seeking to improve social inquiry. What we do claim is a systematic comparison of what qualitative researchers do to strengthen their studies with what conventional research design has defined as canons of reliability and validity. As our summary suggests, these canons cannot be routinely applied to qualitative work without causing more problems than they solve. We see their value in providing a source of checks, considerations, rival explanations, and cautions.

Summary

To an extent, determining quality is intuitive and subjective. Like Pirsig (1974), who compares judging motorcycles with judging technical manuals, scholars simply know quality when they see it. However, the scientific endeavor requires more than intuition. Evaluative criteria must be stated clearly so that they can be scrutinized and assessed by the community of scholars. If evaluative criteria are identified and codified, they can then be used, judiciously, to assess single studies or to evaluate the comparative merit of a group of related studies.

Assessing qualitative studies is difficult because of the inherent diversity of the designs. Research endeavors like ethnographies, characterized by phenomenological perspectives, naturalistic factors, multimodal strategies, eclectic approaches to theory, and participation of the researcher as instrument, resist simplistic recipes for evaluation.

On the other hand, the comparative applications intended and sought by most researchers require legitimate means for weighing the relative merits of observations, findings, conclusions, and interpretations. As Rist (1980) notes so aptly, the competent ethnographer demystifies the research process through open and public revelation, self-monitoring, and self evaluation. This contributes to comprehending complex phenomena and understanding how that comprehension has been achieved.

As we have illustrated in the preceding section, addressing all of the sources of contamination and bias in qualitative design mandates contradictory measures. For example, although we often use the term *ethnography* to refer to a research process, ethnography also is the product of a research effort. As we emphasized in Chapter One, it is defined by anthropologists as an analytic description of an intact cultural scene (Spradley & McCurdy, 1972), delineating the shared beliefs, practices, artifacts, folk knowledge, and behaviors of some group of people. Its objective is the holistic reconstruction of the culture of phenomena investigated. Given this goal, the ethnographer's primary commitment is to a faithful and accurate rendition of the participant's life ways. These may be eccentric, singular, or idiosyncratic when compared to other groups, but they still require, and perhaps necessitate, reporting. As a consequence, some ethnographers resist formulation of the comparable constructs and postulates translatable to other groups prerequisite for establishing conventional external validity and external reliability. They believe that tailoring these abstractions for cross-group comparisons distorts their derivation. Thus, they risk the possibility of obtaining noncomparable data in the service of the unique research setting.

Such dilemmas, discussed as dichotomous choices between subjective or objective data and data analysis processes, between replicability or authenticity, between representativeness of samples or purposive selection, between generalizability or uniqueness of results (Filstead, 1979; Rist, 1977; Wilson, 1977), are shared across social science research designs as divergent as experimental research and ethnography. Although dichotomous conceptualization of these issues is useful pedagogically, it distorts research practice; few studies, whether qualitative or quantitative, fit neatly into the either–or slots of the dichotomies (Reichardt & Cook, 1979). Unfortunately educational researchers and scholars in other professional fields are susceptible to viewing these alternatives as mutually exclusive choices. In a shared commitment to the improvement of curriculum, instruction, and other practices, we seek research designs that answer questions and solve problems. In addition, public and academic concern for direct applicability of educational research overshadows investigation in the field and provokes simplistic interpretations of design and result. The inevitable outcome is research results rarely functional in or applicable to real classrooms.

Our position is that transforming these issues into dichotomous choices is unnecessary, inaccurate, and ultimately counterproductive. Many research studies include the collection of both objective and subjective data. Similarly, a single investigation may use data analysis strategies that range from subjective to objective (Scriven, 1972). Replicability, often viewed as merely a function of standardization of instruments and procedures and therefore inapplicable to ethnography, is a complex issue to be addressed by multiple strategies. Sampling is only one form of selection. If it is viewed as a collection of overlapping alternatives to a variety of design problems, then its assessment depends on how well problems are solved rather than on conformity to a randomness seldom achieved even in quantitative studies. The extent to which results are generalizable or unique, reliable, and valid depends on such factors as the level of abstraction addressed and varies by the constructs or relationships posited, rather than by the degree to which a design conforms to research stereotypes.

The Lord High Executioner in the Mikado demanded that "the punishment fit the crime." With apologies to Gilbert and Sullivan, we believe that design should fit lines of inquiry. Qualitative research can be used in many contexts; what is reprehensible is using it inappropriately or executing it poorly. We hope that the preceding pages assist neophyte as well as experienced researchers in sharing with us the exhilaration of doing qualitative research. It is, after all, generated by curiosity about people in both everyday and extraordinary situations; it leads to investigations of the most complex of social phenomena. The word *ethnography* literally means "writing about people"; in our minds, there is no more intriguing task.

References

Adler, P. A., & Adler, P. (1987). *Membership roles in field research.* Newbury Park, CA: Sage Publications.

Adler, P. A., & Adler, P. (1991). *Backboards and blackboards: College athletes and role engulfment.* New York: Columbia University Press.

Agar, M. H. (1980). *The professional stranger: An informal introduction to ethnography.* New York: Academic Press.

Aiello, J. R., & Jones, S. E. (1971). Field study of the proxemic behavior of young school children in three subcultural groups. *Journal of Personality and Social Psychology,* **19,** 351–356.

Aisenberg, N., & Harrington, M. (1988). *Women of academe: Outsiders in the sacred grove.* Amherst: University of Massachusetts Press.

Albrecht, G. L. (1985). Videotape safaris: Entering the field with a camera. *Qualitative Sociology,* **8,** 325–344.

Altheide, D. L. (1987). Ethnographic content analysis. *Qualitative Sociology,* **10,** 65–77.

Ambrose, S. E. (1991). Ike and the disappearing atrocities. *The New York Times Book Review,* **96**(8), 1, 35–37.

American Anthropological Association (1971). *Principles of professional responsibility.* Washington, DC: American Anthropological Museum.

American Educational Research Association (1991). Council minutes: Ethical standards. *Educational Researcher,* **20**(5), 32–33.

American Psychological Association (1981). *Ethical principles of psychologists* (Revised ed.). Washington, DC: American Psychological Association.

American Sociological Association (1989). *Code of ethics.* Washington, DC: American Sociological Association.

Amidon, E. J., & Flanders, N. A. (1963). *The role of the teacher in the classroom: A manual for understanding and improving teachers' classroom behavior.* Minneapolis: Amidon.

Ammar, H. (1954). *Growing up in an Egyptian village: Silwa, province of Aswan.* London: Routledge & Kegan Paul.

357

Anastasi, A. (1982). *Psychological testing* (5th ed.). New York: Macmillan.

Anderson, C. A., & Bowman, M. J. (Eds.) (1965). *Education and economic development.* Chicago: Aldine.

Anderson, C. H. (1971). *Toward a new sociology: A critical view.* Homewood, IL: Dorsey Press.

Anderson, G. L. (1989). Critical ethnography in education: Its origins, current status and new directions. *Review of Educational Research,* **59**(3), 249–270.

Anderson, G. L. (1989). Toward a critical constructivist approach to school administration: Invisibility, legitimation and the study of non-events. *Educational Administration Quarterly,* **26**(1), 38–59.

Anderson, G. L., & Herr, K. (1991). *Oral history for student empowerment: Capturing student voices.* Paper presented at the Second Interamerican Symposium on Classroom Ethnographic Research, June. C.I.S.E., Autonomous University of Mexico, Mexico City.

Anderson, N. (1923). *The hobo.* Chicago: University of Chicago Press.

Anyon, J. (1983). Workers, labor and economic history, and textbook content. In M. W. Apple, & L. Weis (Eds.), *Ideology and practice in schooling* (pp. 37–60). Philadelphia: Temple University Press.

Apple, M. W. (1978). The new sociology of education: Analyzing cultural and economic reproduction. *Harvard Educational Review,* **48,** 495–503.

Apple, M. W. (1986). *Teachers and texts: A political economy of class and gender relations in education.* New York: Methuen.

Apple, M. W., & Weis, L. (Eds.) (1983). *Ideology and practice in schooling.* Philadelphia: Temple University Press.

Applebaum, R. P. (1970). *Theories of social change.* Chicago: Markham.

Argyris, C. (1952). Diagnosing defenses against the outsider. *Journal of Social Issues,* **8**(3), 24–34.

Asad, T. (1986). The concept of cultural translation in British social anthropology. In J. Cifford & G. E. Marcus (Eds.), *Writing Culture* (pp. 141–165). Berkeley and Los Angeles, CA: University of California Press.

Au, K. H. (1980). Participation structures in a reading lesson with Hawaiian children: Analysis of a culturally appropriate instructional event. *Anthropology and Education Quarterly,* **11,** 91–115.

Au, K. H., & Jordan, C. (1981). Teaching reading to Hawaiian children: Finding a culturally appropriate solution. *Anthropology and Education Quarterly,* **11,** 91–115.

Babbie, E. R. (1973). *Survey research methods.* Belmont, CA: Wadsworth.

Bales R. F. (1950). *Interaction process analysis: A method for the study of small groups.* Chicago: University of Chicago Press.

Ball, S. J. (1990). Self-doubt and soft data: Social and technical trajectories in ethnographic fieldwork. *Qualitative Studies in Education*, **3**, 7–171.

Ball, S., & Goodson, I. (Eds.) (1985). *Teachers' Lives and Careers*. London: Falmer Press.

Bandura, A. (1977). *Social learning theory*. Englewood Cliffs, NJ: Prentice-Hall.

Banta, M., & Hinsley, C. M. (1986). *From site to sight: Anthropology, photography, and the power of imagery*. Cambridge, MA: Peabody Museum Press.

Barker, R. G. (Ed.) (1963). *The stream of behavior: Explorations of its structure and content*. New York: Appleton Century-Crofts.

Barker, R. G., & Gump, P. V. (1964). *Big school, small school: High school size and student behavior*. Stanford, CA: Standford University Press.

Barker, R. G., & Wright, H. F. (1951). *One boy's day: A specimen record of behavior*. New York: Harper.

Barker, R. G., Gump, P. V., Friesen, W. V., & Willems, E. (1970). The ecological environment: Student participation in non-class settings. In M. W. Miles & W. W. Charters, Jr. (Eds.), *Learning in social settings: New readings in the social psychology of education* (pp. 12–42). Boston: Allyn and Bacon.

Barnhardt, C. (1982). *Tuning-in: Athabaskan teachers and Athabaskan students*. Paper presented at the Annual Meeting of the American Anthropological Association, Washington, D.C.

Bateson, M. C. (1985). *With a daughter's eye: A memoir of Margaret Mead and Gregory Bateson*. New York: Washington Square Press.

Bateson, M. C. (1989). *Composing a life*. New York: Penguin.

Beals, A. R., Spindler, G. D., & Spindler, L. (1973). *Culture in process* (2nd ed.). New York: Holt, Rinehart, and Winston.

Beck, L. W. (1949). The "natural science ideal" in the social sciences. *Scientific Monthly* **68**, 386–394.

Becker, H. S. (1958). Problems of inference and proof in participant observation. *American Sociological Review*, **23**, 652–660.

Becker, H. S. (1986). *Writing for social scientists: How to start and finish your thesis, book, or article*. Chicago: University of Chicago Press.

Becker, H. S., Geer, B., Hughes, E. C., & Strauss, A. L. (1961). *Boys in white: Student culture in medical school*. Chicago: University of Chicago Press.

Becker, H. S., Geer, B., & Hughes, E. C. (1968). *Making the grade: The academic side of college life*. New York: Wiley.

Belenky, M. F., Clinchy, B. M., Bellack, N. R., Arno, A., Kliebard, H. M., Hyman, R. T., & Smith, F. L., Jr. (1966). *The language of the classroom*. New York: Teachers College Press.

Belenky, M. F., Clinchy, B. M., Goldberger, N. R., & Tarule, J. M. (1986).

Woman's ways of knowing: The development of self, voice, and mind. New York: Basic Books.

Bellack, N. R., Arno, A., Kliebard, H. M., Hyman, R. T., & Smith, F. L., Jr. (1966). *The language of the classroom.* New York: Teachers College Press.

Bellman, B. L., & Jules-Rosette, B. (1977). *A paradigm for looking: Cross-cultural research with visual media.* Norwood, NJ: Ablex.

Benedict, R. (1934). *Patterns of culture.* Boston: Houghton Mifflin.

Benedict, R. (1938). Continuities and discontinuities in cultural conditioning. *Psychiatry,* **1,** 161–167.

Benedict, R. (1943). Transmitting our democratic heritage in the school. *American Journal of Sociology,* **48,** 722–727.

Benedict, R. (1946). *The Chrysanthemum and the sword: Patterns of Japanese culture.* Boston: Houghton Mifflin.

Bennett, K. B., & LeCompte, M. D. (1990). *The way schools work: A sociological analysis of education.* White Plans, NY: Longman.

Bernstein, B. B. (1971). *Class, codes and control.* London: Routledge & Kegan Paul.

Berreman, G. D. (1962). Behind many masks: Ethnography and impression management in a Himalayan village. *Monographs of the Society for Applied Anthropology,* No. 4.

Birdwhistell, R. L. (1970). *Kinesics and context: Essays on body motion communication.* Philadelphia: University of Pennsylvania Press.

Blackwood, B. (1935). *Both sides of Buka passage: An ethnographic study of social, sexual, and economic questions in the north western Solomon Islands.* Oxford: Clarendon.

Blau, P. M. (1955). *The dynamics of bureaucracy: A study of interpersonal relations in two government agencies.* Chicago: University of Chicago Press.

Blau, P. M. (1964). *Exchange and power in social life.* New York: Wiley.

Blau, P. M., & Duncan, O. D. (1967). *The American occupational structure.* New York: Wiley.

Bloor, M. J. (1983). Notes on member validation. In R. M. Emerson (Ed.), *Contemporary field research: A collection of readings* (pp. 156–172). Prospect Heights, IL: Waveland.

Boardman, S. K., Harrington, C. C., & Horowitz, S. V. (1987). Successful women: A psychological investigation of family class and education origins. In B. A. Gutekl & L. Larwood (Eds.), *Women's career development* (pp. 66–85). Newbury Park, CA: Sage Publications.

Boas, F. (1911). *The mind of primitive man: A course of lectures delivered before the Lowell Institute, Boston, MA, and the National University of Mexico, 1910–1911.* New York: Macmillan.

Boas, F. (1928). *Anthropology and modern life.* New York: Norton.

Boas, F. (1938). Living philosophies, II: An anthropologist's credo. *The Nation* **147,** 201–204.

Bogdan, R. (1972). *Participant observation in organizational settings.* Syracuse, NY: Syracuse University Division of Special Education and Rehabilitation and the Center on Human Policy.

Bogdan, R. (1989). *Learning by doing: Techniques of teaching and doing qualitative research.* Keynote address at the second annual Conference on Qualitative Research in Education. Athens, GA.

Bogdan, R. C., & Biklen, S. K. (1992). *Qualitative research for education: An introduction to theory and methods* (2nd ed.). Boston: Allyn and Bacon.

Bogdan, R. & Taylor S. J. (1982). *Inside out: The social meaning of mental retardation.* Toronto: University of Toronto Press.

Bond, G. C. (1990). Fieldnotes: Research in past occurrences. In R. Sanjek (Ed.), *Fieldnotes: The making of anthropology* (pp. 273–289). Ithaca, NY: Cornell University Press.

Borg, W. R., & Gall, M. D. (1983). *Educational research: An introduction* (4th ed.). New York: Longman.

Borman, K. M. (1978). Social control and schooling: Power and process in two kindergarten settings. *Anthropology and Education Quarterly,* **9,** 38–53.

Borman, K. M. (Ed.) (1982). *The social life of children in a changing society.* Hillsdale, NJ: Erlbaum.

Borman, K. M. (1991). *The first "real" job: A study of young workers.* Albany, NY: State University of New York Press.

Borman, K. M., LeCompte, M. D., & Goetz, J. P. (1986). Ethnographic research design and why it doesn't work. *American Behavioral Scientist,* **3**(1), Sept/Oct, 43–57.

Bossert, S. T. (1979). *Tasks and social relationships in classrooms: A study of instructional organization and its consequences.* Cambridge, England: Cambridge University Press.

Bottomore, T. (1984). *The Frankfurt school.* London: Tavistock.

Boudon, R. (1974). *Education, opportunity, and social inequality: Changing prospects in Western society.* New York: Wiley.

Bourdieu, P. & Passeron, J.-C. (1977). *Reproduction in education, society and culture* (translated by R. Nice). London: Sage Publications.

Bowen, E. S. (Pseudonym for Laura Bohannon.) (1954). *Return to laughter.* New York: Harper.

Bowles, S., & Gintis, H. (1976). *Schooling in capitalist America: Educational reform and the contradictions of economic life.* New York: Basic Books.

Bradburn, N. M. (1983). Response error. In P. H. Rossi, J. D. Wright, &

A. B. Anderson (Eds.), *The handbook of survey research* (pp. 289–329). New York: Academic Press.

Bradburn, N. M., & Sudman, S. (1988). *Polls and surveys: Understanding what they tell us.* San Francisco: Jossey-Bass.

Brameld, T. (1957). *Cultural foundations of education: An interdisciplinary exploration.* New York: Harper.

Brameld, T. (1958). Explicit and implicit culture in Puerto Rico: A case study in educational anthropology. *Harvard Educational Review,* **28,** 197–213.

Brameld, T. (1959). *The remaking of a culture: Life and education in Puerto Rico.* New York: Harper.

Brameld, T. (1968). *Japan: Culture, education, and change in two communities.* New York: Holt, Rinehart, and Winston.

Brameld, T., & Sullivan, E. B. (1961). Anthropology and education. *Review of Educational Research,* **31,** 70–79.

Bredo, E., & Feinberg, W. (Eds.) (1982). *Knowledge and values in social and educational research.* Philadelphia: Temple University Press.

Brenner, M., Brown, J., & Canter D. (Eds.) (1985). *The research interview: Uses and approaches.* New York: Academic Press.

Brinberg, D., & McGrath, J. E. (1985). *Validity and the research process.* Newbury Park, CA: Sage Publications.

Brodkey, L. (1987). Writing critical ethnographic narratives. *Anthropology and Education Quarterly,* **18,** 67–76.

Bronfenbrenner, U. (1970). *Two worlds of childhood: U.S. and U.S.S.R.* New York: Basic Books.

Bronfenbrenner, U. (1976). The experimental ecology of education. *Teachers College Record,* **78,** 157–204.

Brown, M. J. M. (1982a). *Implementation of a state mandated economics course in one large school system: A case study.* Doctoral dissertation. Department of Social Science Education, University of Georgia.

Brownstein, L. (1972). *Education and development in rural Kenya: A study of primary school graduates.* New York: Praeger.

Bruner, J. S., Goodnow, J. J., & Austin, G. A. (1956). *A study of thinking.* New York: Wiley.

Bruyn, S. T. (1966). *The human perspective in sociology: The methodology of participant observation.* Englewood Cliffs, NJ: Prentice-Hall.

Bryson, L. (1939). Anthropology and education. In D. D. Brand & F. E. Harvey (Eds.), *So live the works of men: Seventieth anniversary volume honoring Edgar Lee Hewett* (pp. 107–115). Albuquerque: University of New Mexico Press.

Bucher, R., & Stellings, J. G. (1977). *Becoming professional.* Beverly Hills, CA: Sage Publications.

Burger, D. (1991). *The use of case method in educating professionals.* Unpublished doctoral dissertation. University of Colorado, Boulder.

Burgess, R. G. (1982). Keeping field notes. In R. G. Burgess (Ed.), *Field research: A sourcebook and field manual* (pp. 191–194). London: Allen & Unwin.

Burgess, R. G. (1984). *In the field: An introduction to field research.* London: Allen & Unwin.

Burnett, J. H. (1969). Ceremony, rites, and economy in the student system of an American high school. *Human Organization, 28,* 1–10.

Burnett, J. H. (1973). Event description and analysis in the microethnography of urban classrooms. In F. A. J. Ianni & E. Storey (Eds.), *Cultural relevance and educational issues: Readings in anthropology and education* (pp. 287–303). Boston: Little, Brown.

Burnett, J. H. (1974a). *Anthropology and education: An annotated bibliographic guide.* New Haven, CT: Human Relations Area Files Press.

Burnett, J. H. (1974b). On the analog between culture acquisition and ethnographic method. *Anthropology and Education Quarterly, 5*(1), 25–29.

Burns, A. F. (1975). An anthropologist at work: Field perspectives on applied ethnography and an independent research firm. *Anthropology and Education Quarterly, 6*(4), 28–33.

Burns, A. F. (1976). On the ethnographic process in anthropology and education. *Anthropology and Education Quarterly, 7*(3), 25–33.

Camilleri, S. F. (1962). Theory, probability and induction in social research. *American Sociological Review, 27,* 170–178.

Campbell, A. (1984). *The girls in the gang: A report from New York City.* New York: Basil Blackwell.

Campbell, D. T. (1979). "Degrees of freedom" and the case study. In D. Cook & C. S. Reichardt (Eds.), *Qualitative and quantitative methods in evaluation research* (pp. 49–67). Beverly Hills, CA: Sage Publications.

Campbell, D. T., & Fiske, D. W. (1959). Convergent and discriminant validation by the multitrait–multimethod matrix. *Psychological Bulletin, 56,* 81–105.

Campbell, D. T., & Stanley, J. C. (1963). *Experimental and quasi-experimental designs for research.* Chicago: McNally.

Carew, J. V., & Lightfoot, S. L. (1979). *Beyond bias: Perspectives on classrooms.* Cambridge, MA: Harvard University Press.

Carin, A., & Sund, R. B. (1978). *Creative questioning and sensitive listening techniques: A self-concept approach* (2nd ed.). Columbus, OH: Merrill.

Carnoy, M. (Ed.) (1972). *Schooling in a corporate society: The political economy of education in America.* New York: McKay.

Carr, E. H. (1961). *What is history?: The George MacCauley Trevelyan lectures delivered in the University of Cambridge, January–March 1961.* New York: Knopf.

Carroll, T. G. (1975). Transactions of cognitive equivalence in the domains of "work" and "play." *Anthropology and Education Quarterly,* **6**(2), 17–22.

Carroll, T. G. (1977). *Work and play: A probe of the formation, use and intersection of adult and child activity domains.* Doctoral dissertation, Department of Anthropology, State University of New York at Buffalo. (Dissertation Abstracts International 37:5211A-5212A. University Microfilms No. 77-3520.)

Carspecken, P. F., & Apple, M. (1992). Critical qualitative research: Theory, methodology and practice. In M. D. LeCompte *et al.,* (Eds.), *The handbook of qualitative research in education* (pp. 507–555). San Diego, CA: Academic Press.

Cassell, J. (1978). *A fieldwork manual for studying desegregated schools.* Washington, D.C.: The National Institute of Education.

Caudill, H. M. (1963). *Night comes to the Cumberland: A biography of a depressed area.* Boston: Little, Brown.

Cazden, C. B., John, V. P., & Hymes, D. (Eds.) (1972). *Functions of language in the classroom.* New York: Teachers College Press.

Center for New Schools (1972). Strengthening alternative high schools. *Harvard Educational Review,* **42,** 313–350.

Center for New Schools (1976). Ethnographic evaluation in education. *Journal of Research and Development in Education,* **9**(4), 3–11.

Chagnon, N. A. (1974). *Studying the Yanomamo.* New York: Holt, Rinehart, and Winston.

Chang, H. (1991). *American high school life and ethos: An ethnography.* New York: Falmer Press.

Christian-Smith, L. (1988). Romancing the girl: Adolescent romance novels and the construction of femininity. In L. Roman & L. Christian-Smith with E. Ellsworth (Eds.), *Becoming feminine: The politics of popular culture* (pp. 76–101) London: The Falmer Press.

Cicourel, A. V. (1964). *Method and measurement in sociology.* New York: Free Press.

Cicourel, A. V., & Kitsuse, J. I. (1963). *The educational decision-makers.* Indianapolis: Bobbs-Merrill.

Clement, D. C., Eisenhart, M. A., & Harding, J. R. (1979). The veneer of harmony: Social-race relations in a southern desegregated school. In R. C. Rist (Ed.), *Desegregated schools:Appraisals of an American experiment* (pp. 15–52). New York: Academic Press.

Clement, D. C., & Harding, J. R. (1978). Social distinctions and emergent student groups in a desegregated school. *Anthropology and Education Quarterly,* **9,** 272–282.

Clifford, J. (1986). On ethnographic allegory. In J. Clifford & G. E. Marcus (Eds.), *Writing culture: The poetics and politics of ethnography* (pp. 98–121). Berkeley, CA: University of California Press.

Clifford, J. (1990). Notes on (field) notes. In R. Sanjek (Ed.), *Fieldnotes: The makings of anthropology* (pp. 47–71). Ithaca, NY: Cornell University Press.

Clifford, J., & Marcus, G. (Eds.) (1986). *Writing culture: The poetics and politics of ethnography.* Berkeley, CA: University of California Press.

Clignet, R. P., & Foster, P. (1966). *The fortunate few: A study of secondary schools and students in the Ivory Coast.* Evanston, IL: Northwestern University Press.

Cole, M., & Scribner, S. (1974). *Culture and thought: A psychological introduction.* New York: Wiley.

Cole, M., Gay, J., Glick, J., & Sharp, D. (1971). *The cultural context of learning and thinking.* New York: Basic Books.

Coleman, J. S., Campbell, E. Q., Hobson, C. J., McPartland, J., Mood, A. M., Weinfeld, F. D., & York, R. L. (1966). *Equality of educational opportunity.* Washington, D.C.: U.S. Government Printing Office.

Coles, R. (1967). *Children of crisis: A study of courage and fear.* Boston: Little, Brown.

Coles, R. (1971a). *Children of crisis: Migrants, sharecroppers, mountaineers* (Vol. II). Boston: Little, Brown.

Coles, R. (1971b). *Children of crisis: The south goes north* (Vol. III). Boston: Little, Brown.

Collier, J., Jr. (1973). *Alaskan Eskimo education: A film analysis of cultural confrontation in the schools.* New York: Holt, Rinehart, and Winston.

Collier, J., Jr., & Collier, M. (1986). *Visual anthropology: Photography as a research method* (revised ed.). Albuquerque: University of New Mexico Press.

Colson, E. (1954). The intensive study of small sample communities. In R. T. Spencer (Ed.), *Method and perspective in anthropology: Papers in honor of Wilson D. Wallis* (pp. 43–59). Minneapolis: University of Minnesota Press.

Cook, T. D., & Campbell, D. T. (1979). *Quasi-experimentation: Design and analysis issues for field settings.* Chicago: McNally.

Corbett, H. D. (1984). School context, the field researcher role, and achieving data comparability in multisite research. *Anthropology and Education Quarterly,* **15**(3), 202–211.

Corwin, R. G. (1973). *Reform and organizational survival: The Teacher Corps as an instrument of educational change.* New York: Wiley.

Cox, T. V. (1980). *Kindergarten, a status passage for American children: A microethnography of an urban kindergarten classroom.* Doctoral dissertation, Department of Anthropology, University of Georgia. (Dissertation Abstracts International 41:1668A-1669A. University Microfilms No. 8023196.)

Crain, R. L. (1977). Racial tension in high schools: Pushing the survey method closer to reality. *Anthropology and Education Quarterly,* **8,** 142–151.

Cusick, P. A. (1973). *Inside high school: The student's world.* New York: Holt, Rinehart, and Winston.

D'Souza, D. (1991). *Illiberal education: The politics of race and sex on campus.* New York: Free Press.

Dagenais, J. J. (1972). *Models of man: A phenomenological critique of some paradigms in the human sciences.* The Hague: Martinus Nijhoff.

Daniels, A. K. (1980). Getting in and getting on: The sociology of infiltration and ingratiation. In M. Mackie (Ed.), *Sociology's relations with the community* (pp. 85–97).

Davidson, J. (1981). *The long road north.* Austin, TX: Texas Monthly Press.

Davis, L. (1984). *Pupil power: Deviance and gender in school.* London: Palmer Press.

Deal, T. E. (1975). An organizational explanation of the failure of alternative secondary schools. *Educational Researcher,* **4**(4), 10–16.

Dean, J., & Whyte, W. F. (1958). How do you know if the informant is telling the truth? *Human Organization,* **17**(2), 34–38.

Dean, J. P., Eichhorn, R. L., & Dean, L. R. (1967). Fruitful informants for intensive interviewing. In J. T. Doby (Ed.), *An introduction to social research* (2nd ed.) (pp. 284–286). New York: Appleton Century-Crofts.

Deegan, M. J. (1988). *Jane Addams and the men of the Chicago School.* New Brunswick, NJ: Transaction Books.

Delamont, S. (1989). *Knowledgeable women: Structuralism and the reproduction of elites.* New York: Routledge & Kegan Paul.

Delgado-Gaitan, C. (1988). The value of conformity: Learning to stay in school. *Anthropology and Education Quarterly,* **19,** (4), 354–382.

Deloria, V., Jr. (1969). *Custer died for your sins: An Indian manifesto.* New York: Macmillan.

Deng, F. M. (1972). *The Dinka of the Sudan.* New York: Holt, Rinehart, and Winston.

Denzin, N. K. (1978). *The research act: A theoretical introduction to sociological methods* (2nd ed.). New York: McGraw-Hill.

Dewey, J. (1916). *Democracy and education: An introduction to the philosophy of education.* New York: Macmillan.

Deyhle, D. M. (1986). Break dancing and breaking out: Anglos, Utes and Navajos in a border reservation school. *Anthropology and Education quarterly,* **17,** 111–127.

Deyhle, D. M. (1989). Pushouts and pullouts: Navajo and Ute school leavers. *Journal of Navajo Education,* **6,** 36–51.

Deyhle, D. M. (1991). Empowerment and cultural conflict: Navajo parents and the schooling of their children. *Qualitative Studies in Education,* **4,** 277–297.

Deyhle, D. M. (1992). Constructing failure and maintaining cultural identity: Navajo and Ute school leavers. *Journal of American Indian Education.* January, 24–47.

Dillon, D., and Searle, D. (1981). The role of language in one first grade classroom. *Research in the Teaching of English,* **15,** 311–328.

Dilthey, W. (1988). *Introduction to the human sciences: An attempt to lay a foundation for the study of society and history* (translated by R. J. Betanzos). Detroit: Wayne State University.

Dobbert, M. L. (1976). Another route to a general theory of cultural transmission: A systems model. In J. I. Roberts & S. Akinsanya (Eds.), *Educational patterns and cultural configurations: The anthropology of education* (pp. 205–211). New York: David McKay Co., Inc.

Dobbert, M. L. (1982). *Ethnographic research: Theory and application for modern schools and societies.* New York: Praeger.

Dobbert, M. L., & Kurth-Schai, R. (1992). Systematic ethnography: Toward an evolutionary science of education and culture. In M. D. LeCompte, W. Millroy, & J. Preissle (Eds.), *The handbook of qualitative research in education* (pp. 93–161). San Diego: Academic Press.

Dollard, J. (1935). *Criteria for the life history, with analyses of six notable documents.* New Haven, CT: Yale University Press.

Dore, R. P. (1965). *Education in Tokugawa Japan.* Berkeley, CA: University of California Press.

Douglas, J. D. (1976). *Investigative social research: Individual and team field research.* Newbury Park, CA: Sage Publications.

Douglas, J. D. (1985). *Creative interviewing.* Beverly Hills, CA: Sage Publications.

Dreeben, R. (1968). *On what is learned in school.* Reading, MA: Addison-Wesley.

Dunkin, M. J., & Biddle, B. J. (1974). *The study of teaching.* New York: Holt, Rinehart, and Winston.

Durkheim, E. (1947). *The division of labor in society* (translated by G. Simpson). Glencoe, IL: Free Press.

Durkheim, E. (1951). *Suicide: A study in sociology* (translated by J. A. Spaulding & G. Simpson). G. Simpson (Ed.). Glencoe, IL: Free Press.

Durkheim, E. (1961). *Moral education: A study in the theory and application of the sociology of education* (translated by K. Wilson & H. Schnurer). E. K. Wilson (Ed.). Glencoe, IL: Free Press.

Dworkin, A. G. (1987). *Burnout in the public schools: Structural causes and consequences for children.* Albany, NY: State University of New York Press.

Dworkin, R. J. (1992). *Researching the mentally ill.* Newbury Park, CA: Sage Publications.

Eckerd, P. (1988). *Jocks and burnouts: Social categories and identity in the high school.* New York: Teachers College Press.

Eddy, E. M. (1967). *Walk the white line: A profile of urban education.* New York: Praeger.

Eddy, E. M. (1969). *Becoming a teacher: The passage to professional status.* New York: Teachers College Press.

Eisenhart, M. A., & Graue, M. E. (1990). Socially constructed readiness for school. *Qualitative Studies in Education, 3*(3), 253–269.

Eisenhart, M. A., & Holland, D. C. (1988). Moments of discontent: University women and the gender status quo. *Anthropology and Education Quarterly, 19*(2), 115–138.

Eisenhart, M. A., & Holland, D. C. (1990). Gender constructs and career choice: The influence of peer culture on women's commitments in college. In A. Whitehead & B. Reid (Eds.), *The cultural construction of gender.* Champaign, IL: University of Illinois Press.

Eisenhart, M. A., & Howe, K. R. (1992). Validity in educational research. In M. D. LeCompte, W. L. Millroy, & J. Preissle (Eds.), *The handbook of qualitative research in education* (pp. 643–680). New York: Academic Press.

Eisner, E. W., & Peshkin, A. (Eds.) (1990). *Qualitative inquiry in education: The continuing debate.* New York: Teachers College Press.

Elkin, A. P. (1937). Native education, with special reference to the Australian Aborigines. *Oceania, 7,* 459–500.

Elkins, S. M. (1959). *Slavery: A problem in American institutional and intellectual life.* Chicago: University of Chicago Press.

Ellsworth, E. (1989). Why doesn't this feel empowering? Working through the repressive myths of critical pedagogy. *Harvard Educational Review, 59*(3), 297–324.

Ely, M. (1991). *Doing qualitative research: Circles within circles.* London: Falmer Press.

Embree, J. F. (1939). *Suye Mura: A Japanese village.* Chicago: University of Chicago Press.

English, F. W. (1988). The utility of the camera in qualitative inquiry. *Educational Researcher, 17*(4), 8–15.

Erchak, G. M. (1977). *Full respect: Kpelle children in adaptation.* New Haven, CT: Human Relations Area Files Press.

Erickson, F. (1973). What makes school ethnography "ethnographic?" *Anthropology and Education Quarterly, 4*(2), 10–19.

Erickson, F. (1977). Some approaches to inquiry in school-community ethnography. *Anthropology and Education Quarterly, 8,* 58–69.

Erickson, F. (1984). School literacy, reasoning and civility: An anthropologist's perspective. *Review of Educational Research, 54,* 525–546.

Erickson, F. (1986). Qualitative methods in research on teaching. In M. C. Wittrock (Ed.), *The handbook of research in teaching* (3rd ed.) (pp. 119–161). New York: MacMillan.

Erickson, F. (1992). Ethnographic microanalysis of interaction. In M. D. LeCompte *et al.*, (Eds.), *The handbook of qualitative research in education* (pp. 201–227). San Diego, CA: Academic Press.

Erickson, F., & Mohatt, G. (1982). Cultural organization of participation structures in two classrooms of Indian students. In G. D. Spindler (Ed.), *Doing the ethnography of schooling: Educational anthropology in action* (pp. 132–174). New York: Holt, Rinehart, and Winston.

Erickson, F., & Shultz, J. (1982). *The counselor as gatekeeper: Social interaction in interviews.* New York: Academic Press.

Erickson, F., & Wilson, J. (1982). *Sights and sounds of life in schools: A resource guide to film and videotape for research and education.* East Lansing, MI: Institute for Research on Teaching, College of Education, Michigan State University.

Erikson E. H. (1939). Observations on Sioux education. *The Journal of Psychology, 7,* 101–156.

Erikson, E. H. (1962). *Young man Luther: A study in psychoanalysis and history.* New York: Norton.

Erikson, E. H. (1968). *Identity: Youth and crisis.* New York: Norton.

Erikson, E. H. (1969). *Ghandi's truth: On the origins of militant nonviolence.* New York: Norton.

Evans-Pritchard, E. E. (1962). Social anthropology: Past and present. In *Essays in social anthropology* (pp. 13–28). New York: Free Press.

Everhart, R. B. (1975). Problems of doing fieldwork in educational evaluation. *Human Organization, 34,* 205–215.

Everhart, R. B. (1976). Ethnography and educational policy: Love and marriage or strange bedfellows? *Anthropology and Education Quarterly, 7*(3), 17–25.

Everhart, R. B. (1977). Between stranger and friend: Some consequences of "long term" fieldwork in schools. *American Educational Research Journal, 14,* 1–15.

Evertson, C., & Green, J. (1986). Observations as inquiry and method. In M. C. Wittrock (Ed.), *The handbook of research in teaching* (3rd ed.) (pp. 162–214). New York: MacMillan.

Evetts, J. (1989). Married women and career: Career history accounts of primary headteachers. *International Journal of Qualitative Studies in Education, 2,* 89–105.

Faraday, A., & Plummer, K. (1979). Doing life histories. *Sociological Review, 27*(4), 773–789.

Ferrell, B., & Compton, D. (1986). The use of ethnographic techniques for evaluation in a large school district: The Vanguard case. In D. Fetterman & M. A. Pitman (Eds.), *Educational evaluation: Ethnography in theory, practice and politics* (pp. 171–192). Beverly Hills, CA: Sage Publications.

Feshbach, N. D. (1969). Student teacher preferences for elementary school pupils varying in personality characteristics. *Journal of Educational Psychology,* **60,** 126–132.

Fetterman, D. M. (1979). *Ethnographic techniques and concepts in educational evaluation.* Paper presented at the Annual Meeting of the American Anthropological Association, Cincinnati.

Fetterman, D. M. (Ed.) (1984). *Ethnography in educational evaluation.* Beverly Hills, CA: Sage Publications.

Fetterman, D. M. (1988a). *Excellence and equality: A qualitatively different perspective on gifted and talented education.* Albany, NY: State Universtiy of New York Press.

Fetterman, D. M. (1988b). *Qualitative approaches to evaluation in education: The silent revolution.* New York: Praeger.

Fetterman, D. M. (1989). *Ethnography: step by step.* Newbury Park, CA: Sage Publications.

Fetterman, D. M., & Pitman, M. A. (Eds.) (1986). *Educational evaluation: Ethnography in theory, practice, and politics.* Beverly Hills, CA: Sage Publications.

Filstead, W. J. (1979). Qualitative methods: A needed perspective in evaluation research. In T. C. Cook & C. S. Reichardt (Eds.), *Qualitative and quantitative methods in evaluation research* (pp. 33–48). Beverly Hills, CA: Sage Publications.

Fine, G. A., & Sandstrom, K. L. (1988). *Knowing children: Participant observation with minors.* Beverly Hills, CA: Sage Publications.

Fine, M. (1987). Silencing in public schools. *Language Arts,* **64**(2), 157–174.

Fine, M. (1991). *Framing dropouts: Notes on the politics of an urban high school.* Albany, NY: State University of New York Press.

Fine, M., & Zane, N. (1989). Bein' wrapped too tight. Why low-income women drop out of high school. In L. Weis, E. Farrar, & H. Petrie (Eds.), *Dropouts from school: Issues, dilemmas and solutions.* Albany, NY: State University of New York Press.

Finnan, C. R. (1982). The ethnography of children's spontaneous play. In G. D. Spindler (Ed.), *Doing the ethnography of schooling: Educational anthropology in action* (pp. 356–380). New York: Holt, Rinehart, and Winston.

Firth, R. (1936). *We, the Tikopia: A sociological study of kinship in primitive Polynesia.* London: Allen and Unwin.

Fitzgerald, F. (1979). *America revised: History schoolbooks in the twentieth century.* Boston: Little, Brown.

Fitzsimmon, S. J. (1975). The anthropologist in a strange land. *Human Organization,* **34,** 183–196.

Flanders, N. A. (1970). *Analyzing teaching behavior.* Reading, MA: Addison–Wesley.

Florio, S., & Walsh, M. (1981). The classroom teacher as colleague in classroom research. In H. T. Trueba, G. P. Guthrie, & K. H. Au, (Eds.), *Culture and the bilingual classroom.* Rowley, MA: Newbury House.

Foley, D. (1990). *Learning capitalist culture: Deep in the heart of Tejas.* Philadelphia: University of Pennsylvania Press.

Forston, R. F. (1975). Proxemic research: A check on the validity of its techniques. In P. Hockings (Ed.), *Principles of visual anthropology* (pp. 373–380). The Hague: Mouton.

Fortune, R. (1963). *Sorcerers of Dobu.* New York: E. P. Dutton.

Foster, P. J. (1965). *Education and social change in Ghana.* Chicago: University of Chicago Press.

Fowke, G. (1910). *Antiquities of central and southeastern Missouri.* Smithsonian Institution Bureau of American Ethnology Bull. No. 37. Washington, D. C.: United States Government Printing Office.

Fowler, F. J., Jr. (1984). *Survey research methods:* Newsbury Park, CA: Sage Publication.

Fox, L. K. (1948). *The rural community and its school.* New York: King's Crown Press.

Freed, R. S., & Freed, S. A. (1981). Enculturation and education in Shanti Nagar. *Anthropological Papers of the American Museum of Natural History,* **57,** 49–156.

Freeman, D. (1983). *Margaret Mead and Samoa: The making and unmaking of an anthropological myth.* Cambridge, MA: Harvard University Press.

Freilich, M. (Ed.) (1970). *Marginal natives: Anthropologists at work.* New York: Harper and Row.

Fuchs, E. (1966). *Pickets at the gate.* New York: Free Press.

Fuchs, E. (1969). *Teachers talk: Views from inside city schools.* New York: Doubleday.

Furlong, V. (1976). Interaction sets in the classroom: Towards a study of pupil knowledge. In M. Stubbs & S. Delamont (Eds.), *Explorations in classroom observations* (pp. 23–44). London: Wiley.

Gallimore, R., Boggs, J. W., & Jordan, C. (1974). *Culture, behavior and education: A Study of Hawaiian-Americans.* Beverly Hills, CA: Sage Publications.

Gans, H. J. (1962). *The urban villagers: Group and class in the life of Italian Americans.* New York: Free Press.

Gans, H. J. (1967). *The Levittowners: Ways of life and politics in a new suburban community*. New York: Random House.

Gay, J., & Cole, M. (1967). *The new mathematics and an old culture: A study of learning among the Kpelle of Liberia*. New York: Holt, Rinehart, and Winston.

Gearing, F. O. (1973). Where we are and where we might go: Steps toward a general theory of cultural transmission. *Anthropology and Education Quarterly,* **4**(1), 1–10.

Gearing, F. O. (1975). Overview: A cultural theory of education. *Anthropology and Education Quarterly,* **6**(2), 1–9.

Gearing, F. O., & Epstein, P. (1982). Learning to wait: An ethnographic probe into the operations of an item of hidden curriculum. In G. D. Spindler (Ed.), *Doing the ethnography of schooling: Educational anthropology in action* (pp. 240–267). New York: Holt, Rinehart, and Winston.

Gearing, F. O., & Tindall, B. A. (1973). Anthropological studies of the educational process. *Annual Review of Anthropology,* **2,** 95–105.

Gee, J. P., Michaels, S., & O'Connor, M. C. (1992). Discourse analysis. In M. D. LeCompte *et al.,* (Eds.), *The handbook of qualitative research in education* (pp. 227–293). San Diego, CA: Academic Press.

Geer, B. (1964). First days in the field: A chronicle of research in progress. In P. E. Hammond (Ed.), *Sociologists at work: Essays on the craft of social research* (pp. 322–344). New York: Basic Books.

Geertz, C. (1973). *The interpretation of cultures: Selected essays*. New York: Basic Books.

Geertz, C. (1988) *Works and lives: The anthropologist as author*. Stanford, CA: Stanford University Press.

Georges, R. A., & Jones, M. O. (1980). *People studying people: The human element in fieldwork*. Berkeley, CA: University of California Press.

Gibson, M. A. (1976). *Reputation, respectability and school achievement in the Virgin Islands*. Paper presented at the Annual Meeting of the American Anthropological Association, Washington, D.C.

Gibson, M. A. (1982). Reputation and respectability: How competing cultural systems affect students' performance in school. *Anthropology and Education Quarterly,* **13,** 3–27.

Gibson, M. A. (1988). *Accommodation without assimilation: Sikh immigrants in an American high school*. Ithaca, NY: Cornell University Press.

Giles, J., Compton, D., & Ferrell, B. (1982). *Evaluating magnet schools: Expanding the information base for decision makers*. Paper presented at the Annual Meeting of the American Anthropological Association, Washington, D.C.

Gill, E., III (1982). *The learning activities of illiterate adults*. Unpublished doctoral dissertation. Department of Adult Education, University of Georgia.

Gilligan, C. (1982). *In a different voice.* Cambridge, MA: Harvard University Press.

Ginsburg, M. B. (1989). *Contradictions in teacher education and society: A critical analysis.* New York: Falmer Press.

Ginsburg, M., & LeCompte, M. D. (1980). *Passive and active models of occupational socialization: The case of teachers.* Paper presented at the Annual Meeting of the Southwestern Sociological Association, Houston, TX.

Ginsburg, M. B., Meyenn, R. J., & Miller, H. D. R. (1980). Teachers' conceptions of professionalism and trade unionism: An ideological analysis. P. Woods (Ed.), *Teacher Strategies: Explorations in the sociology of the school* (pp. 178–212). London: Croom Helm.

Giroux, H. A. (1981). *Ideology, culture, and the process of schooling.* Philadelphia: Temple University Press.

Giroux, H. A. (1988). Critical theory and the politics of culture and voice: Rethinking the discourse of educational research. In R. R. Sherman & R. B. Webb (Eds.), *Qualitative research in education: focus and methods* (pp.190–210). London: Falmer Press.

Giroux, H. A., & Simon, R. (1989). *Popular culture: Schooling and everyday life.* Westport, CT: Bergin and Garvey.

Gitlin, A., & Smyth, J. (1989). *Teacher evaluation: Educative alternatives.* Philadelphia: Falmer Press.

Gitlin, A., Siegel, M., & Boru, K. (1989). The politics of method: From leftist ethnography to educative research. *International Journal of Qualitative Research in Education,* **2,** 237–253.

Glascock, A. P. (1976). Dominance interaction in a first-grade ILP class. *Journal of Research and Development in Education,* **9**(4), 61–68.

Glaser, B. G., & Strauss, A. L. (1965). *Awareness of dying.* Chicago: Aldine.

Glaser, B. G., & Strauss, A. L. (1967). *The discovery of grounded theory: Strategies for qualitative research.* Chicago: Aldine.

Glaser, B. G., & Strauss, A. L. (1968). *Time for dying.* Chicago: Aldine.

Glazer, M. (1972). *The research adventure: Promise and problems of field work.* New York: Random House.

Gleick, J. (1987). *Chaos: The making of a new science.* New York: Penquin Books.

Glesne, C., & Peshkin, A. (1992). *Becoming qualitative researchers: An Introduction.* White Plains, NY: Longman.

Goetz, J. P. (1976a). Behavioral configurations in the classroom: A case study. *Journal of Research and Development in Education,* **9**(4), 36–49.

Goetz, J. P. (1976b). *Configurations in control and autonomy: A microethnography of a rural third-grade classroom.* Doctoral dissertation, Department of Social Studies Education, Indiana University. (Dissertation Abstracts International 36:6175A. University Microfilms No. 76–6275.)

Goetz, J. P. (1978). Theoretical approaches to the study of sex-role culture in schools. *Anthropology and Education Quarterly,* **9,** 3–21.

Goetz, J. P. (1981a). Children's sex-role knowledge and behavior. An ethnographic study of first graders in the rural south. *Theory and Research in Social Education,* 8(4), 31–54.

Goetz, J. P. (1981b). Sex-role systems in Rose Elementary School: Change and tradition in the rural-transitional South. In R. T. Sieber & A. J. Gordon (Eds.), *Children and their organizations: Investigations in American culture* (pp. 58–73). Boston: Hall.

Goetz, J. P., & Breneman, E. A. R. (1988). Desegregation and black students' experiences in two rural southern elementary schools. *Elementary School Journal,* **88,** 489–502.

Goetz, J. P., & Hansen, J. F. (1974). The cultural analysis of schooling. *Anthropology and Education Quarterly,* 5(4), 1–8.

Goetz, J. P., & LeCompte, M. D. (1984). *Ethnography and qualitative design in educational research.* San Diego, CA: Academic Press.

Gold, R. L. (1958). Roles in sociological field observations. *Social Forces,* **36,** 217–223.

Goode, W. J., & Hatt, P. K. (1952). *Methods in social research.* New York: McGraw-Hill.

Goodenough, W. H. (1976). Multiculturalism at the normal human experience. *Anthropology and Education Quarterly,* 7(4), 4–7.

Goodman, M. E. (1957). Values, attitudes, and social concepts of Japanese and American children. *American Anthropologist,* **59,** 979–999.

Goodman, M. E. (1970). *The culture of childhood: Child's eye views of society and culture.* New York: Teachers College Press.

Goodson, I. (1980–1981). Life histories and the study of schooling. *Interchange,* 11(4), 62–76.

Goodson, I. F., & Walker, R. (1991). *Biography, identity and schooling: Episodes in educational research.* London: Falmer Press.

Gordon, R. L. (1975). *Interviewing strategy, techniques, and tactics* (revised ed.). Homewood, IL: Dorsey Press.

Gouldner, A. W. (1970). *The coming crisis of Western sociology.* New York: Avon Books.

Granqvist, H. (1947). *Birth and childhood among the Arabs: Studies in a Muhammadan village in Palestine.* Helsingfors: Söderström.

Grant, C. A., & Sleeter, C. E. (1986). *After the school bell rings.* Baskingstoke, England: Falmer Press.

Grant, G. (1989). *The world we created at Hamilton High*. Cambridge, MA: Harvard University Press.

Green, J. L., & Wallat, C. (Eds.) (1981). *Ethnography and language in educational settings*. Norwood, NJ: Ablex.

Griffiths, G (1985). Doubts, dilemmas and diary-keeping: Some reflections on teacher-based research. In R. G. Burgess (Ed.), *Issues in educational research: Qualitative methods* (pp. 197–215). London: Falmer Press.

Grindal, B. T. (1972). *Growing up in two worlds: Education and transition among the Sisala of Northern Ghana*. New York: Holt, Rinehart, and Winston.

Guba, E. G. (1978). *Toward a methodology of naturalistic inquiry in educational evaluation*. Los Angeles: Center for the Study of Evaluation, UCLA Graduate School of Education, University of California.

Guba, E. G., (1981). Criteria for assessing the trustworthiness of naturalistic inquiries. *Educational Communication and Technology Journal*, **29**, 75–91.

Guba, E. G. (1982). *The search for truth: Naturalistic inquiry as an option*. Paper presented at the annual meeting of the International Reading Association, Chicago.

Guba, E. G. (1986). *The development of parallel criteria for trustworthiness*. Paper presented at the meeting of the American Educational Research Association, San Francisco.

Guba, E. G., & Lincoln, Y. S. (1981). *Effective evaluation: Improving the usefulness of education results through responsive and naturalistic approaches*. San Francisco: Jossey-Bass.

Guilmet, G. M. (1978). Navajo and Caucasian children's verbal and non-verbal–visual behavior in the urban classroom. *Anthropology and Education Quarterly*, **9**, 196–215.

Guilmet, G. M. (1979). Instructor reaction to verbal and nonverbal–visual styles: An example of Navajo and Caucasian children. *Anthropology and Education Quarterly*, **10**, 254–266.

Gumport, P. (1992). The politics of academic identity and exclusion. Paper presented at the American Educational Research Association meetings, April 20–24, San Francisco, CA.

Guthrie, G. P. (1985). *A school divided: An ethnography of bilingual education in a Chinese community*. (Series: Psychology of Reading and Reading Instruction.), Hillsdale, NJ: Lawrence Erlbaum Associates.

Guttentag, M. (1971). Evaluation and society. *Personality and Social Psychology Bulletin*, **3**, 31–40.

Hadjighasem, M. M. (1980). *Predictors of women's occupational attainment*. Doctoral dissertation, Department of Educational Administration,

University of Houston. (Dissertation Abstracts International 40:6164A. University Microfilms No. 8012720.)

Hakken, D. (1980). Workers' education and the reproduction of working class culture in Sheffield, England. *Anthropology and Education Quarterly*, **11**, 211–234.

Hall, C. S., & Lindzey, G. (1970). *Theories of personality* (2nd ed.). New York: Wiley.

Hall, E. T. (1974). *Handbook for proxemic research*. Washington, D.C.: Society for the Anthropology of Visual Communication.

Hall, G. E., and Loucks, S. F. (1977). A developmental model for determining whether the treatment is actually implemented. *American Educational Research Journal*, **14**, 263–276.

Hall, L. K. (1983). *A qualitative study of the nature of charisma*. Unpublished doctoral dissertation. Department of Educational Psychology, University of Georgia.

Hammond, D., & Jablow, A. (1976). *Women in cultures of the world*. Menlo Park, CA: Cummings.

Hammond, P. E. (Ed.) (1964). *Sociologists at work: Essays on the craft of social research*. New York: Basic Books.

Hanna, J. L. (1982). Public social policy and the children's world: Implications of ethnographic research for desegregated schooling. In G. D. Spindler (Ed.), *Doing the ethnography of schooling: Educational anthropology in action* (pp. 316–355). New York: Holt, Rinehart, and Winston.

Hansen, J. F. (1979). *Sociocultural perspectives on human learning: An introduction to educational anthropology*. Englewood Cliffs, NJ: Prentice-Hall.

Harbison, F., & Myers, C. A. (1964). *Education, manpower and economic growth: Strategies of human resource development*. New York: McGraw-Hill.

Harding, S., & Hintikka, M. B. (1983). *Discovering reality: Feminist perspectives on epistemology, metaphysics, methodology, and philosophy of science*. Boston: D. Reidel Publishing Co.

Hargreaves, A., & Woods, P. (1984). *Classrooms and staffrooms*. Milton Keynes, England: The Open University Press.

Haring, D. G. (Ed.) (1956). *Personal character and cultural milieu: A collection of readings* (3rd revised ed.). Syracuse, NY: Syracuse University Press.

Harley, G. W. (1941). *Notes on the Poro in Liberia*. Papers of the Peabody Museum of American Archaeology and Ethnology, Vol. 19, No. 2.

Harper, I. S. (1979). *From student to nurse: A longitudinal study of socialization*. New York: Cambridge University Press.

Harrell-Bond, B. (1976). Studying elites: Some special problems. In M. A. Rynkiewich & J. P. Spradley (Eds.), *Ethics and anthropology: Dilemmas in fieldwork*. New York: Wiley.

Harrington, C. C. (1979). *Psychological anthropology and education: A delineation of a field inquiry.* New York: AMS Press.

Harrington, C. C., & Gumpert, P. (1981). *Negative prediction defiers: Educational antecedents of success—proposal to the Spencer Foundation.* Unpublished manuscript. Files of the Authors, Department of Anthropology, Teachers College, Columbia University.

Harris, M. (1976). History and significance of the emic/etic distinction. *Annual Review of Anthropology, 5,* 329–350.

Harris, M. (1979). *Cultural materialism: The struggle for a science of culture.* New York: Random House.

Harris, M. (1980). *Culture, people, nature: An introduction to general anthropology* (3rd ed.). New York: Harper and Row.

Hartshorne, E. Y. (1943). Undergraduate society and the college culture. *American Sociological Review, 8,* 321–332.

Hartsock, N. M. (1983). The feminist standpoint: Developing the ground for a specifically feminist historical materialism. In S. Harding & M. B. Hintikka (Eds.), *Discovering reality: Feminist perspectives on epistemology, metaphysics, methodology, and philosophy of science.* Boston: D. Reidel Publishing Co.

Havighurst, R. J. (1961). Education and social mobility in four societies. In A. H. Halsey, J. Floud, & C. A. Anderson (Eds.), *Education, economy and society: A reader in the sociology of education* (pp. 105–120). New York: Free Press.

Hayes, H. R. (1958). *From ape to angel: An informal history of social anthropology.* New York: Capricorn Books.

Heath, S. B. (1983). *Ways with words: Language, life, and work in communities and classrooms.* Cambridge University Press.

Heckel, B. (1935). The Yao tribe: Their culture and education. *University of London Institute of Education Studies and Reports, 4,* 9–53.

Heider, K. G. (1976). *Ethnographic film.* Austin, TX: University of Texas Press.

Helfgot, J. (1974). Professional reform organizations and the symbolic representation of the poor. *American Sociological Review, 39,* 475–491.

Hendricks, G. (1974). *The Dominican diaspora: From the Dominican Republic to New York City—Villagers in transition.* New York: Teachers College Press.

Henry, J. (1955). Docility, or giving teacher what she wants. *Journal of Social Issues, 11*(2), 33–41.

Henry, J. (1957). Attitude organization in elementary school classrooms. *American Journal of Orthopsychiatry, 27,* 117–133.

Henry, J. (1959). The problem of spontaneity, initiative, and creativity in suburban classrooms. *American Journal of Orthopsychiatry, 29,* 266–279.

Henry, J. (1960). A cross-cultural outline of education. *Current Anthropology*, **1**, 267–305.

Henry, J. (1963). *Culture against man*. New York: Random House.

Herr, K. (1991). Portrait of a teen-age mother. In R. Donmoyer & R. Kos (Eds.), *Students at-risk: Portraits and policies*. Albany, NY: State University of New York Press.

Herriott, R. E. (1977). Ethnographic case studies in federally funded multidisciplinary policy research: Some design and implementation issues. *Anthropology and Education Quarterly*, **8**, 106–115.

Herriott, R. E., & Gross, N. (Eds.) (1979). *The dynamics of planned educational change: Case studies and analyses*. Berkeley, CA: McCutchan.

Herskovits, M. J. (1943). Education and cultural dynamics. *American Journal of Sociology*, **48**, 737–749.

Hess, D. (1989). Teaching ethnographic writing: A review essay. *Anthropology and Education Quarterly*, **20**, 163–177.

Hess, G. A. (1991). *School reform Chicago style*. Newbury Park, CA: Corwin Press.

Hewett, E. L. (1904). Anthropology and education. *American Anthropologist*, **6**, 574–575.

Heyneman, S. P. (1976). Influences on academic achievement: A comparison of results from Uganda and more industrialized societies. *Sociology of Education*, **49**, 200–211.

Hilgard, E. R., & Bower, G. H. (1966). *Theories of learning* (3rd ed.). New York: Appleton Century–Crofts.

Hilger, Sister M. I. (1966). *Field guide to the ethnological study of child life* (2nd ed.). New Haven, CT: Human Relations Area Files Press.

Hockings, P. (Ed.) (1975). *Principles of visual anthropology*. The Hague: Mouton.

Hoffman, J. E. (1980). Problems of access in the study of social elites and boards of directors. In W. B. Shaffir, R. A. Stebbins, & A. Turowitz (Eds.), *Fieldword experience: Qualitative approaches to social research* (pp. 45–56). New York: St. Martin's Press.

Hoffman, N. (1981). *Women's 'true' profession: Voices from the history of teaching*. New York: McGraw-Hill.

Holecek, B. G. (1983). *Nova: Anthropology on trial*. Boston, MA: WGBH Transcripts.

Holland, D., & Eisenhart, M. (1990). *Educated in romance: Women, achievement and college culture*. Chicago: University of Chicago Press.

Holland, D., & Quinn, N. (Eds.) (1987). *Cultural models in language and thought*. Cambridge, England: Cambridge University Press.

Hollingshead, A. B. (1949). *Elmtown's youth*. New York: Wiley.

Hollingshead, A. B. (1975). *Elmtown's youth and Elmtown revisited*. New York: Wiley.

Homans, G. C. (1964). Contemporary theory in sociology. In R. E. L. Faris (Ed.), *Handbook of modern sociology* (pp. 951–977). Chicago: McNally.

Homans, G. C. (1967). *The nature of social science.* New York: Harcourt, Brace, and World.

Honigmann, J. J., & Honigmann, I. (1965). *Eskimo townsmen.* Ottawa, Canada: Canadian Research Center for Anthropology, University of Ottawa.

Hostetler, J. A., & Huntington, G. E. (1971). *Children in Amish society: Socialization and community education.* New York: Holt, Rinehart, and Winston.

House, E. R. (1979). The objectivity, fairness, and justice of federal evaluation policy as reflected in the Follow Through evaluation. *Educational Evaluation and Policy Analysis,* **1**(1), 28–42.

Howard, A. (1970). *Learning to be Rotuman: Enculturation in the South Pacific.* New York: Teachers College Press.

Howe, K., & Eisenhart, M. (1990). Standards for qualitative (and quantitative) research: A prolegomenon. *Educational Researcher,* **19**(4), 2–9.

Huberman, A. M., & Miles, M. B. (1983). *Innovation up close: A field study in 12 school settings.* Andover, MA: The Network.

Huberman, M. (1990). Linkage between researchers and practitioners: A qualitative study. *American Educational Research Journal,* **27**(2), 363–391.

Hughes, H. S. (1964). *History as art and as science: Twin vistas on the past.* New York: Harper and Row.

Hunkins, F. P. (1972). *Questioning strategies and techniques.* Boston: Allyn and Bacon.

Hurn, C. J. (1978). *The limits and possibilities of schooling: An introduction to the sociology of education.* Boston: Allyn and Bacon.

Hymes, D. (1967). Models of the interaction of language and social setting. *Journal of Social Issues,* **23**(2), 8–28.

Hymes, D. (Ed.) (1972). *Reinventing anthropology.* New York: Vintage Books.

Ianni, F. A. J. (1976). Anthropology and educational research: A report on federal agency programs, policies and issues. *Anthropology and Education Quarterly,* **7**(3), 3–11.

Inkeles, A. (1974). The school as a context for modernization. In A. Inkeles & D. Holsinger (Eds.), *Education and individual modernity in developing countries* (pp. 7–23). Leiden, The Netherlands: Brill.

Inkeles, A., & Smith, D. H. (1974). *Becoming modern: Individual change in six developing countries.* Cambridge, MA: Harvard University Press.

Jackson, B. (1987). *Fieldwork.* Urbana, IL: University of Illinois Press.

Jackson, J. E. (1990). "I am a fieldnote": Fieldnotes as a symbol of profes-
    sional identity. In R. Sanjeck (Ed.), *Fieldnotes: The making of anthropol-
    ogy* (pp. 3–33). Ithaca, NY: Cornell University Press.
Jackson, M. (1989). *Paths toward a clearing: Radical empiricism and ethno-
    graphic inquiry.* Bloomington, IN: Indiana University Press.
Jackson, P. W. (1968). *Life in classrooms.* New York: Holt, Rinehart, and
    Winston.
Jackson, P. W., & Lahaderne, H. M. (1967). Inequalities of teacher–pupil
    contacts. *Psychology in the Schools,* **4,** 204–211.
Jacobs, G. (Ed.) (1970). *The participant observer: Encounters with social reality.*
    New York: Braziller.
Jaeger, R. M. (1988). *Complementary methods for research in education.* Wash-
    ington, D. C.: American Educational Research Association.
Jagger, A. (1983). *Feminist politics and human nature.* Totowa, NJ: Rowman
    and Allenheld.
Janes, R. W. (1961). A note on phases of the community role of the
    participant observer. *American Sociological Review,* **26,** 446–450.
Jencks, C., Smith, M., Acland, H., Bane, M. J., Cohen, D., Gintis, H.,
    Heyns, B., & Michelson, S. (1972). *Inequality: A reassessment of the effect
    of family and schooling in America.* New York: Basic Books.
Jo, M. S. (1991). *A domain analysis.* Unpublished class paper. School of
    Education, University of Colorado, Boulder, CO.
Jocano, F. L. (1969). *Growing up in a Philippine barrio.* New York: Holt,
    Rinehart, and Winston.
Johnson, A., & Johnson, O. R. (1990). Quality into quantity: On the
    measurement potential of ethnographic fieldnotes. In R. Sanjek
    (Ed.), *Fieldnotes: The making of anthropology* (pp. 161–186). Ithaca, NY:
    Cornell University Press.
Johnson, J. M. (1975). *Doing field research.* New York: Free Press.
Johnson, N. B. (1980). The material culture of public school classrooms:
    The symbolic integration of local schools and national culture. *Anthro-
    pology and Education Quarterly,* **11,** 173–190.
Johnston, M. (1990). Experience and reflections on collaborative re-
    search. *International Journal of Qualitative Studies in Education,* **3,**
    173–183.
Jones, J. P. (1983). *The effects of increasing physical fitness levels on locus of
    control, self-concept, and reported changes in life-style dimensions.* Unpub-
    lished doctoral dissertation. Department of Counseling and Student
    Personnel Services, University of Georgia.
Jorgensen, D. L. (1989). *Participant observation: A methodology for human
    studies.* Newbury Park, CA: Sage Publications.
Jorgensen, J. G. (1971). On ethics and anthropology. *Current Anthropology,*
    12, 321–334.

Kaestle, C. F. (1998). Recent methodological developments in the history of American education. In R. M. Jaeger (Ed.), *Complementary methods for research in education* (pp. 61–171). Washington, D.C.: American Educational Research Association.

Kahl, J. A. (1953). Educational and occupational aspirations of "common man" boys. *Harvard Educational Review*, **23**, 186–203.

Kahl, J. A. (1968). *The measurement of modernism: A study of values in Brazil and Mexico.* Austin, TX: University of Texas Press.

Kahn, R., & Mann, F. (1952). Developing research partnerships. *Journal of Social Issues*, **8**(3), 4–10.

Kalton, G. (1983). *Introduction to survey sampling.* Newbury Park, CA: Sage Publications.

Kapferer, J. L. (1981). Socialization and the symbolic order of the school. *Anthropology and Education Quarterly*, **12**, 258–274.

Kaplan, A. (1964). *The conduct of inquiry: Methodology for behavioral science.* Scranton, PA: Chandler.

Kaplan, D., & Manners, R. A. (1972). *Culture theory.* Englewood Cliffs, NJ: Prentice-Hall.

Karabel, J., & Halsey, A. H. (Eds.) (1978). *Power and ideology in education.* New York: Oxford University Press.

Kawharu, I. H. (1975). *Orakei: A Ngati Whatua community.* Wellington, New Zealand: New Zealand Council for Educational Research.

Kaye, B. (1962). *Bringing up children in Ghana: An impressionistic survey.* London: Allen & Unwin.

Keddie, N. (1971). Classroom knowledge. In M. F. D. Young, (Ed.), *Knowledge and control: New directions for the sociology of education* (pp. 133–160). London: Collier-Macmillan.

Keller, E. F. (1983). Gender and science. In S. Harding & S. Hintikka (Eds.), *Discovering reality: Feminist perspectives on epistemology, metaphysics, methodology and philosophy of sciences.* Boston: D. Reidel Publishing Co.

Keller, E. F., & Grontkowski, C. R. (1983). The mind's eye. In S. Harding & S. Hintikka (Eds.), *Discovering reality: Feminist perspectives on epistemology, metaphysics, methodology and philosophy of sciences.* Boston: D. Reidel Publishing Co.

Kelley, J. H. (1978). *Yaqui women: Contemporary life histories.* Lincoln, NE: University of Nebraska Press.

Kelly, G. P., & Nihlen, A. S. (1982). Schooling and the reproduction of patriarchy: Unequal workloads, unequal rewards. In M. Apple (Ed.), *Cultural and economic reproduction in education* (pp. 162–201). London: Routledge and Kegan Paul.

Kidd, D. (1906). *Savage childhood: A study of Kafir children.* London: Black.

Kimball, R. (1990). *Tenured radicals: How politics has corrupted our higher education.* New York: Harper and Row.

Kimball, S. T. (1956a). Anthropology and education. *Educational Leadership,* **13,** 480–483.

Kimball, S. T. (1956b). The role of education in community development. *Teachers College Record,* **57,** 386–391.

Kimball, S. T. (1965). The transmission of culture. *Educational Horizons,* **43,** 161–186.

Kimball, S. T. (1974). *Culture and the Educative Process: An anthropological perspective.* New York: Teachers College Press.

Kimball, S. T., & Burnett, J. H. (Eds.) (1973). *Learning and culture: Proceedings of the 1972 American Ethnological Society Symposium on Learning and Culture.* Seattle: University of Washington Press.

Kimball, S. T., & McClellan, J. E., Jr. (1962). *Education and the New America.* New York: Random House.

King, A. R. (1967). *The school at Mopass: A problem of identity.* New York: Holt, Rinehart, and Winston.

King, A. R. (1974). The teacher as a participant–observer: A case study. In G. D. Spindler (Ed.), *Education and cultural process: Toward an anthropology of education* (pp. 399–410). New York: Holt, Rinehart, and Winston.

King, J. R. (1991). Collaborative life history narratives: Heroes in reading teachers' tales. *International Journal of Qualitative Studies in Education,* **4,** 45–60.

King, R. (1978). *All things bright and beautiful? A sociological study of infants' classrooms.* Chichester, England: Wiley.

Kirby, P. L. (1982). *Interpersonal relationships between floor nurses and surgery patients in a mid-size county hospital.* Unpublished master's thesis. Department of Speech Communication, University of Georgia.

Kirk, J., & Miller, M. L. (1986). *Reliability and validity in qualitative research.* Beverly Hills, CA: Sage Publications.

Kleinfeld, J. S. (1979). *Eskimo school on the Andreafsky: A study of effective bicultural education.* New York: Praeger.

Kluckhohn, C. (1944). *Mirror for man: A survey of human behavior and social attitudes.* New York: McGraw-Hill.

Knapp, M. S. (1979). Ethnographic contributions to evaluation research: The experimental schools program evaluation and some alternatives. In T. C. Cook & C. S. Reichardt (Eds.), *Qualitative and quantitative methods in evaluation research* (pp. 118–139). Beverly Hills, CA: Sage Publications.

Koppelman, K. L. (1979). The explication model: An anthropological approach to program evaluation. *Educational Evaluation and Policy Analysis,* **1**(4), 59–64.

Kounin, J. S. (1970). *Discipline and group management in classrooms*. New York: Holt, Rinehart, and Winston.

Kress, M. (1982). *Thinking skills addressed in HISD's curriculum for gifted students*. Unpublished manuscript. Files of the Author, Houston Independent School District Department of Special Populations, Houston, TX.

Krueger, R. A. (1988). *Focus groups: A practical guide for applied research*. Newbury Park, CA: Sage Publications.

Kuhn, T. S. (1970). *The structure of scientific revolutions* (2nd ed.). Chicago: University of Chicago Press.

Kvale, S. (Ed.) (1989). *Issues of validity in qualitative research*. Sweden: Studentlitteratur.

La Belle, T. J. (1975). Liberation, development, and rural nonformal education. *Anthropology and Education Quarterly*, **6**(4), 20–26.

La Belle, T. J., & Verhine, R. E. (1975). Nonformal education and occupational stratification: Implications for Latin America. *Harvard Educational Review*, **45**, 160–190.

La Belle, T. J., Moll, L. C., & Weisner, T. S. (1979). Context-based educational evaluation: A participant research strategy. *Educational Evaluation and Policy Analysis*, **1**, **(3)** 85–194.

Lacey, C. (1970). *Hightown Grammar: The school as a social system*. Manchester, England: Manchester University Press.

Lancy, D. F. (1980). Becoming a blacksmith in Gbarngasuakwelle. *Anthropology and Education Quarterly*, **11**, 266–274.

Landy, D. (1959). *Tropical childhood: Cultural transmission and learning in a rural Puerto Rican village*. Chapel Hill, NC: University of North Carolina Press.

Langness, L. L., & Frank, G. (1981). *Lives: An anthropological approach to biography*. Novato, CA: Chandler and Sharp.

Langreth, R. (1991). Engineering dogma gives way to chaos. *Science*, **252**(5007), May 10, **776**(3).

Larkins, A. G., & Oldham, S. E. (1976). Patterns of racial separation in a desegregated high school. *Theory and Research in Social Education*, **4**(2), 23–38.

Lather, P. (1986). Research as praxis. *Harvard Educational Review*, **56**, 257–277.

Lave, J. (1988). *Cognition in practice*. Cambridge: Cambridge University Press.

Laye, C. (1959). *The African child* (translated by J. Kirkup). London: Fontana Books.

Leacock, E. B. (1969). *Teaching and learning in city schools: A comparative study*. New York: Basic Books.

Leacock, E., & Safa, H. I. (Eds.) (1986). *Women's work: Development and the division of labor by gender.* South Hadley, MA: Bergin and Garvey.

LeCompte, M. D. (1969). *The dilemmas of inner city school reform: The Woodlawn Experimental School project.* Unpublished master's thesis. University of Chicago.

LeCompte, M. D. (1970). The uneasy alliance of community action and research. *School Review,* **79,** 125–132.

LeCompte, M. D. (1975). *Institutional constraints on teacher styles and the development of student work norms.* Doctoral dissertation, University of Chicago. (Dissertation Abstracts International 36:43A.)

LeCompte, M. D. (1978). Learning from work: The hidden curriculum of the classroom. *Anthropology and Education Quarterly,* **9,** 22–37.

LeCompte, M. D. (1980). The civilizing of children: How young children learn to become students. *The Journal of Thought,* **15**(3), 105–127.

LeCompte, M. D. (1981). The Procrustean bed: Public schools, management systems, and minority students. In H. T. Trueba, G. P. Guthrie, & K. H.-P Au (Eds.), *Culture and the bilingual classroom: Studies in classroom ethnography* (pp. 178–195). Rowley, MA: Newbury House.

LeCompte, M. D. (1987). Bias in the biography: Bias and subjectivity in ethnographic research. *Anthropology and Education Quarterly,* **18**(1), 43–52.

LeCompte, M. D. (1990). Review of *Designing qualitative research* by C. Marshall & G. P. Rossman. *Qualitative Studies in Education,* **3**(3), 295–298.

LeCompte, M. D. (1993). Frameworks for hearing silence: Why are we telling stories when we are supposed to be doing science? In W. Tierney & D. McLaughlin (Eds.), *Naming Silenced Lives.* New York: Routledge (in press).

LeCompte, M. D., & Dworkin, A. G. (1988). Educational programs: Indirect linkages and unfulfilled expectations. In H. R. Rodgers (Ed.), *Beyond welfare: New approaches to the problem of poverty in America* (pp. 135–167) Armonk, NJ: M. E. Sharpe.

LeCompte, M. D., & Dworkin, A. G. (1991). *Giving up on school: Teacher burnout and student dropout.* Newbury Park, CA: Sage/Corwin.

LeCompte, M. D., & Goebel, S. D. (1987). Can bad data produce good program planning? An analysis of record-keeping on school dropouts. *Education and Urban Society,* **19**(3), 250–268.

LeCompte, M. D., & Goetz, J. P. (1982). Problems of reliability and validity in ethnographic research. *Review of Educational Research,* **52,** 31–60.

LeCompte, M. D, & Preissle, J. (1992a). Toward an ethnology of student life in schools and classrooms: Synthesizing the qualitative research tradition. In M. D. LeCompte, W. L. Millroy, & J. Preissle (Eds.), *The handbook of qualitative research in education*. San Diego: Academic Press.

LeCompte, M. D., & Preissle, J. (1992b). Qualitative research: Basic distinctions and data analysis options. In B. Thompson (Ed.), *Advances in social science methodology* (Vol. 3). New York: Jai Press.

LeCompte, M. D., Millroy, W. L., & Preissle, J. (1992). *The handbook of qualitative research in education*. San Diego: Academic Press.

Lee, D. (1955). Discrepancies in the teaching of American culture. In G. D. Spindler (Ed.), *Education and anthropology* (pp. 163–176). Stanford, CA: Stanford University Press.

Leemon, T. A. (1972). *The rites of passage in a student culture: A study of the dynamics of transition*. New York: Teachers College Press.

Leis, P. E. (1972). *Enculturation and socialization in Ijaw village*. New York: Holt, Rinehart, and Winston.

Lesko, N. (1986). Individualism and community: Ritual discourse in a parochial high school. *Anthropology and Education Quarterly, 17*(1), 25–40.

Lesko, N. (1988). *Symbolizing society: Stories, rites and structure in a Catholic high school*. New York: Falmer Press.

Levis-Pilz, G. (1982). Uncovering the "hidden dimension": Proxemic research techniques applied to teacher preparation. *Action in Teacher Education, 4*(1), 46–51.

Lewin, K. (1951). *Field theory in social science: Selected theoretical papers*. D. Cartwright (Ed.). New York: Harper and Row.

Lewis, C. (1970). *Indian families of the northwest coast: The impact of change*. Chicago: University of Chicago Press.

Lightfoot, S. L. (1988). *Balm in Gilead: Journey of a healer*. Reading, MA: Addison-Wesley.

Lincoln, Y. S. (1986). *The development of intrinsic criteria for authenticity: A model for trust in naturalistic research*. Paper presented at the meeting of the American Educational Research Association.

Lincoln, Y. S. (1990). The making of a constructivist: A remembrance of transformations past. In E. Guba (Ed.), *The paradigm dialog* (pp. 67–87). Newbury Park, CA: Sage Publications.

Lincoln, Y. S., & Guba, E. G. (1985). *Naturalistic inquiry*. Beverly Hills, CA: Sage Publications.

Lincoln, Y. S., & Guba, E. G. (1988). *Criteria for assessing naturalistic inquiries as reports*. Paper presented at the Annual Meeting of the American Educational Research Association, New Orleans.

Lincoln, Y. S., & Guba, E. G. (1990). Judging the quality of case study reports. *International Journal of Qualitative Studies in Education, 3,* 53–59.

Lindesmith, A. R. (1947). *Opiate addiction.* Evanston, IL: Principia Press.

Lindesmith, A. R. (1968). *Addiction and opiates.* Chicago: Aldine.

Lindzey, G. (1961). *Projective techniques and cross-cultural research.* New York: Appleton Century-Crofts.

Linton, R. (1945). *The cultural background of personality.* New York: Appleton-Century.

Little, K. (1951). *The Mende of Sierra Leone: A West African people in transition.* London: Routledge & Kegan Paul.

Lofland, J. (1971). *Analyzing social settings: A guide to qualitative observation and analysis.* Belmont, CA: Wadsworth.

Lofland, J., & Lofland, L. H. (1984). *Analyzing social settings: A guide to qualitative observation and analysis* (2nd ed.). Belmont, CA: Wadsworth.

London, H. B. (1978). *The culture of a community college.* New York: Praeger.

Lortie, D. C. (1975). *Schoolteacher: A sociological study.* Chicago: University of Chicago Press.

Louis, K. S. (1982). Multi-site multi-method studies. *American Behavioral Scientist,* **26**(1), 6–22.

Lundgren, U. P., & Pettersson, S. (Eds.) (1979). Code, context and curriculum processes: Seven papers presented at the annual meeting of the American Educational Research Association, 1979. *Studies in curriculum theory and cultural reproduction* (Vol. 3). Lund, Sweden: Liberlaromedel/Gleerup.

Lutz, F. W. (1982). *Witches and witchcraft in educational organizations.* Paper presented at the Annual Meeting of the American Anthropological Association, Washington, D. C.

Lynd, R. S. (1964). *Knowledge for what?* New York: Grove Press Edition.

Lynd, R. S., & Lynd, H. M. (1929). *Middletown: A study in contemporary American culture.* New York: Harcourt Brace.

McCall, G. J. (1969). Data quality control in participant observation. In G. J. McCall & J. L. Simmons (Eds.), *Issues in participant observation: A text and reader* (pp. 128–141). Reading, MA: Addison-Wesley.

McClelland, D. C. (1961). *The achieving society.* New York: Van Nostrand.

McCracken, G. (1988). *The long interview.* Beverly Hill, CA: Sage Publications.

McCutcheon, G. (1981). On the interpretation of classroom observations. *Educational Researcher,* **10**(5), 5–10.

McCutcheon, G. (1990). Ruminations on methodology: Of truth and significance. In E. G. Guba (Ed.), *The paradigm dialog* (pp. 277–285). Newbury Park, CA: Sage Publications.

McLaren, P. (1980). *Cries from the corridor: The new suburban ghettos.* Toronto: Methuen.

McLaren, P. (1986). *Schooling as a ritual performance: Towards a political economy of educational symbols and gestures.* London and Boston: Routledge and Kegan Paul.

McLeod, J. (1987). *Ain't no making it: Leveled aspirations in a low-income neighborhood.* Boulder, CO: Westview Press.

McNeil, L. M. (1988a). Contradictions of control II: Teachers, students and curriculum. *Phi Delta Kappan,* **69**(6), 432–438.

McNeil, L. M. (1988b). Contradictions of control III: Contradictions of reform. *Phi Delta Kappan,* **69**(7), 478–485.

McNeil, L. M. (1988c). *Contradictions of control: School structure and school knowledge.* New York: Routledge.

McPherson, G. H. (1972). *Small town teacher.* Cambridge, MA: Harvard University Press.

McRobbie, A. (1978). Working class girls and the culture of femininity. In Women's Studies Group, Center for Contemporary Cultural Studies (Ed.), *Women take issue: Aspects of womens' subordination* (pp. 96–108). London: Hutchinson.

Madge, J. (1953). *The tools of social science.* London: Longmans, Green.

Magoon, A. J. (1977). Constructivist approaches in educational research. *Review of Educational Research,* **47,** 651–693.

Malinowski, B. (1922). *Argonauts of the Western Pacific: An account of native enterprise and adventure in the archipelagoes of Melanesian New Guinea.* New York: Dutton.

Malinowski, B. (1927). *Sex and repression in savage society.* New York: Harcourt Brace.

Malinowski, B. (1929). *The sexual life of savages in North-Western Melanesia: An ethnographic account of courtship, marriage and family life among the natives of the Trobriand Islands, British New Guinea.* New York: Liveright.

Malinowski, B. (1935). *Coral gardens and their magic: A study of the methods of tilling the soil and of agricultural rites in the Trobriand Islands.* New York: American Books.

Malinowski, B. (1967). *A diary in the strict sense of the term.* Stanford, CA: Stanford University Press.

Manheim, H. L. (1977). *Sociological research: Philosophy and methods.* Homewood, IL: Dorsey Press.

Manners, R. A., & Kaplan, D. (Eds.) (1968). *Theory in anthropology: A sourcebook.* Chicago: Aldine.

Manning, P. K. (1987). *Semiotics and fieldwork.* Newbury Park, CA: Sage Publications.

Marcus, G. E., & Fischer, M. M. J. (1986). *Anthropology as cultural critique:*

An experimental moment in the human sciences. Chicago: University of Chicago Press.

Marshall, C. (1990). Goodness criteria: Are they objective or judgment calls? In E. G. Guba (Ed.), *The paradigm dialog* (pp. 188–197). Newbury Park, CA: Sage Publications.

Marshall, C., & Rossman, G. (1989). *Designing qualitative research.* Newbury Park, CA: Sage Publications.

Maxwell, J. A., Bashook, P. G., & Sandlow, L. J. (1986). Combining ethnographic and experimental methods in educational evaluation: A case study. In D. Fetterman & M. A. Pitman (Eds.), *Educational evaluation: Ethnography in theory, practice and politics* (pp. 171–191). Beverly Hills, CA: Sage Publications.

Mead, M. (1928). *Coming of age in Samoa: A psychological study of primitive youth for Western civilisation.* New York: Murrow.

Mead, M. (1930). *Growing up in New Guinea: A comparative study of primitive education.* New York: Morrow.

Mead, M. (1935). *Sex and temperament in three primitive societies.* New York: Morrow.

Mead, M. (1942). *And keep your powder dry: An anthropologist looks at America.* New York: Morrow.

Mead, M. (1943). Our educational emphases in primitive perspective. *American Journal of Sociology, 48,* 633–639.

Mead, M. (1951). *The school in American culture.* Cambridge, MA: Harvard University Press.

Mead, M. (1956). New lives for old: Cultural transformation—Manus, 1928–1953. New York: Morrow.

Mead, M. (1959). *An anthropologist at work: Writings of Ruth Benedict.* Boston: Houghton Mifflin.

Mead, M. (1972). *Blackberry winter: My earlier years.* New York: Morrow.

Medley, D. M., & Mitzel, H. E. (1963). Measuring classroom behavior by systematic observation. In N. L. Gage (Ed.), *Handbook of research on teaching* (pp. 247–328). Chicago: McNally.

Mehan, H. (1976). Assessing children's school performance. In M. Hammersley & P. Woods (Eds.), *The process of schooling: A sociological reader* (pp. 126–132). London: Routledge & Kegan Paul, in association with the Open House Press.

Mehan, H. (1978). Structuring school structure. *Harvard Educational Review, 48,* 32–64.

Mehan, H. (1979). *Learning lessons: Social organization in the classroom.* Cambridge, MA: Harvard University Press.

Melrose, L. (1989). *The creative personality and the creative process: A phenomenological perspective.* Lanham, MD: University Press of America.

Mercurio, J. A. (1979). Community involvement in cooperative decision making: Some lessons learned. *Educational Evaluation and Policy Analysis,* **1**(6), 37–46.

Merriam, S. B. (1988). *Case study research in education: A qualitative approach.* San Francisco: Jossey-Bass.

Merton, R. K. (1967). *On theoretical sociology: Five essays old and new.* New York: Free Press.

Metz, M. H. (1978). *Classrooms and corridors: The crisis of authority in desegregated secondary schools.* Berkeley, CA: University of California Press.

Metz, M. H. (1981). *Procedures, perspectives, and responsibility in an ethnographic study.* Paper presented to the Annual Meeting of the American Educational Research Association, Los Angeles.

Miles, M. B., & Huberman, A. M. (1984). *Qualitative data analysis: A sourcebook of new methods.* Beverly Hills, CA: Sage Publications.

Miles, M. B., & Lake, D. G. (1967). Self-renewal in school systems: A strategy for planned change. In G. Watson (Ed.), *Concepts for social change* (pp. 81–88). Washington, D.C.: National Training Laboratories, National Education Association.

Milgram, S. (1974). *Obedience to authority: An experimental view.* New York: Harper and Row.

Milgram, S., Mann, L. & Harter, S. (1965). The lost-letter technique: A tool of social research. *Public Opinion Quarterly,* **29**, 437–438.

Miller, J. L. (1990). *Creating spaces and finding voices: Teachers collaborating for empowerment.* Albany, NY: State University of New York Press.

Miller, S. M. (1952). The participant observer and "over-rapport." *American Sociological Review,* **17**, 97–99.

Millroy, W. L. (1990). *An ethnographic study of the mathematical ideas of a group of carpenters.* Unpublished doctoral dissertation. Cornell University, Ithaca, NY.

Mills, C. W. (1959). *The sociological imagination.* London: Oxford University Press.

Minuchin, P., Biber, B., Shapiro, E., & Zimiles, H. (1969). *The psychological impact of school experience: A comparative study of nine-year-old children in contrasting schools.* New York: Basic Books.

Mishler, E. (1986). *Research interviewing: Context and narrative.* Cambridge, MA: Harvard University Press.

Modiano, N. (1973). *Indian education in the Chiapus highlands.* New York: Holt, Rinehart, and Winston.

Moerman, M. (1988). *Talking culture: Ethnography and conversational analysis.* Philadelphia: University of Pennsylvania Press.

Mohatt, G., & Erickson, F. (1981). Cultural differences in teaching styles in an Odawa school: A sociolinguistic approach. In H. Trueba, G. Guthrie, & K. Au (Eds.), *Culture in the bilingual classroom: Studies in classroom ethnography* (pp. 105–120). Rowley, MA: Newbury House Publishers.

Moll, L. C., & Greenberg, J. B. (1990). Creating zones of possibilities: Combining social contexts for instruction. In L. C. Moll (Ed.), *Vygotsky and education: Instructional implications and applications of sociohistorical psychology* (pp. 319–349). Cambridge: Cambridge University Press.

Monroe, M. (1932). *Children who cannot read: The analysis of reading disabilities and the use of diagnostic tests in the instruction of retarded readers.* Chicago: University of Chicago Press.

Montessori, M. (1913). *Pedagogical anthropology* (translated by F. T. Cooper). New York: Stokes.

Moore, G. A., Jr. (1967). *Realities of the urban classroom: Observations in elementary schools.* Garden City, NY: Doubleday.

Moore, G. A., Jr. (1973). *Life cycles in Atchalán: The diverse careers of certain Guatemalans.* New York: Teachers College Press.

Morgan, D. L. (1988). *Focus groups as qualitative research.* Newbury Park, CA: Sage Publications.

Murray, A. V. (1929). *The school in the bush: A critical study of the theory and practice of native education in Africa.* London: Longmans, Green.

Nadel, S. F. (1942). *A black Byzantium: The kingdom of Nupe in Nigeria.* London: Oxford University Press for the International Institute of African Languages and Cultures.

Nader, L. (1972). Up the anthropologist—Perspectives gained from studying up. In D. Hymes (Ed.), *Reinventing anthropology* (pp. 286–311). New York: Vintage Books.

Naroll, R. (1962). *Data quality control—A new research technique: Prolegomena to a cross-cultural study of culture stress.* New York: Free Press.

Newman, K. K. (1979). *Middle-aged experienced teachers' perceptions of their career development.* Doctoral dissertation, Department of Curriculum and Supervision, Ohio State University. (Dissertation Abstracts International 39:4885A-4886A. University Microfilms No. 7902196.)

Newman, K. K. (1980). Stages in an unstaged occupation. *Educational Leadership, 37,* 514–516.

Nihlen, A. S. (1992). Los maestros como investigadores cualitivos: Reflexion y accion (Teachers as qualitative researchers: Reflection and action). In M. R. Beltran & M. A. Campos (Eds.), *Investigacion Ethnografia en Educacion* (pp. 89–105). Mexico, D. F.: Universidad Autonoma de Mexico.

Nisbet, R. A. (1966). *The sociological tradition.* New York: Basic Books.

Ogbu, J. U. (1974). *The next generation: An ethnography of education in an urban neighborhood.* New York: Academic Press.

Ogbu, J. U. (1978). *Minority education and caste: The American system in cross-cultural perspective.* New York: Academic Press.

Ogbu, J. U. (1988). *Community forces and educational strategies study: A preliminary coding guide.* Unpublished manuscript.

Oja, S. N., & Smulyan, L. (1989). *Collaborative action research: A developmental approach.* New York: Falmer Press.

Opler, M. E. (1941). *An Apache life-way: The economic, social and religious institutions of the Chiricahua Indians.* Chicago: University of Chicago Press.

Ottenberg, S. (1990). Thirty years of fieldnotes; Changing relationships to the text. In R. Sanjek (Ed.), *Fieldnotes: The makings of anthropology* (pp. 139–161). Ithaca, NY: Cornell University Press.

Ouchi, W. (1982). *Theory Z: How American business can meet the Japanese challenge.* New York: Avon.

Parmee, E. A. (1968). *Formal education and culture change: A modern Apache Indian community and government education programs.* Tucson, AZ: University of Arizona Press.

Partridge, W. L. (Ed.) (1984). *Training manual in development anthropology.* (Series: American Anthropological Association Special publication, No. 17.). Washington, D.C.: American Anthropological Association.

Patton, M. Q. (1978). *Utilization-focused evaluation.* Beverly Hills, CA: Sage Publications.

Patton, M. Q. (1980). *Qualitative evaluation methods.* Newbury Park, CA: Sage Publications.

Patton, M. Q. (1990a). Ethical dimensions of qualitative inquiry: Cultural and research contexts. In M. J. McGee-Brown (Ed.), *Processes, applications, and ethics in qualitative research* (pp. 7–38). Athens, GA: College of Education, University of Georgia.

Patton, M. Q. (1990b). *Qualitative evaluation and research methods* (2nd ed.). Newbury Park, CA: Sage Publications.

Pearson, J. (1982). *On the nature of congruency and incongruency between teachers' cognitive reality and their observed behavioral reality.* Unpublished doctoral dissertation. Department of Educational Foundations, University of Houston.

Pearson, J. (1986). Are teacher beliefs congruent with their observed classroom behavior? *The Urban Review, 17,* 128–146.

Pelto, P. J., & Pelto, G. H. (1978). *Anthropological research: The structure of inquiry* (2nd ed.). Cambridge, England: Cambridge University Press.

Persell, C. H. (1977). *Education and inequality: The roots and results of stratification in America's schools.* New York: Free Press.

Peshkin, A. (1972). *Kanuri schoolchildren: Education and social mobilization in Nigeria.* New York: Holt, Rinehart, and Winston.

Peshkin, A. (1978). *Growing up American: Schooling and the survival of community.* Chicago: University of Chicago Press.

Peshkin, A. (1982). The Researcher and subjectivity: Reflections on an ethnography of school and community. In G. D. Spindler (Ed.), *Doing the ethnography of schooling: Educational anthropology in action* (pp. 48–67). New York: Holt, Rinehart, and Winston.

Peshkin, A. (1986). *God's choice: The total world of a Christian fundamentalist school.* Chicago: University of Chicago Press.

Peshkin, A. (1989). *A postnote: Tales from the rear.* Paper presented at the Alternative Paradigms Conference, San Francisco.

Peshkin, A. (1991). *The color of strangers, the color of friends: The play of ethnicity in school and community.* Chicago: University of Chicago Press.

Peterson, P. L., Wilkinson, L. C., & Hallinan, M. (Eds.) (1984). *The social context of instruction: Group organization and group processes.* New York: Academic Press.

Petrie, H. G. (1976). Do you see what I see? The epistemology of interdisciplinary inquiry. *Educational Researcher,* **5**(2), 9–15.

Philips, S. U. (1972). Participation structures and communicative competence: Warm Springs children in community and classroom. In C. B. Cazden, V. P. John, & D. Hymes (Eds.), *Functions of language in the classroom* (pp. 370–394). New York: Teachers College Press.

Philips, S. U. (1983). *The invisible culture: Communication in classroom and community on the Warm Springs Indian Reservation.* New York: Longman.

Phillips, D. C. (1990a). Postpositivistic science: Myths and realities. In E. G. Guba (Ed.), *The paradigm dialog* (pp. 31–45). Newbury Park, CA: Sage Publications.

Phillips, D. C. (1990b). Subjectivity and objectivity: An objective inquiry. In E. Eisner, & A. Peshkin (Eds.), *Qualitative inquiry in education: The continuing debate* (pp. 19–37). New York: Teachers College Press.

Phillips, D. L. (1971). *Knowledge from what? Theories and methods in social research.* Chicago: McNally.

Piaget, J., & Inhelder, B. (1969). *The psychology of the child.* New York: Basic Books.

Pike, K. (1967). *Language in relation to a unified theory of the structure of human behavior* (2nd ed.). The Hague: Mouton.

Pirsig, R. M. (1974). *Zen and the art of motorcycle maintenance: An inquiry into values.* New York: Morrow.

Pitman, M. A., & Maxwell, J. A. (1992). Qualitative approaches to evaluation: Models and methods. In M. D. LeCompte, W. L. Millroy, & J. Preissle (Eds.), *The handbook of qualitative research in education* (pp. 729–770). New York: Academic Press.

Pitman, M. A., Eisikovitz, R., & Dobbert, M. (1989). *Culture acquisition: A holistic approach to human learning.* New York: Praeger.

Pitt, D. C. (1972). *Using historical sources in anthropology and sociology.* New York: Holt, Rinehart, and Winston.

Pitts, J. R. (Eds.) (1965). *Theories of society: Foundations of modern sociological theory.* New York: Free Press.

Polkinghorne, D. E. (1991). *Generalization and qualitative research: Issues of external validity.* Paper presented at the American Educational Research Association, April 3–7, Chicago.

Popkewitz, T. S. (1990). Whose future? Whose past? Notes on critical theory and methodology. In E. G. Guba (Ed.), *The paradigm dialog* (pp. 46–66). Newbury Park, CA: Sage Publications.

Popkewitz, T. S., & Tabachnick B. R. (Eds.) (1981). *The study of schooling: Field based methodologies in educational research and evaluation.* New York: Praeger.

Popper, K. R. (1968). *The logic of scientific discovery* (revised ed.). New York: Basic Books.

Powdermaker, H. (1933). *Life in Lesu: The study of a Melanesian society in New Ireland.* New York: Norton.

Powdermaker, H. (1966). *Stranger and friend: The way of an anthropologist.* New York: Norton.

Precourt, W. (1982). Ethnohistorical analysis of an Appalachian settlement school. In G. D. Spindler (Ed.), *Doing the ethnography of schooling: Educational anthropology in action* (pp. 440–453). New York: Holt, Rinehart, and Winston.

Preissle-Goetz, J., & LeCompte, M. D. (1990). Qualitative research in social studies education. In J. P. Shaver (Ed.), *Handbook of research on social studies teaching and learning* (pp. 56–66). New York: Macmillan.

Prost, J. H. (1975). Filming body behavior. In P. Hockings (Ed.), *Principles of visual anthropology* (pp. 325–363). The Hague: Mouton.

Puckett, J. L. (1989). *Foxfire reconsidered: A twenty year experiment in progressive education.* Urbana, IL: University of Illinois Press.

Punch, M. (1986). *The politics and ethics of fieldwork.* Beverly Hills, CA: Sage Publications.

Quantz, R. A. (1992). On critical ethnography (with some post-modern considerations). In M. D. LeCompte, W. L. Millroy, & J. Preissle (Eds.), *The handbook of qualitative research in education* (pp. 447–505). San Diego: Academic Press.

Quantz, R. A., & O'Connor, T. W. (1988). Writing critical ethnography: Dialogue, multivoicedness, and carnival in cultural texts. *Educational Theory*, **38**, 95–109.

Quay, H. C., & Werry, J. S. (1979). *Psychopathological disorders of childhood* (2nd ed.). New York: Wiley.

Radcliffe-Brown, A. R. (1965). *Structure and function in primitive society: Essays and addresses.* New York: Free Press.

Radin, P. (1933). *The method and theory of ethnology: An essay in criticism.* New York: McGraw-Hill.

Rappoport, A. (1970). Modern systems theory—An outlook for coping with change. *General Systems,* **15,** 15–25.

Raum, O. (1940). *Chaga childhood: A description of indigenous education in an East African tribe.* London: Oxford University Press for the International Institute of African Languages and Cultures.

Read, M. H. (1955). Education in Africa: Its pattern and role in social change. *The Annals of the American Academy of Political and Social Sciences,* **298,** 170–179.

Read, M. H. (1959). *Children of their fathers: Growing up among the Ngoni of Nyasaland.* New Haven, CT: Yale University Press.

Reason, P. (Ed.) (1989). *Human inquiry in action: Developments in new paradigm research.* Newbury Park, CA: Sage Publications.

Redfield, R. (1930). *Tepoztlán—A Mexican village: A study of folklife.* Chicago: University of Chicago Press.

Redfield, R. (1943). Culture and education in the Midwestern highlands of Guatemala. *American Journal of Sociology,* **48,** 640–648.

Redfield, R. (1945). A contribution of anthropology to the education of teachers. *School Review,* **53,** 516–525.

Reichardt, C. S., & Cook, T. D. (1979). Beyond qualitative versus quantitative methods. In T. D. Cook & C. S. Reichardt (Eds.), *Qualitative and quantitative methods in evaluation research* (pp. 7–32). Beverly Hills, CA: Sage Publications.

Reiter, R. R. (Ed.) (1975). *Toward an anthropology of women.* New York: Monthly Review Press.

Reyes M. L., & Laliberty, E. A. (1992). A teacher's "Pied Piper" effect on young authors. *Education and Urban Society,* **24**(2), 112–127.

Rich, J. (1968). *Interviewing children and adolescents.* New York: Wiley.

Richards, A. I. (1956). *Chisungu: A girls' initiation ceremony among the Bemba of Northern Rhodesia.* New York: Grove Press.

Richardson, M. (1990). *Cry lonesome and other accounts of the anthropologist's project.* Albany, NY: State University of New York Press.

Richardson, V., Casanova, U., Placier, P., & Guilfoyle, K. (1989). *School children at-risk.* Philadelphia, PA: Falmer Press.

Richberg, J. A. (1976). Dual jurisdiction and political conflict: A case of the Choctaw Follow Through program. *Journal of Research and Development in Education,* **9**(4), 91–101.

Riner, R. D. (1979). American Indian education: A rite that fails. *Anthropology and Education Quarterly, 10,* 236–253.

Risenborough, G. F. (1988). The great Heddekashun War: A life historical cenotaph for an unknown teacher. *International Journal of Qualitative Studies in Education, 1,* 197–223.

Rist, R. C. (1970). Student social class and teacher expectations: The self-fulfilling prophecy in ghetto education. *Harvard Educational Review, 40,* 411–451.

Rist, R. C. (1973). *The urban school: A factory for failure—A study of education in American society.* Cambridge, MA: MIT Press.

Rist, R. C. (1977). On the relations among educational research paradigms: From disdain to detente. *Anthropology and Education Quarterly, 8,* 42–49.

Rist, R. C. (1978). *The invisible children: School integration in American society.* Cambridge, MA: Harvard University Press.

Rist, R. C. (Ed.) (1979). *Desegregated schools: Appraisals of an American experiment.* New York: Academic Press.

Rist, R. C. (1980). Blitzkrieg ethnography: On the transformation of a method into a movement. *Educational Researcher, 9*(2), 8–10.

Rist, R. C. (1981). *The youthwork national policy study.* Paper presented at the Annual Meeting of the American Educational Research Association, Los Angeles.

Rivlin, A. M. (1971). *Systematic thinking for social action.* Washington, D.C.: The Brookings Institution.

Roberts, J. I. (1970). *Scene of the battle: Group behavior in urban classrooms.* Garden City, NY: Doubleday.

Robinson, W. S. (1951). The logical structure of analytic induction. *American Sociological Review, 16,* 812–818.

Rogers, D. (1968). *110 Livingston Street: Politics and bureaucracy in the New York City school system.* New York: Random House.

Romagnano, L. (1991). *Managing the dilemmas of change: A case study of two ninth grade general mathematics teachers.* Unpublished dissertation, University of Colorado–Boulder.

Roman, L. G. (1988). Intimacy, labor and class: Ideologies of feminine sexuality in the punk slam dance. In L. G. Roman & L. Christian-Smith (Eds.), *Becoming feminine: The politics of popular culture* (pp. 143–184). London: Falmer Press.

Roman, L. G. (1989). *Double exposure: The politics of feminist materialist ethnography.* Paper presented at the American Educational Research Association, San Francisco, CA.

Roman, L. G. (1992). The political significance of other ways of narrating ethnography: A feminist materialist approach. In M. D. LeCompte,

W. L. Millroy, & J. Preissle (Eds.), *The handbook of qualitative research in education* (pp. 555–594). San Diego: Academic Press.

Roman, L. G., & Apple, M. W. (1990). Is naturalism a move away from positivism? Materialist and feminist approaches to subjectivity in ethnographic research. In E. W. Eisner & A. Peshkin (Eds.), *Qualitative inquiry in education: The continuing debate* (pp. 38–73). New York: Teachers College Press.

Rorty, R. (1985). Solidarity or objectivity? In J. Rajchman & C. West (Eds.), *Post-analytic philosophy* (pp. 3–19). New York: Columbia University Press.

Rosaldo, M. Z., & Lamphere, L. (Eds.) (1974). *Women, culture, and society.* Stanford, CA: Stanford University Press.

Rosenblatt, P. C. (1981). Ethnographic case studies. In M. B. Brewer & B. E. Collins (Eds.), *Scientific inquiry and the social sciences: A volume in honor of Donald T. Campbell* (pp. 194–225). Washington, D.C.: Jossey-Bass.

Rosenfeld, G. (1971). *"Shut those thick lips!": A study of slum school failure.* New York: Holt, Rinehart, and Winston.

Rosenshine, B., & Furst, N. (1973). The use of direct observation to study teaching. In R. M. W. Travers (Ed.), *Second handbook of research on teaching* (pp. 122–183). Chicago: McNally.

Rosenstiel, A. (1954). Educational anthropology: A new approach to cultural analysis. *Harvard Educational Review,* **24,** 28–36.

Rossi, P., Wright, J., & Anderson, A. (1983). *Handbook of survey research.* San Diego: Academic Press.

Rowley, E. A. (1983). *Ethnographic study of a desegregated north Georgian county elementary school twelve years post de jure.* Unpublished doctoral dissertation. Department of Social Science Education, University of Georgia.

Royal Anthropological Institute of Great Britain and Ireland (1951). *Notes and queries on anthropology* (6th ed.). London: Routledge & Kegan Paul.

Rynkiewich, M. A., & Spradley, J. P. (Eds.) (1976). *Ethics and anthropology: Dilemmas in fieldwork.* New York: Wiley.

Safter, H. T. (1992). *Exiting from within: Case studies of highly gifted and creative adolescents.* Buffalo, NY: Bearly Limited.

Said, E. (1978). *Orientalism.* New York: Pantheon.

Sampling: How to Fix the Odds—Part I. (1980). *How To: Evaluate Educational Programs,* July: 1–2.

Sanders, N. M. (1966). *Classroom questions: What kinds?* New York: Harper and Row.

Sanjek, R. (1990). A vocabulary for fieldnotes. In R. Sanjek (Ed.), *Field-*

notes: The making of anthropology (pp. 92–139). Ithaca, NY: Cornell University Press.

Schatzman, L., & Strauss, A. L. (1973). *Field research: Strategies for a natural sociology.* Englewood Cliffs, NJ: Prentice-Hall.

Schein, E. H. (1987). *The clinical prospective in fieldwork.* Newberry Park, CA: Sage Publications.

Schensul, J. J., & Schensul, S. (1992). Collaborative research: Methods of inquiry for social change. In M. D. LeCompte, W. L. Millroy, & J. Preissle (Eds.), *The handbook of qualitative research in education.* San Diego: Academic Press.

Schensul, J. J., Schensul, S. L., Gonzales, M., & Caro, E. (1981). Community-based research and approaches to social change: The case of the Hispanic health council. *The Generator, 12*(2), 13–36.

Scheppler, M. L. D. (1980). *A field study of a state social studies supervisor: Patterns of decision making, communication, and leadership.* Doctoral dissertation, Department of Social Science Education, University of Georgia. (Dissertation Abstracts International 41:622A-623A. University Microfilms No. 8017178.)

Scherer, S. E. (1974). Proxemic behavior of primary-school children as a function of the socioeconomic class and subculture. *Journal of Personality and Social Psychology, 29,* 800–805.

Scherer, S. E. (1975). A photographic method for the recording and evaluation of cross-cultural proxemic interaction patterns. In P. Hockings (Ed.), *Principles of visual anthropology* (pp. 365–371). The Hague: Mouton.

Schoem, D. (1982). Explaining Jewish student failure. *Anthropology and Education Quarterly, 13,* 308–322.

Schofield, J. W. (1982). *Black and white in school: Trust, tolerance or tokenism?* New York: Praeger.

Schwartz, F. (1981). Supporting or subverting learning: Peer group patterns in four tracked schools. *Anthropology and Education Quarterly, 12,* 99–121.

Schwartz, M. S., & Schwartz, C. G. (1955). Problems in participant observation. *American Journal of Sociology, 60,* 343–353.

Scriven, M. (1972). Objectivity and subjectivity in educational research. In L. G. Thomas (Ed.), *Philosophical redirection of educational research* (pp. 94–142). Chicago: National Society for the Study of Education.

Scriven, M. (1974). Evaluation perspectives and procedures. In W. J. Popham (Ed.), *Evaluation in education: Current applications* (pp. 1–93). Berkeley, CA: McCutchan.

Sewell, W. H., Haller, A. O., & Portes, A. (1969). The educational and early occupational attainment process. *American Sociological Review, 34,* pp. 82–42.

Shaffir, W. B., & Stebbins, R. A. (Eds.) (1991). *Experiencing fieldwork: An inside view of qualitative research.* Newbury Park, CA: Sage Publications.

Shaffir, W. B., Stebbins, R. A. & Turowitz, A. (Eds.) (1980). *Fieldwork experience: Qualitative approaches to social research.* New York: St. Martin's Press.

Sharp, R. (1981). Marxism, the concept of ideology, and its implications for fieldwork. In T. S. Popkewitz & B. R. Tabachnick (Eds.), *The study of schooling: Field based methodologies in educational research and evaluation* (pp. 112–154). New York: Praeger.

Sharp, R., & Green, A. (1975). *Education and social control: A study in progressive primary education.* London: Routledge & Kegan Paul.

Shaver, J. P., & Larkins, A. G. (1973). Research on teaching social studies. In R. M. W. Travers (Ed.), *Second handbook of research on teaching* (pp. 1243–1262). Chicago: McNally.

Shaw, C. R. (1930). *The jack roller: A delinquent boy's own story.* Chicago: University of Chicago Press.

Sherman, R., & Webb, R. (Eds.) (1988). *Qualitative research in education: Focus and methods.* Philadelphia, PA: Falmer Press.

Shils, E. (1965). Toward a modern intellectual community in the new states. In J. S. Coleman (Ed.), *Education and political development* (pp. 498–518). Princeton, NJ: Princeton University Press.

Shimahara, N. K. (1971). *Burakumin: A Japanese minority and education.* The Hague: Martinus Nijhoff.

Shostak, M. (1981). *Nisa: The life and words of a !Kung woman.* Cambridge, MA: Harvard University Press.

Shultz, J., & Florio, S. (1979). Stop and freeze: The negotiation of social and physical space in a kindergarten/first grade classroom. *Anthropology and Education Quarterly,* **10,** 166–181.

Shunk, W. R., & Goldstein, B. Z. (1964). Anthropology and education. *Review of Educational Research,* **34,** 71–84.

Sieber, R. T. (1979a). Classmates as workmates: Informal peer activity in the elementary school. *Anthropology and Education Quarterly,* **10,** 207–235.

Sieber, R. T. (1979b). Schoolrooms, pupils, and rules: The role of informality in bureaucratic socialization. *Human Organization,* **38,** 273–282.

Sieber, R. T. (1981). Many roles, many faces: Researching school–community relations in a heterogeneous American urban community. In D. A. Messerschmidt (Ed.), *Anthropologists at home in North America: Methods and issues in the study of one's own society* (pp. 202–220). Cambridge, England: Cambridge University Press.

Sieber, R. T., & Gordan, A. J. (Eds.) (1981). *Children and their organizations: Investigations in American culture.* Boston: Hall.

Siedman, I. E. (1991). *Interviewing as qualitative research: A guide for researchers in education and the social sciences.* New York: Teachers College Press.

Sikes, P., Measor, L., & Woods, P. (1985). *Teacher careers: Crises and continuities.* London: Falmer Press.

Silberman, M. L. (1971). Teachers' attitudes and actions toward their students. In M. L. Silberman (Ed.), *The experience of schooling* (pp. 86–96). New York: Holt, Rinehart, and Winston.

Sinclair, J. McH., & Coulthard, R. M. (1975). *Towards analysis of discourse: The English used by teachers and pupils.* London: Oxford University Press.

Sindell, P. S. (1969). Anthropological approaches to the study of education. *Review of Educational Research, 39,* 593–605.

Sindell, P. S. (1974). Some discontinuities in the enculturation of Mistassini Cree children. In G. D. Spindler (Ed.), *Education and cultural process: Toward an anthropology of education* (pp. 333–341). New York: Holt, Rinehart, and Winston.

Singleton, J. (1967). *Nichu: A Japanese school.* New York: Holt, Rinehart, and Winston.

Siskind, J. (1973). *To hunt in the morning.* New York: Oxford University Press.

Smith, D. E. (1987). *The everyday world as problematic: A feminist sociology.* Boston: Northeastern University Press.

Smith, J. K. (1984). The problem of criteria for judging interpretive inquiry. *Educational Evaluation and Policy Analysis, 6,* 379–391.

Smith, J. K. (1990). Alternative research paradigms and the problem of criteria. In E. Guba (Ed.), *The paradigm dialog* (pp. 167–188). Newbury Park, CA: Sage Publications.

Smith, L. M. (1974). Reflections on trying to theorize from ethnographic data. *Anthropology and Education Quarterly, 5*(1), 18–24.

Smith, L. M. (1979). An evolving logic of participant observation, educational ethnography, and other case studies. *Review of Research in Education, 6,* 316–377.

Smith, L. M., & Brock, J. A. M. (1970). *"Go, bug, go!": Methodological issues in classroom observational research.* St. Louis: Central Midwestern Regional Educational Laboratory.

Smith, L. M., & Carpenter, P. C. (1972). *General reinforcement package project: Qualitative observation and interpretation.* St. Louis: Central Midwestern Regional Educational Laboratory.

Smith, L. M., & Geoffrey, W. (1968). *The complexities of an urban classroom: An analysis toward a general theory of teaching.* New York: Holt, Rinehart, and Winston.

Smith, L. M., & Keith, P. M. (1971). *Anatomy of educational innovation: An organizational analysis of an elementary school.* New York: Wiley.

Smith, L. M., & Pohland, P. A. (1976). Grounded theory and educational ethnography: A methodological analysis and critique. In J. T. Roberts & S. K. Akinsanya (Eds.), *Educational patterns and cultural configurations: The anthropology of education* (pp. 264–279). New York: McKay.

Smith, L. M., & Schumacher, S. (1972). *Extended pilot trials of the aesthetic education program: A qualitative description, analysis, and evaluation.* St. Louis: Central Midwestern Regional Educational Laboratory.

Smith, L. M., Dwyer, D. C., Prunty, J. J., & Kleine, P. F. (1986). *Educational innovators: Then and now. Book 1 of the trilogy.* New York: Falmer Press.

Smith, L. M., Dwyer, D. C., Prunty, J. J., & Kleine, P. F. (1987). *The fate of an innovative school: The history and present status of the Kensington School. Book 2 of the trilogy.* New York: Falmer Press.

Smith, L. M., Dwyer, D. C., Prunty, J. J., & Kleine, P. F. (1988). *Innovation and change in schooling: History, politics and agency. Book 3 of the trilogy.* New York: Falmer Press.

Snow, C. P. (1963). *The two cultures and the scientific revolution: A second look.* New York: Mentor Books.

Snow, D. A. (1980). The disengagement process: A neglected problem in participant observation research. *Qualitative Sociology, 3,* 100–122.

Spindler, G. D. (1955a). Education in a transforming American culture. *Harvard Educational Review, 25,* 145–156.

Spindler, G. D. (Ed.) (1955b). *Education and anthropology.* Palo Alto, CA: Stanford University Press.

Spindler, G. D. (1959). *Transmission of American culture.* Cambridge, MA: Harvard University Press.

Spindler, G. D. (Ed.) (1963b). *Education and culture: Anthropological approaches.* New York: Holt, Rinehart, and Winston.

Spindler, G. D. (Ed.) (1970). *Being an anthropologist: Fieldwork in eleven cultures.* New York: Holt, Rinehart, and Winston.

Spindler, G. D. (1973). *Burgbach: Urbanization and identity in a German village.* New York: Holt, Rinehart, and Winston.

Spindler, G. D. (1974a). Beth Anne—A case study of culturally defined adjustment and teacher perceptions. In G. D. Spindler (Ed.), *Education and cultural process: Toward an anthropology of education* (pp. 139–153). New York: Holt, Rinehart, and Winston.

Spindler, G. D. (1974b). Schooling in Schönhausen: A study in cultural transmission and instrumental adaptation in an urbanizing German village. In G. D. Spindler (Ed.), *Education and cultural process: Toward an anthropology of education* (pp. 230–271). New York: Holt, Rinehart, and Winston.

Spindler, G. D. (Ed.) (1974c). *Education and cultural process: Toward an anthropology of education.* New York: Holt, Rinehart, and Winston.

Spindler, G. D. (1982a). General introduction. In G. D. Spindler (Ed.), *Doing the ethnography of schooling: Educational anthropology in action* (pp. 1–13). New York: Holt, Rinehart, and Winston.

Spindler, G. D. (Ed.) (1982b). *Doing the ethnography of schooling: Educational anthropology in action.* New York: Holt, Rinehart, and Winston.

Spindler, G. D. (Ed.) (1987). *Education and cultural process: Anthropological approaches* (2nd ed.). Prospect Heights, IL: Waveland Press.

Spindler, G. D., & Spindler, L. (1971). *Dreamers without power: The Menomini Indians.* New York: Holt, Rinehart, and Winston.

Spindler, G. D., & Spindler, L. (1982). Roger Harker and Schönhausen: From familiar to strange and back again. In G. D. Spindler (Ed.), *Doing the ethnography of schooling: Educational anthropology in action* (pp. 20–46). New York: Holt, Rinehart, and Winston.

Spindler, G. D., & Spindler, L. (Eds.) (1987). *Interpretive ethnography education at home and abroad.* Hillsdale, NJ: Lawrence Erlebaum Associates.

Spindler, G. D., & Spindler, L. (1992). Cultural process and ethnography: An anthropological perspective. In M. D. LeCompte, W. L. Millroy, & J. Preissle (Eds.), *The handbook of qualitative research in education.* San Diego, CA: Academic Press.

Spindler, L., & Spindler, G. D. (1958). Male and female adaptations in culture change. *American Anthropologist,* **60,** 217–233.

Spiro, M. E. (1958). *Children of the kibbutz.* Cambridge, MA: Harvard University Press.

Spradley, J. P. (1970). *You owe yourself a drunk: An ethnography of urban nomads.* Boston: Little, Brown.

Spradley, J. P. (Ed.) (1972). *Culture and cognition: Rules, maps, and plans.* New York: Chandler.

Spradley, J. P. (1979). *The ethnographic interview.* New York: Holt, Rinehart, and Winston.

Spradley, J. P. (1980). *Participant observation.* New York: Holt, Rinehart, and Winston.

Spradley, J. P., & McCurdy, D. W. (Eds.) (1972). *The cultural experience: Ethnography in complex society.* Chicago: Science Research Associates.

Srinivas, M. N. (1976). *The remembered village.* Berkeley, CA: University of California Press.

Stake, R. (1988). Case study methods in educational research: Seeking sweetwater. In R. M. Jaeger (Ed.), *Complementary methods for research in education.* Washington, D.C.: American Educational Research Association.

Stake, R. E., & Easley, J. A. (Eds.) (1978). *Case studies in science education.* (2 Vols. Prepared for the National Science Foundation.) Washington,

D.C.: U.S. Government Printing Office. (ERIC Document Reproduction Service Nos. ED 166 058 and ED 166 059.)

Stambler, S. (1982). Herodotus. In T. J. Luse (Ed.), *Ancient writers: Greece and Rome* (Vol. 1) (pp. 209–232). New York: Scribner's.

Stayb, H. A. (1931). *The BaVenda.* London: International Institute of African Languages and Cultures, Oxford University Press.

Stein, M. R. (1960). *The eclipse of community: An interpretation of American studies.* Princeton, NJ: Princeton University Press.

Stewart, D. M., & Shamdasani, P. (1990). *Focus groups: Theory and practice.* Newbury Park, CA: Sage Publications.

Stinchcombe, A. L. (1964). *Rebellion in a high school.* Chicago: Quadrangle.

Stocking, G. W., Jr. (1968). Franz Boas and the culture concept in historical perspective. In *Race, culture, and evolution: Essays in the history of anthropology* (pp. 195–233). New York: Free Press.

Stocking, G. W., Jr. (1983). The ethnographer's magic: Fieldwork in British anthropology from Tylor to Malinowski. In G. W. Stocking, Jr. (Ed.), *Observers observed: Essays on ethnographic fieldwork* (pp. 70–120). Madison, WI: University of Wisconsin Press.

Strodtbeck, F. L. (1961). Family integration, values, and achievement. In A. H. Halsey, J. Floud, & C. A. Anderson (Eds.), *Education, economy and society: A reader in the sociology of education* (pp. 315–347). New York: Free Press.

Stubbs, M., & Delamont, S. (Eds.) (1976). *Explorations in classroom observation.* London: Wiley.

Studstill, J. D. (1979). Education in a Luba secret society. *Anthropology and Education Quarterly, 10,* 67–79.

Stufflebeam, D. L. (1978). *Philosophical, conceptual and practical guides for evaluating education.* Unpublished manuscript. Files of the author. The Evaluation Center, College of Education, Western Michigan University, Kalamazoo, MI.

Sudman, S., & Bradburn, N. M. (1989). *Asking questions: A practical guide to questions of design.* San Francisco: Josey-Bass.

Sykes, C. J. (1988). *ProfScam: Professors and the demise of higher education.* New York: St. Martin's Press.

Tabachnik, B. R., Zeichner, K. M., Adler, S., Densmore, K, & Egan, K. (1982). *The impact of student teaching experience on the development of teacher perspectives.* Paper presented at the Annual Meeting of the American Educational Research Association, New York.

Talbert, C. (1970). Interaction and adaptation in two Negro kindergartens. *Human organization, 29,* 103–114.

Terman, L. M. (Ed.) (1925). *Mental and physical traits of a thousand gifted children.* Stanford, CA: Stanford University Press.

Terman, L. M., & Oden, M. H. (1947). *The gifted child grows up: Twenty-five years' follow-up of a superior group.* Stanford, CA: Stanford University Press.

Terman, L. M., & Oden, M. H. (1959). *The gifted group at midlife: Thirty-five years follow-up of the superior group.* Stanford, CA: Stanford University Press.

Tesch, R. (1990). *Qualitative research: Analysis types and software tools.* London and Philadelphia: Falmer Press.

Tharp, R. G. (1989). Psychocultural variables and constants: Effects on teaching and learning in schools. *American Psychologist,* **44**(2), 349–359.

Tharp, R. G., & Gallimore, R. (1988). *Rousing minds to life: Teaching, learning, and schooling in social context.* Cambridge University Press.

Thomas, L. (1983). *The youngest science: Notes of a medicine-watcher.* New York: Viking Press.

Thompson, L. (1941). *Guam and its people: A study of culture change and colonial education.* Studies of the Pacific, No. 8. San Francisco: American Council, Institute of Pacific Relations.

Tierney, W. (1991). *Official encouragement, institutional discouragement: Minorities in academe.* Norwood, NJ: Ablex Press.

Tierney, W., & McLaughin, D. (Ed.) (1992). *Naming silenced lives.* New York & London: Routledge.

Tikunoff, W. J., Berliner, D. C., & Rist, R. C. (1975). *Special study A: An ethnographic study of 40 classrooms of the BTES known sample.* San Francisco: Far West Laboratory for Educational Development. (ERIC Document Reproduction Service No. ED 150 110.)

Tobin, J. J., Wu, D. Y. H., & Davidson, D. H. (1989). *Pre-school in three cultures: Japan, China and the United States.* New Haven, CT: Yale University Press.

Tranel, D. D. (1981). A lesson from the physicists. *The Personnel and Guidance Journal,* **59,** 425–429.

Trend, M. G. (1979). On the reconciliation of qualitative and quantitative analyses: A case study. In T. C. Cook & C. S. Reichardt (Eds.) *Qualitative and quantitative methods in evaluation research* (pp. 68–86). Beverly Hills, CA: Sage Publications.

Turnbull, C. M. (1972). *The mountain people.* New York: Simon and Schuster.

Turner, J.H. (1978). *The structure of sociological theory* (revised ed.). Homewood, IL: Dorsey Press.

Tuthill, D., & Ashton, P. (1988). Improving educational research through development of educational paradigms. *Educational Researcher,* December: 6–14, Vol. 12, No. 12.

Vaillant, G. E. (1977). *Adaptation to life*. Boston: Little, Brown.

Valli, L. (1986). *Becoming clerical workers*. Boston: Routledge & Kegan-Paul.

Valli, L. (1988). *The parallel curriculum at Central Catholic High School*. Paper presented at the American Educational Research Association, New Orleans.

Vanderwalker, N. C. (1898). Some demands of education upon anthropology. *American Journal of Sociology*, **4**, 69–78.

Van Gennep, A. (1960). *The rites of passage* (translated by M. B. Vizedom & G. L. Caffee). Chicago: University of Chicago Press.

Varenne, H. (1982). Jocks and freaks: The symbolic structure of the expression of social interaction among American senior high school students. In G. D. Spindler (Ed.), *Doing the ethnography of schooling: Educational anthropology in action* (pp. 210–235). New York: Holt, Rinehart, and Winston.

Vico, G. (1968). *The new science of Giambattista Vico*. Ithaca, NY: Cornell University Press.

Vidich, A. J. (1955). Participant observation and the collection and interpretation of Data. *American Journal of Sociology*, **60**, 354–360.

Vidich, A. J., & Bensman, J. (1958). *Small town in mass society: Class, power, and religion in a rural community*. Princeton, NJ: Princeton University Press.

Vogt, L. (1985). *Rectifying the school performance of Hawaiian and Navajo students*. Paper presented at the American Anthropological Association, Washington, D.C.

Vygotsky, L. (1962). *Language and thought*. Cambridge: Cambridge University Press. (Originally published in 1934.)

Walker, R. S. (1983). *Daniel Levinson's concept of the dream in the lives of selected southern Baptist ministers*. Unpublished doctoral dissertation. Department of Adult Education, University of Georgia.

Walker, R., & Wiedel, J. (1985). Using photographs in a discipline of words. In R. G. Burgess (Ed.), *Field methods in the study of education* (pp. 191–216). Philadelphia, PA: The Falmer Press, Taylor and Francis, Inc.

Waller, W. (1932). *The sociology of teaching*. New York: Wiley.

Ward, M. C. (1971). *Them children: A study in language learning*. New York: Holt, Rinehart, and Winston.

Warner, W. L., Low, J. O., Lunt, P. S., & Srole, L. (1963). *Yankee city*. New Haven, CT: Yale University Press.

Warren, C. A. B. (1988). *Gender issues in field research*. Beverly Hills, CA: Sage Publications.

Warren, R. L. (1967). *Education in Rebhausen: A German village*. New York: Holt, Rinehart, and Winston.

Warren, R. L. (1982). Schooling, biculturalism, and ethnic identity: A case study. In G. D. Spindler (Ed.), *Doing the ethnography of schooling: Educational anthropology in action* (pp. 383–409). New York: Holt, Rinehart, and Winston.

Watkins, M. H. (1943). The West African "bush" school. *American Journal of Sociology,* **48,** 666–675.

Watson, L. C., & Watson-Franke, M. B. (1985). *Interpreting life histories: An anthropological inquiry.* New Brunswick, NJ: Rutgers University Press.

Wax, M. L. (Ed.) (1979). *Desegregated schools: An intimate portrait based on five ethnographic studies.* Unpublished report to the National Institute of Education. Files of the editor, Social Science Institute, Washington University, St. Louis.

Wax, M. L., & Wax, R. H. (1980). Fieldwork and the research process. *Anthropology and Education Quarterly,* **11,** 29–37.

Wax, M. L., Diamond, S., & Gearing, F. O. (Eds.) (1971). *Anthropological perspectives on education.* New York: Basic Books.

Wax, M. L., Wax, R. H., & Dumont, R. V., Jr. (1964). Formal education in an American Indian community. *Supplement to Social Problems,* **11**(4), 1–126.

Wax, R. H. (1971). *Doing fieldwork: Warnings and advice.* Chicago: University of Chicago Press.

Weaver, T. (Ed.) (1973). *To see ourselves: Anthropology and modern social issues.* Glenview, IL: Scott Foresman.

Webb, B. (1926). *My apprenticeship.* London: Longmans, Green.

Webb, E. J., Campbell, D. T., Schwartz, R. D., & Sechrest, L. (1966). *Unobtrusive measures: Nonreactive research in the social sciences.* Chicago: McNally.

Weber, M. (1947). *The theory of social and economic organization* (translated by A. M. Henderson & T. Parsons). T. Parsons (Ed.). New York: Oxford University Press.

Weber, M. (1949). *The methodology of the social sciences* (translated and edited by E. Shils and H. Finch). New York: Free Press.

Weber, M. (1968). *Economy and society.* G. Roth & C. Wittich (Eds.). New York: Bedminster Press.

Weis, L. (1988). *Class, race, and gender in American education.* Albany, NY: State University of New York Press.

Weis, L. (1990). *Working class without work: High school students in a deindustrializing economy.* New York: Routledge.

Weller, S. C., & Romney, A. K. (1988). *Systematic data collection.* Newbury Park, CA: Sage Publications.

Wengle, J. L. (1988). *Ethnographers in the field: The psychology of research.* Tuscaloosa, AL: University of Alabama Press.

Werner, O., & Schoepfle, G. M. (1987). Foundations of ethnography and interviewing. *Systematic Fieldwork* (Vol. 1). Newbury Park, CA: Sage Publications.

Wertsch, J. V. (Ed.) (1985). *Culture, communication and cognition: Vygotskian perspectives.* Cambridge: Cambridge University Press.

Whitford, L. (1986). Effects of organizational context on program implementation. In G. W. Nolbit & W. T. Pink (Eds.), *Schooling in social context: Qualitative studies.* Norwood, NJ: Ablex Press.

Whiting, B. B. (Ed.) (1963). *Six cultures: Studies of child rearing.* New York: Wiley.

Whiting, B. B., & Edwards, C. P. (1988). *Children of different worlds: The formation of social behavior.* Cambridge, MA: Harvard University Press.

Whiting, B. B., & Whiting, J. W. M. (1975). *Children of six cultures: A psycho-cultural analysis.* Cambridge, MA: Harvard University Press.

Whiting, J. W. M. (1941). *Becoming a Kwoma: Teaching and learning in a New Guinea tribe.* New Haven, CT: Yale University Press.

Whiting, J. W. M., Child, I. L., & Lambert, W. M. (1966). *Field guide for a study of socialization.* New York: Wiley.

Whyte, W. F. (1955). *Street corner society: The social structure of an Italian slum* (2nd ed.). Chicago: University of Chicago Press.

Whyte, W. F. (1984). *Learning from the field: A guide from experience.* Newbury Park, CA: Sage Publications.

Wieder, A. (1988). Possibilities, lost possibilities, no possibilities: Images of middle-class children and lower-class adults. *International Journal of Qualitative Studies in Education,* **1,** 225–238.

Wilkinson, L. C. (Ed.) (1982). *Communicating in the classroom.* New York: Academic Press.

Williams, T. R. (1967). *Field methods in the study of culture.* New York: Holt, Rinehart, and Winston.

Williams, T. R. (1969). *A Borneo childhood: Enculturation in Dusun society.* New York: Holt, Rinehart, and Winston.

Willis, G. (Ed.) (1978). *Qualitative evaluation: Concepts and cases in curriculum criticism.* Berkeley, CA: McCutchan.

Willis, P. E. (1976). The class significance of school counter-culture. In M. Hammersley & P. Woods (Eds.), *The process of schooling: A sociological reader* (pp. 188–200). London: Routledge & Kegan Paul.

Willis, P. E. (1977). *Learning to labour: How working class kids get working class jobs.* Farnborough, England: Saxon House.

Wilson, S. (1977). The use of ethnographic techniques in educational research. *Review of Educational Research,* **47,** 245–265.

Wolcott, H. F. (1967a). Anthropology and education. *Review of Educational Research,* **37,** 82–95.

Wolcott, H. F. (1967b). *A Kwakiutl village and school.* New York: Holt, Rinehart, and Winston.

Wolcott, H. F. (1971). Handle with care: Necessary precautions in the anthropology of schools. In M. L. Wax, S. Diamond, & F. O. Gearings (Eds.), *Anthropological perspectives on Education* (pp. 98–117). New York: Basic Books.

Wolcott, H. F. (1973). *The man in the principal's office: An ethnography.* New York: Holt, Rinehart, and Winston.

Wolcott, H. F. (1974). The teacher as an enemy. In G. D. Spindler (Ed.), *Education and cultural process: Toward an anthropology of education* (pp. 411–425). New York: Holt, Rinehart, and Winston.

Wolcott, H. F. (1975). Criteria for an ethnographic approach to research in schools. *Human Organization, 34,* 111–127.

Wolcott, H. F. (1977). *Teachers versus technocrats: An educational innovation in anthropological perspective.* Eugene, OR: Center for Educational Policy and Management, University of Oregon.

Wolcott, H. F. (1980). *How to look like an anthropologist without really being one.* Paper presented at the Annual Meeting of the American Educational Research Association, Boston.

Wolcott, H. F. (1982). Mirrors, models, and monitors: Educator adaptations of the ethnographic innovation. In G. D. Spindler (Ed.), *Doing the ethnography of schooling: Educational anthropology in action* (pp. 68–95). New York: Holt, Rinehart, and Winston.

Wolcott, H. F. (1988). Ethnographic research in education. In R. M. Jaeger (Ed.), *Complementary methods for research in education* (pp. 185–249). Washington, D.C.: American Educational Research Association.

Wolcott, H. F. (1990). On seeking—and rejecting—Validity in qualitative research. In E. Eisner & A. Peshkin (Eds.), *Qualitative inquiry in education: The continuing debate* (pp. 121–152). New York: Teachers College Press.

Wolf, D. R. (1990). *The Rebels: A brotherhood of outlaw bikers.* Toronto: University of Toronto Press.

Woods, P. (1992). Symbolic interactionism: Theory and method: In M. D. LeCompte *et al.,* (Eds.), *The handbook of qualitative research in education* (pp. 337–405). San Diego: Academic Press.

Wooton, F. C. (1946). Primitive education in the history of education. *Harvard Educational Review, 16,* 235–254.

Wright, H. F. (1960). Observational child study. In P. H. Mussen (Ed.) *Handbook of research methods in child development* (pp. 71–139). New York: Wiley.

Wrong, D. H. (1961). The oversocialized conception of man in modern sociology. *American Sociological Review, 26,* 183–193.

Wylie, L. (1957). *Village in the Vaucluse: An account of life in a French village.* Cambridge, MA: Harvard University Press.

Wylie, L. (1974). *Village in the Vaucluse* (3rd ed.). Cambridge, MA: Harvard University Press.

Wyndham, H. A. (1933). *Native education: Ceylon, Java, Formosa, Philippines, French Indo-China, and British Malaya.* London: Oxford University Press.

Yinger, R. (1987). *By the seat of your pants: An inquiry into improvisation and teaching.* Paper presented at the American Educational Research Association meetings, Washington, D.C.

Yoors, J. (1967). *The gypsies.* New York: Simon and Schuster.

Young, M. F. D. (Ed.) (1971). *Knowledge and control: New directions for the sociology of education.* London: Collier-Macmillan.

Zeigler, H., & Peak, W. (1970). The political functions of the educational system. *Sociology of Education, 43,* 115–142.

Zelditch, M., Jr. (1962). Some methodological problems of field studies. *American Journal of Sociology, 67,* 566–576.

Zetterberg, H. L. (1966). *On theory and verification in sociology* (3rd ed.). Totowa, NJ: Bedminister Press.

Znaniecki, F. (1934). *The method of sociology.* New York: Farrar and Rinehart.

Zukav, G. (1979). *The dancing Wu Li masters: An overview of the new physics.* New York: Morrow.

Author Index

Numbers in parentheses are the pages where the author is cited in the references.

409

Subject Index

ISBN 0-12-440575-4